Private pages

Cp.2 pb.

7.99

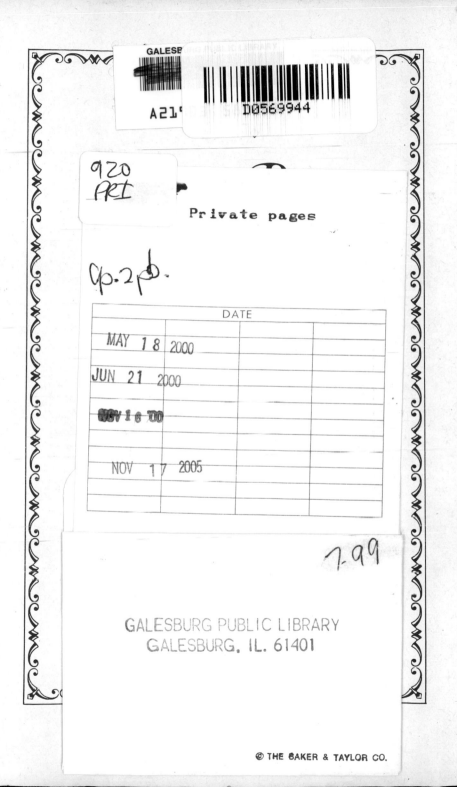

Private Pages

◇ ◇

Diaries of American Women
1830s–1970s

◇ ◇

EDITED BY

PENELOPE FRANKLIN

BALLANTINE BOOKS ◇ NEW YORK

Library of Congress Catalog Card Number: 85-90885
ISBN: 345-31471-9

Cover design by James R. Harris
Interior design by Ann Gold

Manufactured in the United States of America

First Edition: July 1986

10 9 8 7 6 5 4 3 2 1

This book is for my grandmother,
Shirley Levy Luttinger

Contents

Locations of Manuscripts

The Diaries of Yvonne Blue, Marie Barrows Streeter,
"Marion Taylor" and Winifred Willis
The Schlesinger Library, Radcliffe College,
Cambridge, Massachusetts.

The Diaries of Martha Lavell and Azalia Emma Peet
The Sophia Smith Collection, Smith College,
Northampton, Massachusetts.

The Diary of Martha Shaw Farnsworth
The Kansas State Historical Society, Topeka, Kansas.

The Diary of Deborah Norris Logan
The Historical Society of Pennsylvania,
Philadelphia, Pennsylvania.

The Diary of "Kate Tomibe"
The Bancroft Library, the University of California at Berkeley.

Transcript of the Diary of Eleanor Cohen Seixas
The American Jewish Archives, Cincinnati, Ohio.

The Diary of Carole Bovoso
Private Collection

The Diary of Annie Burnham Cooper
Private Collection

The Diary of Ethel Robertson Whiting
Private Collection. Microfilm copy in the Bancroft Library.

Acknowledgments

I have indeed been fortunate in having the assistance and support of some remarkable women. I would like to thank my agent, Lynn Seligman, for believing in me from the start; and Joëlle Delbourgo and Michelle Russell, my editors at Ballantine Books, for the patience and wisdom to see the project through.

I am grateful to the three living diarists: Carole Bovoso, Martha Lavell, and Yvonne Blue Skinner, for so generously sharing their lives with me. Nancy Willey (daughter of Annie Cooper), Margaret Stewart Oxley (granddaughter of Ethel Robertson Whiting), and Harriet Sabine (sister of Winifred Willis) provided a wealth of knowledge on those women.

Thanks are also due to the New York Feminist Art Institute, for the chance to teach journal writing; and to the many librarians and archivists across the country who helped in my research, most especially Susan Boone of The Sophia Smith Collection and Eva Mosely of The Schlesinger Library.

Last but not least, I'd like to thank my family for their love and patience. And to Elliott Swift, who provided moral support and editorial suggestions, and saw to it that I ate properly—my heartfelt gratitude.

Introduction

It's happened to all of us: we find unguarded, abandoned on a desk, by a bedside, or in an attic—someone else's diary. It lures us seductively. The desire to read it, to know intimately this hidden side of the writer, is almost irresistible.

"If she really didn't want it to be read, she wouldn't have left it lying around," we may think. This fascination with "private pages" extends to those of people we don't know and people we can never know, except through the medium of the printed word.

What's so fascinating about diaries? The lure of the forbidden may have something to do with it, but it's more than that. It has to do with what is revealed in a diary, levels of awareness that most people hide even from their most intimate friends. It has to do with why the diarist is what she is—and like Gretel's bread crumbs, it gives us a way to retrace her path. In the process, we may learn as much about ourselves as we do about the writer.

One might as well admit it: there's a bit of the voyeur in all of us. Who hasn't had the delicious thrill of eavesdropping on a private conversation? The details of other people's lives are intriguing because, after all, everyone's life is a variation on the same theme. It's our theme, too.

I've been fascinated with diaries for a number of years, especially those of women. This interest began very early in my life, although I didn't actually keep a journal until my twenties. I remember writing my name, the date, and a message on a slip of paper, and pushing it down a crack in the wall of my bedroom closet when I was about twelve. My primitive time capsule is still there, I guess, and I'm still intrigued by the question of who will find it, and when.

My interest in such "time capsules" increased when, grown

up, I moved into a house built in 1804. Beginning 170 years before, other women had left parts of their lives in that house. Those women were long dead, but they came alive to me as I shared the secrets of their lives for long hours in the dusty attic. I had stumbled upon the "diary" of a family, told in notebooks, letters, deeds, schoolbooks, faded photos, and tattered clothes.

That was in the 1970s, a time when women's lives were beginning to be taken more seriously. More women's writing began to be published, and I read it with excitement—both as a woman and in my professional capacity as an editor. About that time, a friend's mother showed me the nineteeth-century diaries of a New York State woman that she was preparing for publication. I was intrigued, and did some research into the publishing history of women's diaries.

What I found amazed me. The vast majority of published journals were those of men. Thousands of unpublished women's diaries were in archives across the country—thousands more, I realized, were in attics like my own. I noticed that the men's diaries published were often tales of exploration, war, politics, or adventure; or were those of famous literary or historical figures.

The women's diaries published were sometimes by famous women, but very often they were by the wife, mother, or sister of a famous man. Since women weren't, for the most part, climbing mountains or running for public office, no one had considered their personal diaries particularly interesting in themselves. But as I read more and more women's journals in manuscript, I became convinced that some of them were potentially more important than any man's journals of exploration in foreign lands.

These women, too, had recorded their adventures in uncharted territories. But their experiences, and the knowledge gathered along the way, could be of value to anyone—woman or man, young or old. They had described their travels over the common ground which we all tread in the passages of our lives; yet such encounters are rarely found in print with their fresh emotion intact.

My research began to focus on diaries that dealt with the "inner landscape," as opposed to the outer one. Such journals do not merely record events; they tend to become an integral part of the diarist's way of looking at and moving in the world. Often, everyday happenings merely trigger the reflections that are the diaries' real substance. These journals capture the process of living, with its ups and downs, enthusiasms and depressions, dreams and disappointments. They communicate the immediacy and the energy of daily life.

I use the terms "diary" and "journal" interchangeably. Both are related to words meaning "day", as Webster's will attest:

DIARY (from the Latin: *diarium*, day):
    A record of events, transactions or observations kept daily or at frequent intervals: journal; especially a daily record of personal activities, reflections, or feelings.
JOURNAL (from the French: *journal*, daily):
    An account of day-to-day events. A record of experiences, ideas or reflections kept for private use.

Both "diary" and "journal," in their present usage, refer to records that are kept regularly, but not necessarily every day. In fact, diarists often go for months, even years, between making entries.

The journal form's flexibility is part of its appeal. Diaries are not necessarily kept in bound books; entries may be made on loose sheets of paper, on the backs of envelopes, between the lines of an almanac—even on the endpapers of a novel. Their subject matter is absolutely unlimited: they can, and do, discuss everything from the weather to a lovers' spat to the existence of God. Some diarists write for hours a day, while others make the briefest possible notations. And diaries are kept for all kinds of reasons, as we shall see.

"How do you find these diaries?" I'm often asked. There's a very simple answer: they are everywhere.

"My mother kept a diary," says an elderly woman at a cocktail party. Or, "One of my neighbors found some notebooks in the trash," a fellow teacher reports. Many of the women you know probably keep journals, or did once. Go to any local library, and you're likely to find at least a few women's diaries. Visit any of the large university libraries or especially one of the major women's history collections and you will be overwhelmed by the wealth of women's diaries available.

And keep your eyes open. A standard human interest story, found in local newspapers everywhere, is some variation on "Aunt Mary died and we cleaned out the attic and guess what we found?" Strangers on the bus, seeing you write in your journal, will regale you with stories of theirs. Used bookstores have diaries in forgotten corners. And there are always yard sales, where the contents of many attics end up.

My research for this book has included all of these. Chance and luck have played their part. Of necessity, I've concentrated my efforts in major regional archives; at these libraries I could look at hundreds of diaries over the course of a few days. I also corresponded with smaller archives, relying on the librarians to send copies of journals that sounded interesting; and with a number of scholars, who generously shared manuscripts found during their own research.

Sifting through old manuscripts is, to me, one of the most exciting aspects of the work. Holding a diary in its worn cover and imagining the woman who wrote in it so long ago . . . touching the photos or clippings or faded flowers she pasted in . . . seeing the way her handwriting changed over the course of her life . . . such experiences have almost convinced me, at times, that I've known the woman herself.

At a library, I would thumb through the catalog, eliminating certain types of journals from the start. Travel diaries, for instance, are rarely introspective. Pioneer journals have been widely published, and are pretty much alike. Well-known women were out; I wanted "ordinary" diarists. Since I was aiming for geographical balance, as time went on I deliberately bypassed regions that were already well represented in my collection. I also decided against any journals that had been published already.

Each time I asked a librarian for a diary, I was filled with anticipation. I could never tell in advance what I might find. There might be one or two slim volumes that would fit into an ordinary file folder. Or there might be seventy or so large volumes, filling a number of cartons which taxed the strength of the student who had retrieved them from the basement. I was not popular, in such cases, as I peeked into the first heavy carton, only to quickly close the lid and say no thanks! But there were certain kinds of diaries that were rejected just that quickly. The "line a day" type, five days to the page, often kept in the tiniest handwriting for perhaps fifty years, was such. Any journal that couldn't be photocopied was unusable for my purposes: this included those that were physically fragile or seriously faded. And of course anything totally illegible wouldn't do, though I became adept at deciphering illegible words in otherwise readable handwriting.

All researchers have "Eureka!" stories, and I am no exception. After three exhausting days at a California library, one of the last manuscripts on my list was on microfilm. I almost didn't look at it—too impatient to face a struggle with the infernal machine—but I did, and dashed back to the reading room rejuvenated, excited by what I'd found. This was the diary of Ethel Whiting, and I'd only had to read a few pages to see that she was a natural writer, with a keen eye for detail and a wry sense of humor.

Some discoveries are quieter. A dignified-looking woman introduced herself to me at a party. Her mother's journals, tucked away in an old sea chest, seemed interesting, she said; and they were in her house, just around the corner. Would I care to drop by? Annie Cooper's diaries were funny, touching, and sad, and they made me completely reevaluate my concept of a Victorian girlhood.

Winifred Willis's journal arrived at my home neatly typed, edited after her death by her sister and a friend. The thick volume was intimidating at first; it covered over forty years in the difficult life of a sensitive, articulate writer. Its tortuous self-analysis was obviously too complex to condense easily. But I realized that the first year of the journal formed a self-contained and fascinating story—one embodying the classic conflict between love and work.

Together, the diaries in *Private Pages* trace the life cycle of women from adolescence through old age. The book begins with the diary of a thirteen-year-old California schoolgirl and ends with that of a seventy-seven-year-old Pennsylvania Quaker. It records schoolgirl crushes, love affairs, and friendships; marriages, pregnancies, the births and deaths of children; identity crises, career struggles, accomplishments and failures; motherhood, wifehood, divorce, and widowhood.

The diarists here lived at various times during the last two centuries. They were Americans from the West, the Midwest, the Northeast, and the South. They were students, farmers, homemakers, tradespeople, and professionals. They were of different ethnic, religious, and economic backgrounds. Yet all these differences quickly recede in the face of their similar emotions and experiences.

Why did these women keep diaries, and what did their journals mean to them? Marion Taylor adored hers:

"How nice a diary is. I could not get along without one. I enjoy writing what has happened as much as I enjoy the happenings themselves almost—thinking about them—living them over again and putting them in words. . . .

"I love to express my thoughts in writing. I like to analyze myself and things in general. It gives me great satisfaction to catch my thoughts on paper where they can't get away. It makes things clearer in my mind, to write them." (Summer 1919)

While Yvonne Blue was ambivalent:

"I picked up this book out of curiosity, while I was cleaning my closet; and as always the old nostalgic desire to write here seized me. . . . It's a strange kind of conceit that makes a totally unimportant person want to record for posterity all his pathetic little feelings and hopes and desires." (1931)

Martha Lavell, on the other hand, felt at times that journal-writing was a mistake:

"Somehow I feel that this book of thoughts will not survive

much longer. I am beginning to realize that it's rather bad for one's character. I have lately been accused of being ego-centric. Perhaps writing my thoughts is one proof of it." (April 24, 1931)

The reasons for diary-keeping are perhaps as numerous as diaries themselves have been. Women's journals are usually quite different from men's, and not merely because their everyday lives have been different. Women's diaries have special functions for them which are related to social expectations and the various limitations they impose.

A diary can be a "safe place" where new roles can be tried out, protected from censure; a sounding board for ideas or emotions that may not be acceptable to friends or family; a testing ground where creative experiments of all kinds can be tried, with no one to laugh if they fizzle; a means of regaining balance when caught by conflicting emotions; a valuable record of progress and growth; a place where past, present, and future live together—and all under one's control.

The diary often evolves into a friend, a confidante, the first place to run with an exciting secret and a last refuge when other people can't or won't listen. This has been especially important to women, who are often isolated physically by the conditions of their lives or psychically by restraints placed on the expression of their feelings. Annie Cooper voiced a common sentiment,

"I may as well put in one more line to my history. . . . Then too the old longing seems to be upon me to *tell* someone—and that I never do—so I resort again as when a child to you my Diary.

"Three years almost of life have passed since I last looked upon this book. They have been years of prosperity, years of comfort, years of *outward* free-heartedness and yet—to you *alone*, my Diary, I confess—they have been years of mute suffering." (May 28, 1892)

The act of keeping a journal is often a way for the writer to get in touch with and develop hidden parts of herself—often those aspects for which little support is given by others—and establish emotional stability and independence. The process can even be a means of keeping the personality intact under great stress—as the diaries of prisoners and invalids attest.

As a focus for complaints, anger, and bitterness, the diary can be a useful emotional safety valve. For Martha Shaw this was a way of shielding her family:

"I know it makes them all feel badly, to see me grieving. So I give them my smiles, write my sorrow here, [and] save my tears for the night hours." (August 13, 1892)

The journal allowed Eleanor Cohen to voice doubts about her fiancé, without seeming disloyal:

"There is a pang deep and sore at my heart . . . it seems strange to me that he should willingly as it were separate himself from me. To no human being would I express this thought for though it looks strange to me I doubt not he knows best . . . I pray to God to grant me strength, not to murmur or repine." (March 30, 1865)

Diarists often write in attempts at self-improvement, as did Annie Cooper:

"I have yielded to the world this past quarter very much more than I realized, but now . . . I start again on a clean page, & may God help me to keep it pure, full of good deeds, actions & thoughts." (March 1, 1885)

And a journal can preserve the satisfaction of accomplishment:

"I have three short stories that I have written—and finished!—since I have been here. My poems are selling better than might have been expected, and in every way my writing is improving." (Winifred Willis, July 13, 1923)

In time, to the diarist, the diary often develops a personality and is addressed directly: "Grand news dear old book, I guess this is the last entry Eleanor Cohen will make in this book . . . I will become Mrs. B.M. Seixas, this event long looked for is at hand." (July 26, 1865)

"How did I ever think I could give you up? Though I shall never go back to driveling I shall come to you at intervals. I shall always need you. I need you now." (Winifred Willis, September 9, 1923)

Many diarists, adolescent girls in particular, give the diary a name and compose entries as letters to this "friend." The friend may be an imaginary figure, such as a fairy godmother; a real person, idealized; or another girl much like herself. It may be a person the diarist hopes to meet (such as a future husband), or a descendant not yet born. One's future self is always an imagined audience, and sometimes this self is consciously addressed:

"I have discovered your personality, Diary. I was rather disturbed for a while before I did. You are Marion of the Future. I always knew it in a way but never realized it clearly." (Marion Taylor, August 1919)

The diarist is often concerned with how her audience perceives her, although that audience may be an amorphous presence whose character alters according to her mood. Deborah Norris Logan sometimes seemed to notice a reader over her shoulder:

"Dear reader . . . Invest me with all the dignity and wisdom which your conscience can allow. And in no account consider me in the light of a vain or foolish old woman." (April 27, 1835) "My future acquaintances, I mean readers (perhaps now unborn) . . . I must hope such will not figure me as morose, melancholy and adverse to the innocent enjoyments of life. . . . This is not the case at all." (January 6, 1837)

The parallels between the lives of these women are endlessly fascinating. The same themes arise over and over again: a longing for someone who is unattainable; the feeling that one is not "modern" enough; the conflict between "duty" and "freedom"; a feeling of alienation from one's peers; the longing for someone "who will understand"; the worry that the diary isn't well written or expressive enough; the fear of "going crazy"; the desire to "do something"—make one's mark in the world; and guilt at "neglecting" the diary.

So reading diaries from the past can challenge one's sense of time. It's something like traveling to a foreign country: one anticipates that everything in a new place will be different, yet so often the similarities far outweigh the differences. People are much the same everywhere. If this realization is disappointing, it is also reassuring. Like the traveler who feels unaccountably at home in a distant land, the reader of these diaries will experience no culture shock. Customs and technologies change, but human emotions remain the same. Today's reader may not recognize a butter churn when she sees one, but she can easily recognize jealousy, naiveté, or heartache in a diarist of 150 years ago. She may believe that Martha Shaw's loyalty to an alcoholic husband who abuses her for years is misplaced; but everyone knows what loyalty feels like, so Martha is not an alien being after all.

Their finished diaries were important to all these women. How do we know this? For one thing, they preserved the volumes they'd created for the rest of their lives. The diary can be of continuing interest to the writer, even long after it is written; in fact diarists often alter their journals years later. Sometimes lines are crossed out or pages cut away; often explanatory notes are added. When diarists type out their handwritten diaries they often take the opportunity to rewrite or edit, or disguise names or identities. Winifred Willis cut out whole sections of her journals when she typed them: years later, she restored some, but left a few omissions with the careful note, "this page removed by W.W." Martha Lavell removed several pages of her journal, bridging the gaps by inserting an equal number of pages on which she wrote a modified version (in larger handwriting to take up the space).

Indeed, the question of honesty seems to intrigue diarists.

"What is it about diaries, I wonder? You can't be honest in them—these pages are one long succession of poses of one kind or another—and if you were honest I don't know whether it would be much better." (Yvonne Blue, 1931)

"Once in a while I catch myself trying to fool myself—the silliest thing one can do. Sometimes when things are not quite what I would like them, I refuse to admit it in my diary, and write as if they were." (Marion Taylor, summer 1919)

"I have read, and I am afraid it is true, that people always give themselves away to their readers, in writing about themselves. I mean, let them strive ever so hard to prevent it, to hide the egotism, the littleness, the inconsistencies they absurdly do not want to see in themselves—they steal their way through." (Ethel Robertson Whiting, March 1924)

It seems that the longer a diary is kept, the harder it is for the diarist to conceal herself. "A succession of poses" cannot fool a reader for long. And in fact, as a diary progresses, the need for such poses becomes less. The diarist comes, more and more, to express herself just as she is.

Talking with diarists has taught me a lot about women's self-images. For several years in the early 1980s I taught journal writing to small groups of women, with participants ranging in age from late teens through late middle age. At the first class meeting, I always asked the women to share their journal writing history: to discuss what sorts of diaries they had kept in the past, and what the process meant to them.

Some had kept journals since childhood; others had just begun, or wanted to begin. Many had written for months or years and then stopped; they missed it, but felt a hesitancy to start again. Some were distressed because a friend, mate, or parent had read the diary without permission; sometimes the diarist had destroyed the books as a result. Often, since then, she'd been unable to write in a journal at all.

One kind of comment cropped up over and over again: "I'm not doing it right," i.e., "I don't write every day," "my entries are too emotional (or unemotional)," "my writing isn't descriptive enough," "it's too factual," "too mundane," "there's too much detail (or not enough)," "I write too fast," "too slowly," and so forth. Again and again, the feeling of a standard unmet.

Then, one by one, each diarist would read a few passages from her journal. Often a hushed silence followed each reading. We would stare at the reader, moved and unsure of what to say; each diary had a distinctive and powerful voice, yet seemed so little valued by the writer. "I can't really write," she might say, "I only write in my journal." Such reservations are expressed in many of the women's diaries I've read—regardless of when and where they were written.

I've noticed that, although the social role of women has changed over time, women's responses to their role (as expressed in their journals) have a repetitive ring. For hundreds of years women have confided to their diaries the fear that they don't match society's current ideal of womanhood.

Annie Cooper prays to become a better daughter; Ethel Whiting wishes she could be a better wife; Azalia Peet struggles to submit to God and Deborah Logan criticizes her own housekeeping. Martha Lavell wonders how to attract a "Prince"; Marion Taylor wants to be charming and Yvonne Blue wants to be thin. This state of affairs seems to be quite constant over time; only the fashions in beauty, duty or acceptable aspiration seem to change.

Yet it's easy to see that diarists have a common strength of character. Journal writing, after all, is a form of self-assertion. It's a way of saying "look at me, I'm here, I'm important," and if kept up for any length of time, it actually helps the writer become a stronger individual with clearer goals.

Mary Ellen Moffat in *Revelations: Diaries of Women*, expresses one view of women's journals:

> The form has been an important outlet for women partly because it is an analogue to their lives: emotional, fragmentary, interrupted, modest, not to be taken seriously, private, restricted, daily, trivial, formless, concerned with self, as endless as their tasks.

But there is a more positive view. Why not substitute: realistic, self-contained, patient, assertive, serious, individual, liberating, constant, accessible, flexible, proud, limited only by one's imagination?

The diary is all of these. What is more, these qualities mirror the strengths women admire in others and strive for in their own lives. Journal writing serves to reinforce these strengths. It is a refuge, but it need not be a means of hiding from the world.

The diarist may have real practical or emotional difficulties to overcome. Or perhaps she must learn to adjust her demands on herself. The diary is a valuable ally in these struggles: It is a way of gaining perspective and control. Journal writing can help to clarify the need to remain in a situation (such as Martha Shaw's marriage); to summon reasons for moving on (as Azalia Peet does as she decides to leave home to become a missionary); or to begin the process of change (like Carole Bovoso as she explores her dreams).

Editing and publishing diaries raises intriguing issues. Yvonne Blue pinpointed one at the age of fourteen:

"My diary is of interest only to myself. But possibly in years to come they might publish it. It makes my blood boil. It would have, of course, facsimilies of pages, illustrations, prefaces, introductions, explanations, notes and all the rest. . . . They correct ungrammatical phrases, and put down what they *think* you meant, and switch sentences around, and leave out the most interesting parts. . . . They would write a lot of junk in the front about me, and make me seem silly and sentimental and senseless. I don't want *anyone* to have fun out of what I sweated for, after I am dust and ashes. I don't *want* them to say, 'What a curious person! This book is a treasure.' . . . I'm not writing all this for them to read, and get pleasure from in after years. I'm writing it for *myself*, and for no one else."

Yet six years later, she comes to the conclusion: "All diary writers hope for posthumous publication."

Is publishing journals an invasion of privacy? There is a paradox here. While almost all diarists keep their journals private at the time they are written, most eventually view these earlier selves with some detachment, even amusement. With the passage of years, the journal is often shared with friends or family. Even when diarists keep their old volumes hidden, it is quite likely done to protect other people who were mentioned there, rather than the diarist herself.

Of the diarists in this book, four are known to have explored the idea of publication. One of them asked only that all names in the journal be changed, one specified that her diary be published posthumously, and two made their journals available virtually without restriction. In several cases too, the diarist's immediate family sought publication after her death. A number of these diarists personally donated their journals to researchers or archives, thus opening the way for publication.

Some years ago, I attended a journal workshop which raised for me an issue of editing. The leader opened the session with a reading from her own diary—a document so polished and lucid that it took everyone's breath away, along with whatever confidence each woman might have had in her own journals. It wasn't until the end of the workshop that the leader explained that she'd read carefully edited excerpts—not sections lifted verbatim from her diary. At this, there was a collective sigh of relief from the group. Each woman, it seemed, had been mentally comparing that precise, pristine journal with her own. And in every case she had found her journal wanting, and was understandably intimidated.

It's true that journals in the raw can be hard to read. They are repetitious; they make no sense at times; they talk in circles, never getting to the point; they go on interminably about some details while leaving out others. Editing a journal is, of necessity, creating something new—cleaner and somewhat clearer than the original document. Yet one must be careful to edit the diary without editing the life itself.

For if the framework of the diarist's life is somewhat askew, it's probably a fairly typical life. If the diarist is confused and uncertain at times; if she contradicts herself; if she breaks good resolutions or fails to carry out her worst threats—and if she details these things in her diary—it's all to the good. The diary will be a better one for all that and the reader will appreciate it. Such inconsistencies should not be removed, for they are part of what makes a diary so valuable. Journals are the opposite of autobiographies or memoirs, which invariably gloss over or eliminate most of life's irregularities. A diary brings the reader much closer to the ebb and flow of real life.

For this reason, reading well-edited diaries can be very reassuring. Many of us have unrealistic expectations of ourselves, partly because the lives of people we admire, as we've read about them, have had the wrinkles taken out. Those lives have often appeared seamless, so much tidier than ours. We've tried to imitate them and, of course, we couldn't. And yet, everyone's life holds contradictions, inconsistencies, insecurities, messy stops and starts. Journals can teach us this. Perhaps this is the secret of the fascination of diaries: These private pages can give us, their readers, permission to be human.

A Note About the Diaries
in this Book

Each of the diarists in this book has a distinctive writing style. Sometimes that style isn't technically perfect, but attempting to impose one set of rules on all would spoil their individual flavor. Therefore, I have corrected only those grammatical errors which interfered with meaning. I have left all original spelling, except in cases of obvious slips of the pen or typographical errors.

Since each of the excerpts printed here has been edited from a much longer document, there would be thousands of ellipses had I chosen to use them. Ellipses have been used only occasionally where a lengthy anecdote has been shortened. Paragraphing has been left virtually unchanged, except in a few cases where the original was unnecessarily confusing. In no case have I changed the meaning or order of the diarist's words. Added words or phrases have been indicated with brackets.

Some of these diaries were edited from typed transcripts rather than original manuscripts. I have checked the accuracy of the transcripts wherever possible; however, in some cases the original no longer exists. I have indicated each diary's origin in a list at the front of the book.

THE DIARY OF

Marion Taylor

Los Angeles, California
1915–1920

$\diamond$ $\diamond$

Introduction

At the age of nine Marion Taylor, a California schoolgirl, received a small pocket diary as a Christmas gift from her grandmother. For the first three days of the new year, 1912, she wrote of her Papa's new auto, school, her sister, and her doll. "It seems as if everything was new, and I want to be new, too," she says.

Marion Taylor (not her real name) had been born in 1902 in Illinois, the first child of Hannah and Donald Taylor, respectively a former schoolteacher and dentist. Her sister Caroline was born four years later; the family moved to California when Marion was almost seven.

Marion's first attempts at journal writing did not hold her interest for long. An eighteen-month gap follows the first three entries; the next is dated July 16, 1913:

"Dear Diary: We are living in Glendale now. Pape doesent live with us any more, but we are living very happiley in a beautiful little house"

Marion's parents had separated. Years later she remembered:

"After ten or eleven years of married life my father decided that he must be free to marry his pretty sixteen year old office girl and insisted on a divorce . . . it was a great blow to my mother. I remember hearing the news from her as she lay weeping in bed that Papa didn't love her anymore and that we were going to move away."

Marion had been much closer to her father, but she took her mother's side in the dispute. Mrs. Taylor, a cool and reserved person at best, was now pressed and overworked by financial difficulties. Nor was Marion close to her sister Caroline. Her need for a sympathetic friend was filled by her journals. By the age of twelve, Marion had developed the habit of writing at least once a day—a habit she was to maintain for the next twenty years.

Marion's mother enjoyed writing (she had kept "Baby Books" for both her daughters and published nature articles in the local paper), and at first she encouraged Marion to keep the diary. Later, however, when this writing assumed a major role in Marion's life, her mother "became exasperated with me for the hours I devoted to it," Marion

3

wrote. "A diary to her is the epitome of all that is foolish, impractical and idle."

In spite of, and perhaps partially because of, this lack of understanding on her mother's part, Marion wrote more and more. As time went on, she began to keep many different types of notebooks. After several of her schoolmates discovered and exposed her original diary, she began a second, more secret one, addressed to her adored teacher Miss Green and titled, at first, *Ego Amor Miss Veridis*, later *Letters She Never Sent (to Miss Green the Beloved)*. She always kept this secret diary with her, in her desk at school and under her pillow at night. During her adolescence Marion also kept notebooks of poetry she liked, comments on books read, nature observations, religious ideas, and stories she wrote.

Nature was another special interest, and by her early teens Marion had become a local authority on birds, answering queries from neighbors and contributing articles to the town newspaper. She was also a talented artist and storyteller. "My stories are in great demand," she wrote in April of 1914.

In December of the same year, she noted that she and a friend, Ruth Brewster, "have spent all our spare time writing love stories." Marion's mother disapproved of this (partly, perhaps, because of her own romantic disillusionment), but Marion was not dissuaded; she and three friends formed a "secret story writing club" and continued to create. (This later evolved into the "I.Q." club, prominent in the diary's early years.)

And so in February of 1915, "Marion stands on the threshold of adolescence with a well-established habit of writing in her diary; a strong inner need for such an outlet has not yet arisen, but the path of expression is ready—very important in the year to come when Marion finds herself suddenly in the maelstrom of adolescent emotions, with experiences and cravings she can confide to no human ear. Then Dear Diary comes to her rescue, becomes vitalized, ready to receive those precious confidences."—Gordon W. Allport

Marion Taylor's adolescent diaries came to the attention of Harvard psychologist Gordon Allport in the late 1930s, through mutual friends. Allport had long been interested in journals—his mother's and grandmother's diaries were valued and preserved within his family—and he saw the Taylor manuscript as a unique means of exploring the development of a personality in depth.

The grown-up Marion Taylor, who had a professional as well as a personal interest in psychology, gave her full cooperation to the study; she contributed autobiographical writings, took personality tests, and allowed friends and family to be interviewed about her. Allport's extensive notes, partially quoted here, describe Taylor in depth and trace elements of her mature personality back to their earliest manifestations in her adolescent diaries.

Allport envisioned the Taylor study as the first in a projected series to be used for teaching purposes. Unfortunately, it was never completed. The original source material (including Taylor's journals), along with Allport's research notes, were donated to The Schlesinger Library by his family after his death. In editing the Taylor diaries, I have drawn from Allport's transcriptions of the various notebooks which she often kept simultaneously, and arranged them as closely as possible according to date. All names in the diary have been changed.

◇ *1915* ◇

FEBRUARY 9. Dear Friend, Today I am thirteen (13) years old! I am in my teens. I had the I.Q. up and oh the fun we had! What I.Q. means has never been written on paper until now. As a great secret I will tell you what it means. It means Ingenious Quartet. Well when we got home we played valentine games and we had a programe and had a jolly time. We had a beautiful birthday cake. There was a dime, a thimble, and a ring baked in it.

Charlotte Foote got the dime, Caroline got the ring and the thimble wasn't found. I was in hopes I'd get it cause I am going to be an old maid. I made a solemn vow never to be married this morning and I intend to keep it.

I feel very aged today. I am in my "teens"!

FEBRUARY 23. How I love school! I would die without it. I used to hate it but the work is so easy and I get such fine marks and it is so intresting and theres the I.Q. and above all my teacher Miss Green!

MARCH 19. Today the I.Q. outright quarreled. I came home bauling and mama saw my eyes were red and someway she managed to worm it out of me. They are all down on me cause I talk about Miss Green so much. Talk about that for a grudge! And I'm not so silly as Ruth. She acts dead silly over a boy! A boy of all things! I think that though they say they don't like Miss Green, they are secretly jealous. Ruth is awful silly about Harold Russel, her affinity. I never could abhor boys anyway! Anyone would love Miss Green! Mother said that!

MARCH 22. Today what do you think happened? It fairly stunned me. I cant realize it. A horrible tradgedy. The girls (Ruth and Molly but not Charlotte) went and, for some mean and unacountable reason *told Miss Green that I was crazy over her ect.* They went up at noon and Ruth told me later that they told her that they wanted her advise on the subject. Think of telling her that! She said that it would soon wear off, ect. Well—there's where she's mistaken! My love, adoration, and reverance and

6

respect of her will never "wear off." Never! I shall always, always, adore her. How I should like to shake those girls.

MARCH 24.   *Members of the I.Q.*
                    Ruth Brewster
                    Charlotte Foote
                    Molly Whiteman
                    Marion Taylor

Ruth is my especial chum. She is Welsh and very literary and we are kindred spirits. Charlotte is very pretty. Dimples and curly hair and brown eyes. She says she is going to be a movie actress. Molly is very dignified and a perfect dear. She has light hair and blue eyes and she keeps the rather rowdy I.Q. nicely balanced.

Miss Green was a dream today. Just lovely. She wears the lovliest clothes, simple, appropriate, ellegant and lovely. She has beautiful humorous twinkling brown eyes that seem to take in everything at a glance and fluffy brown hair, and an aristocratic nose—as aristocratic as a princesses'. She is different from other teachers and people. She knows just *everything*, I believe. She is *wonderful*. (She is 26 or 28 I *think*! I wish I knew for sure!)

APRIL 1. Ah! Only a girl knows the sensation of being crushy! I am not boy struck as yet although Ruth and Charlotte are. Molly is to dignified to be either although she sometimes mentions so and so back in Michigan.

APRIL 9. Miss Green was a dream today! She wore a beautiful new pink dress and she looked lovely. A soft, frilly dainty little dress that looked lovely with her pretty soft flyaway hair blowing abought her face and with her bright dark brown eyes full of humourous twinkles, her whole beautiful face alight! Mother went to the Parent Teachers association and saw Miss Green and talked to her abought the time those girls went and told cause I felt awful abought it and Miss Green said that she liked it! Miss Green is the most wonderful thing! Oh how I adore her! Anyone would.

I must have somebody to confide in. The girls of our I.Q.

laugh and sneer at me and it is sacred and it shall *not* be laughed or sneered at.

I was reading a book at the library, *The Lass of the Silver Sword*, and it gave me the idea of this book [special secret diary], only this book shall *not* be discovered.

I just *must* have someone to adore and love!

I don't think it is a crush—from what I know of crushes, they are very, very silly.

I respect and revere Miss Green and I do not love her in a silly way. Of all things I desire most, is her good opinion of me.

APRIL 13. Im going to tell you an awful secret—I hate to write it and I can never let anybody see this diary if I do. I have got some papers or have had, pinned to my waist (underwaist) abought her (M.G.) what I think abought her ect. and now I've got my natural science test paper with her writing on it. It's a great comfort to know that dear papers there. No one knows. Someday I'll think that's awful silly but I don't now.

And I have a shrine. Hidden and secret with some papers buried there and flowers on it. Those are my most secret of secret secrets.

APRIL 14. Every once in a while I will hear a suppressed giggling and looking over see those crazy I.Q. girls (the horrid old dears) just bursting with laughter whenever they catch me looking at her, M.G., and dreaming. They actually upset my dignity.

Molly, Charlotte and I and two other girls took a long tramp in the Hills. We had a heavenly time. We ate our lunch looking down in the valley from the hills. I kept bumping into things cause I was dreaming and dreaming of her.

APRIL 20. Last night Ruth and I walked home together and Ruth told me one of her day dreams and I told her one of mine. It was a very fanciful dream about M.G. and I.

I have so many dreams like them. M.G. never lets *me* help her. Ruth helps her and everything. Oh Well! Such is life.

R. and I have established a *very* secret club—the C.C. standing for Confidential Club. The other members of the I.Q. know nothing of it. It is for the purpose of confidential confidings.

I feel just like crying. Silly goose that I am! I misplaced this book a minute ago and I was simply wild for a minute. Then again M.G. has been near all noon and never said a word to me. Just looked at me once. And I love her so! I would do anything in the world for her—I want to please her so! Nearly every thought of mine is abought her.

Prehaps the reason she kind of avoids me is because prehaps I unconsciously act stiff or cold in her presence.

Well I'm always embarressed and self conscious and excited and tongue tied when I'm with her anyway. Well I'll try my best to act natural because I do want her to like me—more than anything else in the world! Whenever I pass her my heart beats wildly and I act as if I diden't see her.

One time I went in to show M.G. a book on leaves of mine and the other girls (the big horrids!) all of them—followed me in and stood acting only as girls can, giggling and laughing at me until I could hardly keep my self-control. My face was as *red*. I just rushed out and came as near bauling as I have.

APRIL 21. Tonight on the way home from school Ruth told me something. Now sometime ago (abought two weeks) she wrote a note to me asking me to write "Why I love Miss Green," all abought it you know saying that she wanted it for a souviner. I wrote it—one paper on both sides expressed as plainly as in this book. Well Ruth said that a few days ago she felt mischievous and she—took—that—paper—and—gave—it—to—Miss—Green. Well—She said that she (Ruth) said "Miss Green, I have a paper here I think you'd like to see," and Miss Green said, "Certlnly." So she began reading it and when she had read a little she said I haven't time to read any more (for the bell rang just then) but who wrote this? "Look on the other side," Ruth said. And there my name signed in full—Marion Taylor to her Chum Ruth Brewster. "Why bless her dear hart"! said Miss Green (or something to that effect) "to think she would have written such a thing abought me! Marion doesn't come around here very much. I wonder why." "I don't know," said Ruth, "I think Marion is rather researved." "Yes, prehaps that's it," said Miss Green. (Bless her heart). Dear, dear, dear Miss Green!

APRIL 22. If I ever am fool enough to marry I shall marry a quiet grave, serious, man; literary in his tastes and a great deal older than I. If I ever have children I want my baby (I hope I don't have more than one!!) quiet and the kind that likes to be cuddled and loved and not a rembunktious kid like some. But I do want to be an old maid! My disposition is not suited to marriage. I am dignified and unaffectionate, and not soft and giggly and cute like the ones that are fit for marriage.

MAY 1. This morning I left the May Basket on her desk. It was a little brown basket with Roses in it and candy ect.

This noon she came and sat down beside me and laid her cheek against mine (Bless her dear loving Heart!) and I got as red as a beet or so the girls said I did. But I liked it! Oh yes! No one ever did such a thing to me before! My Mother is the only one who even ever kissed me (and Dad). She said a lot of nice things. I asked her how she knew I gave it to her and she said "A little bird told me." Oh Dear! Oh Dear! Why can't I act natural! She probably classes me as a silly, bashful country Jake.

MAY 2. How I love her! She is so lovely to everyone and no one else ever treats me (big grown up, *over* grown, long legged, awkward *me*) like that. (Bless her warm loving heart!)

Oh my greatest wish is to be as wonderful and loving and lovely as she is when I get big. I get loved so very little that a little affection like that means a great deal to me, and especially when its from her.

MAY 8. I am very ill [with chicken pox] and absolutely misable and all I can do is *think*! Sometimes I get to thinking this book is disgustingly sentimental but it's just the way I feel—therefore *I* must be sentimental. My dear sensible non sentimental mother would be horrified! (if she knew)

This book is such a comfort to me! When I feel lonesome and desperate and am thinking of her and when I feel selfish and jealous (that concerns one of the secrets I can't tell even here. It's one I'm ashamed to tell.) why I read over a few pages and write a few and I feel lots better.

MAY 15. I have been thinking that I want more than a high school and Normal education. I want a college education. Miss Green has a college education. I'm afraid I can't be a Natural Science teacher which is what I specially want to be without it. Well that is all in the far away future!

This is Study period with her, next best to Natural Science period. Every time I look up at her I feel someone looking and giggling and there that dear, crazy I.Q. will all be watching me and giggling.

Oh Well! I suppose I will have to look out of the window and dream. I have been writing a long story, a Boarding School story and a teacher, one of the most prominent characters is Miss Green. I make her just like Miss Green. I have her say the same funny things and I have her with the same "fluffly fly away brown hair and twinkling bright humourous brown eyes" and everything. I'm getting envious of the heroine Betty Brooks cause M.G. treats her so lovely. But its a great comfort. I pretend I am Betty.

I get so excited sometimes writing about Betty and She.

It is extremely interesting. I think (mabe) I will write a novel—herone—Helen Green. Charming! That idea, I mean.

MAY 27. Sunday morning we went down to Papa's [office]. (Just us kids went.) He said I'd grown a foot. He told us to come down in the afternoon and he would take us for a ride. We did and went riding all around. He took us all over in the auto, got us ice-cream, gum and candy.

JUNE 2. We lay in [Charlotte's] hammock and look up into the arch of branches above and it is cool and dreamy and quiet and wonderful. Well, Ruth was charmed with it and we laid in that hammock squeezed in like sardines and dreamed and whispered and told imaginings and had a fine time. Then we went in and made divinity candy and oh it was delicious! and ate it in the hammock and Charlotte and Ruth played on the piano and we all felt dreamy because we were in dreamy moods.

JUNE 3. I am in a turmoil of feeling! I am angry (mad) discouraged, lonesome and tearful. M.G. treats me perfectly *all right.* Almost like the others (on the top it looks just as she treats

the other girls but it *isen't*!) She treats me *very* cooly (more so
than anyone else) She kind of looks at me in a mocking, you-
are-ver-y-annoying sort of way. I *can't* stand it! I love her so and
it cuts me to the heart to have her treat me so.

I don't love, really love, many people—I am not very affectionate but when I really *love* anyone I *love* them and I love
them deeply, more than anyone knows.

And when you love as I love her it hurts you deeply, cuts
you to the heart—to have that person distinctly show dislike.
It matters a great deal wheather they like you or not and it
hurts—it hurts awfully when they dont.

JUNE 4. Something has happened so that it is necessary to
keep this book in the farthest corner of my locker at school and
hidden in a drawer at home for awhile at least. Something that
cant be explained here—something that I dont want to explain.

I dont think I will write in here for a little while, little book.
I haven't the heart to. But I *must* express my thoughts and tell
them to somebody so prehaps I will write them on loose paper
and then destroy them. All I can say to explain is that a low,
cruel, unkind trick has been played on me. As soon as possible
I will come back and write in you dear book.

JUNE 6. Dear Me! We *are* getting sentimental aren't we!

I am in a particularly healthy joyous state of mind this evening
and this book disgusts me beyond measure! Sickeningly sentimental! I shall get a new one tomorrow and it shall be a sensible
healthy optimissistical one.

Great Guns and little fishes! Save us all! Instead of raising
her opinion of me as has been my greatest wish no dought I've
lowered it!

Thank Goodness I've come to my right (sane) mind at last.

Farewell to *disgusting* sentimentalty, Oh hail to a healthy kind!

Your *now* Sane and sensible Author with Heartfelt apologies
for this piece of disgusting sentimentlety.

JUNE 10. I am afraid I have been too open in this book—
that is, telling and revealing my most sacred, tender, secrets—
the ones that are dear to me and nearest my heart, but no one
has ever read this book—and no one ever will so I guess my

secrets are safe. No one will ever know them, they will remain secret in my heart and in this book.

She will never know. And not all of my secrets abought her are written in this book. Some of my day dreams abought her, some of my feelings and thoughts of her are sacred, so sacred and dear that I cannot write them even here.

JUNE 13. I feel that this book *is* a little bit "too much" and the reason I feel so is this; I would be ashamed to have Her see it and some of its silliness therefore it must not be all it should be. And so I am not going to write—it is not necessary and my feelings and emotions are more than I can explain. They have become so great and so un-understandable to me that I will not attempt to write them down.

JUNE 14. Papa is going to be married again sometime this month and it is only on the 8th of this month and he gets the final divorce decree and *can* get married! Do you wonder that I am determined to be a Bachelor maid?

JUNE 15. Vacation seems such a waste of time. So useless. There is nothing expecial to live for. Oh I can never settle down to a quiet married life and work and the monoteny. You get up in the morning and do dishes three times then to bed again with a vision of countless days just the same. If I had to look forward to a life of it! Oh! My hope and salvation is next fall— school.

JUNE 23. I am getting old—going on fourteen. I get to feeling rather old when I recolect that in a very few years I must be earning my own living! Dear me! I can't imagine lazy, book-worm, dreamy unsensible *me* earning my living.

Mother says that I'd better be getting sensible some of these days. There's plenty of time to do that! When I get big.

My ambitions are daily reaching higher. A college education now. Papa tells me to get that "bee out of my bonnet". He says colledge isen't good for girls! Nonsense! *I'm* not going to be a "wifie" and household drudge! But I'm going to have the College education! If I have to work my way through (which I probly will.)

JULY 4. Papa told us that he was married and had been for

three weeks. We have suspected but didn't know for sure. Well I hope he's contented and got what he wants at last! Papa is trying more and more as Caroline and I get older to make us believe that the separation ect. wasn't his fault. We, at least I, refuse to be convinced!

JULY 13. My Hero. If I marry which I hope I never shall do as I think I am too old maidish to get along well with a man I shall marry no younger than at twenty five (by then I ought to have a little sense) And I shall marry a middle aged man (in late thirtys or early forties), with more sense than I so as not to get mad at me whenever I do anything wrong. He shall be patient and literary and fond of books and love me enough to not mind my homliness. I will not expect any romantic ravishing love like in books. I shall never have children.

JULY 14. I go over to the playground all the time now. Miss Howe [playground supervisor] is dear but she is not unusual. She hasn't much of a sense of humor and has no personality and charm like Miss Green and I can't help comparing her with M.G. (Oh how I long to see the said M.G.!!) But she is a darling and a regular sport in playing.

JULY 23. Miss Howe was over for dinner. She looked too dear for anything! She is very pretty. English I think. She has been through college. She is a dear!

JULY 26. I was over at the playground all day. I played seven games of volley ball with four different boys. I'm a regular shark in volley ball.

There are a couple of swings and we pump up (standing up) way up high. Charlotte (she goes over there all the time now and its' just because of the boys there!) won't pump up unless its' with a boy. She's simply sickening over the boys but the funny part of it is the boys like her silly baby ways!—I can't see why a girl can't be comradely and nice with a boy without getting silly. She giggles and giggles at whatever they say and acts so babyish and they *like* it!!

JULY 27. Two things I'm going to learn and they are dancing and tennis. Then I shall learn to play cards and play croquet ball, and basket ball if I can. I am not pretty nor am I witty or clever nor charming and I *must* know something to make up for it.

I am pretending that I have a Fairy Godmother—and perhaps I have, for all I know!

I want someone in whom to confide my secrets and who as good as she? So I am going to write her a letter and unburden my heart of the subject that is oftenest present in my mind.

Dear Fairy Godmother:—

I feel that you are a person that can understand and sympathize so I am writing to you.

I am at the age of Hero Worship. I have Heroes galore and they of course are the persons with whom I come in contact.

Therefore my heroes are mostly teachers—school teachers. Towards each of that kind of person I feel most lovingly inclined.

Of course there is an especial hero—in this case Heroine. Instead of boys on whom a great many girls lavish their affection I have a heroine and I jolly well make up for not being silly over boys! In short as you have doughtlessly understood already—I have a crush on a teacher.

Now Fairy Godmother—you are a fairy and you must be able to see things more clearly than a person.

Under my pillow each night is her letter to me that she wrote when I was ill and when I feel tired and unhappy and bad at night I get into bed and with my hand under my pillow on the letter I feel better and I forget my woes and think of Her.

I pray each night that I may be charming and beautiful and witty that she may like me and I pray that she will know just the least little bit how I love her.

And now dear Fairy Godmother you know it all and I know you understand as well as I do though I can't express it so Good Bye and God Bless Her!

Your Godchild
Marion Taylor

[Undated] I can't for the life of me refrain from nearly splitting with laughter over this passionate, lovelorn epistle although I know very well I was deadly in earnest when I wrote it! Oh Marion of the future I hope you have a sense of humour! (if you ever read this!) Realy I think this thing is *insulting* to her— a perfectly sensible, respectable woman.

Some day when I get the 'big-head' and feel terribly sensible or when I feel disgusted with some 'Sentimental Jane of a Girl' I hope I shall read this. I reckon it will lessen my opinion of myself somewhat. But still I was dreadfully in earnest and Miss Green is very dear and I still love her and I'm not beyond a little silliness now.

JULY 30. Tomorrow is Caroline's great day. She is going to the music teachers big recital in which she is to play. Mother and she will be gone all day tomorrow and I will spend my day at the playground. Thank my stars I stopped my music. What if I had to play in a recital!

AUGUST 2. I was over at the Playground practically all day. Miss Howe is the dearest, the prettiest, cutest, sweetest, darlingest thing! I have more fun at that playground. Caroline acted awful over her lesson this evening. Caroline is so everlasting sure of herself and hates to be told anything.

AUGUST 3. Miss Howe is adorable! Why I almost forget Miss Green for hours at a time over there! Oh, no! She's not to compare with Miss Green! and I don't get such crushes as I have on M.G. every day but shes mighty nice just the same.

I certainly am at a dangerous age! The age of Hero worship. Why I worship every moderately young (from 18 to 40) person in skirts!

AUGUST 5. As a general rule I do not like boys. There such funny creatures! I much prefer females! Thank my stars I'm not a boy!

I intend to be ladylike and dignified and girlish and sensible and not go out of my way for the boys and if they don't like it they don't have too, and if they do—alright!

AUGUST 7. I had to sew a lot this morning. Mother says if I don't finish that negligee, before we go to the beach I'll have to do it there! I don't take any interest in my clothes at all and it makes mother so mad.

AUGUST 11. We left for the beach at 9:00 this morning. Miss Howe was passing near our house on her way to the playground and I ran out to say goodbye to her. She was so nice and she kissed me goodbye! I shall most probly never see her again but I shall always remember her!

AUGUST 14. My ambition this summer is to become athletic. I want to be strong and healthy and athletic looking. I saw a woman in the surf today who was the finest example of health and strength I have seen. Big muscular, brown limbs and so straight and tall.

AUGUST 16. My nose is the trial of my life. It is big and shapeless and usualy pimpeled and always red. Oh for a nose like Miss Green's! Hawked! Hawked noses like hers are aristocratic. How I long for one. I wish I was back with the Playground and Miss Howe! And oh I wish school would begin!!!!

AUGUST 25. I just paused in my writing to lend my ear to a lecture from mother. I say snappy things to Caroline all the time and mother says I'm getting to be an awful (lemon) old maid. She says I'd be just the same to my husband. No dought. For that very reason I'll not have a hub. There awful bothers anyway. I can make lots of friends (I've got lots of girl friends) when their just very dear friends like chums and I don't know them *too* intimatly. I don't think I could get along with a man though. I can see so many things abought men, rather childish, babyish things that I'd be sure to say some sarcastic bity thing. Men are so funny. Theyre so boyish—oh well you know what I mean. I'm a born old maid—that's what I am.

SEPTEMBER 2. I've had a spell of meloncholy (I guess thats what it is) lately. It is very unpleasant. I have morbid fears and am perfectly miserable.

SEPTEMBER 3. I had one of my awful sick headaches today. Too little exercise and too much reading and writing. I love to write letters, storys, anything and it isn't good for me.

SEPTEMBER 10. Charlotte certainly does have a good time with the boys. She usualy is quite comradly and chummy with them as she should be but sometimes she does get awful silly! She is more of a little girl in her tastes and likes and everything than the rest of the I.Q. She plays and cuts up and is so lively and giggly. She's not as deep nor as serious as Ruth or I but I think she stands a better chance of being happy in life than either of us too. She will never be melancholy and she'll never take things too seriously. And sometimes I think those frivalous, merry, lively, 'cute', giggly, free kind make better wives when they get older! My kind is too serious.

SEPTEMBER 13. SCHOOL! It has begun! I've looked forward to today all vacation. Miss Howe was just *lovely* and darling but Miss Green beats her to smash. She held my hand all the time she was talking and was so nice to me! We talked abought fifteen minutes in the hall.

[An imaginary reply from Fairy Godmother]

Dear Marion:

I am writing to you at the beginning of the new school year for I think you need help in forming new resolutions and you need good advice and sympathy and some plain speaking more than at any other time.

Now we will treat the most important subject first: Miss Green. Do remember my child that she is only a humane being! A humane being like yourself. Worship her, adore her, admire her, love her—if I know you as well as I think I do you cannot help it, but have a wholesome, healthy love for her. She is a wonderful woman and you are a romantic young girl.

Now remember this Marion. Now I am speaking out plainly and it is for your sake; strive to overcome your love of making an impression. You like to impress people—You know what I mean so we will not go into details.

Don't be loose-mouthed—Keep things to yourself—it is a good test of your emotions and feelings if you feel the same [way] without imparting it to anyone. This will be harder for you than anything else. If you cannot do it then it is not genuine feeling and is not worth while.

Whenever you are doing anything or saying anything or striking an attitude for the benefit of anyone else, just remember this and forget yourself—act natural.

Try to over-come your self-consciousness.

A Few of the Most Important Rules for the New School Year.

Keep it your ambition to get the highest [report] card in the room.

Do not talk abought M.G. You know it antagonises the girls (I.Q.) and don't make up for not talking abought her by talking abought M.H. (Miss Howe).

Don't think abought M.G. any more than you can help. Remember you mean nothing to her though she may mean the world to you. And she will go out of your life forever when you leave this school. The more you think of her the harder it is going to make it for you when you leave.

Don't make rash and silly statements.

Smile! Smile! Look animated and pleasant. You're an awful lemon when you don't.

Be sure of yourself. Be confident in yourself. Just think who you are and throw back your shoulders.

Be very very neat in your personal appearance. A lady is always neat!

Speak low and softly.

Don't show off.

Say pleasant things about people. Never say unkind things.

Cultivate a charm. Make your conversation interesting. To be a perfect lady, to be charming, interesting, delightful, be as like your M.G. as possible and you will succeed!

SEPTEMBER 22. Jelly-cake! Say that one word to the I.Q. and they will laugh, sigh or cry according to how they feel. Charlotte brought a jelly-cake, ten sandwitches, and five peaches. Molly brought 2 hard boiled eggs, two peaches, ten sandwitches, and I brought two pears, one banana and five sandwitches (Ruth diden't bring anything extra). All this was for our lunch with Miss Green and—she never came!

We waited and waited and we began to think she wasn't at Intermediate today, but in the afternoon we saw her here. We got tired of waiting so we ate our lunch. If we weren't disappointed. It was no joke I can tell you. We felt awful. She just forgot that's all. And she diden't know we were going to make such a big thing of it and that we were so excited. We call Miss Green "Jelly cake" now. The I.Q. will never forget this. We don't know wheather to consider it a joke or not.

SEPTEMBER 23. When M.G. saw us in the hall today she ran into the office and then peeked out. She said she was ashamed to face us. She coulden't come because when she got back from the school she was at in the morning it was after one o'clock and she had to go right in and teach! "Well, some night after school you four girls will have to go with me to a drug store [soda fountain] and talk this over," she said. Just think!

OCTOBER 6. I showed M.G. my class picture and she whispered to me that it was the nicest class in school and she liked it best! Really I think she favors the I.Q. She is such a dear! M.G. had her arm around me all the time we were talking and she squeezed me and put her cheek up to mine. I not affectionate? I not like affection? I not like a little 'loving' (by the right people)??? Don't you worry! Mother thinks I *don't*. Well I *do*. I just love it! And I get very little of it too.

OCTOBER 9. I've been feeling meloncholy again of late. I get meloncholy and have morbid fears that I might or am going crazy. It's awful.

OCTOBER 14. I'm having my monthly now. It isen't regular yet. I think thats why I have meloncholy spells. I'm just growing. I'm 5 ft. 5 and I only weigh 99 lbs.

OCTOBER 16. I've worked like sixty. And written in my story book. Mother doesen't approve of my writing—she doesn't like the stories nor the fact that I spend all my time on them but I do love to write and if I get an idea for a story I just have got to write it down.

OCTOBER 22. Natural Science today. Miss Green is so dear and so lovable! You don't know and you can't understand how I love her! I have toned down a lot. I am not so effusive and crazy in my adoration but I love her more than ever in more sensible way. Next to my mother she is the very lovliest woman in the world and I love her next. I'm getting sensible awful fast.

NOVEMBER 2. I had a sick headache today and my sick headaches are pretty bad. My head aches so and I can't strain my eyes so I can't read and this writing is all Mother will let me do. Mother says here's where the story writing stops—not enough exercise to digest my food.

NOVEMBER 3. I think the reason girls are silly (over boys and teachers) is because there is a certain sentimentality and romanticness and dramaticness in their hearts they've got to lavish on *somebody*. They woulden't be girls if they were *normal*.

NOVEMBER 5. Oh, I hope I have a sense of humour when I grow up or I shall be so ashamed of myself upon looking back over girlhood and my M.G. case, I shall never recover.

I'm glad my affection for her is getting more sensible. M.G. is too very lovely and free from silly sentiment and too frank and sweet to have anyone moping over her in silliness like *that*!

NOVEMBER 27. I am very glad I'm not crazy over the boys for if I were I should have to act like Charlotte does—do some of the 'chasing' for believe me *they'd* never do any of after me unless I did a good deal of it too! But I never worry abought my popularity with the *boys!*

DECEMBER 11. I recieved a compliment today. Mother told me that a boy on our street (he's just thirteen), his mother told her that he liked Marion for she was sensible and diden't talk abought the boys all the time. She is tall and sweet like her mother, he said. Oh I *do hope* lots of people think as well of me as that! I do *hope* I appear sweet and sensible.

DECEMBER 18. This diary is awfully conceited! Awful big important "me's" and "I's" in it!

Mother says I'm getting awfuly affected in my talk, and manner, ect. She says nothing is so detestable as an affected girl. It's come upon me quite unconciously. I'll be glad when I'm grown up and safely out of all the dangerous ages and settled for good.

DECEMBER 31. Caroline told me that mother said to the doctor when they were down there that "the other girl," (meaning me) was so differant from Caroline "She" (meaning me) "is stupid. Stupid Physically."

Well that isen't a very nice thing to have true abought you but just so it isen't stupid *mentaly* why I don't care!

This is the last page in this diary; I begin my new one tomorrow. A diary is just the kind of a confidente to have—one who never tells anything.

◇ *1916* ◇

JANUARY 7. Miss Green told us in our lesson about the wonderful nature story and in such a wonderful, beautiful way. Some vulgar, silly girls were saying afterwards she shouldn't have given such a lesson, and it made me furious.

It is a beautiful story and it is they that make it wicked in the way they talk of it. They had better learn it from a good noble woman like she, than from bad companions in an ugly, vile way!

JANUARY 8. Miss Green told us yesterday, to say each morning before we got out of bed: "I'm so glad I'm alive!" and on rainy mornings to say it twice. "It works like a charm but you want to be sure and say it before you begin to get out of bed and get your feet on the cold floor, that takes away some of the charm," she said. I tried it this morning and it worked fine. I just think about *her* and it makes *me* glad I'm alive anyway.

JANUARY 10. We are reading Merchant of Venice in play form and I am Portia in the dialogues. I don't admire Portia, she was such a "gentle lady" with "pretty speeches" "befitting an obedient wife." I hope I'll never be an "obedient wife" or any other kind for that matter.

JANUARY 11. Half of the time Ruth and I get along just grand, and are certain we're made for each other and the rest of the time we're stiff and so afraid we'll be nice to the other. It's a good thing we don't see each other any oftener than we

do or we'd never get along at all. She's so sure of herself and
determined and bossy.

I.Q. program

I. Dramatic recital by the world renowned dramatist, Miss
Ruth Brewster. Miss Brewster makes tragedies and love stories
her specialties.

II. A thrillingly entrancing piece played by the most famous
musician the world has produced, Miss Charlotte Foote. Miss
Foote has studied in Hong Kong under Paderewski.

III. A beautiful selection read by the well known elocution-
ist, Miss Molly Whiteman. Miss Whiteman has studied in Africa
until she can readily bring tears to the eye or convulse a funeral.

IV. A poem read by the author, the beloved, admired Miss
Taylor. The poem entitled "School Days," will bring back to
each one half forgotten memories dear to the heart of their
childhood.

V. A touching little lullaby by one of America's model mothers, Miss Caroline Taylor. When she played this in N.Y. all the
dolls were found asleep.

JANUARY 24. When we graduate from Intermediate we will
have a class party. And at these parties the boys take the girls.
Mother says that *I* can't go with any boy! It isn't the *boy* that I
want but all the other girls are going with them and I don't want
to be the *only one* and a left out. I simply won't go to the party
at all if I can't go like the other girls! Maybe fourteen *is* too
young but I don't care.

There was one girl this year that refused to go to the party
with a boy and everybody is talking about her and calling her
a prig. I'm not so specially anxious to go with a *boy* but I don't
want to be the only one that doesn't and be a wall-flower. The
other girls are all going and they laughed at me when I told
them what mother said. I won't go to that class party at all then!
I'll let them think I'm ill. I *won't* be talked about and pitied by
an outsider!

JANUARY 25. I got a compliment today. They're so rare so
I appreciate them extra. A girl said her mother said that I was

sweet looking and had such a sweet face and such a pleasant one. Wasn't that nice? I hope it's true.
[unsent letter]
    Dear M.G.,

    I wish you understood my unhappy disposition. I'm afraid you've noticed how affected I act. I never knew I acted that way until someone told me; it's perfectly unconscious. And I don't want anybody, especially you, to think badly of me.

    If I act affected and put-on and all that it is because I'm so everlastingly self-conscious! I want so much to be nice and pleasant and have you think well of me, and I am not exactly in *awe* of you, but someway or other I think of you as totally different from ordinary people and I get embarrassed, and tongue-tied or try to look indifferent and put on airs and altogether make a f—— of myself when I talk to you. I couldn't act ordinary and natural to save my neck.

    I shall be very glad when I'm safely grown up and staid, unemotional, and sensible! I'm glad you don't know how sentimental and silly I am! You don't know how I admire and love you and I want you to like me and I know very well you'd be disgusted and despise me if you knew how very sentimental and silly I am.

FEBRUARY 3. We I.Q. quarreled today and I guess for the last time. We were all hopping mad at each other and when they said they had something important to tell me I wouldn't go. I never dreamed what it was and didn't find out till later. They wanted to adopt a new girl into our charmed circle. To think of another girl in the I.Q.! And this girl whom we hardly know. As mother says it's silly but I can't bear to think of sharing my secrets and our good times with another girl. It would just be awful. And we've all vowed never to take a new member. Well they went ahead and adopted her into the club and of course I wasn't on speaking terms and wasn't there. I'd far rather not be in the I.Q. at all than with a new member.

    I've got a glorious secret which I wouldn't tell anybody for the world for they *wouldn't* believe it! And they'd think me vain!

It's this: I'm going to be pretty! I feel it in my bones and see it in the mirror. I'll never be a raving beauty nor *very* pretty but I'm going to be nice looking. I'm not vain—I've been homely for so long that the promise of looking better is mighty nice. Even mother said "You're getting better looking every day!" And one of the neighbor ladies said (it was very much exaggerated!) "Why Marion is getting positively beautiful!"

I think it's just because I'm young and girlish looking, and healthy and happy. Every girl wants to be nice looking and I certainly do!

But my greatest wish is to be unusual looking, refined, above the common and out of the ordinary looking like Miss Green.

FEBRUARY 4. Not a word did the I.Q. exchange today. We never looked at each other nor spoke. The new girl ate with them. You don't understand that the I.Q. can never be the same again. This is our last quarrel, I guess.

FEBRUARY 7. Never spoke to the I.Q. or they to me today. Mother is very angry at me. She says of course it's my fault if they're mad, if they're *all* against me.

FEBRUARY 8. We I.Q. girls were in study period and all sitting around one of the tables. It is rather embarrassing to be sure. Molly just said (for the first time in three days that she nor any of them have spoken). "Well, what ails you anyway. Have *we* done anything?" I answered with great dignity such as befitted the occasion, "You're pretty thick I'm sure if you can't see." I then handed her a page-long note I'd written sometime ago on my ideas on the subject and she's writing an answer. A regular post office correspondence has been started no doubt. It's rather ridiculous!!

I answered her note and said that I didn't care to be in it with any other girl but I didn't see why we had to feel so bitter toward each other.

FEBRUARY 9. Just think! I am fourteen. Papa sent me a lovely bag. And then in the evening Miss Green came. After dinner we sat around the fire and she had me sit in her lap. Who says I don't like to be loved and cuddled a little once in a while even if I *am* fourteen and awful big! I'm as big if not bigger than Miss Green. I had my arms around her neck and my head on her shoulder and her arms were around me. We talked and had such a cozy time. She told me she thought I had such poise! and that the other teachers did too and I *know* I act so self-conscious and embarrassed! Oh, I am so glad she thinks I have poise and act decent.

FEBRUARY 14. Today was Valentines Day. I got *only one* valentine! I felt rather badly at first when all the other girls got so many. I'm friendly and on good terms with everybody but you see I never had any intimate friends but the I.Q. and I never went with anyone else and when they fail me why there you are!

FEBRUARY 18. I had a great longing today to be petted and loved and hugged. I wanted it especially bad; I wanted someone to hug *me*. Needless to say no one has yet! Since no one would hug *me* I had to hug someone else so I tried Miss Turnbridge. She bore it bravely.

FEBRUARY 21. Mother keeps at me about the I.Q. quarrel. "Marion, why don't you make up? It is unladylike and un-christian. Apologize to them" etc. Apologize! We may be on speaking terms but we can never be on the terms we were before.

Papa hasn't written us for ever so long nor sent our allowance and I've written him *three* letters. He makes me tired! Oh I wish we didn't have to depend on him for everything and then we wouldn't have to "keep on his good side" and humour him all the time!

FEBRUARY 22. Last night who should appear after mother had gone to polytechnic [evening class] but *papa*! He just came to spy! He saw mother down town one night and he told us he didn't approve of the idea of our staying alone at night. And he doesn't even know where mother goes and he knows we're perfectly safe; he just wanted to *kick*. Well, just so's he wouldn't cause trouble we had to get a woman to stay with us. He just came last night to see if we were alone. Well he took us to a show and we had quite a nice time. He was there when mother came home and it was embarrassing for her let me tell you, as

well as for the neighbor lady who was staying with us. He just
did it to be smart! Mother was so indignant that she could hardly
keep from telling him what she thought of him. Oh I shall *never*
never never get married!

MARCH 3. We had a class meeting and I was nominated for
president and lost by two votes. I wore my new red middie
(turkey red—like all the fad now) and every one of the I.Q.
complimented me on how it looked and were really astonish-
ingly nice considering how they've been lately. Charlotte and
I have quite forgotten the feud in our interest over [my] petition
to get Miss Howe back [to the playground].

MARCH 7. I'm not on such good terms with the I.Q. except
Charlotte. But soon will be no doubt and if I don't look out I'll
be giving in and going back in the club. But I really mustn't
do that! Why you just can't understand how awful it would be
to have that simp of a Lily in the club! I could never be decent
to her and it would be miserable.

MARCH 31. Some day I'm fully trusting and hoping I'll meet
another chum.

I want a chum that I can get along with a little better than
with Ruth yet somebody I respect quite a good deal. I know
I'll meet her someday—and I'm going to try to be amiable and
unselfish and not ever quarrel and I'll be so glad when I do
meet her because I can't be real happy without a chum and one
whom I think of as an equal.

APRIL 2. What I said quite a long time ago about how I
thought I was getting nice looking is all a fake! I'm just as puggy
and smuggy as ever and lankier and sicklier and sallower and
there's no getting around it. It wasn't meant that I should be
nice looking. Oh how I wish I was! Miss Green would think
more of me if I wasn't so blame homely, I'm sure. I've got some
brains anyway even if I *don't* look it! Well, I'm not crippled or
disfigured and I *might* be worse.

There have been several times in my youthful career when
I've felt like *two cents*. And I'm going to relate the worst one.
(Thank goodness this book is private.) Well, one night after
school (it was at a meeting) Miss Green came in the library

rather late and I got up and offered her my chair. She sat down and made me sit in her lap and I'm no airy fairy being and I was perfectly willing to stand but she didn't realize what she was undertaking and made me sit still. In about ten minutes the poor creature (oh it makes be blush to write it) could stand it no longer and she said, "I guess you'll have to get up, Marion; my feet are going to sleep." I'm cured forever of wanting to sit in anybody's lap! I've got it through my head at last that I'm quite past the age to be held. It took courage to look poor Miss Green in the face. But I survived and am living down the shame. I'll bet she's stiff in the legs yet.

APRIL. 28. I just don't know what to do without a chum! I'm just lost without one. I suppose I don't deserve one quarreling with my last one but I'll be nice as can be if I can have another.

I wish that a certain person I loved, loved me one-tenth as much as I do them. But I suppose there isn't much in a sentimental, self-conscious, gawky, common, ordinary little girl for a charming, witty, wonderful woman like M.G. to like when there's many interesting, lovely girls in the school.

MAY 10. Oh, you can't guess the awful news! It's unbelievable—my first real, great disappointment. Miss Howe isn't coming. I worked so hard on that petition and I thought we were going to have her and I do love her so and I don't know what I shall do all summer! Oh I'm so disappointed! I just can't keep from crying and I cried and cried when I found it out. I just won't go near the playground this summer.

MAY 15. My average of 96 3/4 is the highest in all the [class]! I tell you I'm mighty proud.

And of course I had to tell somebody and the two or three girls I told showed me very plainly that they begrudged me it. I suppose I act awfully swelled up over my high marks but I haven't anything else to be swelled up over. I'm not popular nor cute, nor attractive or interesting or pretty. And I'm not in the [class] play (which is a very high honor) nor in the Glee Club so why should anyone begrudge me this.

MAY 16. There is a girl in school and her name is Helen Baxter. I met her mother Sunday (Helen wasn't there) and she said that Helen was always talking about Marion. "She's just the nicest girl mother! And she certainly can draw," etc. and that all they heard at their house was Marion Taylor, Marion Taylor! That certainly did make me feel good. It tickled me to death. I wonder if Miss Green was anywheres near as delighted when she found out that I liked her! I never thought *I'd* be admired very much—I always thought I'd do all the admiring.

JUNE 17. Miss Green came this evening for dinner. We talked about what I am planning to take in High School and then she said there was one fault in me she wished to talk to me about. "It seems as if you are just about perfect except for this" she said. "For the last four or five months since your 'I.Q.' broke up, you have been practically alone. Now I know nothing whatever about what caused the 'I.Q.' scrap so I am perfectly neutral. But the teachers seem to think that you held back when the others were willing to make up. Is it so Marion?" Those are her words almost exactly. "The girls—not the I.Q. only, but all the girls at school like you and admire you so much but you seem to repel their advances. You have a great influence for good with the girls if you only will, Marion. It isn't right you should keep all to yourself. The teachers and the girls think so much of you. You are a sweet, lovely, darling girl, but people who do not know you will misunderstand you. I've never been more interested in any girl I have known, Marion, and I am telling you this because I am so interested in you. I want to save you the heart-ache I suffered when I was in High School. I was miserable because I couldn't find one girl who was congenial. Just love all the girls and look for the best in them." That is what she said as near in her words as I can remember. She held my hand and she was so kind and loving and what she said meant so much more in her own dear voice than it does when I write it down.

She looked at my hand and at my thumb and said, "You dream lots more than you carry out, don't you dear? Your thumb shows it. You have been very lonely this year—I know it and you mustn't be next year." That talk has done me so much good! And it makes me want to try my best to do better because she cares and is interested.

"Don't say that you are not going to get married. It is a wonderful thing to marry the right man. Maybe some day you will meet the dearest man in the world." I haven't told you half she said and you can't know the way she said it all—so kind and loving.

JUNE 18. What a privilege it is to know women like my mother and Miss Green—mother is just as wonderful as Miss Green but what we are used to and expect we take for granted and do not appreciate.

JUNE 21. Miss Green made it out nicely about my drawing within myself and made it out that it was such a pity because I was such "lovely girl" and all that, but it's just plain selfishness and grouchiness and ugliness but it's just natural I guess. I never put myself out to be nice to people.

Miss Waterbury [Sunday school teacher] believes that the heathen are going to hell if they aren't Christians and that their not being Christian is going to be counted against us. It seems the first and most important thing the churches believe in doing when they go to the heathens is to convert them and preach the gospel. Miss W. would be actually pained if she heard this— I think we should think first of educating and helping the heathen and then when their minds are sufficiently developed they can take the religion they like best. Religion isn't going to clothe them and keep them from disease and misery.

And what does it matter whether they believe in wooden idols if it gives them comfort and if they live up to their religion and their conscience why they stand as great a chance of heaven (if there is such a place like the Presbyterian Church teaches about though privately I think our heaven or hell is made right here on this earth by each individual).

It seems almost hopeless when I try to be good but I haven't tried any too hard yet and I *can do it.* I will be more unselfish! I've got the brains to do it and I *will.* It is just a constant fight and selfishness is just naturally born in me.

JULY 4. This evening we went to the beach to see the fire

works. I was miserable. It was icy cold and I didn't enjoy watching tough girls dance. I'll be considered a "stick" by boys all my life I suppose but I don't care. I like to stay at home and read and write and draw and study birds and go to school and study and adore teachers and have firm friends among girls. I'm not interested in clothes, boys or dancing.

No matter what Miss Green says I've got to have a chum. I've absolutely got to. I hope to goodness I find one at High School.

JULY 13. Caroline was at Papa's [office] all day yesterday. He asked her if she wouldn't like to live with him. Wasn't that mean of him! He's trying hard to get her. She told him she'd rather live with mother. Papa's always tried to get Caroline. Caroline is the favorite with her affectionate disposition and she's cute. I'm a stick and not interesting. I'm not lively enough to suit him and mother loves the baby best.

JULY 15. I love to write things! Diaries, letters, stories! Anything. I love to write in my bird notebook and in my little notebook of good thoughts and helpful things I get from New Thought [church]. I love to express my thoughts and I am perfectly contented with lots of things to write. I may be odd but I don't care. Other girls don't like to write and read and they aren't dippy over teachers and school, etc. But I should worry!

JULY 16. At night instead of praying I go to my open window and just look out on the flowers in the moonlight. It rests me instantly. It's queer but it soothes me and rests me and makes me feel quieted just to breathe the cool night air and everything looks so mysterious and quiet and peaceful in the moonlight.

I just *rest* for a minute. Some nights I feel happy and I just say "I am so happy!" And other nights I feel tired or out of sorts or sad and I ask God to help me be good and unselfish. I affirm my four great wishes. I am unselfish. I am healthy and strong. I am charming. I am wise with a keen mind. And I imagine myself those things. Then I say goodnight to Miss Green wherever she may be which is probably silly and sentimental but I can't help it.

While I'm feeling confidential, I'll tell you something else.

Now you know I'm not affectionate in disposition like Caroline but just the same lately I've just longed to be cuddled. I don't think it's bad or silly but at night I just want to hug up tight to somebody. Now with mother I never kiss her and I'd feel dreadfully silly if I hugged her or anything, though I love her more than anybody else in the world. But with Papa I could kiss him and act soft and never mean a thing by it nor think of it. I haven't a spark of love in my heart for papa sad to say though from outward appearances I might love him like everything. And Caroline too. I love her a lot in spite of her bickering, but I'd no more kiss her! I'm a funny girl I guess. But it's people I love a great deal though not as much as mother that I'd love to hug! I can't easily show affection. I'm not made that way and I'm so clumsy and bashful about it!

But at night I just long for some of my girlfriends or my teachers! to just hug up to close. I imagine Miss Green's arms are around me and she's holding me tight at night. It may seem silly but it's nothing bad I know and it might seem ridiculous to some people.

But enough for such stuff.

I'm awful afraid if I ever met a man that I loved half as much as I love Miss Green I'd forget my resolutions and marry. In fact I know I would. Some of these things are pretty silly but what's a diary for if you can't be confidential!

AUGUST 5. An article of mine on birds came out in the evening paper. I never told mother anything about it so as to surprise her. They must have thought it was pretty good for it was on the front page. Mother was so surprised! It sounded lots better to me, in print, than it did when I wrote it. It was just an outline of the common birds about here.

AUGUST 19. I'm selfish, self-centered, unaffectionate and cold in disposition, lazy, uninteresting—everything unlovely. The only thing I like about Marion Taylor is that she's got a good bit of brains—at least I think so. And she's sensible in not liking the boys, etc. It seems like almost all girls are the domestic kind. They are usually plump and pretty and love to dress and are so interested in their clothes. I am not the domestic girl at all and as most girls seem to be that kind perhaps it's the right kind. I suppose it's the way women should be but some of it doesn't appeal to me. I wish I was more like that but if I had to be entirely interested in home affairs and never care to read or write or anything like that I'd much rather be like I am.

I'm stupid physically and I'm not at all vivacious or pretty. I'd never be content to keep house and take care of babies forever and ever and I'd never interest a man for two minutes. Ruth Brewster was my kind. I think the reason we didn't get along very well was because we were too much alike. It really was a shame we had to quarrel. We were just made for each other when we were on good terms.

Every once in a while I write reams and reams and rant and rant like tonight. I'm like mother—I have to express my feelings on paper every once in a while.

◇ *1917* ◇

MAY. Oh what is God! It suits me now, this scientific, abstract idea of him because I havn't any troubles. All the miracle of nature and life, and love, that is my idea of God. But when people grow up they always have troubles so they say, and just must have someone to go to and it must be inexpressibly lonely when there's no one. A personal God would be comforting when your in trouble. I wish I could accept that instead of my reason forcing me to believe in that just but cruel and inexorable law "Whatsoever a man soweth, that shall he also reap." After all I wish I were one of those people who can accept without questioning, any old views. They are more content and happier, I believe. They can pray for troubles to be averted etc. They can pray to have a loved one guarded, or to be saved from a disease but I couldn't—because I'd be thinking if that person is coming to danger he's coming to it, if I've been exposed to that disease I'll take it and God isn't going to interfere—God is a force, not a person. I'm afraid to grow up—I'm a coward—I fear the trouble and sorrow. I wouldn't mind dying before I grow up and before I've had any sorrow.

I wish I had a clearer idea of God, one that I could pray to. My God isn't very comforting—a personal God is—you can talk to them and feel that they understand, and that they love you like a mother loves a child.

But when I get big I will need a real God and I want to find him now so I won't have to hunt very long then.

I am very analytical and I am always hunting for my motives in everything and distrusting myself.

SEPTEMBER 10. School today. Just in the morning I had a sick headache! And couldn't see straight all morning and how my eyes hurt. There are lots of new teachers—I'm in love with two of them—one especially—my biology teacher, Miss Graham.

SEPTEMBER 19. I don't know which I like best—Miss Graham or Miss Macey. They are as different as two people could be. I love Miss Graham—she's my kind—the quiet sort—I imagine she would take things more seriously. But it's M. Macey that makes you have a tight feeling in your solar plexus— that you adore from afar, that gives you that hopeless feeling because she is "so beautiful beyond compare." She makes you have a lump in your throat. I haven't seen Miss Green yet. I'm wild to see her.

SEPTEMBER 22. I saw her! Mary and I decided to go over to Intermediate—we just couldn't stay away any longer. We ran all the way over. At least we saw her!!!!!! I'm afraid we nearly broke her in two the way we pounced on her. It's an inspiration to see her. My circulatory system didn't get to going regular again all afternoon.

SEPTEMBER. I can't wait till I grow up! I know girlhood is the best time and I appreciate it. I wish I could have stayed fourteen forever. But still I want to be independent! To have money to do things! I want to go places. With my first money that I am free to spend I shall go to Yosemite! I shall spend every summer in the mountains—I shall travel a little. I shall have an artistic house and buy beautiful pictures and books— I shall go to the plays and things I long to do. If I can teach nature-study it will be ideal—work will be a joy.

Things like religion and books etc. appeal to me—to my mind but not to my heart. New Thought appeals entirely to my mind. Religion to me has to be something that's reasonable, scientific. I can't take a single thing for granted. Mother gets shocked at some of my infidel views.

OCTOBER 1. Miss Green was up last night. Mother asked her about Mr. Wood and said that Marion had been worrying about him. Then she tried to persuade me that even if she did marry him what difference would it make and that she would have a nice little home where I could come see her etc. Piffle!

OCTOBER 2. I am so happy! so contented! I don't long constantly for Miss Green. I have lovely teachers at High that though not nearly so wonderful as she, are very interesting. Oh it's so nice to just be content! To not have an ache and unquiet in your heart all the time. Now my existence doesn't center around the glimpses of her. It's a restful feeling—a relief. I loved her too much. One shouldn't love a teacher any more than I love Miss Macey—just enjoying her, admiring her, and getting the excitement but not get so wrapped up in them and adoring them so passionately. I have lived in the past or rather in a dream world—always hoping, never realizing. It's a relief! I am content in the present.

OCTOBER. I feel so sorry for myself! I often feel pity for poor abused me. I guess I was out of sorts today, but everything went wrong. In the first place they got out the honor list of people who will receive pins and everybody is asking everybody else whether they are going to get one or not. And I'm not, and Ruth is, and Mary and everybody else with the slightest brains. You don't know how ashamed I feel. It's awfully humiliating, and I feel murderous to Ruth—she acts so mean about it. She acts very condescending and patronizing and I could slap her!

Well, while I was feeling in this sweet mood, we had a big spelling match, and trust me to get spelled down and Ruth to carry off the honors. So I sulked like a baby.

Oh I'm jealous and sour and sulky, but it's hard when you've been used to being more. I've lost all respect for myself I ever did have. I'm usually quite conceited, but believe me it's knocked out tonight.

NOVEMBER. Oh and wouldn't it be lovely to meet a young man (when I grow up) that was real serious-minded and that cared for intellectual things and liked me and I liked him and he liked scientific things and books and we'd have so much fun nosing around in museums, art stores, and book stores, and go to see plays and operas and things, and go on nature hikes and we could read together and do serious things and with occasional dances etc. and then when we were real old, to plan a nice little house with lovely pictures and books and all artistic, and we'd travel and write nature books, and after quite a while have a little girl to spoil and bring up all sweet and dainty.

DECEMBER 2. I dream and build air castles so much lately— I have very sentimental thoughts I fear—but no matter how sentimental they are they don't make me interested in the boys. I wonder if anywhere in the world there are boys like me.

DECEMBER 14. Mary and I have such good times together. We talk about teachers and all sorts of nonsense and nothing at all and go around hugging each other and giggling. I think I spend too much time thinking about myself and that's why I enjoy Mary. It's a sort of relaxation to be with Mary—she's smarter in her studies than I yet she seems sort of simple in manner—we do have such nice times together. What will I do when she goes away.

The thing I like to do best in all the world is a combination of the four things I like best—reading, nature study, writing, and drawing. It is making up notebooks on nature, reading up on it and writing what I learn, adding my personal observations, and illustrating with sketches, diagrams, etc.

◇ *1918* ◇

JANUARY 1. How on earth do people like me when I'm such an awful cuss?! Of course people outside of the family don't see much of my selfishness and meanness, but I act so unpleasant with the girls; I rant and rave and hate everybody, but a few people. But Charlotte and Mary like me best! Say I oughta reform! It's a seven days wonder that they do. I'm going to reform! I'm getting badder and badder all the time—the easiest thing to begin reforming on would be the way I act at school—the way I act at home is too darn hard to begin on.

I know I've got an ornery disposition, but I think Mother might not make out that Caroline is a dear sweet thing though just impulsive, while I'm hard and cold and selfish and mean.

JANUARY 11. I haven't seen Miss Green for three weeks—I'm not going to hunt her up either; I guess she's getting bored with me—she didn't act very cordial last time I saw her.

JANUARY 16. Miss Green called up this evening. And what do you think! She said "Do you want to trade photographs?" Won't that be great! She talked about Mr. Wood. Darn him! (That's the man that likes her you know!)

JANUARY 22. I went over to Intermediate and she wasn't a bit nice! I think if I only see her once in seven weeks, she might be nicer. I'm never going to hunt her up anymore!

[Unsent letter] *JANUARY 27.* Really I've been acting very young, lately—getting so worked up because you [Miss Green] aren't crazy to see me—I love you better than that, so I shall try to maintain poise and equanimity. Someday I'm going to be great—That is I'm going to be known of in the literary world—not a second George Elliot, but someday I'm going to write. How does that strike you? And someday I'm going to write the story of my life.

You know I've got to have money for traveling, the lovely house and college—how am I going to get it teaching school? And since I like to express my opinions as you well know and if I could express them so people would read them—why not?

It was not very long ago that I believed in angels and hell etc.—but how impossible they seem now! I think heaven and such things are too grand and wonderful to be all figured out down to such details—such material details as wings and golden streets—I think man's mind is not capable of realizing the truth—only such truths as we need here—and unselfishness is about as much as we can handle here—I can not accept any ideas at all about God or the next world—either orthodox or otherwise—because why should *we* have discovered the truth when millions before us have not. Theosophy appeals to me—reincarnation, etc. but why should that be right? Any more than other ideas. God would not select a chosen few to whom to reveal the truth.

FEBRUARY 4. A girl was telling me that she kept a diary—she said she had such a dreadful time trying to think what to put in it. I'll venture hers runs "Got up at seven—ate breakfast, had mush and biscuits, went to school came home, etc."

FEBRUARY. Say I wish you could tell me whats the matter with me. I have an inane longing to be loved and to cuddle up with someone—isn't that crazy—but I never kiss or hug any-body and I long for some loving sometimes—I haven't kissed mother for a year I guess—isn't that awful—but really I can't help it—I feel like a boy—embarressed and you couldn't hire me to kiss Caroline.

But every time I do try to love people something disasterous always happens and I feel like a fool. So I confine it to imaginings.

It seems to me from my vast experience in life that there are three kinds of love. Of course there are different kinds like a mothers love, love between friends and love between man and wife.

But there seems to be different kinds in the latter. The great-est kind is that wonderful love we can't quite understand—soul love; then heart love—love of a person's virtues, congeniality, personality, mind, etc. and then nature love—physical love. I should think heart love would have to come first before soul love. There may be soul love between friends or between man and woman.

Does that sound silly? From a 16 year old—? It's just one of the fancies that enter my head. All I know of life is what I get from books and thats what I think. What else is it if not a wonderful soul-love between a man and woman who have little in common—it can't all be physical—at least I hope not.

FEBRUARY. As to a future existence I never was much interested. We don't know anything about the next world so why
worry. If we behave ourselves here we'll get the best of what's
coming to us there. I don't want to go to heaven; eternal bliss
sounds rather stupid. It doesn't seem fair to the people who
look forward to meeting loved ones. If heaven is spritual, why
how could you meet people? Just souls floating around is a little
too vague. Even the purest, greatest loves are earthly. Some
way it is the person we love; their virtues, their disposition,
their mind, their personality and a soul hasn't mind or disposition. No, I'd rather not go to heaven. And I shouldn't like to
be reincarnated; it would be tiresome to keep on living all the
time; and have to have pains and sorrows all over again. I'd
rather die with my body—just rest and oblivion.

FEBRUARY. I wish I were a man—then I would not be expected to be lively and feminine and domestic. Men get it easier
anyhow. One can't blame men for liking feminine women.
Young ladies are such adorable things, if I were a man I'd make
love to them all. The main reason I object to the scheme of
things in general, is because I'm not feminine or cute or ap-
pealing or anything, I guess. I don't see why I wasn't made so,
since I'm a woman kind, or else made a man.

What do you think I'm doing! I'm falling in love with Miss
Macey like I did over Miss Green. She is so wonderful, so
unattainable, and beautiful that it just makes you miserable.
Isn't that crazy?

FEBRUARY. I just hate Miss Green! I'm mad at her forever.
I'll never like her anymore. I met her tonight, and I haven't
seen her for a month, and she nodded and wouldn't walk with
me and was utterly hateful. She thinks she's too good for other
people! She was rude. I just hate her! It's absolutely sickening
the way I've acted over her. I've absolutely no more interest in
her. I tore up her pictures and packed away everything that
reminds me of her!

[Unsent letter] I'm dissapointed in you—of all things I didn't
think you were snubbish. But I can't smooth it over and make
it look all right, I guess it's true. Mother has said before that

when she meets you you avoid speaking to her. You don't need to speak to Mother if you don't want to! She's just as good, and better, than you are!

I reckon you're one of those people—like a man, that doesn't like to be loved—too much affection bores them. I'm not that kind and I can't understand those people. I feel just now as if I never wanted to see you and bore you again. I could cry.

I'm delighted to worship at your feet, but when you get bored I get off my knees as fast as possible. As Mother says, you must learn to depend on yourself—other people always fail you.

Later: It doesn't seem so terrible as it did this morning—My pride still hurts but I love you! If you were mean and hateful I just couldn't help loving you—It scares me I love you so. I love you passionately—it isn't natural. Why do I love you so!!

I've come to the conclusion that you have a few microscopic faults—it's a kind of a lost feeling, to find that [my] ideal isn't quite what [I] thought—You have been the main thing in my life—unconsciously in my mind I turn to you in everything—now when I do so there is a little feeling of disappointment. Oh I must see you and dispel my doubts!

MARCH. I've been wishing a most unChristian wish; that I might meet Miss Green, so that I might cut her, like she cut me. But upon thinking it over, she would not care if I acted mad at her, but if when I meet her I act very polite, but disinterested, that might make her feel bad just a little (Ain't I childish?)

From a psychological standpoint I should be interested in what I would do upon meeting Miss Green. If she was nice I'm afraid should relent, but if she was mean I should hate her in earnest and the last little spark of love for her would be extinguished. It would be better for me doubtless, and fortunate for her, if she was mean.

I took M. Macey a beautiful bunch of roses. She was darling!

APRIL. All I can think about now is Italian art and art in general. I wrote twenty pages in my history notebook on da Vinci and Michelangelo. Oh it is *so* interesting! I never appreciated the old masters before.

APRIL. What do you think I did? I am perfectly shameless. And have no proper pride. Or common sense. Or decency. Or good taste. Or self-respect. Or will-power. *I wrote a letter to Miss Green!* It's been two months since that fatal meeting and I haven't seen her since. Absence is a good cure for grouches.

APRIL. Miss Green stopped in a minute today. I wasn't here. Mother said she said she enjoyed the letter so much and that my letters helped her! (If I wrote all I wanted to she sure would have plenty of help!) She said she was green with jealousy about Miss Macey.

SEPTEMBER. I wrote papa a while ago, about how I wanted to go to college, and a little concerning my opinions on matrimony. I got *some* letter from him today. He said if I wanted college, I should have to get it for myself, and that I took life too seriously, and that when the time comes "he" will care more about the cute little curl behind my ear than for my opinions on the whyness of the unknowable, if he loves me as he should. Those are his very words. What do you think of that for a father's words to his daughter. Oh more than ever I realize that if I marry it must absolutely be a serious-minded congenial man. How terrible to be married to an "animal" that cared only for your physical charms—a silly thing, that only thought about "the cute little curl behind your ear." It makes me positively ill to think about it!

With a father with such ideals, how can I help but feel bitter and old maidish? Papa has his virtues too; he's no different from the average man I guess, and how can I help but think men are funny creatures. Since most of the people in this world are made like that I suppose that way is right, but I'm very different.

OCTOBER. I read a poem today, and I thought and thought about it. This the part:

> *God knows 'twere better to lie deep*
> *Pillowed in silk and scented down*
> *Where love throbs out in blissful sleep*
> *Pulse nigh pulse, and breath to breath*
> *Where hushed awakenings are dear.*

Was it silly of me to think of it? If it was, I can't help it. I'm just hungry for something—I don't know what, but that poem has something to do with it. It unsettled me so. Love is a wonderful something—is that why people marry—for the thing in the poem? Oh is it bad of me to think so? At night I dream of arms about me—of cuddling up *close, close* to some one. And I dream of Him too. I blush to write this even in my diary—but my diary is as secret as my thoughts except for one stranger who reads it—Marion of the future—Marion grown up—I am very anxious about her opinion, so I hesitate to write such things as this.

OCTOBER. Papa was here today. I wish I could never see him again for years. He is absolutely boring—his conversation is so empty—he is so silly, so boyish, so conceited, has no ideals, etc. I have no affection for him whatever. I just can't help it. He is physically disgusting. Isn't it dreadful for a daughter to feel so!

NOVEMBER. I've a dreadful case on Miss Jarvis! Just at present I like her better than Miss Macey! Just think of it! Miss Jarvis is so cultured, intellectual and refined. She knows so much. She has been abroad. She has poise, is broadminded, and is a woman, no young girl as are so many of the High teachers.

NOVEMBER. Saw M. Jarvis down at the library today. Say! I'm more in love with her than I was with Miss Green. I've got it awful bad! Why do I get such violent attachments to people? I don't care if it is silly, I'm going to like her all I want to!

NOVEMBER. Knowing Miss Jarvis, a charming, and fascinating and serious minded woman, has made me hope that by modifying my tastes I may be like her a little some day. Serious minded people are always interesting and worthwhile to me, but M. Jarvis is interesting to everybody, and everybody admires her.

And so I play act off by myself, feeling very interesting, and self-conscious and conceited. It isn't good for me. I see that I must not go off by myself. But if only I knew someone—boy or girl—congenial!!

NOVEMBER. Went on a hike in the foothills with Miss Green this afternoon. It was glorious! A lovely day, and the hills were so beautiful. We had a lovely time, and a nice talk. I've calmed down in my affection for her to a great extent, and so can enjoy her company in a more natural and restful way. I didn't find out much that I wanted to know—only that those crazy spells I had a while ago, were only natural.

DECEMBER 12. I'm recklessly extravagant in the matter of diaries. I filled the last up in ten months. A diary is impractical and rather silly no doubt, but I have to have one. I'm getting quite cosmopolitan of late and very gay and sociable for me. I've actually talked with strange girls, and gotten acquainted with several.

DECEMBER. I'm writing out the fifteen subkingdoms of zoology. Oh why do I just love such things so! Papa says he can't understand my liking nature—he thinks my wanting that butterfly book was *crazy*.

He would never get over it if he saw me surrounded by ponderous volumes and writing about memathelminths, platyhelminthes, etenophoro, colenterata, etc. and enjoying it better than anything!

I feel guilty every time I do it. I feel as if it were a dry, bugologisty thing to do—but why do I love it so.

DECEMBER 25. Papa has given us such a nice Christmas this year. Besides the money, he bought Caroline a Christmas tree and trimmings, and this evening he brought over a great basket of fruit and some bacon and eggs. He stayed for dinner. He has taken a great deal of interest in us girls lately, and has seemed less boyish.

◇ *1919* ◇

JANUARY. It is human nature to desire that which one has not, and to disregard that which one has. I once thought that if Miss Green only liked me I should be sublimely happy. I have won her friendship as much as I ever shall, and it does not mean so much to me! I suppose if I ever win M. Jarvis's friendship I will take it quite calmly too. I hope to goodness I will be more constant if I ever marry! I'm beginning to doubt myself! I surely loved Miss Green to distraction and now I have tired of her. I'm sure I should get tired of a husband after a while, no matter how I loved him at first.

But I suppose when I fall in love I shall be worrying far more about whether he will be constant to me! And it doesn't do any good to get tired of one's husband, so I suppose one doesn't.

JANUARY. I feel very much in love with myself tonight—I feel very pleased with myself—I fondly imagine, what a brilliant child I am etc! Isn't it funny because half the time I could kick myself.

JANUARY. Goodness! If I get more serious-minded as I get older, I will have no friends at all! But dear me! I cant help the way I was made. I never knew a girl that was a dreamer, who loved knowledge for its own sake, who loved to read and study and dream. How nice to know a girl that was absolutely indifferent to boys, movies, ball-games, cooking, sewing, and clothes!! But I mustn't pipe-dream about such things—perfect friends are not to be had, and even if I knew a girl like that I probably couldn't get along with her. Even more than I wish for a congenial girl, I should like to know a congenial boy.

FEBRUARY 9. Today was my seventeenth birthday and the long looked forward to event came off, to whit, Miss Jarvis' visit. I had an agonizing time manufacturing conversation. What a birthday supper—I had cake with 17 candles, ice cream, etc. At 7:30, Louise, Henrietta Sommers and Elizabeth came over, but Miss Jarvis had to go at 8:00, drat the luck! I was so excited I actually had a nervous chill and I couldn't keep my teeth from chattering. I'm scared stiff of that woman. She inspires the most awe in me. I'm always uncomfortable while with her, but always longing to be with her when I'm not. I detest polite conversation—I can't talk it, and it's so silly and trivial.

We girls played games and had lots of fun. Henrietta is a very nice girl. She is extremely clever in mathematics, English, history and Latin, is a musician and likes to cook and sew. How do they do it!

FEBRUARY. I go around with Henrietta mostly now. She is plain, but is neat as a pin, and is very quiet and unobtrusive. She is real jolly when you get to know her—she cuts up quite surprisingly. They are very poor, and she works in the school cafeteria noons. She is planning to go to college. I never knew a person so clever in every subject.

FEBRUARY. I've laughed myself sick today. I took a couple of my first story notebooks that I wrote in the seventh grade to school to show Henrietta. I hadn't read them for a long, long time, and we read them together in study period. It's just as if I had never written them, and oh they are so funny. They're rich! Such a mixture of romance and ridiculousness (if there is such a word) and so trashy and sentimental. The spelling is wonderful to behold. Oh, they are screams. Henrietta nearly split laughing and Miss Jarvis changed my seat for disturbing the peace.

I was surely a rare child! I never knew I was such a queer individual.

Henrietta is great! When she was 8 years old her favorite amusement was to get an arithmetic book and do interest problems by the hour! Think of it.

FEBRUARY. Latin is over forever!!!! Two years and a half of suffering ended today. I shall proceed to forget it all. Now school will be lovely. [Latin] has been my bugbear.

FEBRUARY. I'm so happy today! The world is so nice! School is so pleasant. The world is full of delightful books to be read, and the out-of-doors is all sunny and green with birds and flowers. I adore Miss Jarvis passionately and I like Henrietta so very much!

FEBRUARY. Henrietta is the congenial girl I've longed for. She is a kindred spirit. Henrietta is more congenial than Ruth and her disposition is far superior. She isn't bold, aggressive, and domineering like Ruth, but she has a mind of her own and has determination and will power. She is thoughtful and cares for the serious worthwhile things in life. She has high ideals. She is enthusiastic. We walk home nights together and talk about books and things. She loves to read and write and has an interest in nature, though she has never studied it. Oh you can't understand how I enjoy her, diary! I can talk to her as I feel— I can express my thoughts and ideals, and she doesn't think I'm queer. I can talk to her as I could only talk to Miss Green before and there is the great advantage that she is my age and not so much older and wiser as are teachers. She is the only girl I have been perfectly natural with for a long time.

MARCH. I'm very fickle I guess—isn't it funny that at one time anything concerning Miss Green, or later, Miss Macey gave me violent thrills, while now my heart doesn't beat a bit faster on account of either. I suppose some day I shall regard Miss Jarvis as an ordinary mortal too. I wonder if I shall fall in love with any more teachers. I shall be quite lost without adoring any, but I suppose I can't adore them forever. I am an idol worshipper and I think I shall always be setting up idols, and pushing them aside for new ones.

MARCH. Henrietta and I went on a long walk today. We went way up in the hills and it was wonderful. The low, rolling hills were all a tender shimmering green and the sky all blue, and the sun so warm. I was just sublimely happy.

APRIL. It is funny the way I adore first one and then another but it sure is strong while it lasts. I just can't think of anything else when I'm in love, and I love so hard it hurts. It improves my disposition and makes me happier. It may be silly, but it awakens the highest within me. My love for my idols is fleeting and selfish, but it's all I'm capable of.

APRIL. I don't know what's got into me lately. The last three days I've been sentimental and melancholy, and felt perfectly awful. I've been absolutely *crazy* about Miss Jarvis. I even lost my appetite and went so far as to work up a little excitement about a *boy*! I can't settle down, and I don't want to do anything. I don't want to read or study or work or go any place. I just mope around. I crave excitement, but don't care for the only available kind—movies or going places. A little Romance would be a welcome variation of the monotony.

APRIL. There are only two boys I have ever known that I admired or respected in the least and they are far from perfect.

All other boys I have ever seen are big, foolish, conceited empty-
headed babies. These two are fairly grown up for boys—they
have thoughts and ideas of their own, and are not afraid to
express them.

APRIL. Dear Diary! I wish you could tell me what's got into
me lately. I never felt so before in my life. Why I'm so sentimental and melancholy and dreamy and silly. I'm positively
unhappy. I don't think it's all Miss Jarvis—I connect it with
her, but I haven't been so crazy about her before. Why men in
love never get so crazy about a woman, I'm sure. I wish to
goodness I was a man anyway.

I long for Romance—maybe that's it. The Romance over
Miss Jarvis is altogether too one-sided. I wish some other Romance would come my way. I never, never got so worked up
about Miss Green! I'm half ashamed to confess it diary but I
want some Romance in the form of the detested sex!!! It would
be awful exciting! To have some one like you and to go places
with them. But absolutely they must be the right kind and the
right kind is rarer than diamonds.

Now listen diary. Supposing that it would be *possible* for one
of the Right Kind to enjoy my company if I knew him and he
knew me, why how go about it? I assure you I'm not so anxious
as to go after them. But I should very much like to know a
congenial boy and I do want a little excitement. I want it awful,
awful bad. I suppose the only answer is to wait and then probably wait in vain.

I feel half-ashamed of this day's confession. I wish you could
tell me what to do. It's very important I assure you, though it
may seem trivial. It's something you can't ask anyone but a
diary.

[Unsent letter to Miss Green] I can scarcely wait for the trip
next week—to talk things over. I have so many questions to
ask, and I shan't mind asking them at all—on the contrary, I
shall rather enjoy it.

I've had another spell—when I can think of nothing but how
I long to love someone. I wish I knew whether it was wrong or
not—Those spells make me feel so queer, it must be.

How much I have to ask you! Things that have worried me so long.

Well! The phone rang the very minute I wrote that—and it was you. But you forgot all about the trip!! You never said a word about it, and it's all I've thought of for two days! Oh well. I'll keep my questions to myself. There's a book at the library that will tell me or I can ask somebody else.

APRIL 24. Well, my pulse is almost normal again. I can go home nights and *almost* forget about Miss Jarvis instead of being miserable and moping about her. Shall I tell you how this miracle came about? Most of it was just natural—it was only a bad spell and did not last long, thank goodness. But I used *great will power* and helped cure it. Every time I started to think about her, which was every two minutes, I would think about M. Macey instead. I took M. Macey flowers and talked to her a lot, and she was awfully sweet and dear as usual, so thus I relieved the strain. Now let's hope and pray that I don't fall violently in love again with Miss Macey! If I can keep my susceptible heart divided between the two, I can be reasonably happy I think. Just so I don't fall as wildly in love with *both* of them at once, as I was with both separately! Oh Dear! I inherit my susceptibility from papa. He was always fond of the ladies!

APRIL. In sewing I was making a pair of drawers—they were in two pieces and I hadn't the slightest idea how they went together and when I went to join the pieces together, I found that the ruffles, instead of being around the legs, ran up the middle of the front and back! My teacher thinks I'm an inspired idiot. I've spent four periods, ripping those ruffles out. I spend most of my time in sewing ripping things out. How I hate sewing. It nearly drives me wild.

APRIL. The girls say I'm unnatural because I don't like boys. Pshaw! It's all right if you never like them. But if ever the Right One came along and was crazy about me, I should fall with a reverberating *Thump!* And I wish he would! It would be exciting and interesting, and I wouldn't feel like I was queer and unnatural—it would give one confidence in oneself! Womenfolks is contrairy creatures, ain't they?

MAY. Last night I went with the Brewsters to a movie (it was perfectly punk!) and afterwards we went across the street where there was a big festival going on and dancing on the tennis court etc. and Ruth and I had the time of our lives. That's what I've been longing for, excitement—dancing and romance etc. I adore to dance.

MAY. I was informed today by a girl that I was conceited, that I talked too much and was very cold in disposition. I know I'm conceited but I didn't think I showed it so much. Sometimes I feel very conceited, and sometimes very much the other way. I shall try to keep still in future. As to my cold disposition I was born with that and I can't change it. How much am I responsible for my disposition? Should I ever get married? At first I should be wildly in love, but after a while I think I should get cold and indifferent, and have that physical repugnance though I still loved him. I don't understand myself.

MAY. I enjoyed that dancing last week, but I've enjoyed *Mill on the Floss* a hundred times better. When I'm feeling happy, then any little thing can make me blissful—I'm just in love with life then. The depths of my disposition are awful blue and miserable but the heights are grand. But I don't think the heights make up for the depths. The depths are so terrifying and the heights are few and far between. My greatest happiness is not in doing things—it's in thinking things.

JUNE. I've got to change myself a lot this summer or I shall have a miserable time of it. I've got to stop dreaming so much, and try to be more interested in practical things. I've got to go places and do things and keep busy. Dreaming makes one unhappy. I dream of things that are not, or of unattainable, impossible things.

JUNE. Mother is working again. She comes home at night just worn out, and yet she will work. She's just wearing herself out. Papa won't give us more money. And it makes me so mad to think she has to work like that. And she worries and worries to make ends meet and is pessimistic and nervous.

JUNE. When I get hold of a good book, I'm good for nothing as mother will testify. I do nothing but read it no matter what

else I should do. Mother gets very exasperated with me. I'm
perfectly irresponsible—I don't listen to what mother says—
she orders me to put it up, but I can't leave it alone. She "hid"
Little Minister today and I had a dreadful time to find it. Nothing
under the sun could have lured me away from that until I finished it.

JUNE. For the last few days I've been going around mentally
furnishing a house. It's to be my future abode with the Serious
Man. It is planned to every stick of furniture, rug, picture and
book, and the design of wallpaper. It is so much fun.

JUNE. I was so surprised today—I received a letter from Miss
Green. I was surprised that she would condescend to write to
me when I have not written to her. I immediately sat down and
answered at length—*16* pages! I hope I shall see Miss Green
soon. As soon as Miss Jarvis is beyond my reach, I begin to
think of Miss Green again!

JUNE. How nice a diary is. I could not get along without one.
I enjoy writing what has happened as much as I enjoy the happenings themselves almost—thinking about them—living
them over again and putting them in words. A good book, an
interesting letter, a new bird, a beautiful picture, a visit with
my girlfriends, a new thought or idea about something, anything
connected with my Lady Loves, a new daydream or a day close
to Mother Nature—those are the chief events in my life that I
have to chronicle here—they are the things I enjoy most. The
only value of a diary is the pleasure one has in writing in it, and
a diary would surely be a dismal failure if you kept it for any
other reason. Very few people would really enjoy keeping one
I think—only impractical dreamy speculative people enjoy
them very much I should think.

JULY. I like books that give me new ideas about life. Some
day I am going to write a book. It is going to be based on my
diary. I think it will be interesting in showing development.
Just the interesting parts, and connected by a plot. My early
diaries are so funny. But before I can produce said masterpiece
I must be older. I know how I should like it to end—that the
self-centered, rather heartless, dreamy, impractical, one-sided

girl should become an unselfish, caring, helpful, strong, wide-awake, well-balanced, intelligent woman.

JULY. Papa was over today and I told him I was going to work in the cannery because I had to have some money for clothes. It had a good effect. He talked to mother and said he didn't want [me] to work there and ended up by telling me to buy a suit and charge it to his account. Mother gave him some plain talk about how we need more money, and he said he would try to give us more. Poor mother is just wearing herself out to make ends meet.

Mother told him that it was most important that I have college education because I haven't gumption enough (Ahem!) to get along and earn my living without the best preparation, because I'm so impractical etc. Papa seemed to agree.

I'm so happy I don't have to work in the cannery and I can have a swell new suit!!

JULY. Diary, let me whisper something in your ear. I am hoping awfully much that I will meet Him my Senior year!

JULY. I have decided never to get married. I'm quite discouraged. Mother says that when a woman marries, she must submerge her personality. I think that's bosh. I don't intend to submerge mine. She says it's all nonsense to think I could ever meet a man who cared for books and the things I do. I don't think it is. Marriage would be Hell if the man wasn't congenial.

Mother won't let me read. I have to sew. I simply hate to sew, and I don't accomplish anything. I am so lazy. I don't like to move around, I hate housework. I just like to read and write. It's awful. Oh dear. Why am I so awful. Why wasn't I a man. I suppose I would be a poor sort of man, too.

AUGUST. I love to express my thoughts in writing. I like to analyze myself and things in general. It gives me great satisfaction to catch my thoughts on paper where they can't get away, though goodness knows they're not valuable and it never does any good. It makes things clearer in my mind, to write them. And then one little reason I like to keep a diary is because it is interesting to read in the future. Once in a while I catch myself trying to fool myself—the silliest thing one can do. Sometimes when things are not quite what I would like them, I refuse to admit it in my diary, and write as if they were. Imagination throws a bit of glamor over things and makes them more ideal.

AUGUST. I have discovered your personality Diary. I was rather disturbed for a while before I did. You are Marion of the Future. I always knew it in a way but never realized it clearly.

AUGUST. I should like some real excitement—some Romance and adventure—dancing and the theatre and fun. It must come to me. I couldn't enjoy it if I went after it. Do you know I think it would be very interesting though if some gentle man manifested an interest in me, regardless of his literary tastes! Just to know that one was interested for a moment—it would give one so much confidence in oneself. I would feel like an ordinary, normal girl—not like an old maidish queer individual, entirely unfeminine.

SEPTEMBER 14. I feel so happy to think I haven't had a fit of the blues—the real serious kind—all summer. I think and I hope they were connected with adolescence. How terrible they are—the awful fear of going insane! I pray that I may never have them again.

SEPTEMBER 15. I have one wish—a Twentieth Century Maiden's Prayer. It is something which I cannot realize through any efforts of my own—something the charm of which is in its coming to one. *Romance!!* Oh that it may come this year! Mildly of course. Really one's high school course is not complete without a little wee bit of Romance. I will be eighteen in February. I want some boy to like me. I wish I were a man, but since Fate has decreed otherwise I want to make a thorough job of being a woman!

How shocked and surprised some of my friends would be to know that I had such sentiments. I do think that marriage is a bad proposition, and that if one used her head and not her heart, she wouldn't get married. I am *so* contrairy and inconsistent!

SEPTEMBER 17. I was reading the life of George Eliot tonight, and it discouraged me completely. Oh if I were only clever! I have given up literary aspirations long ago. I would be supremely happy if I could ever be reasonably cultured and well educated. I have such a poor memory, and I am so slow and dull witted. It makes me desperate.

SEPTEMBER 30. There is a boy in our history class, and he looks awfully nice. He is very clever in history, and he expresses himself well. He has an intelligent, refined face and such nice eyes. I wish he would manifest an interest in me! I am sure I should like him very much.

OCTOBER 1. I am getting altogether too much interested in that boy. It makes me angry that I am, when he scarcely knows that I exist. I should like to know him so much. I wish I were a boy, and then if I liked the looks of someone of the opposite sex, I could seek her acquaintance. Of course, I can't make any move. I've never spoken to him in my life. The main charm in such a friendship would be that he was attracted by me. That would be nice because no one was ever particularly attracted by me—never a boy. It's so humiliating to one's pride to like a boy when he is not interested in you.

OCTOBER 2. Our house has been sold over our heads, and we must get out. It's the worst calamity that could happen. We have been paying a ridiculously low rent and we absolutely can't get anything less than *twice* what we've been paying. There isn't a decent house for rent. And we *absolutely* can't afford to pay more rent. I don't know what we are going to do. We shall have to go into something not half so nice. Oh dear!

OCTOBER 6. I am simply crazy. It was prophesied by M. Green, M. Jarvis and other wiseacres that when I fell for a member of the other sex, I would fall hard! I have fallen hard. I do not think for a moment that I am in love in the mildest degree with that boy (never having spoken to him in my life!). I am in love with Romance and excitement. 75% of the reason I wanted Romance was the gratification it would be to my vanity to think I was attractive to one of the other sex. So this is only 25% satisfactory. I determine each day to speak to him but get cold feet.

OCTOBER 7. Oh Diary! Such exciting things happened today. I spoke to him! Diary, I must confess all, though I blush to do so. The latter part of noon he goes in the history room and studies all by his lonesome. And so do I! I haven't dared speak to him until today.

It was about 5 minutes before I dared say anything. At last I blurted out this profound and brilliant question: "Do you think Mr. Howe will give us that test he threatened?" It nearly choked me—my heart was in my mouth. He looked surprised but responded bravely. We discussed Mr. Howe's merits as a teacher, and ancient history as compared with modern, the cultural value of history, and kindred subjects. He talks so well! He is so serious minded. He loves history. He has so much poise. He is *so handsome.* I'm wild about him. He says "hello" every time we meet, now. Tomorrow I am going in history room very early! Oh diary! I never thought I should sink so low as to fall for a mere man! I blush to think of my unmaidenly conduct. A month ago I never should have believed it. My equilibrium is entirely upset.

OCTOBER 9. Isn't it funny what a difference it makes in a thing which one disapproves of in another person, when one does it oneself!! I could probably not have tolerated a girl who was inclined to romantic attachments for members of the opposite sex a while ago, but now that I have conceived such an attachment, I could probably forgive such failings. In fact it seems quite a natural and interesting thing!! When one does a thing himself, he immediately sees how natural it is, and can at once sympathize with the people he has thought ill of!

A certain person wasn't at school today, much to my regret. Really it left the day rather dull.

I sure have it bad. Some of my intriguing is too shameful to record here, for Marion of the Future to blush over.

OCTOBER 13. It seems like I should choke with excitement when I think of Him. I just can't stand to study most of the time. I just sit and dream.

OCTOBER 14. Well, things have come to a *Crisis.* I can go no further. Men folks don't like to think someone likes them. They like elusiveness. Now it's up to him. I have aroused his curiosity, but now I must act quite indifferent. If he doesn't evince an interest in me, why I can do no more and my little Romance will die a natural death, I suppose.

OCTOBER 15. Well, I shall promptly forget the silly business. And I must never allow myself to be infatuated again. There's no use in a woman liking a man unless he is attracted by her first.

OCTOBER 16. Oh dear I feel so miserable today. Things are dull. I am not interested in anything. I wish I had never had this dangerous taste of Romance. I shall never be content again.

OCTOBER 17. Oh to think I have fallen so low. But I don't care. I'm a different person. If I don't get some Romance and excitement now, Nature will reap her revenge later. I think I had better get it now as gradually as possible, or if it is longer deferred, I will get the Romance bug in its most virulent form and it might prove fatal. Oh this is the life! This is real life. I must, I will get acquainted with Harold Pomeroy!!

OCTOBER 20. My romance progresses slowly, but it progresses. Any other girl than me would have progressed as far as I have in 5 weeks, in one day. But I am new to the game. I have learned valuable information. I have learned that the discussion of the cultural value of history and kindred topics, will not get one very far, no matter how clever and apparently serious-minded the gentleman may be. I have learned that one must talk vivaciously, and on such subjects as foot-ball. One must laugh and talk about trivial and foolish things.

OCTOBER 21. I am getting *awfully* silly! All I think of is Romance. H.P. makes me mad! He is so utterly indifferent. I wish, oh I wish someone, I don't care who, would fall violently in love with me. I'm tired of being violently in love with people who don't give a rap for me.

OCTOBER 28. Oh this is the life! But is it? One minute I am deliriously happy, and the next I am in despair. This affair is perfectly stationary. And the doubts are *awful*.

Oh I'm getting real interested in the sex in general. I notice them all, and I see a great many that look nice and whenever one gives me a passing glance, I immediately imagine a Romance, and imagine he is falling in love with me.

OCTOBER 31. I shall not think about him so much or try to see him and all, as I have done. Well, I shall be a gay bird, and go to games and learn how to dance and not be afraid to talk to boys in general. I spoke to *three* of *them* today!! I'm scared stiff of them all. I'm getting to be a desperate character!

NOVEMBER 1. Henrietta is a dear. She wears so well. She hasn't a strong personality—she submerges hers to whoever she is with. She is certainly unselfish and dear. You know how I wear a subject out, when I'm interested in it. Well, I have talked about nothing else but H.P. for six weeks, and she has acted as interested as if it were *her* Romance. I wish I had a disposition like that.

NOVEMBER 4. Isn't it interesting how that thing has come which I most needed in development? Really what could have done more to make my sympathies broader, and to make me a more all-around girl than to fall in love with a Prince Charming, and to have him quite indifferent to me!!

NOVEMBER 10. I'm not going to languish over Harold Pomeroy anymore. The book he is reading is *Stover at Yale*, a trashy boys' book—if not trashy at least it is very light. He looks more imposing than he is. I guess he's not a demigod after all.

NOVEMBER 25. Oh Diary! What do you think of me. Have you yet recovered your breath from the first shock occasioned by the startling developments of the past two months. Am I not a different person? But don't you think it's good for me? How will I turn out, Diary? You know, for you are Marion of the Future. Will I attain my desire and be a cultured, well-educated, well-balanced fine woman? I think that in order to become well-balanced one goes to one extreme and then to another like a pendulum and finally a happy medium is obtained. So don't be unduly alarmed at my escapades. Oh I'm sure it's good for me. Do you know that I can't look on a member of the sterner sex without having designs on his life! Isn't it shocking. And I feel so bold and adventurous and full of life and if I knew how, I should flirt!!!

◇ *1920* ◇

JANUARY 5. Mother and I have had several fights over the subject of my recent romantic tendencies. I never tell her anything about my affairs in that line because she lectures me every time I do. She says that if I'm getting silly and boy-struck, there isn't any use planning for college! Just because a girl of 18 who has never known any boys in her life wants to know some she talks that way! It makes me so mad that I am rendered fairly speechless. This Romance bug, albeit somewhat unsettling, is good for me. I don't see as it's any worse than being mushy about a teacher.

JANUARY 18. Isn't it funny how I was so madly in love with Miss Jarvis last year, and this year she causes me no uneasiness whatever! I admire her as much as ever, but I scarcely think of her outside of class. It's just that I have a new object for my fickle affections.

FEBRUARY 18. I have been so much happier and contented lately—not nearly so happy as I was at times a while back, but not at all so dissatisfied and restless as I was most of the time. Life is very uneventful again—I can settle down to my studying better. Oh I hope and pray that it lasts. That restlessness is so dreadful.

MARCH 24. I'm feeling quite tender towards Athena again. In other words my worthy pedagogue, Miss Jarvis. I have to adore someone.

APRIL 21. I feel so happy tonight. The pendulum has swung back again. I have been trying to be gay and frivolous all year. I am not going to try any more. There's lots more real joy in life being yourself. Why should I lose my individuality in trying to be normal and well-balanced!!

MAY 25. I received a compliment today—they are rare. Henery told me that a girl told her that her mother said she thought I was such a nice-looking girl and would be a handsome woman! I never got one like that before in my life! I've tried to believe it but I can't. I never used to care what I looked like but I do more now. [Mother] said the only reason anyone might think I was nice looking was because I have more character in my face than most girls my age. I had rather have character in my face and be downright homely, than pretty and without any. But alas! I cannot believe that either. I have such a pudgy expressionless face, and my nose! Vulgarly it would be called pug, and more politely retroussée. And that is quite contradictory to my character. I am not a retroussée person at all. An aquiline nose would be more fitting.

JUNE 7. I was so happy when I wrote here last. And today I feel that life may possibly be worth living, but yesterday I felt that all things had come to an end. Papa came over and staged the biggest farce that was ever pulled off. He arrived in an apparently fainting condition, gasping for breath and saying that the doctors had said he couldn't live a year at the rate he was going now. Said I would have to get out and work. He couldn't support us any longer. But in a little while he recovered completely from his dreadful condition, and was laughing and cutting up with Caroline just as usual. Oh the dirty hypocrite! He told Mother that I must get out and work in a telephone office. He would not support me through college or Normal. He was very decided and stubborn about it. Think! If I should have to go into a telephone office the rest of my life, and have no further education! What a dismal failure my life would be. I was just stunned. Unless mother can get permanent work of some kind I *shall* have to get out and work, and give up school. I *must* have Normal at least. I *will* have it.

How I despise my father. No doubt his health *is* bad, but mother isn't half as strong, and she works much harder. He has always been opposed to higher education. He is so selfish. Maybe I am, too, but oh I must have college. I'm such a good-for-nothing dreamer that I can never make good without it.

JUNE 19. I got a letter from Miss Green this morning. She is going to bring that young man she spoke of once before, to graduation and make him take me home afterwards! She's awfully romantic! In spite of the fact that I know the gentleman (his name is Mr. Trevor and he's 22) is doing the escorting by compulsion I am very much excited.

JUNE 24. Well, Mr. Trevor called. I must admit I was disappointed. He is short, and has a little bullet head and stiff yellow hair closely cropped, and a red face. It was rather embarrassing having to introduce ourselves. I felt so awkward and uneasy. I don't know how to meet the ordinary little gallantries. He sprang at me to help me on with my cloak, and I didn't want it on in the least and got so flustered. And he edged around for the outside of the sidewalk, and I forgot that the gentleman is supposed to do that and I nearly knocked him off because I started to walk on the outside too. At last he fell all over himself and I knew my family was enjoying the spectacle immensely from the window! And crossing the streets he would seize my arm in a vise-like grip and shove me over. I talked a blue streak because I was afraid to keep still—I dread those awful silences. He wouldn't talk much. He isn't a bit interesting or unusual.

Well it was the first time I have ever been escorted anyplace by a fellow, *and where are the thrills?!?* I fully expected to be thrilled to the core. And I wasn't a bit. I was just rather excited and rather ill at ease. Isn't Romance thrilling after all? I'm so surprised and disappointed! What if Romance isn't anything after all!

We discussed *politics* on the way home. I was embarassed half to death when we reached the house. Do you ask 'em in? I didn't. I walked in and he followed. That's him—he follows! Do you ask 'em to sit down? I didn't. I wanted him to go, it was so embarrassing. I made various lame remarks and there were several harrowing pauses. He asked for my phone number and said he'd call me up some evening. I breathed a sigh of relief when he was gone. I hope to goodness he doesn't call. An evening talking to him would bore one to tears. He is engaged in the manufacture of soda pop and ginger beer!!!!

JULY 2. Well, this diary is full. It was just big enough for my Senior year. It has had a happy happy year to record. I shall feel quite lonesome in a big empty new diary!

Let's go back to the first page a minute. There is a noble

resolve to be less self-centered and broader in sympathies. Has it been achieved. Yes, I think it has to quite an extent. But not so much through any efforts of mine. It just came naturally and pleasantly. Opportunity for the development we need does come naturally I think. Isn't it a wonderful thing that it does.

And as to the Twentieth Century Maiden's Prayer—the Maiden has learned a lesson or two and doesn't waste her time praying for such things. She has been cured of her foolish desire—no, not cured, but she can behave herself and wait. Her prayer wasn't granted, but the desire was taken away, which amounts to the same thing in a way. But she hasn't lost her faith in Romance after all.

Goodbye

◇　◇

Afterword

Marion's diaries of her college years at U.C.L.A. show an increasing romantic interest in men, although she continued to have close emotional ties to women friends and teachers. In May of 1922 she wrote, "There is a Jewish fellow whom I knew last year. . . . I shall cultivate the acquaintance. He is intellectual in tastes . . . a good sense of humor. . . ."

And in June, "I have developed quite a romantic admiration for that Pre-med in my zoology class. . . . One can be oneself with Jack. . . . I like him more than any man I've ever known."

In 1933 Marion and Jack were married.

She had continued to keep a journal but, as she noted at the age of 29, "This diary has outlived its function and become a mere catalog of events rather than an opportunity for self expression as it used to be."

Marion attended graduate school at the University of California, Berkeley, and eventually secured a job teaching natural science at Marin County College, a junior college in Northern California. For his study, Gordon Allport described her at the age of 36: "She has an abundance of wavy light brown hair and a fresh complexion . . . a freshness and naturalness in clothes and appearance. Her strongest interest is botany, with literature, art and psychology running close for favor. She has an unusual ability to arouse the interest of others in whatever she is interested in . . . her friends express gratitude for her contagious enthusiasms. She dislikes intolerance and injustice. She is a sensible, straightforward, objective person with a shrewd estimate of herself."

Neither Marion nor Jack wanted children. In a personality sketch of herself written in 1938 for Allport, Marion noted her "over-reaction to the subject of maternity." She attributed this to its "threat to individuality . . . with no conceivable reward. The somewhat painful process of achieving maturity is not something I want to watch or be responsible for. I would resent the bodily role of mother, bodily distortion and discomfort.

"I have been sluggish and disinclined to physical activity all my life," she continued. "Life as it has been experienced seems worthwhile, though a good many fears as to possible physical catastrophes or economic [ones]. World insecurity and unrest depresses.

"Marriage happy. Few interests in common with husband but attitudes and background similar, and emotionally congenial. Well adjusted to job . . . difficulties with foreign languages, mathematical inability, lack of interest in experimentation are factors against real accomplishment in psychology and biology."

Apparently this lack of what she considered "real accomplishment" began to weigh more heavily on Taylor; the following year she wrote, "I don't think I'm particularly happy. It's the fact that I'm stale on the job, that I regard it as completely futile, that it's too strenuous, but that I can't quit it. . . . I feel plenty tired and middle-aged lately. I've just come through a period of adjusting to the idea of getting old. I am distinctly afraid of the sickness and disgusting dilapidation of age. My fears tie up to my particular physical disability." Evidently she had a heart condition.

Little is known of Taylor's life after this period. Toward the end of her life she acknowledged, to herself and a few close friends, that she was a Lesbian. She and her husband were separated; the last years of her life were spent living with another woman.

With this change in her lifestyle, she told friends, she began grappling with a new fear—that she would be "discovered" and lose her teaching job. Marion Taylor died rather suddenly of a heart attack in 1960, at the age of 58.

THE DIARY OF

Yvonne Blue

Chicago, Illinois
1926–1927

Yvonne Blue (*The Schlesinger Library, Radcliffe College*)

◇   ◇

Introduction

Yvonne ("Eve") Blue was born on May 9, 1911, in Chicago, to a moderately well-off professional family. Her father, an ophthalmologist, was a religious Methodist; her mother had been raised as an atheist. Yvonne and her two much younger sisters, Boo and Tickey, spent their early years in the city, but when Yvonne was in high school the family moved to the suburb of Flossmoor. She continued to attend the University High School in Chicago, but missed city life and hated the long commute to and from school.

Yvonne was two years younger than her classmates; she had learned to read at the age of four, and had started school early. Always physically behind the others in development, she was awkward and shy. She had two close friends, Bobbie and Ginny, but felt otherwise lonely and misunderstood.

The diaries were begun when Blue was twelve. The portion included here, started at age fourteen, began an ambitious project—a large red leather ledger book, much more imposing than the small pocket diaries she had kept in previous years.

For days I have pondered upon a fitting beginning for this glorious diary. If I intended this for publication, I should begin something like this :—

"I, Yvonne Blue, being in the fourteenth year of my life, and feeling that I am old enough to convey my impressions on paper, am going to write faithfully herein, and make this book a lasting memorial of me, for those who live after I die.

I have been thinking seriously today about my past life, and it is but right that I record my youthful recollections. Foremost in my mind is . . . . . etc. — etc. — etc."

But I most emphatically do not intend this for publication, so I shall begin merely by recording the events of the past hours instead of the past years.

At about three o'clock today, Grandpa, Grandma, Aunt Elaine, Uncle George, Bonnie, and Bobbie, arrived. [note — If I intended this for publication I should tell who Bonnie and Bobbie are, but as I don't, that is unneccessary] I hardly expected Bobbie to come. I said to my self, "If you don't expect anything, you won't be disappointed", and I was sure that her mother would repent and keep her home. But she came, luckily. Soon after they got here we sat down to the table, ten of us. (Bonnie was sick and Aunt Elaine put her to bed) We had turky, a big fifteen pound fellow. Mother said he didn't weigh more than ten, but I carried him from the station to the house, a whole half-mile, and I guess I know!

Immediately after dinner Bobbie and I set out for the Haunted House. Her mother had said that we couldn't go thru it alone, so we took, Button, the collie pup next door with us. He was more trouble than help tho, because he has never been trained, and every time a car passed

The diary of Yvonne Blue (*The Schlesinger Library, Radcliffe College*)

◇ *1926* ◇

JANUARY 1. For days I have pondered upon a fitting beginning for this glorious diary. If I intended this for publication, I should begin something like this:

"I, Yvonne Blue, being in the fourteenth year of my life, and feeling that I am old enough to convey my impressions on paper, am going to write faithfully herein, and make this book a lasting memorial of me, for those who live after I die.

I have been thinking seriously today about my past life, and it is but right that I record my youthful recollections. Foremost in my mind is . . . . etc. etc. etc."

But I most emphatically do *not* intend this for publication, so I shall begin merely by recording the events of the past hours instead of the past years.

At about three o'clock today, Grandpa, Grandma, Aunt Elaine, Uncle George, Bonnie, and Bobbie, arrived (note—If I intended this for publication I should tell who Bonnie and Bobbie are, but as I don't, that is unneccessary).* [After dinner] Bobbie and I went up to my room. We put my big Buddha stand and Buddha on the floor with an Indian candle on each side and the small Buddha incense burner before it. And we locked the door and turned out the main light and turned on the lamp and burned incense and read about the Taj Mahal from my India book.

JANUARY 13. Some people try to write differently, but there isn't any *very* different type: of course there is backhand, and beautiful writing like Grandma's, and queer writing like Grandpa's but—oh everything is like that. Everybody has to come under something classified before Cleopatra reigned. It's not fair to the present age. There aren't any *terribly* different people.

Whenever anyone *does* try to be different, he is ousted—kicked out. There is no room for originality in anything. Once in a while someone writes something rather different, and then

---

* Bonnie was her cousin, daughter of Aunt Elaine and Uncle George. Bobbie (Valerie) was Yvonne's closest friend.

he is critisized. And I critisize too. But they are different in a weird, terrible way, not in a beautiful one. They think that the more disgusting and wicked things they write, the more different they are. I don't see why we can't imagine what life on other planets is like. I suppose its just because we can't imagine anything *different*. They say that the moderns are different— bosh—they are not more modern than Cleopatra,—she would have smoked if tobacco had been discovered, and she did everything else that they do, and more too. Nothing is *different*. Of course there are all the inventions, that make our life different now. But Cleopatra was just as well off. —I can't imagine a different person—a *tremendously* different person,—and neither can anyone else, for no characters in books are very different. That word is tired, it has been worked long enough—I wish there was a different word. There it goes again.

And I don't know what I've been trying to say. . . . I had intended to say a little about the different sorts of handwriting,—and Something just turned it all about, and made me write a lot of nonsense that I don't understand. A whole page of it! Why—it—almost frightens me. . . .

JANUARY 16. I read in study the other day, a few entries from two diaries of very different types,—Samuel Pepys' Diary,—and *A Diary from Dixie*,—the diary of Mrs. John Rutledge. And mine is a third "type",—if it can be called such. Samuel Pepys' diary, deals with political matters, mostly, but there are things recorded there that he wouldn't want his wife to see. That is why he wrote it in code. And he didn't want it to be published, but they utterly, disregarded his wishes, and revised it and published it in book form with sundry notes and prefaces and introductions and stories of the author. And people have it in beautiful editions in their homes, and they show it to other people and exclaim "so interesting! I think it is lovely to have in a library, and so nice to have a book not meant for publication! I feel so thrilled when I read all his secrets and think how surprised he would be if he knew it."

A Diary from Dixie is rather uninteresting because it was the intention on the part of the author to have it published after her death. And it also has prefaces and pictures and facsimiles of pages in the original. And in a note in front it says, "Some few entries have been omitted because they were personal, and of local rather than general interest."

Just the nicest parts of course. And they leave in the political parts. (It was written during the Cival War.)

My diary is not in the slightest degree, of political interest. Perhaps if I had been fourteen years old during the World's War, and had lived in Belgium or France, it *might* have been. But I'm not much on politics. My diary is of interest only to myself. But possibly in years to come they might publish it, and people would say of it the same as they say of Samuel Pepys' now. It makes my blood boil. It would have, of course, facsimilics of pages, illustrations, prefaces, introductions, explanations, notes and all the rest. But the worst thing is the way they correct ungramatical phrases, and put down what they *think* you meant, and switch sentences around, and leave out the most interesting parts. When *I* read a diary I want to know just the errors the author made, and the personal parts and so forth. It's not fair. They would leave out my pet parts and write a lot of junk in the front about me, and make me seem silly and sentimental and senseless. I don't want *anyone* to have fun out of what I sweated for, after I am dust and ashes. I don't *want* them to say, "What a curious person! This book is a treasure, as a relic. But I can't imagine anyone writing as much, can you?" I don't even want my decendents to have it in the original. *I don't want them to! Horrid Horrid Horrid* people! I know they will say such things because that is what I should say if I were in their place. I'm not writing all this for them to read, and get pleasure from in after years. I'm writing it for *myself*, and for no one else. They have no business to correct mistakes. When one writes stories he scratches out and scratches out and copies over and over again, or else thinks out every sentence ahead of time. But in a diary, one doesn't stop for that. It is spontaneous. (at least mine is.) If I rewrote passages, I naturelly would perfect them. But *they* don't understand.

I know what I'll do! When I'm on my death bed I'll throw *all* my diaries in the fire!

FEBRUARY 8. I told Bobbie of my determination to burn my diaries, and she said not to because she thinks it best to have something left of us, when we die. There are arguments for both sides,—I will think it over. Bobbie wants her diary published, but I don't.

FEBRUARY 15. I like things that I don't exactly understand. I like to listen to the beauty of the words and phrases, as I like to listen to harmonious music. And not to understand a thing completely, elevates it,—makes it more lofty.

FEBRUARY 18. This year, for the first time in the history of the University High School, each teacher wrote a paragraph on the work of each pupil he taught. These reports were all sent home to the parents. There is no use in trying to hide the fact that I am not a marvellous person at school. So in case I should ever get "cocky" and say to children,—my neices and nephews, for I am never going to marry,— "Now when I was a girl I *always* had my lessons well. I can never remember a time when I wasn't the star of the class etc. etc. etc."—in case I should say that, I shall copy the report down word for word,— "without softening one defect", as Jane Eyre tells herself, when she draws her picture and Blanche Ingram's.

FEBRUARY 28. Yesterday I drove to Chicago Heights with Daddy, and when we were half way there, Daddy stopped the car, and showed me how to work it in first and neutral, and then he let me drive! He is going to teach me how to drive, and when I am 16 I can take it out alone. Someday I can have it for my own. I adore to drive.

MARCH 3. I have had two queer feelings within the last week. One was on a Sunday. There is a large expanse of land behind us, and there was a patch of ice there Sunday, so I took my sisters, and went skateing on the tiny smooth patch at the end of the larger place. We had taken the waste-basket to empty in our back yard, and had carried it to the ice. I sat on the over-turned waste-basket, with my head on my arms which rested on my knees, and thought that how little I dreamed when I was in my old home, that some bright sunshiny winter day, I would sit alone in the center of a great waste of rough ice, on an overturned waste-basket with my head in my lap. It was such a queer detached feeling—like I was inside my own mind,—or outside, looking down at myself.

The other time was tonight at nine o'clock, after Mother and I had finished the dishes. I was terrifically hot, and it was so cool and clear outdoors that I thought I would run outside a minute. I sat on the back doorstep, looking at the myriads of stars. Then I ran around in front. It was darker there and so beautiful and fresh,—like a wet white rose, at night. Then I ran out to the road,—a long way from the house. I went to the very middle of the road, where there was a little depression or hollow in the gravel,—and there I sat, gazing at the stars overhead, and the grayish blackness of the fields before me, and the lights of the houses behind me. . . . I felt again, then, that queer detached feeling, just like I had before.

MARCH 5. This afternoon I went to the dentists to have my teeth filled. I took gas. It was so queer! I was scared to death, when he stuck a big thing over my nose, and told me to breathe deeply. It had a queer dark red-brown smell too. At first I didn't feel anything, and then all of a sudden I felt all tingly,—like my foot had gone to sleep, only all over. I seemed to be sinking down and at each breath I sank down deeper. I lost consciousness then. I didn't feel like a person at all. I seemed to see, or be, I don't know which, a funny light irregular shaped thing against a patch of darkness. It jumped up and down too like the reflection of the sun, thrown on the wall by a mirror. I heard a noise too, one short noise, and two long. . . . Even the drill went like that. Then finally, Dr. Maginnis took it off, and filled the teeth. I am to go again every Monday until all my teeth are filled. I am going to take gas too. I rather like it. I imagine it is a little like opium. I read Sax Rohmer's book called *Dope*; it is trashy, I suppose, but oh, so interesting! It describes every step of taking *chandu* which is an oriental name for opium which is smoked.

I would like to take opium once, if I were sure I could stop at once. Everyone thinks he has the will-power,—very often he hasn't.

APRIL 3. We had supper at the Tower Building, Mother, Daddy, and I, and then we went to the theater. I love the city at night! I love to walk along the lighted streets and watch the people pass, or stand in the doorways of sea food places, sunk below the level of the pavements, billiard rooms, and theater lobbies. I love to look up at the colossal buildings with their occasional yellow squares of light. I love to feel that I am part of the pulsing city night-life, and among the poor, walking the streets, aimlessly, and the rich driving grandly up to the lobbies of the opera-houses. I like the queer people who pass—perhaps murderers, theives, Bohemians, artists, poets, novelists, plea-sure seekers, job hunters, college youths, loafers.

APRIL 4. Bobbie and I are planning to be *wonderful!* —to improve ourselves. We want to be very thin and silent, but to say unusual things when we speak, and have people hang on our words. We will wear our hair straight. We want very pale faces, and red lips, and we will dress nicely. We shall be aloof,— above the common mass, and cynical, sarcastic, sardonic, sa-tirical, ironic. Delicious words! I would love to have a skin like Lord Byron's—with a pallor like moonlight—the genius shining thru. *He* fasted. We want to read illuminating books—like Oscar Wilde.

But oh! how we want to be wonderful—and thin. When it gets warmer, I shall go on a four day fast. Not a bite for four days, and see if it does any good. We want to be deep too, and perhaps, a trifle obscure.

We will go queer places, and do queer things. We are going to be newspaper reporters together, come what may. Maybe they will send us to Europe and we will go around there, and live in Bohemia in London, like in Arthur Ransome's book of that name. If we can do all that, we shall have achieved our heart's desire.

APRIL 10. When we die, Bobbie and I would like to be burned and have the ashes put in little jars, and each jar put in

the heart of an apple tree. On the cover of my jar, I would like
to have written:

> *"Here she lies where she longed to be,*
> *Home is the sailor, home from the sea,*
> *And the hunter home from the hill."*
>
> *[Robert Louis Stevenson]*

It was Bobbie's idea of having the ash-jar put in the heart of
an apple tree,—but I like it, so I'm copying it. If she doesn't
want me too, I want them scattered on the wind, part on land
and part on sea. But I like the apple tree better. I would feel
horribly with part of me one place and part another. Why how
could I ever get up when (?) blows the horn? It's a good thing
I don't believe in the Bible.

APRIL 18. Monday Bobbie asked me to spend the night at
her house. I was sure Mother wouldn't let me, but she said that
I could! Bob had our night all planned out. We each got into
our pajamas at about 9 o'clock, and crawled into her big double
bed, after saying our prayers. We wanted to awake at 12:00 at
night, but we had a hard time getting to sleep and it was 1:10
when we woke up. *Then* comes the nicest part of all. We crept
downstairs in the kitchen, and Bobbie put slices of cheeze between bread, and fried them in butter—Cheeze Dreams—or—
Dream Sandwitches. Then we took them, with some animal
crackers and peanuts upstairs. We sat cross-legged on the bed,
lit the lamp, and ate the lovely soggy, melt-in-your-mouthy-
buttery sandwiches, and the rest, and read Oscar Wilde.

APRIL 29. There are so many Londons! There is Sax Rohmer's London—Limehouse, mostly—a dirty yellow, shading
at the edges into "pure luminous color." And there is Frances
Hodgson Burnett's London in "The Lost Prince"—shabbi-
ness—and rain. And there is Conan Doyle's London—Sherlock
Holmes—Baker Street—and Oscar Wilde's London—but-
lers—late dinners, epigrams. And Arthur Ransome's London—
Bohemia—an artists pallate—scrawled papers, and tankards of
ale—

And there is R.L.S.'s [Robert Louis Stevenson] in "New Arabian Nights"—adventures—and Robert Hitchen's in "December Love"—which is a mixture of them all.

And Dickens' London! Historic London!
LONDON!
I want to go to London!

MAY 15. [Uncle] Gil was telling me all about the cabarets today—he has been to lots. But girls can't go alone, damn it—they can in Paris. Ah, but I shall go, never-the-less. Gil says that everyone should go. Gil is rather sophisticated, I fear. He can't sit thru a movie any more, and he has been all over and has had all manner of experience.

But I don't exactly want to be sophisticated. Grandma says that no one can live in a large city, and be *un*sophisticated.

I can never say—"Now when *I* was a girl, I didn't say things like that"—this book is too frank entirely, I think.

Anyway I want to die before I'm 30.

JUNE 1. I'm way behind in all my school work. But somehow I don't care if I flunk everything. What's school? Everyone that's good in school isn't good in his chosen work, and everyone that is poor in school isn't poor outside of it.

JUNE 16. School is over—and I have an Incomplete in French,—an incomplete that I will be two months in working off next year. But, hell's bells! (a pet expression of Bobbie's and mine just now) I don't care! School is over!

But I am rather sorry too. Bobbie and I have been thinking over the nice things about school—things that we will miss. There will be no more Golden Moments! We have had just three of them—moments when we both had work at home, but when leaving was painful—like tearing ribs from our bodies. Lingering, delicious *Golden* Moments—like amber colored wine that goes to the head, and makes one feel estatically uplifted with the Beauty of Youth and the Thrill of Life.

When we came back after our Freshman year the Pirate Passion had burned dim—when we came back after our Sophmore year the India Passion was flickering low, and I suppose that when we came back after our Junior year, the Oscar Wilde Passion (though I can't conceive of such a thing now) will have almost died out. And I don't want it to! But Bobbie and I have always had something—some interest—and I suppose that next year a fourth interest—the oldest of all will replace the interests of this year.

Oh, it is horrible to grow up! I would suffer in hell throughout eternity if I could only be Peter Pan in this life!!!

JUNE 23. Ginny [a close friend] is leaving Chicago July 1st. She sails for Europe and Asia the 3rd. I'll never get to Europe. Nice things always happen to other people—I get all the horrid ones. That is more truth than poetry—I mean it terribly. I get Flossmoor flunks in French—no vacation—maybe California— I haven't been really happy since last summer before I went to camp.

JUNE 25. Today I went to the Jackson Park [Theatre] and saw Adolph Menjou in "The Social Celebrity." It was a good picture, but I'm not going to that theatre alone, again. I sat in a row all by myself, when the play began, but after a time I became aware of a young man sitting beside me. I thought it rather odd, because if I wanted to sit in a row with only one person in it, I would sit at least a seat away. But I didn't like to move, so I just sat still. Finally I stole a look at him. He was a nice looking blond with tortose shell glasses. He said to me, "I have never seen this girl on the screen before. What is her name?" I replied as shortly as possible, "I don't know." "The man is Adolph Menjou, isn't he?" he asked. (as if Adolph Menjou isn't one of the best known and most easily recognized actors on the screen!) "Yes", I replied, determined to say no more than was necessary. He didn't say anything else, but I caught him looking at me, every time I looked away from the screen. Then I became interested in the picture, and forgot all about him until he began crowding over in his seat. I looked down at my lap. His arm was hanging over the seat-arm, and his hand was almost touching mine. I moved as far away as I could, but finally his hand did touch mine. I, of course moved mine. I thought it was an accident and I didn't like to change my seat.

But it wasn't an accident. Every time I looked down and moved my hand he would take his away, and then he would put it back again, but not noticeably. First he would put it on his chair arm. And then he would slowly move it over. I still thought it was an accident, and once I waited for him to move his first. But he didn't!—at least not in the right way. Finally it dawned on me, that he intended to take my hand. I was a fool. I didn't know what to do, and I determined that he shouldn't drive me from my seat. I was there first! But as soon as it was over I got up. I saw him waiting in the lobby and I didn't want to pass him. I thought that there was another exit, but there wasn't so I finally left quickly and ran to a waiting street car.

JULY 3. I have just finished reading this diary. A more tedious, uninteresting, sentimental, forced, slushy book, it has never been my ill-fortune to read. But still, I think I have improved since I spouted this choice bit, in all seriousness, a little more than a year ago:—(speaking of my cuckoo clock)— ". . . . . . If you open the little door at the top the cuckoo peeps out, and if you touch his head he will bow, flap his wings and open his beak, but alas, time has silenced his bell-like voice, and not a sound issues forth from those opened lips."

Still, the part about the Golden Minutes sounds suspiciously like it. From now on, I'm going to be less sentimental, and more interesting.

I'm so tired of being fat! I'm going back to school weighing 119 pounds—I swear it. Three months in which to lose thirty pounds—but I'll do it—or die in the attempt. There its said— whenever I weaken I'll look at this, and then I'll *have* to keep on starving. Tomorrow we have a picnic in honor of the fourth— but just the same I'm not going to eat a single bite all day. I wish there was a pair of scales in Flossmoor.

JULY 9. But of course the next morning I took a chunk of bread and ate it before I thought of my resolution. And that day I *ate*, and *ate*. But today I am keeping it. It is now a quarter to four, and so far not a crumb of food has passed my lips—not even tooth paste—or water. But I'm not at all thirsty. I've the queerest feeling though—emptiness—and rather like my stomack is contracting, and I want food terribly. Some delicious cookies came just now—all my favorite kinds. I put eight away—four lucious marshmallow cocoanut covered ones and four smaller ones also of marshmallow and mounted on vanilla wafers, but covered with malted milk chocolates. I smelled them, but somehow it didn't help so awfully much.

Of course I know I can't get thin in a single day—but I can start to.

It is now just seven. I am starving. I keep close watch on the clock, I can tell you—the days don't pass any too quickly for me. And I haven't weighed myself. But tomorrow we go out for dinner. While the family goes in, I'll sit in the car and read a movie magazine. When I go in to buy it, I'll weigh myself.

I feel queer all over and oh! so hungry. And yet I can smell the food cooking down stairs and not snatch at it furiously the way heroes in novels who haven't eaten for two days always do. I imagine myself eating hot crusty sugary cinnamon rolls or the cookies and two bars of candy that mother bought me, which are in my bottom drawer, and I *want* them. But I'm not mad with hunger. I sent for Antionette Donnelly's book telling just how many calories each food has. "If you are trying to reduce", she says, "you would better keep your food consumption for the day down to at least 1,500—1,200, if possible."

So (after the four days)—I am going to keep them down to about 50 per day.

And thats absolutely *all*, at least till I lose noticeably. No cake or pie or ice-cream or cookies or candy or nuts or fruits or bread or potatoes or meat or anything. If I could *only* drink tea without cream or sugar. It has *no* calories.

I have been exercising very little. 100 jumps with a jump-rope a day, is all, and I'm scarcely strong enough for that.

JULY 11. I ruined the good work today. I was so weak I could hardly pull myself out of bed. My hands shook terribly and I grew hot and cold by turns. I managed to dress, but when I went downstairs Mother said I looked so shaky and pale and sick that she *made* me eat. And to tell the truth I wasn't sorry, I had gone 60 hours without food. I ate an immense breakfast—

two large peaches, a cup of cocoa with three marshmallows and two pieces of toast. I don't know what to do. I weighed myself yesterday and I've lost 5 pounds—I weigh 144. But I'll get thin yet!

JULY 27. Mother and Daddy make me so mad! They *make* me eat. Last week I had an average of less that 140 calories a day and I lost 7 pounds. And now they won't let me diet. Last night I dropped most of the meat in my lap, rolled it in my napkin and fed it to Tar Baby [cat]. and at breakfast I put half my orange and bread in my napkin and throw it away later. I hate to do it, but what am I to do. I *won't* eat it.

If "The Good Fäery" on my desk should take it into her pretty head to grant me three wishes I should need no time in which to make my decision. I would say:

> Eternal Youth
> Genius, and
> to be a boy.

I read an article by Fans Messan, a French sculptor who won recognition by dressing as a boy. Oh how I would love it if Bobbie and I could dress like boys, steal rides on freight trains to New York, go as stowaways to the Latin Quarter of Paris, or the Bohemian Quarter of London, rent a studio as boys, visit the queer restaurants, and write and become famous like Chatterton and Villon and all the rest of the vagabond poets.

I'd like sometime to write a book and call it, "The Thrill of Life." The book would be the story of my life as I would like to have it.

AUGUST 1. Today ends the second week of dieting. I haven't counted my calories this week, but I've eaten as little as Daddy let me—and not a sweet thing for two weeks! At the races they had my favorite candy—and tonight at the Sing which is to be held here, they'll have lemonade, cookies, cake and candy. But I have a will! Thats what I say when I am tempted (and I have been often!)—and I also say—"I'll be glad tomorrow that I held back"—and "Get thin first—eat afterwards." I wonder if I'll *ever* weigh 119!

AUGUST 13. I like Cleveland! [Yvonne was visiting her Uncle George and Aunt Elaine.] I'm having a good time. But my weight bothers me. I am eating very little, and exercising a goodly amount. But I weigh the same—131 in the altogether. If I eat an ordinary meal I know I'll gain.

Wednesday, Lura H. came over. She is nineteen, but she looks sixteen, because she is small and thin. She is a fool over boys—anything in pants will do. And yet she is homely—homlier than I. Her light blue eyes are hidden behind tortous shell glasses. Her nose is very broad, she has very little upper lip, her teeth stick out a little, she has a receding chin, round shoulders and a complextion that reminds me of the outside of a cantalope. And to top it all, she has a permanent wave—a horrible one—fuzzy, kinky and unmanageable.

Lura wanted me to go to the Bandbox Burlesque with her the next day. It is a cheap and rather vulgar show for a quarter with a comedy and feature motion picture. Her mother wouldn't let her go, so she wanted me to sneak off with her. Aunt Elaine said I could go if we didn't talk to any boys—as *if*. Lura said she knew two boys who sold peanuts and candy and pop between the acts, but she wouldn't talk to anyone else.

I met Lura at 3:30 and we went. The last part of a punk comedy was on when we entered, and I couldn't see very well. But I led the way, because Lura said she always sat down by boys, and I didn't want to take any chances. So I sat by an old man and she sat on the aisle. We were almost the only females in there, and all the people looked vulgar. Finally the curtain was raised, and the Burlesque began. About 15 girls in very scant, dirty costumes came out and did a little dancing. Then a couple of comedians came out, and "cracked" what Lura calls, "dirty jokes." One act was terribly coarse and vulgar. and right afterwards they turned on the lights and one of the men said "hello" to Lura and me. I wanted to die—especially after that vile act. It was too awful—that act—I can't write about it. But the Burlesque was exciting and interesting and I'm awfully glad I went. Lura said afterwards that her boys weren't there— "There wasn't much use in *my* going." "Why", I said, "Is *that* why you went? Pay a quarter to see a *boy?*" "Sure" she laughed, "I'd pay more than that." Poor perverted Lura.

On the way home we passed a place where there were queer machines. You go in for a dime and see something or other— I don't know what. But Lura wouldn't even let me look at the outside, because she said its a terrible place. Aunt Elaine is going to take me there before I go.

AUGUST 16. [At a restaurant] I ordered French Pastry. Aunt Elaine didn't want all her ice-cream, so she put a third of it on my cake. And I afterwards ate—4 pieces of candy, 5 marshmallows, 15 cookies, 1 plum, 1 banana, 1 bunch of grapes, 3 peanuts, and a half a pretzel. I knew I'd gain, so the next day, I didn't eat a thing.

AUGUST 20. I've gained two pounds! But I'll lose them. I'm not eating today. When we had supper at the Hitchcocks, I ate like a hog. I keep saying to myself "Eat, drink, and be merry, for tomorrow we die-t." But "O that this too, too solid flesh would melt!"

AUGUST 23. I have only seven pounds to go, *if* I don't gain. I've lost over 20 pounds. Aunt E. and I went to the dime museum but there were just men there. There were pistols and rifles hanging all around, and a great many slot machines where by inserting a penny, nickel or dime, motion pictures could be seen of girls not especially characterized by superfluous clothes. So we didn't stay. I would have liked to look in one of the slot-machines, but I didn't dare with all the men around.

OCTOBER 3. [*Chicago*] School! I *hate* it. It is a seething red-hot hell where tortured souls are crushed beneath despicable work. Underneath the lively chatter, underneath the hundreds of spectacled senior boys and round-eyed bewildered freshmen and laughing slim "popular" girls, underneath the apparently pleasant surface there is an iron hand that bends the students ruthlessly and molds them in a common pattern.

I *hate* to go back. I know what I am getting into. I see the winter ahead of me—long hours after school in the depressing— deadly study-hall, grinding over French verbs in the cheerless November afternoons—waiting frozen-footed on the cold,

windy train platforms—reading in dull history books about battles I don't understand—cramming for tests—trying to memorize page after page of scientific fact. Summer is gone! blue
skied—green-lawned. wild, free summer. And tomorrow—
school.

OCTOBER 11. Ginny, Bobbie and I told each other, (not
without much persuasion, promises not to get mad, etc) our
faults, and oh horrors!—I have learned that I am obstinate,
crude, loquacious, that I walk like a gorilla, and act too terribly
natural. On the other hand I am self possessed. (I'm not really.
Whenever we have floor-talks I clench my fist and murmer—
"Be self-possessed. That's the whole art of living", but much
good it does me!) fearless, "beauty-having" and have the mak-
ings of personality. (Their words) So tomorrow I revolutionize
my character. I shall walk as if I owned the world—talk slightly
condesendingly, be extremely self-possessed, spout scintillating
sophistication (assumed) and develop subtility. In short, I shall
be supermagnaglorious personified.

Here are ten little things I should like to have, even tho they
may not all be good—

1. Self possession & control
2. Superiority
3. Cynicism
4. Will power
5. Silentness
6. Differentness
7. Subtlety
8. Immense range of knowledge
9. Supreme indifference
10. Great independence

OCTOBER 23. After school Bobbie, Ginny and I went to the
Tivoli *in a taxi!* The movie was poor, but they had wonderful,
thrilling music and dim lights. That music made *us* feel wonderful and perhaps by lingering in our subconcious minds, paved
the way for what was to come. . . .

It was dark when Bobbie and I alighted from the taxi at her
door . . . I stayed and Bobbie and I curled up on the bed and
talked. Bobbie's parents weren't there, so we decided to do
things on a deluxe scale.

We each got into pajamas—symbol of ease—of sleep—of

everything that's nice, combed our hair behind our ears, whitened our faces and reddened our lips to a startling degree, and adorned ourselves with jingling ear-rings, necklaces, rings, clashing bracelets and anklets. We pulled the spread of the wide bed back, piled numberless cushions on the down comforter, tyed a red kerchief over the bed lamp, and lit incense. We lay there among the soft pillows, in the magic rosy light, in our quaint dress, with Wilde's poems and Rossetti's pictures beside us and watched the sporls of incense mounting upward in fascinating spell-weaving shapes while we talked. For hours we lay in that still room in perfect harmony. Never had we felt like that before. It was an exquisite rose-colored feeling that comes only once in an eon and weaves a mystic spell around one, and to prove that life is not always cruel, gives one for the time—everything—Beauty—youth—genius—peace—immortality—all were in the soft rosy glow of the lamp—in the incense-laden air—in each other.

We talked. We cannot recall the things we said now. We were perfectly frank—(one *could* be in that marvelous atmosphere) and we did that which so few mortals can—we *understood* each other.

Never shall I forget the light and shadow—the mysterious incense—never the perfect contentment of those enchanted hours.

NOVEMBER 4. I wonder if anyone in the world has ever hated himself as I hate myself. It is just recently that I have. Formerly I thought more of myself. I thought I could write, and now that illusion too has been shattered. No one has said anything, but I have tried to write recently, and I can't—I can't. I never could. It was just illusion. Yet, tho I can form sentences better than some of those at school, they don't worry or care. And I do. I want to be able to write more than I want anything else in the world. I am not modest. I haven't an inferiority complex. I am just seeing things right for the first time, and trying to view myself detachedly, cooly, impersonally. It's not pleasant—this shattering of illusions. This last week or so I've been horribly depressed. For all my life has been bound up with illusions,

and now that they have vanished I see life as it really is. It is
hell. Even my own life is horrible. I hate myself. I really do.
But oh why are my emotions theatrical! *This* seems theatrical—
but it is one of the sincerest things I've ever written. I have a
disagreeable personality, yet no one hates me as I hate myself.
This fall when I came back to school I was different. It wasn't
just thinness. Ginny said I was a little like Peter Pan. I was.
But now I am a fat, crude, uncouth, misunderstood beast. The
prospect of thinness was not the only reason for my fasting this
summer. I wanted to come nearer to the Ancient Greek ideal
(only I didn't know it was Greek then)—to regard eating as an
unavoidable evil—to use food only as a means of sustaining life
that I might attain to higher things. I wanted to be spiritual—
to cast off the bonds of material things. In part I succeeded.
But now!—now I drown myself,—I flounder in a sea of meat
and drink. I am obscene, earthly. I am a gibbering, blundering
stupid creature. That is what my teachers and everyone at school
thinks of me. I am poor in my studies. But if I fail to graduate
this year I will run away, dress like a boy, vagabond to the four
corners of the earth. I will get thin and be a Peter Pan, a Don-
atello, and forget my shattered illusions. Life is sordid, hard,
cruel, here. But in sunny Italie, in Classic Hellas, life should
be ideal, beautiful. I used to crave knowledge, but now I care
little for education. The more intelligent people are, the more
miserable they are. I shall be ignorant—and happy.

NOVEMBER 7. Chicago! There could never be another city
like it. It is the modern Bagdad, the Arabian Night City where
anything can happen. The slender black buildings lit by occasional yellow squares, the flashing sign-lights which seem to
play hide and seek with one another, the brilliant theater lobbies, the Bohemian restaurants, the motley crowds all reek of
adventure. It is like an oriental prince arrayed in sparkling, bar-
baric jewels. It has something that no other city however large
or risqué could ever have—something symbolized by the old
Field Museum. I love Chicago! I love it! I love it because it is
a city of illusion, because it is beautiful and thrilling, because
it is a city that like a golden tawny tiger can bare cruel fangs.

But most of all I love it because it is life—and adventure! I could never be happy away from Chicago—it is in my blood, and if I tried for a thousand years, I could never express half that it means to me.

NOVEMBER 17. I went to Bobbie's for lunch. We both sat in bed, and had more fun! Our lunch was brought up to us, and we cast aside all conventionality and ate naturally. We started with Risotto and goat-cheese. We spilled it on the bed and slung the Risotto we dropped in our laps all over the room. The cat wagged his tail in our plates, and when we got up, the grated cheese covered the bed an inch thick. Then we discovered the soup, and we drank it out of the bowl, while the passers-by in the street below gaped at us thru the open window. We shook the mayonaisse from the bottle on our salads, gulped our fried bananas and spilled our choclate malteds on the floor—but we enjoyed ourselves.

DECEMBER 5. All the adolescents that have even a suggestion of writing ability came to school yesterday to take poetry tests for a young woman who looks like she writes free verse poems in the manner of Amy Lowell, and who is interested in phsycology. I am afraid that if ever I had a poetic reputation, it is sunken in the quicksand of oblivion. First we were given a list of words and we had to find as many rhymes as possible in a minute. . . . She gave us words like "butterfly" and we had to write down as many adjectives for it as we could, in a given time. Then she gave us words like "the sea" and we had to put down things it did, like—"shifts restlessly", or "dashes against rocks". Then she gave us words like "life" and we had to put down symbols, like "a grab bag". But *then* all I could think of was "hell", so I wrote it. It *is* hell when one has one's poetic ability tested by assinine tests given by modern imbeciles, with literary aspirations. Then there were couplets of poetry with words left out, and we had to fill them in ourselves. I filled in the silliest things! I think we stayed *hours*. She dropped a bomb shell when she left us—that some time next week, every person that took the test has to spend an hour with

her alone. I shall collapse if she asks for my latest effort, for
Ginny and I have been trying to write sentimental stuff lately.

Anyway I don't care if I *did* flunk the test—I don't think that
there is any way a person's poetic ability can be tested except
by the poems he writes!

DECEMBER 15. Bobbie and I are going to be wonderful
though. Our new passion is self-improvement. I stayed all night
at her house last night and we made up a wonderful set of rules.
We each have a little blue covered notebook, and we wrote the
rules in India Ink on the cover,

> Keep polished.
> Follow the Health Chart.
> Talk the right amount and clearly.
> Be adventurous and light.
> Realize our own wonderfulness.
> Be decisive and "stick to your guns."
> Go to extremes
> Train Mind
> Be noble—in a princess way
> Have a way with people.

We are going to take one each day and concentrate on it alone.
Today we took the first. If we are good for a week we have
a little spree—a movie and a sundae together, but if we have a
blank space for *one day* we have the most horrible punishment
in the world—doing the dishes for that night. February 1st, if
we're still trying we have the Grand Spree—luncheon at the
Tip-Top and afterwards a real play. If we only keep them!

DECEMBER 22. I wonder if a person could develop an entirely new style if he tried very hard. There is really no use in
my keeping a diary if I can't improve at all. I have just finished
skimming over my last diaries, (*reading* them would have been
too, too, great a strain) and I find that they are all written in
the very same supersalious manner, except that the farther back
you go, the more glaring faults you find.

DECEMBER 31. Its the last day of the old year. 1926. For
exactly a year I've written here at frequent intervals. I wonder

why? For the pleasure it will give me in old age? No, because I know that it will trouble me then with vain longings for youth and health. For future publication? No—that will scarcely do. A published diary is uninteresting at best when genuine, and they are written differently. Because I *must* find some outlet for the genius that is in me? Well, hardly. Because it gives me pleasure? Perhaps. It has been said that a girls day is never complete until she has told someone about it. It may be that being possessed of an interest in writing I choose this way of telling about my more or less interesting experiences. But I think that the real reason that I keep a diary (disgusting word) is so that non omnis moriar [I shall not completely die]. . . . It is futile of course—everything I do is that—life itself is that— but it is the ultimate ideal.

Moi foi! but I was a green little fool! I still am. Writing about life and death! I haven't seen life. Or tasted it. I haven't even smelled it. I'm young. So why worry? And why wah hyat Ullah, write things down? I ask you, why? The non omnis moriar is tommyrot. Romantic Sentimental tommyrot. This year has been a mistake. Anyone courageous enough to read even a few pages will know what I mean. So all I can do is to write on the first page—YAH DAHWATI—And on this last page of the old year I'll inscribe the little word:

. . . . . PECCAVI . . . .
[I have sinned]

◇ *1927* ◇

JANUARY 1. When Montie [family friend] comes, there are three people to order me around. If only she wasn't so old! Some of the things she says to me are downright rude and I could give her as good as she gives me. "You have a lovely mouth" she said, "a perfect bow, and you have good brows and skin but you're getting too big here. Do you eat much candy?" Or again—"Do you like to dance? You should dance—there's nothing like it for the figure—you must take care of your figure." I suffered in silence, of course, but I longed to say—"In the name of Allah, woman, wear shoes that give your toes a chance to breathe! You take pride in wearing a size 2½ AA, but your foot is a mess. Humped up in the middle like a camel's back, and running all over that dainty swade pump. And leave off just a bit of the rouge and don't frizzle your hair so much. Don't talk so much or so sentimentally or so smugly. And above all don't act so much like an old maid—even tho' you are one."

If only it was a year from now! Or last year! No I don't want it to be last year. I'm glad thats finished. I wonder what will happen this year. It feels so queer to turn the blank pages and think of all the things that will be written there and to write that I wonder whats going [to] happen.

Ten years from now an outsider may read this, and all he'll have to do will be to flip the pages over and glance disinterestedly at the writing if *he* is curious. But I don't know at all and if *I* flip the pages I'll find only nothingness.

I swear I won't write here again unless I have something *worth* writing. and you may lay to that.

JANUARY 8. Some time ago in Home Economics I told the teacher that I wrote best when I didn't organize and plan papers. She disagreed, and said that if I did my papers must be very poor. I couldn't very well say anything but Marjorie C. stood up for me and said that I wrote good papers, and the matter dropped.

Yesterday, the teacher said that she wished to see me. . . .

"This paper", said the teacher, "shows as clearly as possible what happens when you fail to organize." I was silent, so she proceeded to tell me what a "wretched" paper it was. . . . apparantly she didn't know that I enjoy the reputation of being able to write, to a small degree, for she told me that being able to express my thoughts clearly would help me later on. But I fear that this diary has ruined me and fitted me at best for "merely clever rambling." Imagine organizing and outlining a diary!

Her poor opinion of my literary abilities mattered not a two-penny damn to me. But she didn't stop pestering me there. Her sermon was organized thusly:

A. Discussion of paper
  1. Critisizm
     a) due to lack of organization
     b) due to lack of interest & attention
  2. How to improve papers
     a) organize
     b) take interest in things.
B. Discussion of *ME*
  1. Critisizm
  2. How to improve myself (Lord! she can't tell me anything about that!)

If I am not mistaken *B* was held in reserve—to be used according to my reaction to *A*. Or again—observing my reaction to *A*—it was spontaneous, and that, perhaps, explains why it was not well organized. Personally I doubt if I had a reaction. I just kept silent and tried to practice my subtle sneer. (only it isn't at *all* subtle). I must have annoyed her, (I'm really talented at that) for she launched into my personality. Apparently I am too decided in my opinions. (but I *tried* to be!) She said that a person couldn't be around me very long without feeling that. I learned that I like my own way—that I resent others' suggestions,—that I immediately accept or reject an idea and no matter how persuasively I am persuaded, I stick to my original decision—that I am self centered and selfish. "You ought to interest yourself more in other people—and do things for them too." "You mean altruism?" I asked a little distastfully and hoping (vainly) that she wouldn't know what it meant. But it appears that the reason she wishes me to do things for others is for the benefit I myself would derive from it. Then she asked me what I lived for and I told her to get all the fun I could. She seemed slightly disappointed but repeated her remark about the fun I would get from knowing other people. "Your life would be fuller and happier." she said "and you would be much more satisfied

with yourself" Surely, I thought, it is a matter for my own choosing. but I said nothing. . . . She told me to hand in the re-
written paper on Monday, and released me. All this is very
interesting, but it hardly teaches me anything except to be very
silent in class and to organize. But I learned to *hate* that mean,
stingy, planning, mundane, sniveling, phlegmatic simpering old
idiot!!!!!

JANUARY 17. I've been home a-bed for a week and I'm
drowning in a sea of school-work. The semester ends very
shortly—in a week or two and I was behind already. I'm worried
sick. If things don't go right I might as well committ suicide
and I would if I wasn't such a damned coward. Why should
school ruin a person's life at it's very start? When I go back
tomorrow I'll face the music and find out where I stand (if at
all.) The disgrace of being another year at school and the infernal
scoldings and naggings I'll get at home if I flunk! Maybe at the
last minute I'll get up an insane courage and commit suicide
after all.

JANUARY 23. Friday I dashed off—

An Experiment to Prove that Carbon Dioxide is given off in
Oxidation
and
The Unification of Germany, Italy and France
and
A Valuation of the Various Account Books for Housewives
and
Romanesque and Gothic Architecture

There is only a week more to the semester and work!
French! Science! Home Economics! Survey of Art! Biology!
Hell!

FEBRUARY 10. I have discovered the person whom I have
never been able to imagine—the female Oscar Wilde. —I have
been reading "Sarah Bernhardt's Philosophy of Love." She was
a friend of Oscar and some of her quips are worthy to stand by
his.

It's funny I didn't get incomplete in anything in school! There was literally not one class that I was not incomplete in and how!

FEBRUARY 20. In Home Economics we are studying calories and Thursday we had to write down everything that we had eaten the previous day. Now as it happens I have been reducing for the past two weeks and my total number of calories for the day was but 635—a sum noticably in arrear of the recognized 2500. I told her I was attempting to make the ol' scales register a trifle less when I mounted them and the up-shot was that I was kept after class while she lectured. She told me:

1. That if I kept it up I'd die
2. That I was not too heavy
3. That thin girls weren't pretty
4. That I was so foolish about this when generally I was so "honest" and "sensible." (heaven forbid)
5. That if I was really overweight, which she doubted, she'd help me reduce, but I must consume 1800 calories a day. She asked me why I wished to reduce and I told her because I felt better that way. She said that she didn't believe me— but it's true.

Now that graduation is pending colleges are being discussed. I hate to think of it—college is—is—worse than high school! I can't bear an American College—I want to go to a convent in Italy—an old old convent with olive trees and flagstone walks with tufts of grass growing between the stones and sunshine, and ivy mantled towers and quiet nuns.

I've been reading *Trilby, The Beloved Vagabond* and *Bohemia in London.* I will not die till I have lived on bread and cheeze in some London or Paris attic with sloping roofs and chimney-pots beyond my casement window—till I have tramped thru sunny Italy. I have said it.

MARCH 10. I just can't loose weight no matter how little I eat. For two weeks I have been existing on next to nothing and I have gained. I am so hungry, and starving in the midst of plenty is worse than awful. For 4 1/2 weeks no bread, potatoes, only thing in the world that matters is the way one conducts onself. Ultimate results are null.

APRIL 17. Good lord, but I made a fuss about not eating for two days, last year! Now I think less than nothing about not eating for a day. I don't feel the slightest bit weak or hungry and I'd just as soon not eat as eat. I fast at least one day each week, and loose two or three pounds. Inbetween times I gorge, but I manage to keep my weight between 128 and 131. I'm not worrying.

MAY 4. Looking over ones ancient diaries may not be a profitable pastime, but it is an amusing, if slightly startling one. In the very brief record of my last year at camp, I find the naive statement ". . . . and I learned to hate Miss Price," (my former crush), but, prigish little fool that I was I neglected to tell why. The truth is, we were on our camping trip, and our bathing suits were wet in the morning when we wanted to take a dip, so Misses Price and Nash decided to go in in their birthday suits. Innocent I, did not understand and my horror was overwhelming when they calmly and slowly undraped before the fire. Modestly I wore a thin pair of B.V.D.'S in the water which proved far worse than nothing. I know now that I missed a priceless opportunity. I regret my uncomfortable sense of the fitness of things.

MAY 10. I was sixteen yesterday. Sixteen. Birthdays are supposed to make one feel old, but sixteen seems an awfully immature age, while fifteen seems absolutely infantile.

JUNE 20. [The] last week of school was one of hectic work and excitement, and I was never sure that I was going to graduate. Even at the last moment when I [was] in white with my boquet of roses, lined up ready to receive my diploma, I feared that someone like in Jane Eyre's wedding would hold up his hand and say "Stop! This ceremony cannot proceed!"

JUNE 23. Tonight five of Boo's and Tickey's friends came over for supper. It was an uproarious mob. I always thought that I hated kids, and I rather prided myself on that fact, but I guess that after all I don't. When both Dode and Buddy [neighbor children] wanted me to sit beside them and I sat between them, Dode hugged me and whispered, "I like you Yvonne." I, of course could only say, "I like you too Dode." "But not as much as I like you." "You don't know," I laughed. It is queer but it made me feel so warm and happy. It's funny—when I completely ignore people they like me—people generally, for whose opinions I do not care. But when *I* make advances, for some reason I fail. There must be something in me that is nice, that these people see—something I don't know about. If I could only find it and cultivate it I might even become popular.

◇   ◇

Afterword

Yvonne entered the University of Chicago the following autumn, at the age of sixteen "and with a characteristic intensity decided to grow up," she wrote.

In an essay on herself and her diary written several years later, Blue gave a vivid picture of her college years. She interspersed descriptions of herself (in the third person) with excerpts from the college diary:

"At first she is shy and afraid. She pledges a club, and describes at length the ceremonies that go with sororities. She misses Bobbie, who has gone to another school, and finds no kindred soul, as she says, in her club. And then there is a lapse of about three months, and we find [in the diary]:

"My god! how different college is from high-school! In class one is treated as a human being—the instructors swear like hell, and they're all atheists. Every damn kid on campus smokes, and so I do, of course, I inhale, and I smoke in public.

"This indeed is a rather startling change. What, I wondered, could cause a timid sensitive girl to become so bumptiously self-assertive. In a novel, no doubt, some soul-shaking experience would account for the metamorphosis. In the pages of the diary no such incident is hinted at. It seems to be part of the painful process, so dreaded in the early part of the book, of growing up.

"For three years, thereafter, the entries are scattered and hurried. When she takes up diary writing seriously again, she tells us that she is still changing:

"It makes me feel rather sad to write here once more. So much has happened to change me from the queer, awkward, eager little high-school girl who thought she was a genius, and the girl who started college—very young, but acting sophisticated with severe black clothes, thick make-up, sleek hair. . . . I used to be freakish, perhaps, but it seems to me I really had more fun then than I do now.

"It frightens me to think of my future. As far as financial returns are concerned, my education has been a complete washout. All I can do is write

a little. I can't type, or take shorthand, or teach, and I doubt if I ever find a man fool enough to want to marry me. I still don't want to get married— at least not for a long time.

"After this entry there is another break of several months, and when she writes again it is to talk of new people, places she has been, parties, and men. From now until the end of the diary men play an increasingly important role."

In July 1936, while visiting friends in Cambridge, Massachusetts, Yvonne met psychologist B.F. Skinner, who was doing post-doctoral research at Harvard. They were married the following November, and took up residence in Cambridge.

The couple has two daughters, Julie Skinner Vargas, a psychologist; and Deborah Skinner Buzan, an artist and writer. Yvonne Blue Skinner has taught for many years at Boston's Museum of Fine Arts, and has written both fiction and essays on art.

THE DIARY OF

Kate Tomibe

Tule Lake Relocation Center
Newell, California
1943

Tule Lake Relocation Center (*Francis Stewart, National Archives*)

◇　　◇

Introduction

Kate Tomibe (not her real name), an American of Japanese descent, started this diary in January 1943. She and her family were among 110,000 Japanese-Americans who had been removed from their homes on the West Coast and interned by the government of the United States, on the grounds that they posed a "security risk."

The hysteria that gripped the United States after the December 1941 bombing of Pearl Harbor by Japan dovetailed with anti-Oriental attitudes that had simmered for over 100 years—especially on the West Coast. In 1941, 127,000 Japanese lived in the continental U.S., mostly in the three West Coast states. The majority of these people were Nisei (American-born). Their parents, the Issei, had been born in Japan, but many had been in this country for decades and had made it their permanent home.

The loyalty of most Issei lay with the United States, where they had worked hard to make lives for themselves. The Issei had made a major contribution to the development of the West, despite the fact that they were legally barred from citizenship. In fact, the economic success of Japanese-Americans contributed to the discrimination against them. There were many who saw them as competition to be removed.

In the United States just after Pearl Harbor, little distinction was made between the Issei, the Nisei, and the foreign enemy. Within hours after that attack, the FBI began to arrest prominent members of the Japanese-American community. Many of these men were treated as criminals and were jailed for months.

Executive Order 9066, signed by President Franklin D. Roosevelt in February 1942, authorized the Secretary of War to "prescribe military areas . . . from which any and all persons may be excluded," and gave the War Department authority to remove people from them. California, Oregon and Washington were declared "strategic areas" on March 2. All enemy aliens and all Japanese-Americans, even if they were U.S. citizens, were ordered to leave. German and Italian aliens, however, were never removed.

There were no facilities for detention of so many people. Temporary "assembly centers" were hurriedly thrown up by the army at such places as racetracks and fairgrounds. The Japanese-American families who were abruptly evacuated from their homes found new quarters in former horse stalls, pigpens and unfinished barracks.

The War Relocation Authority (WRA) was created to provide for the evacuees on a long-term basis. The ten "relocation centers" where they were finally moved were in isolated deserts and swampland. The camps were not even completed when the first evacuees were bussed in, in the summer of 1942. Housing was in standard army barracks, hastily erected. Each family was given a 20 × 25 foot room with army cots as the only furniture. Bathroom facilities were communal and primitive; meals were served in army-type mess halls.

Tule Lake, California, where Kate Tomibe and her family lived, had been built on the sandy bed of a dried-up lake. Summer dust storms were menacing, and winters were extremely cold. Lack of drainage caused seas of mud during wet seasons.

The Tomibe family was from the Seattle, Washington area. Kate was 19; with her were her parents, brother Sam, 16, sister Beth, 14, and brother Ray, 7.

Kate kept several types of journals simultaneously: "In my five-year diary I will briefly record my daily activities with little or no comment. In this [second] day-by-day record I will augment the recording of my activities by impressions of people and events." Some things, she felt, were inappropriate for this journal, "such as jealousy and wanting someone who doesn't care, etc." She also had a third book, "Personal Memoirs," "to write in if I have any petty emotions which should be excluded from this journal."

The diary excerpted here was kept at the suggestion of a teacher and friend, a leading figure in the Tule Lake community. Kate modeled her journal after his, which he let her read; she later gave him her diary for his comments. But he appears to have been the only person she showed it to; "these articles are supposed to be private and confidential," she wrote.

Many of the internees accepted jobs in the centers—not only for cash, but to be of service to others and to keep busy. Pay was very low—a maximum of $16.00 a month for professionals. Kate worked in the Recreation Department; she also acted in the Little Theater and took several classes in the evenings.

The diary bears witness to the constant frustrations of camp life.

The barracks, designed for soldiers, were completely inadequate for families; Kate frequently laments the lack of privacy. Insufficiently insulated, the rooms were too hot in summer and too cold in winter. Food is another frequent subject; meals were nutritionally deficient and boring. It was often hard to obtain necessities such as clothing and toilet articles. Books, recreational equipment, and many household items also had to be ordered and there was often a long wait for delivery.

Like most adolescents, Kate had conflicts with her parents. These difficulties were compounded by the stresses common between immigrant parents, who adhere to traditional old-country values, and their first-generation children who have adopted the ways of the new country. In the case of the Japanese, this cultural barrier was particularly grave; the traditional Japanese values of obedience to authority, respect for parents, and adherence to community standards seemed outmoded to the "zoot-suited jitterbugging Nisei."

The atmosphere of the relocation camps contributed further to this breakdown of family ties. Kate's growing independence was resented by her parents, who could do little to control her since the basis of authority and social life had been shifted away from the family circle.

A typescript of Kate Tomibe's diary is in the Japanese-American Evacuation and Resettlement Records, The Bancroft Library, The University of California, Berkeley.

All names and initials in the diary have been changed.

◇ *1943* ◇

JANUARY 24. As if I don't have enough work to do already; this keeping an hourly account of my daily activities is going to be a terrific strain on me, and all on account of that rogue of a K. He just lets me read a few of his articles in [his] journal but has the nerve to read *all* of mine and tell me that they're too impersonal and not detailed enough. But, all kidding aside, I really think that his advice is just and sound and it's a good idea to try it for a week at least and see the results. I tried doing it once when I was about eight years old and continued it for about three days, but quit because it was too strenuous. This time, with the years of additional experience and knowledge, I'm sure that I could keep it up for a longer length of time.

Mother made me take my kid sister with me, so I went with her and two other girls in our block to the morning service. There was the regular singing of hymns;

"Gloria Patri"
"Glory be to the Father, and to the Son,
and to the Holy Ghost.
As it was in the beginning, is now and
ever shall be;
World without end; amen, amen."

after the responsive reading. After the offering, the hymn

"We give Thee but Thine own,
Whate'er the gift may be;
All that we have is Thine alone,
A trust, O Lord, from Thee. Amen."

Of the entire church service, I like the hymns best. Perhaps the thing I like the least is the prayer. Prayers may be a necessary part of the services, but I don't think too much of some people who give eloquent prayers before the congregation as if they were making an oration. Oftentimes it sounds like a farce because the person's deeds do not conform with his words. And it does say in the Bible that one should not pray out in the crowd so everyone can hear, but to go into the closet and talk to God in private.

It was decided that Sunday breakfasts would be eaten at home in our block. This is a good idea because you don't have to get up as early and can cook the meal more deliciously, although handicapped by the lack of facilities formerly available back home. Sad case, on New Year's day when we had to cook all our meals at home, our soup was cooked in an empty tomato can. However, the breakfast menu isn't very large so it doesn't matter.

In the afternoon I went over to H.'s house for a get-together party. Mostly Tacoma [Washington] kids and some of the members of the cast of "Grandma Pulls the String," the Little Theater one-act play now being presented.

N., a boy from Tacoma, was also [there] looking as suave as ever. It seems so silly now when I think of the crush I had on him long ago. It only lasted several days so it wasn't too serious. He can go jump in the lake for all I care after the dirty deal he gave C.—going steady with her and monopolizing her time for a week then suddenly walking out on her without any explanation. The only reason I can see for his desertion is that he didn't want to go to the dance with her every time. Then he goes necking with any girl that is dumb enough to give him the slightest encouragement.

H.'s mother is so sweet! She goes to all the trouble of preparing the food, even making maki-zushi[1]* and graciously waits on us while we're eating. Then she quietly sits in the corner and knits while we jitterbug on her linoleum, and offers us food from time to time. I certainly admire a woman like that who can adapt herself to modern times and sacrifice her time for the interests of her children.

JANUARY 25. Getting up in the morning is the worst of my trials and tribulations. Last night it was so hot I couldn't sleep

* Notes begin on page 141.

very well. The stove is about six feet from my bed and when Dad puts too much coal in at night it gets too warm. Six-thirty or 7:00 A.M. is an early hour to get up. I like to lie in bed in the morning and meditate because that is about the only time I have to do that. The mess gong and my parents don't give me much time to do that though. I would like to hear a bugle blowing reveille instead of a noisy gong. I have a good notion to get a bugle and blow it myself if some Boy Scout doesn't beat me to it. When I finally dragged myself out of bed, hastily dressed, washed and ran into the mess hall what did we have for breakfast but pancakes! "Sells like pancakes" sounds like a farce here. I never did like pancakes too well, but I just can't stand them anymore; they choke and nauseate me. I wish could have a nice fluffy waffle though.

I couldn't accomplish very much work this morning because the boys in Y.'s orchestra came around and started gabbing about jam sessions, saxophone, clarinet, etc. They're so childish and all they talk about is music and not the classical kind either. When I tell them that they're childish, some of them remind me that they're older than I am, but what difference does chronological age make? Sometimes I give them music tests to see how much they actually know, and they show signs of some knowledge of elementary music. But, after all, I'm just a naive child myself without any too much intelligence so who am I to belittle others?

JANUARY 26. I stopped in at the jitterbug class. The place was just full. It's funny that so many people go to these classes when only a few are interested in taking up the finer forms of dance such as ballet, acrobatic, tap, and modern. A. was thrilled because he said this was one time that I would have to follow him. He thinks I boss him around at the office.

Riding home after the dramatic performance we got front-door service on the panel truck. I didn't say a word, but I noticed that some of the kids talked to the driver as if they were addressing a servant or someone of inferior status. In a place like this I don't think there should be any class distinction because of occupation or education.

On the way back to work in the afternoon I bumped into T. I like T. because she's congenial and not like some girls who paint up, put on airs, and flirt with boys. I certainly think that a few years in Japan improves a person's character. T. said that some women had quit English classes after somebody complained that too much emphasis was being placed on adult education and not enough on the welfare of children. I think it's silly for these women to quit because even if they don't go, the classes are still going on and what good does it do anybody for them to quit. However, I guess appearances are more important than reason to the Japanese.

S. and A. were talking about a date for the Sport Hop. I asked them why they didn't go steady so they wouldn't have to worry about dates, and S. asks, "Do you think it's easy to go steady?" Well, I guess it isn't too easy because I'm not going steady either. I wonder if it's worth it for these boys to go through the agony of getting a date; and they really make it sound like agony. This matter of dates or the lack of them has never worried me too much. There have been times when I have yearned for dates with certain people, and there have also been other times when I have had to run around in circles trying to avoid dates with certain other people.

I managed to find time in the afternoon to go to the post office and get my package. I ordered twelve ounces of black Shetland floss to make a long-sleeved pullover.

This postal situation was really annoying me so I asked the inspector why they didn't deliver the packages to the blocks so the people wouldn't have to go to the post office to get them when everyone was working and roads were so bad. I might know that these uniformed men are only stooges and all they can say is that they're following orders. Even in the assembly center which was one-third the size of this place, packages were delivered to every block with the inspector coming along, and that was a far more effective method.

We're in our second week of [Little Theater] performances and now that the adventure has worn out it's getting to be a nuisance to go down there every night. It will be such a relief when the plays are over this week. The make-up I have to smear on every night isn't any too beneficial to my skin.

JANUARY 27. I went to the clothing canteen to see if they had any boots because the ones I ordered last Saturday won't come for another week or two, I'm afraid. The service is so slow; I don't see why they don't order from Los Angeles instead of from Seattle. The shoe shop didn't have a single pair of boots and the clerk says they probably won't be getting any more in stock for some time because of the rubber shortage, etc. I remember that about three months ago Mother told me to buy a pair of boots, but I said they were too clumsy and I wouldn't need them anyway. Now when I'm running around left and right trying to get ahold of a pair, she's telling me that I should always buy things beforehand and not wait until the last moment. Yes, Mama, you know best.

After I came back to the office [we] went over the budget for 1943. The music department said that it was necessary to get about $200 worth of music books, in addition to various other musical supplies. They got about $160 worth of piano instruction and music textbooks in 1942, and P. thought they were demanding too much. There seemed to be some friction so I kept quiet, but I think that some people really demand too much. They are of the opinion that the government put them in here against their will, so now they'll try to get as much as they can out of the government. As far as the basic needs, such as food, shelter, clothing, medical care are concerned the people should make certain demands, but they shouldn't expect too much in the way of luxuries. Fine arts are more or less of a luxury, and if a person is really interested in taking piano lessons, for instance, the least he could do is buy his own book in view of the fact that they're getting lessons free.

As U. says, if the people have too many things done for them, they'll lose the power to do it themselves and really become wards of the government as the Indians are.

My parents are as nice as any parents could be, but they neglected to give me a thorough education; instead they bought too much candy and toys for me and spoiled me. Ever since I was six years old I have been nagging them to let me take piano lessons, but my father is not musically minded and didn't think private lessons were necessary. Since my older sister died shortly after birth and I am the oldest child, they have more or less used me for a guinea pig. I am now playing second and third grade music and studying from the "Second Solo Book". Most of the music in this book is folk tunes, and they sound so childish. I wish I had brought along all my music books from home.

This morning I suddenly got the idea that I must have my typewriter which I left home along with many other things I should have brought. I told Mother that I was going to write to the man who was taking care of our place and have him send it. She said that if I were going to get my typewriter, she wants her trunk too because it contains many of her precious keepsakes. I thought that if we are going to get the trunk we might as well have the man send the sewing machine too, so that we could do some sewing. At the time of evacuation we had no idea that we would be sending for these things so we left them all boarded up in the junk room and in no condition to be easily packed and sent. Dad seemed frigid to the idea of sending for them when I first told him about it. I told him that if he had any objections please state them now or forever hold his peace, and don't complain after I had written the letter. I reminded him of the time I told them that I wanted to buy a piano. Dad didn't pay any attention to me, but after I got it he raised holy ____ .

Mother later told me that I should show a little more respect for Dad and not talk to him in that tone. I didn't mean to be rude, but I don't like this "beating 'round the bush."

JANUARY 28. As soon as I come to work this morning, some others from the Athletic Department start telling me that I do almost everything. When I asked them for an explanation of what they meant, they said that they had seen me act, dance, play the piano, had heard me sing, and went on complimenting my stenographic ability, etc. I'll add that I can cook and sew too. They're very flattering, and I wish that I were really that versatile but am actually far from it. However, I do think that

I'm trying to do too many things at once, because I am always swamped with things to do and places to go, and as a result of overwork am beginning to feel that I might get hypochondria.

What I need is another love affair. Not any more adolescent infatuations or physical attractions but a beautiful romance which is lasting and based on understanding and companionship. I want somebody to love and understand me, somebody that I can respect and love. Nobody understands me completely, not even my own family. They don't understand, for instance, why I keep a thing like this [diary] or why I should go out of my way to study when I don't have to.

All the girls in the office are excellent knitters, a thing I can't very well say for myself. They seem to take more interest in things domestic than I do because the majority of them attend [pattern] drafting classes three nights a week and keep a hope chest. If I can settle down and get a good cedar chest, I think keeping a hope chest would be fun, but not here where we have to practically live out of our suitcases; and there's no time to make the contents.

There was a block meeting of young people over 18 years of age in the evening with plans to organize a club. I might as well say that I am 19 years old, so I attended the meeting. Election of officers was the main business. After the way I shot off my big mouth saying that the vice-president should do more than merely preside in the absence of the president, I was relieved when I wasn't elected, but then they elected me girls' social chairman which is really a lot more work. They couldn't have chosen a more inefficient person, but we'll see how it turns out.

Mr. L. is an old man about 55 years old who has been more or less a part of our family against our will for the past twenty years. He makes me believe that no man should remain a bachelor. Dad is a decent man, but he used to have the funniest friends before he got married. Ever since I was a child Mr. L. scolded me just like my father did. In more recent years, he has imposed on my father's hospitality and come to live with us. Mother says that she wouldn't mind his coming so much if he would only act decently. But he acts as if we had asked him to come, stationing himself in the best bedroom in the house, and insisting that we treat him like a guest. If it's a matter of only a few days, weeks, or even months, it might be possible, but who can entertain a house guest for years? He liked to drink, so Mother had to make Japanese *sake* for him, although Dad doesn't drink a drop. Sometimes it wouldn't turn out right; then he would be irritable and make insulting remarks about Mother. He finally insisted that Dad buy him some whiskey every week. About once a year he would get mad and leave, saying, "I'll never come back to this house again." We were all hoping that he meant it this time, but a few months later he would come back crying that he didn't have any other place to go or arguing that we must be short of labor so he would help us. Dad is such a kind-hearted soul that he would take him in again, although we put up a protest.

One good thing about evacuation is that we don't have to live in the same house with him because he's living in block 11 in bachelor's quarters. A man like that is happy as long as he is treated with respect and pampered like a child.

JANUARY 29. In the afternoon Miss A. brought over some books which I had requested from the California State Library. I went down last week and asked for a list of available books. In the absence of such a list I asked for some psychology books and a few other non-fiction. I don't think I'll have time to read half of these books, in view of the fact that I'm just beginning to study *The Fundamentals of General Psychology*.

We received a letter from Mr. F. who is taking care of our place. From beginning to end he reiterates on the cold weather and the snow. It really sounds bad; there are no mail deliveries, the schools are closed because the furnace broke and the buses can't run. Under those circumstances perhaps it was asking too much too request him to send our things.

Beth ordered a sweater and skirt to some department store in Chicago, which came today. She's 14, just that age when girls are clothes-crazy. I wasn't that bad five years ago, however. As soon as one thing comes she immediately thinks of something else she wants. The girls she runs around with talk about nothing but clothes and jitterbugging. It amused me when I heard that she was asking Mother, "Why doesn't Kate buy any clothes? Doesn't she care for new dresses?"

I like new clothes as much as anybody else, but I can't stand mail-order clothes because they don't fit and aren't sewed right. Besides, it's no use getting good clothes in here; that's why I don't buy any.

JANUARY 30. When I finally managed to get up at 7:15 A.M. I had a toothache, and also a headache from lack of sleep. The snowball that so-called Leadership Training Officer threw at me, hitting me right where my brain nestles, didn't help much either. I also had a cold, and the bottle of Squirt I had last night didn't do my stomach any good so I didn't go to breakfast. However, I thought that it wouldn't help matters any if I stayed home moping and worked myself up into a mental disorder, so I went to work and felt better after working for a while.

"Inferiority Complex" was the topic of discussion in psychology class today. I used to have inferiority complex when I was small. This came about as a result of my being the eldest child. During the first two and a half years, before my brother Sam was born, my parents pampered and coddled me; then when he was born Dad began saying "I like Sam best." Beth was born, and it was "I like Beth best," etc. I never recall him saying that he liked me best. I used to have fights with Sam very often, and always I would get the blame. "You're older, and besides girls should be quiet."

When I began school I had the language difficulty, and since we had just moved to the community a week before I didn't know anybody. My parents reproached me and compared me with children who got better marks on their report cards. "Look at what good grades so and so gets. Why don't you have good manners like so and so?" I think that comparing children with others is very poor technique, and as I grew older and began to understand, I explained this to my parents, so they don't do it so much any more.

The other day I stopped in at the canteen and got some nail polish, shade young red. I have never used such bright nail polish before, but when I'm working outside I have to be moderate so I might as well use it while I'm here. However, after I got it on it looked a little too flashy, and my parents didn't like it. I don't know why I got it, and I hate to think of having to use up the whole bottle. But perhaps there is something to that "red badge of courage." Some man said that the reason a woman wears lipstick is that when she is down and out, when she has just lost a job, or is disgraced, the flashy lipstick serves as a symbol of courage. If that is true of lipstick, the same should also hold for nail polish. Perhaps when I am depressed my red fingernails will give me courage and inspire me to superior heights.

JANUARY 31. I am a coward. I do not even have the will power to get up early in the morning. Here I wake up before 7 o'clock but have to lie in bed until almost 9 o'clock, wasting two whole hours. No wonder I never get anything accomplished. The mess hall gong clanging early in the morning is a big nuisance, but it's a good thing because otherwise I would stay in bed indefinitely.

Yesterday I did my two weeks' washing after lunch, and today after lunch I was doing my ironing which had been accumulating for over a month. When I had it about half done N. came, so I went to Little Theater with her. When and if I ever get married I faithfully promise to devote my time to domestic work, but while I'm single I might as well enjoy life as much as possible, and there simply isn't enough time to keep up with the housework. I wish I had a nice kitchen to work in; I want to bake pies, cakes, and all those other yummies which I used to make.

After reading over the [diary] contents for the past week, I think that the articles sound very egocentric with all the "me, myself, and I" criticisms of other people as if I were a perfect saint myself. These articles are supposed to be private and confidential, so it doesn't matter very much what I write, but I realize that unconsciously and unintentionally I say things that sound conceited. I argue too much with everyone; perhaps I should be more submissive although sometimes that is impossible. Also, I am afraid that I am of the aloof nature so if the

other person is that way too, we never get very well aquainted.
I want to be humble and make others happy, something like
T. who is now attending School of Theology. He was homely
and holier-than-thou, but the kind of person in whose presence
it is impossible to be morbid.

FEBRUARY 1. V. and G. got word that they had received
their leave clearance,[2] and they were very thrilled and excited.
V. is going to Columbia University in New York, and G. says
he's going to either Michigan or Maine.

My parents still won't let me go out, but I'm not in too much
of a hurry. I am very particular and opportunities seem quite
scarce. The only types of employment I could accept are jour-
nalistic, secretarial, social, or attending college with some kind
of a part-time job. So far I have not gone out of my way to find
employment or enter college.

FEBRUARY 2. This morning Mother and Dad began preaching about getting up earlier for breakfast. I kept quiet because
I knew it was my fault, inasmuch as getting up early was one
of my New Year's resolutions which I have not kept. Dad is
nice enough to start the stove for me, so I should at least get
up early enough not to make myself conspicuous by my belat-
edness at breakfast.

After lunch I went to the hospital to have an x-ray taken of
my tooth. The technician stuck his cigar-smelling hand in my
mouth and nauseated me. There is nothing bad or immoral
about smoking, but there are no advantages to be gained from
smoking; it is a waste of money; the ashes and stubs mess up
the surroundings; its odor permeates into everything within per-
meating distance.

The Issei attitude about girls smoking is unreasonable. It's
natural for a boy to smoke; but if some Nisei girl does, she is
practically an outcast, although some Issei women are profuse
smokers. Smoking isn't good, but it is far worse if a person is
so prejudiced and intolerant as to ostracize someone just because
he or she smokes.

S. is really well versed in Japanese. He's a 23-year-old boy
from Seattle. Since his father was interned,[3] I've never seen

such an openly pro-Japanese person, although he's never been in Japan. P. also goes around saying he's a pro-Jap and states that he isn't going out because he doesn't want to be drafted. He adds, "I'm not afraid of joining the army, but if I'm going to do it, I'll join the Japanese army." You can hardly blame these boys for feeling as they do since their fathers are interned and they've been pushed in here. Anyone who proclaims pro-Americanism is quite unpopular now, but I think that as long as we're in this country it is to our disadvantage to develop this attitude of anti-Americanism. As far as I'm concerned, I think that it was a gross mistake on the part of the government to treat aliens and citizens alike with apparent racial prejudice. However, I feel that mistakes are made by everyone, and if there was some economic selfish motive behind this cry for evacuation, we would be accepting defeat by allowing it to make us bitter. Some people have been hit much harder by evacuation than I have, so I have no right to say such things, but I think that we should face the problem squarely without being handicapped by bitter prejudice.

I have been neglecting my study of Japanese for some time. One translation of a two-page essay took me several days to complete and was enough to wear me thin. Knowledge of Japanese is a weapon which will be advantageous in the battle of the outside world, but it is extremely hard to master to a fine degree.

I have never been among so many Japanese in my life, and since evacuation I am beginning to notice that my speech is starting to sound like a Kibei's.[4] Japanese is a good language to know, but mixing the two isn't very effective. However, it is impossible to refrain from doing it when everyone around me talks that way. I hear such phrases as "*Doko* [where] are you going?" "*Nanji* [what] time?" and saying *ney*[5] on the end of an English sentence.

FEBRUARY 3. I got up before seven this morning, the first time that has occurred in months. Regardless of whether I wanted to or not, I had to because Dad practically yanked me out of bed. Miraculously, we had fried eggs for breakfast. I had almost forgotten what an egg tastes like, and bacon is a thing of the past along with some other commodities.

Today was my piano lesson again. I had to practice an hour in the morning and struggle through my lesson in the afternoon. Every time I have to struggle through those arpeggios, trills, triads, scales, chromatics, diminished and dominant chords, etc. I wish that my parents had let me take lessons when I was 6 or at least 8; then I would have about ten years of experience and by now should be an accomplished pianist.

"Psychology of Women" was the title of a lecture by Freud which I was reading today. Freud places special emphasis on penis-envy and castration complex, but I never experienced anything like that when I was small or at any time in my life and do not understand things like that. Freud also thinks that all women feel inferior to men, but I don't; that's exactly true, although tomboys are more common than sissies.

Around 4:30 in the afternoon I went to voice and diction class. It felt good to be a student once more and walk home, non-chalant and carefree, acting silly. The way we were screaming and singing people must have thought we were going crazy.

I think that in order to gain some experience from my sojourn here I should work some place else. For instance, teaching is an excellent way to learn things, for usually the teacher learns more than the students. Working at the hospital is also good experience for future home life. But I am having too much fun to change to the job of tackling sassy school children or taking care of sick people.

FEBRUARY 4. This water [flooding due to poor drainage] is really getting me down. In fact, I'm developing hypochondria. It's nothing like the beautiful waters of Lake Washington or Puget Sound where we used to go swimming. I'm getting so homesick for a lovely sunset on the Sound; these dirty puddles are nothing but a menace to society.

For many years I have wanted two things, time and money, along with some other things. I still want time, but as long as we have to stay here money hasn't much value to me. About all you can buy besides the bare necessities are extra clothes and perhaps equipment. Since this is only a temporary place, equipment is a burden, and there's no use for fancy clothes. We got our clothing allowance for November yesterday, but these checks are worth as much as a piece of scratch paper. I've still got two other checks uncashed because I haven't had time to run around trying to get them cashed.

Another change that camp life has made is that now I have no desire for food. This mad gulping down of food in the mess hall is ruining my appetite. At home we always had a lot of food lying around the house and sometimes I had to eat things just to keep them from spoiling, but when I got home from school or work around 5 o'clock I was always starving and cleaned out the cookie jar or the refrigerator. Now, when the mess hall gong rings it's just a nuisance. It's just too much of the wrong kind of food, such as two big pancakes in the morning or a big plate full of beans at noon. I still enjoy food when I can eat it slowly and at ease, such as at a tete-a-tete or a party. "Sweets to the sweet," so I like sweets.

FEBRUARY 5. "Boots," that's what I've been trying to get for the last two weeks ever since the wet weather started. Yesterday I was notified that the boots which I ordered two Saturdays ago were all sold out, and due to conditions beyond their control they don't know when another supply would come in. This is too much! This is the last straw, the limit! But "if you don't succeed at first, try, try again," so today I went to the canteen and ordered two other pairs of military and hiking boots. I think rubber ones are more waterproof, but Mother said rubber isn't good for the feet and might give me rheumatism, so I ordered leather ones. If they don't come within two weeks, I'm going to start screaming.

More people left today for points east. The moment when the leave permit arrives is a happy one, a climax to months of waiting, but the moment of departure must be one of joy, sadness, and anxiety combined, the dawn of a new day. I don't think I'll be going for a long time yet. By the end of this year certainly ought to be the limit.

It sounds funny, but until a little over a year ago I didn't even know how babies were born or what intercourse meant. When I asked Mother about these things, she always said, "You'll find out when you grow older." I finally had to get it out of my teacher. I had heard about unmarried mothers and wondered what they did to get that way. For some reason or other sex has always been considered taboo, but I don't see any reason for suppressing talk about the subject because if it is used right it is a beautiful thing. It is only when it is misused that it becomes ugly. Miss S. and I were talking about it one night, and I naively asked her if a woman would get a baby if she married a man and ate with him and slept with him. She said that they'd have to go through intercourse. She couldn't very well explain what that meant in ABC language, but I got a general idea of what it meant. When I was 16, I tried to read Havelock Ellis' *Psychology of Sex* but couldn't get head nor tail out of it. Recently I have read a textbook on marriage and understand most of the things concerned, although I still don't understand the principles of birth control or the strong sexual urge.

I read another one of Freud's lectures on Dreams and he mentions a case where a brother and sister were deeply attached to each other and wished they could get married. Filial love, brotherly love, friendly love, and the one and only love—what is the difference between them? To me filial love means security and gratitude and I owe almost all that I am to my parents. Brotherly love means that you have grown up with your brothers and sisters; they are your own flesh and blood and naturally you have mutual interests. Friendly love means companionship. But from him I want all of these things—companionship, mutual understanding, and if he's the right kind of man eventually security. Besides this, I want his whole-hearted love, kiss, and embrace, not on the promiscuous level but a beautiful romance. Of course, I am prepared to give all these things if I expect to receive them.

When I was in high school I was still naive enough to believe that there was no such thing as racial prejudice although I had been hearing about it. I thought that efficiency was the primary thing in getting employment. After I graduated I went through eight weeks of summer school to take a post-graduate course in geometry and bookkeeping. Then came time to look for a job. I could have gone to college like everybody else did, but I didn't want to struggle my way through financially nor ask my parents for a subsidy, so I pounded the pavement day after day. This was the reality from which I had been sheltered all these years. Some bank presidents and executives were frank enough to tell me the truth about racial prejudice. To others who were hesitant I asked bluntly, "Are you racially prejudiced?" They didn't want to admit it and hemmed and hawed without being able to give a satisfactory explanation. I didn't want to be a quitter so I continued and finally got an office job in the Seattle Public Schools. I was only 17 at the time and just out of high school, so it wasn't too bad as a beginning. About six months later the war had broken out and people were beginning to get hysterical. There were several other Nisei girls working in schools, and some busybody women who said they were PTA members were passing around a petition to have us dismissed because our loyalty was in doubt. I was all prepared to put up a good fight when L., the Nisei JACL[6] leader, advised us that the best thing to do would be to resign graciously because it wasn't wise to let the issue be kicked around like a political football. I had some respect for his judgement, so I quit and for a month worked half-days at the JACL office.

When the curfew[7] went into effect, I had to go home, and since there was nothing else to do I went back to school. By this time evacuation seemed inevitable. Signs were being posted everywhere that all Japanese should clear out within a week. The people in Seattle had already left for Camp Harmony in Puyallup [Washington] and thus we were prepared to go there also, when they sent us to Pinedale Assembly Center near Fresno.

Former classmates of mine, some of whom were on the border line of graduating, are now working at shipyards and defense plants while here I am stuck in this place. Many brilliant college graduates are also here while their duller classmates are earning hundreds of dollars outside.

Last year a Mrs. B. wrote an article in the *Sacramento Bee* complaining that teachers shouldn't be paid $200 a month to teach evacuees in relocation centers music and other fine arts, so I wrote to the *Bee* saying that evacuee teachers who have professional standing are only getting $16 a month and that in a community of 15,000 people education and recreation were a necessity; although handicapped by lack of facilities and equipment, we were doing the best we could. Then two anonymous housewives viciously attacked me, telling me to write [Emperor] Hirohito and ask him what kind of treatment the Japanese were giving American prisoners, and stating that with "limited facilities and equipment" the Americans had fought courageously at Corregidor and Bataan.[8] As it happens almost every other day, another woman wrote an article in the *Bee* protesting the fact that Japanese were permitted to go to colleges while American boys had to join the army. I decided to be more subtle this time, so without mentioning any names I submitted another article stating that the Nisei were loyal and eager to serve but because of their 4-F classification[9] they were unable to do so. However, when the sugar beets were rotting in the field because of lack of labor, hundreds of boys had gone out to help in eastern Oregon, Idaho, Montana, and Utah. I wrote to the editor asking him to exclude my name from this article because I didn't want my name slammed around by misunderstanding people who misconstrued facts and compared American citizens with foreign prisoners of war. From this article I heard no further complaints.

About two weeks later, however, an I.C. from Sacramento who had seen my first signed article, wrote to me, asking for some information about a Mrs. L. who had formerly been her landlady. Although there was no prefix or title, I took it for granted that this person who had written to me was a poor old woman. The letter was very poorly written, about the level of a 10-year-old child, judging from the numerous errors in spelling and grammar. She said that she had read my article in the paper, it was well written, and she admired my courage for saying what

I thought. I wrote to Mrs. C. saying that [the landlady] was hard to contact. Then in elaborate English I wrote several paragraphs attesting to the loyalty of the Nisei and asking her to explain the facts to her friends.

I thought she wouldn't bother me anymore. However, when I got home this afternoon I found a letter from her. She said she admired me very much, my letter was excellently written, and she was sending me some things. I nearly fell out of my rocking chair (if I had such a thing) when at the end of the letter she said that she is not a she, but a he. I began to feel mentally ill. I was going to write a letter telling him bluntly that I couldn't stand second-hand clothing; he had a lot of nerve writing a letter like that to me; and please don't write any more. I told Mother about it, and she said that I shouldn't write anything like that to insult him because his intentions were probably not malicious and I might get into trouble.

I miss my piano very much and have always wanted some musical instrument to take its place. Today I thought that an accordion would be good. Tonight, I played cards with Dad, Ray, and Beth; and we quit after I had skunked them all. Dad seemed to be in a good mood, so I told him that I was planning to buy an accordion. He didn't favor the idea. First, he said that $150 was too much money to spend in here; I should save my money to buy books and study. I told him that I wouldn't ask him for a cent. Furthermore, I wouldn't even spend any of the money I had saved prior to evacuation; I would pay for it from the amount earned after evacuation. After that he didn't have any more to say about finances, but began the argument that I make too much noise at late hours as it is and if I got a musical instrument it would bother the neighbors. I promised Dad that I wouldn't play late at night and would always play it softly.

The next argument he presented was that the accordion was not as refined an instrument as the piano or violin and that I should get something else. There may be some truth to that statement, but the piano is too big and the violin too hard to play.

We finally ended up by his saying that I should be old enough to think for myself, so he wouldn't stop me, but that I should consider the facts carefully before purchasing it.

FEBRUARY 6. I got up early this morning, and Dad said that he thought it was because I was thinking of an accordion, but I told him it was because I was afraid of his yelling at me again.

I., C. and A. asked me about the technique of handling girls. They seemed to think that the reason some boys wait until the last minute before asking for a date is that they're afraid and can't get up enough courage. I told them that if it's the right kind of girl and they use the right technique, there should be no reason for their being turned down unless the girl really had another engagement. I. asked me what I meant by the right kind of girl, and I said that was the kind of girl whom he could take pride in being seen with. I gave them a few other pointers, but after all who am I to be telling them those things when I'm no expert on handling men.

On the evacuation train, Pvt. Al Cohen, one of the soldier guards, after talking to me for a few minutes, told me that I was too naive, that he could read me like an open book, and that in order to attract men I should be more sophisticated and mysterious. But I hate to put on airs and chase after men, and besides I'm not that desperate yet.

K. brought his diary neatly written in shorthand on a steno pad. He said that he had to write it neatly so that S. could read it when she typed it for him. Lucky fellow to have a nice sister to do everything for him.

He seemed reluctant to let me read his journal, but I don't see any reason why. He doesn't have anything about impressions of people in that one as I do in this, and even if he did I could keep it a secret. Anyway, as I told him it's also a means of self defense because if he just read mine he could even blackmail me about exposing some of the contents and I would have no protection. Of course, I know he won't do anything like that, but if he doesn't trust me enough to show me his, what can I expect? Besides, it isn't every day that I get to read someone's diary, and if he wants to help me, he could do it as well by letting me read his as by reading mine and giving suggestions.

As I am writing this day-by-day journal in his style, he thought it was an improvement over my former one. After reading his, one phase of it worries me. He seems to have a psychological interest in people rather than a personal one. People seem to be merely psychological guinea pigs to him and are valuable only insofar as they can benefit his research work. Of course, I may be making an unjust accusation and if so, my sincere apologies, but I wonder, for instance, if he has ever been in love.

I don't know why I should notice appearances so much when I'm not an example of meticulous attire, myself. But I was glad to notice that K. had changed from his afternoon apparel and wore a tie. I think he should get a haircut in a few days. Gee, but I'm getting impudent to say those things, but it's easier to write things that I would never think of saying out loud.

FEBRUARY 7. The snow was about a foot deep this morning, so I said that I couldn't go anywhere in that snow so I would stay in bed all morning. Mother said that I should go to church and it wouldn't look right for me to be in bed if someone should come over. So I got up and after eating a light breakfast, waded in the snow to church. In my younger days snow would have made me very happy, but now I don't care for it so much because the after effects of mud and slush are too much.

When I dropped in at the canteen on Friday, they had some nice ice skates. I wanted to buy a pair, but what's the use because there's no place to skate anyway. Mr. T. has rejected the plan for building a skating rink, and the sewer place is unsanitary. I'd certainly hate to fall in there like some of the kids did.

In spite of the weather there was a surprising number at church. I wonder why some of those people go to church. I don't think it's to show off their clothes because that's silly. They don't look serious enough to go for the purpose of remission of sins. The purpose of meeting people seems the most logical. Why do I go to church? Of course, Mother makes me go, but it's not just because she says so that I do it. The matter of clothes is out because I certainly don't dress up to go to church, and if I had to, I wouldn't want to. I love to dress up in pumps, fur coat, gloves, hat, etc. on the right occasion, but the right occasion never occurs in here. C. told me that she buys a lot more clothes since coming here than she did before evacuation and likes to dress better now. I think a lot of people are like that. Before evacuation they didn't go anyplace and didn't think about clothes much but [now] they figure that they are seen more. It's just the opposite with me. At home I would buy oodles of clothes and material to make clothes. But since coming here, I don't even wear half of the clothes I have, and the simpler the apparel the better I like it.

I don't exactly go to church for remission of sins either because although I realize that I'm not a perfect saint, my conscience never bothers me too much. Maybe it's because I'm a hopeless case.

I now have five books to keep up and have decided that the order of entries will be as follows: In my five-year diary I will briefly record my daily activities with little or no comment. Then I have a book in which I write book reviews and outlines of textbooks. In my other journal I will write essays which will later be translated into Japanese if time permits. In this day-by-day record I will augment the recording of my activities by impressions of people and events. However, I will omit any activity which hasn't much significance, and also keep out petty emotions such as jealousy and wanting someone who doesn't care, etc.

I have never felt intense jealousy because with a little reasoning I know that it doesn't do any good, and there's no reason to feel that way. In a fair contest if someone else is better than I am, that's that. I think equality of mankind means equality of opportunity rather than equality of ability. Some people are naturally better in certain fields than others, and as long as I know that I've done my best I'm satisfied.

I don't think I'll have much use for my book of "Personal Memoirs" because I'm past the adolescent puppy love, crush-

"This mad gulping down of food in the mess hall is ruining my appetite." (*Courtesy of The Bancroft Library*)

a-week stage. However, I'll keep it to write in if I have any petty emotions which should be excluded from this journal.

FEBRUARY 8. Mother said the waiters and waitresses had a meeting yesterday at which they discussed some people whom they had on the "black list." Some of the people they mentioned are Mr. U. who goes in there late, bangs the cup on the table, and complains that the service is poor; Mr. V. who talks to the waitresses as if he were addressing a servant; Mrs. M. who always brings food home for five to seven people who are too lazy to come to eat in the mess hall. Mother said that if she hadn't been there they probably would have talked about me too because I go late and eat slow.

I. and some other boys asked me what I thought about cheek-to-cheek dancing. I told him that if necessary, it might be all right with their one and only but promiscuous if made a habit with every girl. They said that with certain girls it was unavoidable.

After lunch I filled out Dad's selective service questionnaire for him. Some of the ironic questions they asked got on my nerves so I just hastily scribbled out the answers.[10]

FEBRUARY 9. The package from Mr. C. arrived today. I made use of the bandana immediately; the apron is of fancy rayon; the souvenir pillow slip with pictures of scenes in California is all right; and I could make use of the tea bags. I didn't like the second-hand jacket, so I gave it to Dad; but since it was too small for him, Beth said she wants it. This really isn't so bad; it must have been the shock of discovering suddenly that he was a man that upset me when I received the letter. As Mother says, his heart must be in the right place for him to go to the trouble of sending all of those things to a total stranger. In the letter, after listing the items which he was sending, he said that he had a good Buick. It would be wonderful if he would give me that too, although I don't know what use I could make of it here and with tire and gasoline rationing.

At an office staff meeting today, we decided to change jobs. heretofore, I had been taking care of the cash and the supplies but now I will handle the publicity and information. This is just as well because I was getting tired of people bringing me money and asking for this and that. Money is supposed to be one of the dirtiest things and that's no lie.

FEBRUARY 10. It's funny that some people are polite, and it's impossible to find any tangible fault with them, yet you can't get very intimate or friendly with them and relations are always a little strained. There are others who insult you every day and you're always fighting or arguing with them, but they're a lot of fun and nice companions.

After I got home I was reading the rules for selective service. One part says, "We want to give you the opportunity to serve your country along with other Americans. We are sure you wouldn't want to be treated any differently." Is this a farce? What irony! Less than a year ago they were saying, "Everyone of Japanese ancestry clear out within a week."

Animal life is as simple and easy, but not as fun as complex human life. I think the harder the thing the more fun it is and the satisfaction upon achievement is always greater. Life would not be worth living if I had everything I wanted and was always satisfied. Only by being dissatisfied and always striving for something more can we be happy.

FEBRUARY 11. I thought today was just another day but when I got to the office some boys were celebrating *kigensetsu* [Empire Day]. I used to know that this was a Japanese holiday but it's hard to keep up with those things now. April 29 is *tencho setsu* [Emperor's Birthday] but I never celebrated it, and those two days are the only Japanese holidays I know. I think there was another one called *Jimmu tenno sai* [Emperor Jimmu Day], and of course there's *shogatsu* [New Year's Day].

My work hours are being neglected in favor of things which I would otherwise not have the time to do. This afternoon after play rehearsal I went to the post office to get my boots which finally came. I give them two choices and they send me the crumby ones. I wanted browns, but they sent me black ones. However, it's a good thing something came.

We got a card today saying that our freight was here. I was so thrilled that I forgot to take the key when I went to the warehouse. Dad was saying, "They'll probably inspect the trunk from top to bottom." Everything seemed to be in good condition, but I have to go again tomorrow [for inspection] with the keys for the trunk and the typewriter.

In the evening some of the young men got together and suddenly decided to call a block meeting to discuss the selective service questionnaire. [At the meeting] L. was sitting next to me so I asked him what he thought. L. is 23 years old and [was] in Japan 19 years and even attended college there. He said that as an American citizen he would do everything for the United States but expected to be treated like a citizen. He said that it was our duty to fight against all enemies. I asked him if he would join the army and fight against Japan, and he immediately replied "Of course." I told him that was an admirable thing to do and more than some of the nisei would do. L. is living in bachelor's quarters. I had always regarded him as a "stuffed shirt", one of those Sunday school boys, but tonight I saw him smoking and now I have more respect for him. I asked him when he started smoking and he said that he just smoked off and on about once a week. That isn't too bad, and some boys look more virile when they smoke. However, that doesn't mean that I favor smoking; I still have more respect for boys who can refuse a smoke.

G.Y., block manager, and D.G., councilman, thought that there should be no question about answering "yes" to the 28th question which goes something like, "Do you swear allegiance to the United States government and forswear allegiance to the Japanese emperor and any other foreign organization or power?" To the 27th question which asks "Are you willing to do active combat duty and fight at any assigned place?" they thought that it could be answered "no" or with a conditional yes. The conditions would be that nisei solders be allowed to enter any restricted area without any red tape; other nisei would be treated like ordinary American citizens; and our parents be accorded the same privileges as German and Italian aliens. Of course this would not apply to those who were planning to go back to Japan. Such persons should answer no to both questions.

FEBRUARY 12. In the morning I went to the warehouse and got the trunk and typewriter inspected. I was going to tell the inspector a thing or two if he turned the contents inside out but he just looked it over briefly. The typewriter worked perfectly after I had cleaned it a little and the sewing machine was in fine condition too. Mr. F. certainly created them good.

They had a block meeting again about the registration question. The isseis think that the entire block should unite and vote one way. G.Y., block manager, and Mr. O., Planning Board representative, feel that each individual is entitled to [their] own opinion and nobody should be forced to answer either way. While these leaders believe that even as aliens they owe a certain amount of loyalty to the United States after having resided here for so long, most of the issei think that being confined in here they have no reason to readily comply with military orders. The majority of the isseis think that they can solve the problem by going back to Japan. They do not seem to realize that in the course of 30 years Japan is no longer the same place.

FEBRUARY 16. In the evening there was a block meeting. I went in there late and as Mr. O. was making an announcement I didn't want to walk across to the other end of the room. M. and N. and some other boys were sitting on the serving counter so I sat there with them. Dad made me get off and later told me that it's all right for boys to sit on the table but girls shouldn't do it. Gee, I get tired of hearing that boys can do a certain thing but girls can't.

I happened to sit next to U. for lunch so I asked him if he had joined the block club and was coming to the social. He acted bashful and said that he felt out of place because he didn't know many people. I told him that was the reason why he should join, so he could get acquainted with everyone. I said that if he didn't participate, he could stay here five years and still wouldn't know anyone. He seemed convinced and when I went to his place in the afternoon he gave me 40¢ for the dues and social, and his brother also paid 15¢.

FEBRUARY 18. When I got home I found a letter from the Student Relocation Council asking me if I were still interested in continuing my education.[11] I didn't tell my parents about it because I knew they'd just raise a lot of fuss and tell me not to think about going out.

Well, they might as well realize that I'm old enough to take care of myself. In fact, if I had decided to go to Washington, D.C. just before the outbreak I wouldn't even be here for them to fuss over me. I had taken a Civil Service examination in

October, 1941 without telling them about it because I didn't think it would have any significance and they wouldn't offer me a job for a long while even if I passed. About a month later, I got a telegram asking me if I would accept a job in Washington, D.C. so I wired back collect that I would. A few days later they sent me another telegram telling me to report to work at 9:00 A.M. December 8, 1941 at the War Department in Washington. After much deliberation I decided to turn it down because Washington was too far away. It's a good thing I did because beginning work in the War Department on the morning after Pearl Harbor doesn't sound too pleasant.

On the [radio] "Town Meeting of the Air" they discussed the farm question. One of the speakers was Louis Bromfield, author and owner of a large farm in the midwest. All speakers agreed that there was an acute shortage of manpower; what the farmers want in the way of aid from the government is not cash subsidy but skilled labor and fertilizer; an unskilled man would do more harm than good in any phase of farming, dairy, orchard, etc. They don't readily admit it, but they must realize that if the Japanese had been allowed to remain in their homes it would have been far more beneficial to the war effort.

FEBRUARY 21. Instead of the usual [church] sermon, five persons gave their opinion on the pending question. G., who was born in Japan and came to this country when he was four years old, had his based on "If I Were an American Citizen I Would Be Loyal to the United States But I Would Refuse to Register," because registration is the first step toward conscription and conscription goads men into war and makes them robots and puppets in the hands of the military government. However, he thinks that those who are applying for expatriation or re-patriation [to Japan] are acting childish.

Mrs. O. urged everyone to register and proclaim loyalty to the United States. From her experience in Japan she related that Japan is no place for the average nisei because their formal customs are difficult to adjust to for the zoot-suited jitterbugging nisei.

I.P. spoke on "How Much Do We Owe To Our Country and

How Much to Our Parents?" He thought that we should listen to our parents and consider what they have to say but from there on think for ourselves.

Mr. S., one of the high school teachers, gave his opinion on all this. His primary advice was to follow your own conscience and not follow the herd like sheep.

V.N., a boy from Tacoma, gave his reason for answering yes to question 28 as the kindness of American friends and reminiscences of the typical American life he has led.

Reverend U. stated that he didn't like nationalism but as long as there are nations, it's necessary to choose one country and he would choose the United States. "America has many virtues and also has committed many tragic sins but American's sins are our sins."

Beth came home around five and said there was a big riot in block 42. After a block meeting some of the boys put on antiregistration demonstrations and shouted "tenno heika Panzai" ["long live the Emperor"]. The soldiers had come and after using tear gas had carried off some thirty boys to jail.

FEBRUARY 22. Today is Washington's birthday, but the holiday doesn't apply to this project so we had to work.

The girls in our block were supposed to register today, but there was much indecision and vagueness about whether we should or shouldn't. Dad thought that I should wait until the excitement subsided, and since it was raining and snowing I decided that there was no hurry. About half of the girls registered and the others didn't. I hate to walk down there *waza waza* [out of my way], so I'll wait until I have to go that way on some other business.

I got a letter from I.O., who left the project in January for Rochester, Minnesota. She seems to be getting along all right. She's working at the home of a doctor from the Mayo Clinic. If saving money is the prime motive, domestic work is about the best because there is clear profit. The average wage is $50 a month with room and board which really amounts to a lot more than stenographic work at $125 a month. I'm getting rather skeptic about going out for employment because there doesn't seem to be any work that I like which pays enough.

The City Council and Planning Board were in session all day and had come to the conclusion that resignation en masse was the only solution in view of the fact that they were getting no place either with the colonists or the administration. Their request of having the arrested boys returned to the project, conducting registration through the mails or individual blocks, and permitting the registrant to answer all questions without coercion had been rejected by the army officials. There wouldn't have been any harm if the army had agreed to the proposal, but I think they just like to show us who's boss instead of taking orders from the colonists.

Every social and civic function has been cancelled—movies, Little Theater, issei entertainment, private parties, etc. This afternoon we were debating the wisdom of performing our plays as usual. There isn't any reason to drop everything and stay home brooding, but there might be resentful groups who might not like to see anybody having fun at a time like this. After dinner H. came over and told me that we wouldn't perform for awhile and that suits me fine.

FEBRUARY 23. What a wild goose chase! Last night, or rather this morning at 12:30 some kibei boys woke us up and told us to come to a very important block meeting. Mother woke me up so I hastily got dressed and went. Everybody was there looking sleepy-eyed. Some kibeis, mostly from other blocks, said that they had gotten up a petition refusing to register and wanted the signatures of all those who were willing. They were of the mind that they didn't want to be treated as American citizens but as Japanese nationals. Of course, they were acting in sympathy for the boys from block 42 who had been arrested, but those boys had been arrested because they hadn't followed the regular procedure and there's no use in others deliberately making the same mistake. Others put up a protest to signing any such petition of which they had no knowledge. The kibeis finally got it through their heads that they couldn't convince us so they left. All those who signed the petition were supposed to meet at 9 o'clock in the morning but apparently their plan fell through for they didn't have any such meeting. I don't see how such a fantastic plan could have succeeded anyway for they had no organization, but just woke us up at midnight to make us listen to their fanatic tommyrot.

FEBRUARY 24. Today was a gloomy and desolate day and so I stayed home in the afternoon and read Freud's theory on dreams. He thinks that most dreams are wish fulfillments and are of sexual nature. The only dream that I can remember clearly is the one I had about the devil when I was about three years old. When I was small, Mother used to discipline me with "the devil will get you if you don't watch out" stuff so I dreamt that we were on a picnic and a red *oni* [devil] came along and dragged me off to Hades where there were devils of other colors. That didn't scare me very much, but when I was eight years old and had the measles I had a nightmare where I thought that I fell off an airplane. After I was awake I still didn't realize that it was only a dream. Nowadays I seldom have dreams but when I do, they're actually continuations of thought that I may have when falling asleep.

There was another block meeting. A request was made for a representative to attend the kibei meeting, but nobody wanted to go. We thought that it would be fun to see what it was like so I tagged along with the kibeis.

The place was packed, mostly with kibeis. The air was full of smoke and reminded me of a bar room minus the drinks. Everybody was more or less excited, and one man got up and said in a half crying voice, "Some people can't make future plans because they don't know which side will win the war but I'm sure that Japan will win." Somebody else shouted "Japan will never lose!" The gist of the meeting seemed to be to formulate plans for those determined not to register. I.N. was there and explained the rules of registration and stated that we were allowed the rights of citizenship and were compelled to register. Amid all the confusion his voice was calm and steady. I. has such a nice voice, the kind that can bring order out of chaos, and a manner that never offends.

FEBRUARY 25. The kibeis have made up a resolution for non-registration. If they earnestly believe that what they are doing is right, there isn't anything wrong with the stand they have taken. However, their method of beating up anyone who doesn't happen to agree with their policy and trying to keep others from registering with such arguments as, "There is no punishment for not registering" and "Only one-third of the people have registered so far," is very poor sportsmanship. If they have such a firm distrust of the government that they're willing to go to jail for it, that's okay but they don't have to drag others with them. I don't know how much truth there is to their statement that there's no punishment for non-registration but it doesn't sound reasonable. If it's such a hapazard thing why should it be compulsory?

Dad and other isseis are beginning to think that the kibei stand is weak. They were saying today that the action of the kibeis is disgraceful. Most of the kibeis who are active in non-registration activities haven't much education as far as I can see. Some of them are unfortunate enough not to have either a good Japanese or American education. Those who were sent to Japan in their early childhood and perhaps went through elementary school in Japan, then came back here in their teens and because of over-age didn't attend public schools but just bummed around—such incoherence. Heretofore, most of the isseis have more or less sympathized with the kibeis but now they are beginning to say that their manners are coarse and they lack the refinement that most niseis possess to some degree. All the kibeis who I know are Americanized, and I don't know any down-right Japanesy ones too well.

FEBRUARY 26. Among the 180 students who were in my [high school] graduating class, I can remember the following among the outstanding and brilliant students—T., valedictorian and pianist; N., salutatorian and orator, stately manners and rich family; F., studious and conservative. I trailed along fourth because of the below par grades in chemistry and home economics.

Most of these [non-Japanese classmates] are working in de-

fense plants or in the armed forces, even those with most mediocre brains and ability. Some girls got married, and a few
brilliant ones are attending college. Comparatively speaking, on
the average, these people are more sophisticated than the average nisei. I think that the majority of these teen-agers who
were in my class are equal to niseis 20 years or older, not in
intelligence or mental ability but in being worldly wise and
"getting around." Nisei retain their youth very well and are
quite naive.

First Dad tells me to wait until the last moment before registering; then he says that if I must do it I might as well do it
as soon as possible. I had my mind made up since Monday that
I was going to register this afternoon and told him so last night.
Yesterday was the day that the kibeis were passing their non-
registration resolution around, so he tells me to wait again. I
told him that I had my mind made up and wasn't going to be
influenced by every piece of gossip or rumor.

This noon, Mr. M. and Mr. P. were over talking to Dad.
They were saying that helping this country in any way would
be harmful to the Japanese war effort, and no good Japanese
would think of doing a thing like that. It seems that somebody
heard a radio broadcast this morning from Japan in which they
said that all persons of Japanese ancestry whether niseis,
sanseis[12], etc. were considered Japanese citizens and would be
welcome in Japan after the war. Hearing a thing like that may
be more than sweet music to the ears of an issei but doesn't
mean a thing to me. I slipped quietly out of the house and went
to ask V. what she was going to do because she had told me
that she wanted to go with me when I went to register. She
said that her parents intended to go to Japan, and although she
didn't want to go she had no other alternative but to stick to
them since she wasn't independent. I thought that under those
circumstances there was no use in her registering.

V. is an attractive girl but it's too bad that her father is such
a big bully. If I were she I certainly wouldn't submit to his every
will but I guess she has no other alternative.

After I got finished with the dentist I went to the visitor's building to register. There really isn't much to it for everyone to make such a fuss over. Many of the questions are repetitions from the other [leave clearance] form and seemed a waste of time to answer again. I asked the registrar why the extra work, and she admitted that the WRA didn't have the procedure worked out very well. To volunteering for the WAAC I said that I wouldn't volunteer but would be willing to serve if drafted, and answered yes to the 28th question swearing allegiance to the United States.

On the way out I bumped into A. [who] thought that I had gained weight, and I told her not to remind me of such things. I know that since evacuation too much carbohydrates and lack of sufficient excercise is bad.

When I got home Dad asked me if I had registered so I told him I had. He seemed displeased and said I should have waited. I replied, "Wait, wait, how long do you want me to wait? Until doomsday? Am I a worm or a woman?" He was angry and said this was no time to talk that way. I asked him if he planned on going back to Japan and he said there was no way of telling how things were going to be in the future. Well, it's no use crossing the bridge before you get to it.

FEBRUARY 27. There has been much ado during the past week and it hasn't been exactly over nothing, although some people make it more serious than it really is. The question lies in whether or not the person trusts the government. If a person is suspicious of the government's motive that may be just reason for refusing to sign. However, the government trusts us enough to believe everything we write.

It's true that the kibeis and some others are getting overly excited, but the government really used the wrong approach. If this had been handled more discreetly, everyone would have registered peacefully. They shouldn't have conducted the selective service and leave clearance registrations at the same since the two have nothing in common and aren't even handled by the same agency.

Some people think that the entire camp should unite and take one stand but that's impossible because everyone isn't of one mind and it's undemocratic to force anyone. The isseis think that individual interests should be thrown aside in favor of the group benefit. But all human beings have the right to follow their own conscience.

Five or six kibeis in our block were arrested last night. For what I don't know because, although all those boys are very Japanesy and I didn't know them very well, they didn't seem to be overly influential. I feel sorry for them for they were just kids and there are many other eligible candidates who could have been arrested before them.

G. doesn't seem to be concerned about it at all. In fact, he suggested that we have a movie in our block tonight. Many isseis are accusing him of being a spy, working for the FBI and getting $75 a month. I don't know where they got the figure of his salary, or whether there's any truth in the matter.

All these arrests and accusations reminds me of the days before evacuation. Everyone was living in morbid fear of being interned and anyone who acted a little out of step with the others was accused of being a spy. [The local] executive secretary of the JACL was accused of being one just because every issei man on a certain part of Main Street was interned except his father. Those were crucial days of insecurity. Around March of last year, evacuation was inevitable and every day we would gather at the office and talk about nothing else.

I was very much surprised when K. suggested in psychology class today that fear of death was the main reason why the people are refusing to register. I heartily disagree with K. and hope that I am right because otherwise it would be a terrible disillusionment of my conception of mankind. Of course, no sane human being wants to die but when the cause is great and worthy enough they should be willing to give their lives. If everyone were afraid of death to the extent that K. says there shouldn't be any wars. I believe that the reason that the majority of nisei boys and their parents are opposed to induction into the army is the resentment against being pushed around by the government. If they hadn't been evacuated, they would have peacefully complied with selective service orders. There are many plausible reasons for refusing to join the army—lack of patriotic zeal for country, opposition to killing and militarism, unwillingness to bear arms against the country of one's ancestors, etc. However, fear of death doesn't sound manly, and any cowards who feel that way deserve to die.

They are having a general mass strike at Boeing's Aircraft Company in Seattle. The minimum beginning wage is 62½ cents an hour, and the men are striking to have that raised to 95 cents which is the rate for shipyard workers. Here we are, getting less than 10 cents an hour and not complaining. Outsiders use the slightest excuse to accuse us of impeding the war effort. Manufacturing airplanes is one of the most important war industries in the United States. In spite of all the talking they do, these so-called patriotic Americans are only thinking of their own pocketbooks.

Darn those men! Mr. N. and Mr. P. always come over and influence Dad. Mr. N was saying today that when a child disobeys his parents, it's because he wasn't reared right and it's the parent's fault. In self-defense Dad was saying that some children are naturally aggressive and do things their own way no matter what the parents say. Dad says that his heart is definitely in Japan, and if it came to the point of choosing between Japan and me he would choose Japan. Well, I'm not going to worry about anything like that until I get to it. I might even be willing to go to Japan for awhile and see how it is.

There simply isn't any privacy here. I was getting undressed to take a shower when Mr. P. knocks on the door and comes in. They've finally installed a Japanese bath in our shower room but now that the weather is getting warmer it won't do much good. It seems so unsanitary for everyone to use the same water. The rules are that the people are supposed to take a shower and clean themselves before going in the bath, and they can't take their towels or washcloths in there. I didn't think anything of going in the swimming pool even with Negroes but bath is a different matter.

FEBRUARY 28. The weather today was sunny and gay. It makes me homesick because if we were back in Seattle, our

Japanese flowering cherries would be starting to bloom now. All decked out in pink and white, they look as beautiful as the proverbial cherry blossoms in Japan.

MARCH 1. Mother was saying that she's always been afraid of animals, and also snakes and worms. A snake or worm in the house is enough to get her into hysterics. I wonder what difference in bodily or mental structure there is between men and women. Women are afraid of so many things. Perhaps men are afraid too but just don't admit it.

MARCH 2. Today was a drowsy day. Although the wind is cold, it looks like spring is here. I'm getting spring fever and don't feel like doing anything. In love with love.

MARCH 3. Today is the annual Doll Festival in Japan but it went unnoticed here. In the good old days, March 3 meant taking out my Japanese dolls, and especially good Japanese food. However, we had nothing but salted herring for supper today. I certainly won't be sorry if salt is rationed.

The recruiter for the WAAC is here today and tomorrow. If I could meet the minimum requirement I might enlist if it weren't for my parents. Driving a jeep over foreign terrain sounds very thrilling.

I got a letter from D. in Pennsylvania. We've been writing to each other for seven years now. She doesn't seem to be especially intelligent but quite well-to-do. In one previous letter I asked her if the people in her community were racially prejudiced. She misinterpreted the question and said the people were angry at the brutal treatment the Japanese and Germans gave their prisoners. Therefore, I wrote back that I hadn't meant the people's reaction to the propaganda about Axis countries. I elaborated on the fact that here we American citizens were confined in camp while German and Italian aliens roamed around free. She apologized, hoped that I wasn't angry at her, and said the people in her community were not narrow-minded.

MARCH 5. A telegram states that General DeWitt's[13] proclamation makes Gila and Colorado River Projects non-restrictive areas effective March 4. This means that 245 persons may go back to their homes in Arizona. "Another evidence of the WRA's good faith in restoring evacuees to normal life."

MARCH 6. What is it nowadays that makes it difficult for me to concentrate? It is much easier to just sit and talk or knit or sew or just waste time than to read a book or study. I can't even concentrate on the funnies anymore. The reason may be just passed up as spring fever, but the real reason is perhaps the feeling of insecurity and uncertainty. Nobody knows what's going to happen the next minute and every way I turn there is a stone wall. I could just be a nice girl and stay quietly within the stone wall but what a boring life that would be. Man was made to fight for things and it's no fun to just be contented with whatever comes along and never aspire for higher things.

There are several ways out of this stone wall. One would be to go to college which would mean an expense of at least $1,000 a year plus cramming and a nervous breakdown. At the end of four years if I study hard enough I might come out with a degree but four years older. The merits of a college education would be mainly cultural refinement and experience which would be well worth the effort. Another way is to get outside employment, but the obstacle is that the kind of work I like with sufficient pay is unavailable. If saving money were my primary motive I could get domestic work and make a clear profit of $15 a week, but I made up my mind years ago that never again would I stoop so low and money as such doesn't interest me. Secretarial work is the next easiest to get but $125 a month in a strange city would amount to almost nothing. The WAAC sounds like a good thing but Japanese public sentiment and age limit are against me. But the greatest obstacle is my parents. Of course, I'm glad they're here and wouldn't know what to do without them. Their viewpoint is reasonable and if they said they didn't care where I went or what I did, that would be a great shock to my ego. However, they insist that the family should stay together; I'm just a child and shouldn't be out alone in the world. Dad came to this country alone when he was only 19, but "boys are different." What gets me is that they make me feel that I would be committing a crime if I left against their wishes and caused them unnecessary worry. How long am I supposed to stay home? If I knew definitely that it was to be a year or two years, that's a different story but it might be five or ten years or even more.

It's this state of indecision that's causing my restlessness. If I were reconciled to staying here for the duration or for a known length of time or left everything up to my parents, I could be at ease and get down to business.

The past few weeks have been exceptional [at the office] because of the cancellation of all recreational activities. I enjoy the freedom and congeniality but lately it's been getting a little boring.

[In Psychology class] drives and motives was the topic of instruction. Physiological motives are obvious but the social ones are quite complex because in many instances the person doesn't admit his real motive and there's no way of ascertaining the truth.

Sex figures largely in psychology and most psychologists treat it in a most complicated manner. Sexual urge is supposed to be inherent. If that's the case, I must be abnormal or something because I don't see anything inherent about it in my experience which amounts to exactly none. As I mentioned some time before, I didn't even know the process of reproduction until a little over a year ago. If I loved a man enough to marry him I would permit him to do anything but I don't feel that urge myself. Yet, I don't think I'm abnormal because this urge is supposed to be stronger in men but many men go through life as bachelors without experiencing it and don't seem to be any worse off. For me, everything has been learned. In many ways, some boys are more interesting than girls because they are more broad-minded and do not resort to cattiness or petty gossip. If all men were abolished, it wouldn't hurt me so much but it would be very tragic because the other women would become impossible to live with.

In the evening Dad was counting a lot of money so I asked him what it was for. He said that the sympathetic people in the block were donating $1 from each family to purchase food and send to the kibei boys in jail because those boys were being fed poorly. I said, "For the love of Pete" in my surprise and Dad gave me the dirtiest look. We may not approve of their motives, but we can sympathize with them as fellow men and this is a very kind gesture on the part of the block people.

MARCH 9. The leave office has asked for 30 volunteer registrars from our section to register isseis [for leave clearance]. I said that I would be willing, although my knowledge of Japanese is limited. At the staff meeting, [they] read the names of all who volunteered and said that they were not tools of the administration.

MARCH 10. I heard that there was a riot in block 44 last night. Reports were that colonists had punctured the tires of cars and trucks which came to arrest agitators, had called the authorities names and made a big racket. Many of these people are the ones who had been shouting that they're willing to go to jail for Japan's sake so why don't they go quietly. In the afternoon I went to a meeting of volunteer registrars. D. and his wife were there. This is the first time I've seen them but she looks like a woman who believes in feminine rights—freedom of speech and smoking.

MARCH 11. I went this morning to register the aliens for leave clearance. The work isn't hard but it takes almost an hour to register one person. I wish we could type it because it's so messy to write or print by hand, and pressing hard to make the writing go through three carbon copies is hard on the fingers. Most of the questions are easy because most of the isseis bring their alien registration books. However, I feel silly asking them if they've ever been arrested. Some of them start reiterating that they've never committed a crime, yet the government pushes them in camp. When I ask them if they will swear to abide by the laws of the United States and not do anything to obstruct the war effort[14], they say, "How can we do anything when we're stuck in here?" From the second time, before I asked them if they've ever been arrested, I learned to say, "I'm sure that it's unnecessary to ask you such a question and it's rude to doubt your honesty, but since the question is on the form I have to ask you as a matter of routine."

MARCH 12. Mr. G. was the first person whom I registered today. He seems to be quite well educated for his time. He said that he was good in reading, writing, and speaking Japanese and fair in English. I think that education more than occupation marks a person's ability. Regardless of whether they're farmers, miners, laborers, or plumbers, education shows up in a person's reasoning, especially in times of crisis.

MARCH 13. We finally had our block social in the evening. Most of the people were assembled at 8 o'clock so I started them off with a few songs and then ran off to Little Theater. When I got back around 9:30 they had just finished eating. I didn't help prepare the food, but the mess girls whom I appointed had egg and tuna sandwiches, potato salad, delicious fruit jello and tea fixed.

The boys needed some pushing before they began dancing, but after awhile they got into the swing of things. Some people who paid their money didn't come. Undoubtedly, many of them didn't come because of bashfulness. I don't see why some boys are so shy. They're good dancers and there's nothing for them to be so bashful about. If this were Leap Year the girls could really go to town because there aren't as many bashful ones among them.[15]

MARCH 15. M. was asking Z. to speak at the Buddhist service. C. says, "Are you a Bussei? Oh, you old Bussei!" Surprised, Z. asked, "Gee, is it a crime to be a Buddhist?" C. said that since he was teaching Sunday school he had to reform everybody. I assured Z. that Buddhists were as good as Christians, and since the odds were even we thought that it was no use arguing about religion.

We got our identification badges, more commonly known as dog licenses, today. Ours is under Community Services, therefore yellow in color. They're too big and conspicuous but I guess it's supposed to be that way. I feel like a dog wearing a thing like that around.

MARCH 17. Today is the day for the "Wearin' of the Green."

I don't see why we can't celebrate a day for the Japanese as well as a day for the Irish.

I ordered a pair of red play shoes [and] a girdle. I never wore a girdle in my life but they could be rationed because of the rubber shortage so I'd better buy one now to keep for old age.

MARCH 18. In the evening I went to hear Mrs. F.G.'s speech on preparation for marriage. She listed ten points to look for in the prospective partner: closest to ideal, sterling character, confidence, ability to live together, no clashing of tastes, health, skills, worthy to be a parent, brings out the best in yourself, mutual interests. She also emphasized the "give and take" proposition and stated that nobody is perfect, except her husband.

There really isn't much to be said about sex and marriage that hasn't already been said. Mother went to hear her this afternoon when she spoke to the Christian mothers' group on "Sex and Youth Problems." She said the speech was on the same thing that she already knew—promiscuous sex relations, venereal diseases, etc.

I listened to "Town Meeting of the Air" as I do every Thursday evening, and the topic of discussion today was on the subjects to be taught in the schools in war time. The question was whether to discontinue liberal arts and replace it with military training. Most of them thought that liberal arts had its place but war came first.

MARCH 19. I was thinking last night that perhaps it would be a good idea for me to transfer to another job and get out of commercial work for a while. In the recreation center I've had more fun and freedom than at any other place of employment. However, I don't think too much freedom is good for discipline in the future. Since the registration problem came up and most recreational activities have been curtailed, there hasn't been much work to do so most of the people don't exactly come to work but more for social get-together. After due consideration, I came to the conclusion that while I was having fun I wasn't accomplishing much but just signing in for eight hours a day and collecting my pay check.

I like to take shortcuts and don't like to do unnecessary work, but I never was a slacker and I like to work. Usually, the teacher learns more than the students so I decided to try working at the high school and get into academic subjects. I went to the placement office this morning and W. told me that there were teaching positions open so I went to the high school office and talked to Mr. S. He said that I could start out by being an assistant in English or social science. High school is to begin next Thursday so I could begin as soon as I got a termination from my present job. I never hope to take up teaching as a profession. However, practice teaching would be good training for other things, for instance preparation for college study. In order to be a teacher in the outside world, usually a college degree or graduation from a normal school is necessary. In addition, the candidate must serve several years as a cadet teacher. In view of that fact, it isn't too bad for a person like me without a college education to be given an opportunity like that here.

Some people may say that being an assistant teacher is a dog's life, a stooge to another teacher. However, that depends on the way you look at it. It isn't necessary for anyone to become somebody else's stooge if he has the initiative and will power. I'm not intimating that I have that initiative and will power, but at least I could try.

NOTES

1. Vinegared rice and vegetables rolled in seaweed.

2. Students were granted clearance to leave camp if accepted at a college or university.

3. A number of prominent Isseis were designated "dangerous enemy aliens" and interned in prison camps, as opposed to "relocation camps."

4. American-born Japanese who had been sent to Japan for schooling and tended to combine the two languages. In addition, since Japan's educational system had been highly militaristic in the 1930s, the Kibeis who Kate knew were usually vehement supporters of Japan's wartime policies.

5. *Ne* may be added to the end of a Japanese sentence for emphasis.

6. The Japanese American Citizens League, a national Nisei group that had urged cooperation "under protest" with the evacuation in order to prove loyalty.

7. In March of 1942, an 8 P.M. curfew had been imposed on all Japanese-Americans on the West Coast.

8. Sites of important Japanese victories in the Philippines.

9. As of June 1942, most Nisei men were actually classified 4–C—"not acceptable for service because of ancestry."

10. In January 1943 the War Department announced that Japanese-Americans would be accepted into the armed forces. The ensuing Selective Service registration, coinciding with the compulsory WRA Leave Clearance registration, generated great anger and confusion in the relocation camps.

    Two questions in particular caused problems. Question 27, regarding willingness to serve in the armed forces, was resented by many, coming as it did from a government that had denied their most basic rights. Question 28 asked, "Will you swear unqualified allegiance to the United States . . . and forswear any form of allegiance to the Japanese emperor?" Since Isseis had been barred from American citizenship, answering "yes" to this question would have left them without a country.

11. The National Japanese Student Relocation Council helped young people gain college admission and leave clearance.

12. Third generation Japanese-Americans, i.e., children of Niseis.

13. General John DeWitt, Commander of the Western Defense Command, had masterminded the evacuation and set up the "restricted areas."

14. Question 28 had been rephrased for the benefit of the Issei.

15. According to an old American tradition, only during Leap Year could women ask men out.

◇　　◇

Afterword

Kate Tomibe's life after this point can only be guessed at. If she chose to go to college, she was probably accepted because of her excellent academic record, and granted leave clearance after the usual period of waiting. She could have secured a job outside and been granted leave, or she may have remained with her family, who probably eventually returned to the home that they owned near Seattle.

The WRA's official policy was to encourage people to leave the camps, and qualified U.S. citizens had been granted leave clearance as early as July 1942. But this was not as easy as it seemed; permission was only granted if the applicant had a place to go and a means of support outside of the restricted areas. Many of the evacuees had neither. In addition, one had to have answered "correctly" on the Leave Clearance forms, and was subject to FBI and Intelligence investigations. Applicants had to agree to keep the WRA informed of their addresses at all times.

The National Japanese American Student Relocation Council helped thousands of young people leave the camps to enter colleges and universities throughout the country. Quaker and church groups established halfway houses and helped former internees find jobs and housing. Some evacuees entered the armed forces, including the all-Nisei units that earned distinguished service records.

By the end of 1944, 35,000 people had left the camps. But the majority remained until after the government rescinded its mass-exclusion orders, and announced that the camps would be closed within a year. The announcement in December 1944 created an uproar, for there was little government assistance offered to those leaving, many of whom had lost the means to re-establish themselves outside.

Tule Lake itself had been turned into a maximum security facility in the summer of 1943. So-called "disloyals," people who had answered "no" to questions 27 and 28, were brought to Tule Lake from other camps. Six thousand "loyal" Tuleans were moved to other camps in September, but many "loyals" refused to leave, and a great deal of unrest ensued. Tule Lake was the last camp to close; many of those left in the end had renounced citizenship and went to Japan.

The Japanese-Americans had suffered massive economic losses as a result of their imprisonment. Many of their possessions had been hurriedly sold at prices well below market value, and much that they had left behind had been stolen or vandalized. In 1948 a law was passed for government compensation to the evacuees. But ultimately they were paid less than 10% of the value of property lost, and no payments were made for mental or physical suffering.

THE DIARY OF

Annie Burnham Cooper

*Sag Harbor, New York
1881–1894*

Annie Cooper (*Courtesy of Nancy Willey*)

◇   ◇

Introduction

In August of 1880, during the last week of her summer vacation, fifteen-year-old Annie Cooper began the first of her journals in a small school notebook.

"The idea of writing a Diary has not occured to me before," she wrote, "neverless it is not too late now, by any means, so now, on this very page I begin my Diary, in which I shall write my good and bad times, my ways, my thoughts, my troubles, my experiences, any daily occupation, and so forth."

Annie Cooper was the youngest child in a large, prosperous family of Sag Harbor, New York—a Long Island village which had been a bustling whaling port some forty years before. Now, however, the Long Island whaling industry was dead; Sag Harbor was a quiet backwater. Annie's father, the last of three generations of boat builders, had also been in the business of financing and outfitting ships, and had retired with enough investments to keep the family comfortable. The young Annie appears to have lacked for nothing—not material goods: "papa is so good & generous," she often wrote—nor love and attention, for as the "baby" she was pampered and indulged. Her idyllic childhood is well characterized in the first diary entry:

"I have spent my [summer] mostly in *rowing, bathing, sailing, crabbing, fishing, minoing, riding horseback*, sewing buttons on shoes, mending stockings, gloves, and trimming *boating hats, tanning my arms and rists* as brown as a pancake, helping Mama in a few places, when I could, and not helping her in a thousand different ways when I could, and so fourth."

Years later she remembered: "What a jolly rollicing girl I was— ready for fun or any mischief. Skating—ice no thicker than a pane of glass—the thinner, the more fun. And then the day when I first had *my* own boat to row—never a thought of fear—going out alone into our bay when it was white with foam. And then the days spent with a lot of boys crabbing, fishing, etc. They always took me along because they said I was 'as good as a boy.' And the way I learned to sail— stealing away on the sly. I alone in my own little boat, independant

147

& free. Papa finally gave me a side saddle—finding I *would* ride some-how—that he couldn't keep me off of horses backs. . . . My life was full & rich & innocent & happy."

The early volumes of Annie's diary mostly record her actions, rather than her thoughts—and in these, as in her constant admonitions to herself to "be a good girl," she seems much younger than she was. Within a few years, in these excerpts, the diary becames more introspective, and more of a secret confidante.

By her late teens Annie was often perplexed by life; and, as she wrote, she couldn't confide in any person; the little book was her refuge. There, her change from girlhood to womanhood was recorded, marked by a growing sense of guilt—and a feeling of unworthiness which she constantly strives to overcome with resolutions—"I must try & pray to overcome my impulses, impetuousness, thoughtlessness, carelessness." She struggles with her own nature—which she often labelled weak, selfish and un-Christian. A strong-willed child was acceptable in her milieu; a strong-willed woman was not.

Annie Cooper had one pleasure, at least, that was considered proper for a young lady—art. Like many girls of her time she studied drawing and painting, but she took it more seriously than most. She began early to sell her work to friends and family, calling this her "business" and keeping track of her earnings in a ledger patterned after her father's. Her art, like her diary, was a means of preserving the impressions and passions of a deeply-felt life.

◇ *1881* ◇

DECEMBER 11. Alas! alas! the 11 has arrived and crowns me 17 yrs old. I feel as though I were almost loosing my childhood, sweet childhood. And yet I do not feel so old, I feel as though I wish it were only 12 yrs. I hate to grow up. My childhood has been *so* sweet, I hate to part with it.

◇ *1882* ◇

JANUARY 22. I am afraid Mama & Papa think me very hard hearted, here I am 17 years old & have not joined a church yet, they think I am not in at all serious mood I think, but I am, I am weighing the subj. of religion, & dancing in my mind, I know I believe in the Lord Jesus. Christ and I know that I am a sinner Oh! how great a sinner. Oh! If I only could make some of the girls talk of religion, I don't know whether they see as I do or not.

I don't want to Join the church & be a stumbling block to others, when I join I want to be fully decided to lead a christian life and work for my Savior.

MARCH 4. How thankful I ought to be for my beautiful home & the many pleasures & blessings it includes. I can't see why God is so good to me, I am sure I don't deserve it. I ride horseback ever so much most every day, either horseback or in the carriage. I take the girls, all riding, but I don't take some of the poor girls that I know would be so glad to go. God help me & I will the first chance I get. Mama won't let me ride in the woods much alone.

OCTOBER 10. Mama & [sister] Celia went to Hartford last week & I was housekeeper.

Papa & I enjoyed it very much indeed, for I painted nearly all the time. & of course that was bliss for me. Yesterday I began school, & like it very much indeed, for I love study, I have French, Geometry, Algebra, Physolrgy & reading, spelling, music & painting.

DECEMBER 3. I write this sitting in my room with a fire in the stove, & my room is beautifully furnished, Papa is as good & kind as he can be, he gives us nearly every thing we ask for. I am doing a good deal of painting lately, little things for Xmas presents. I enjoy it ever so much, I love it.

DECEMBER 11. Again my birthday has rolled around & I am still spared, well & happy, no care yet hath been put upon me, I am still a happy, joyous, merry, hearty, & healthy, school girl, girl of 16 in feeling, but eighteen in years. I can't bear to think how fast my happy youth & childhood is slipping from me, that I soon will be too big to climb trees & ride horse back straddling, etc. yes, that in fact I *am* too big already, it makes me feel badly, for although I love the deeper & more sound *stuff*, yet too I love *nature*, in all its phases, I love, the woods the air, the birds, the storms, the water, the animals of every description, & I love nature's sports, & I feel that in advancing age I am getting too big to do with propriety all the sports which belong to nature, but thank God who has given them to me, that I still can ride horse back & go boating as much as I please, with propriety, if I can not climb trees (in the front yard.)

◇ *1883* ◇

APRIL 8. I do not seem to care for the "boys" very much. Sometimes I think I care for them too little for my own good, but if girls are going to tend to fellows, they have to be a good deal with them & that takes them away from the private sitting room & home a good deal. that is what I don't want, for if I am not home with Papa & Mamma what comfort can I be to them, & that is my daily prayer, to be a comfort & prop to my parents. Celia being older of cause has fellows & is even now "engaged," but home is the sweetest and dearest place to me in the world, I have nearly every thing that could make me happy, viz the *best* of Fathers & Mothers, & Sister, & four kind brothers, a beautiful home, surrounded by *Nature* in all her *glory*, *pets* viz. hens, chickens, cat, & a horse that we all *almost* "*love to pieces*," & which we, I especially, ride, in the beautiful woods which surround Sag Harbor, to the vast ocean only 6 miles from

here. (Oh! how delightful) large nice grounds, trees, fruit by
the—(all we can eat). Then we have boats, four in number.
One is my boat with my name on it. Then Papa reads to us in
the evening or I play chess with him, & practice on the Piano,
& get my lessons, read the papers, of which we have plenty.

JUNE 2. I went to Brooklyn to visit Annie Rhodes, had a
lovely time, went everywhere nearly, stayed three weeks, went
to my first ball, & a *grand ball* it was! & to four Theaters or
Operas. I had plenty of fellows & attention, and all that sort of
thing! I can't begin to tell how I enjoyed it! I got me a new silk
dress & hat, picked it out myself, & had a good time spending
money generally, in all I spent $33.43 while I was away, & I
did not buy many nicknacks either. Money melts in N.Y. Papa
was so good & generous!

JULY 14. How much has happened since I last wrote in this
book, & how I have neglected it! I don't seem to have any time
to write in it without letting some one know something about
it, & this is private, no one is supposed to know any thing about
this book. If I had time I would like to put down the workings
& thoughts of my heart & mind, but the most of this book is
merely facts of things which have transpired, I think that I could
easily write a book if I should try. It would be my delight.

OCTOBER 14. Since I wrote last in this book, my sister, my
only sister, so loving, so true, so kind & yet always so cheerful
has been married & left me to rule supreme in our room & in
the house. I cannot realize that she is married, she has always
been so kind to me, & so much with me that I have always
considered her as young almost as myself. She was always the
helper to Mamma in the house cares, I must try to fill her place,
Oh! what a mountain it seems like! my filling her place! why
simply impossible! but God helping me, I will fill it as much
as it *ought* to be filled, I will be kind, loving, obedient, patient,
& thoughtful, God help me.

◇ *1884* ◇

DECEMBER 7. 6 months since I wrote in this book, & today I have taken the boldest & best step of my life. I have

joined the church, and am happier and feel freer than I ever did in my life before, I do not feel that wonderful, uncontrollable joy which some people talk about, but I feel a peaceful joy. What I *longed* to do for *months* and *months*, but no one had taken the trouble to *speak* to me upon the subject until lately when Mr. Camp, our minister, came to see me, also Puss [friend]. I have felt no great change, sudden and terrible, but I *do* feel changed. I shall be 20 this week. I am so glad I have taken this step while I can say I am in my teens. I went to the young peoples meeting to-night, Mr. Camp might *almost have* asked me to speak, but I feel it almost wrong for women to speak in church, after reading what Paul says, I mean to ask Mr. Camp about it. I did not speak, & I felt awfully guilty, but still I don't think I did wrong exactly, I read a verse though.

DECEMBER 28. Mr. Camp was down here last night playing chess, I beat him four games. I wish Mr. Camp was a little more dignified outside of the pulpit, he is very gushing, & quite a *society* man, *etc.* he is a wonderful preacher & a very nice pastor.

◇ *1885* ◇

JANUARY 8. I have just returned from prayer meeting, which was well attended & to-day I have been asked if I would come & help in a female prayer meeting, *Oh! my God! how can I?* I do wish I could but have not the gift of "gab," *I don't see how I can.* I, who can not even, to save my life, say a single word at home, how can I brake through the barriers of timidity & natural diffidence to *such an extent as that?* Oh! no—no—no— I should brake down, & yet is it true that *I*, a young *professing* Christian, can not say one word for my Saviour? Oh! God forbid, *I will, God helping me.* Then they want me to take a class in S.S. [Sunday School]. I long to do it but *feel unfit, totally unfit in every way.*

Oh! How I love my room, this room in which I am now writing, it is a great comfort & a great blessing. If it were not for the refuge of my room, I fear I should not ever be able to be good, or think of serious things, if Celia was here, it would seal my lips, & actions, as much as I love her; but the presence of any one however dear, is to me a seal of my best thoughts & feelings. I never could open my heart to anyone yet, I don't think any earthly person knows how I feel, I wish I could talk to Mama & Papa as I would like to, but impossible—, I am exceeding reserve, I mean diffident, about things nearest & dearest to me. If I should ever fall in love, no one would ever know it. I know that my dear kind Godly, Mother, would comfort & help me, & pray with me, but I can not open my heart to her. It is wonder to me, when I see how much she has to bear that she can be so good & cheerful, & patient, when she receives *little or no* help from me, I *do* try to help her, but I don't very much. & Oh! if only I could get beneath the cold & stern exterior of my Fathers heart, to where *I know* it is warm, & all aglow with love, & bring out some of it.

FEBRUARY 7. This afternoon I have been skating on Crooked Pond! Oh, Oh, what fun! It is the most delightful pond anyway! the surroundings are lovely, & it is all turns & inlets & outlets, & islands! Oh! I just love it! We were a party of 12, & rode up in wagons, had a fire on one of the islands.

FEBRUARY 12. Mr. Camp has been down playing chess with me to-night, I imagine I'll not have the trouble to record a similar fact again, I can be awfully hateful & disagreeable when I've a mind to be so, & I find it fearfully hard to be agreeable when I want to sometimes, such a mixture of indignation & scorn is within me & still over powering all this is a desire not to bite my own nose off, as I am doing continually.

FEBRUARY 16. Mr. Camp has been down playing chess this evening, I beat him 2 games out of 3. What *he* comes here for, is *more* than *I can see.* For he does not pay scarcely any attention to Mama & Papa, & I *surely know* he does not *care* about paying any attention to me, for why should he a minister & a man of 43 years old, & a batcholor, care about coming down here to play *chess with me,* a giddy young girl, *scarcely out of my teens.* It is a puzzle to me, for he never talks religion to me, but mostly French de la sorte, "L'amour et le fumee ne prevent pas se cache." et "loin les yeux, pres de coeur." etc. It is very pleasant to have him come, I enjoy it, of course, if he is *goose* enough to waste his time on me, but he has so many charming acquaintances where he is so beloved that I can't understand why he does not stay with them, but—I see,—he feels it his duty to go every where among his parish & keep on the right side of every one, Oh, yes! I see, but then why does he want to play chess every time? I give it up. He is *awfully* nice! but *very* "frivilous" or "giddy" we call him "the destracted young parson" & the "Reverend Idle."

I was going to have such a nice time practising to-night, it rained so hard, when he came & *of course*, I practised in another direction—coque—flirta—etc, chess I mean. He *kindly* informed me that I must not fall in love with him as if I had any *idea* of it!!! *His conceit* is *unparelled*!!! I told him he should not have come here to-night, & I am *sure* I can't see *why* he did!

FEBRUARY 21. How wicked, how utterly wretched I feel! The clock has just struck twelve, & now it is God's holy Sabath Day, & I have but just dismissed my last guest, & somehow, I know that they have had a very stupid, stiff time, Oh! if only I was musical! I feel as if I could cry. Mr. Camp thinks me a little "fool" I have no doubt, & exceedingly rude & pert, & he will not want to come here any more I am afraid, Oh, dear, he is too "giddy" for any thing, I am getting disgusted! he thinks I never have any serious thoughts or feelings, & I can't blame him for that, but he never gives me a chance to show them. I feel *horrid*! wicked! ugly! I am *so* dissatisfied with my life, *so* dissatisfied. It is *so* far below my ideal of a Christian life. Oh, what can I do? If only I could have a good talk with Mr. Camp about myself I feel as if I should feel so much stronger, but he is more of a "parlez-Francais", etc, than anything else. Oh, dear, Oh! Pussie is so sweet & innocent & charming, everybody likes her, & me I am horrid! Oh dear!

FEBRUARY 22. Just returned from church. Oh! what a sermon, but what a change in the man who delivered it, from last night! It does not seem *possible* it is the same man, but alas, it *is*, the depth of thought on the one occasion & the "height" of thought on the other.

FEBRUARY 24. To-day *we, the quartette*, Mr. Camp. & me on the back seat, Puss & Mr. Cook on the front, of Mr. Cook's wagon, went to skate again. Oh, *how entrancing*! A charming day, that great Pond all to our selves, (& the wood choppers) about 3 miles from the village, a real romantic spot! with two old bachelors, one our suprentendant & the other our pastor, with a general understanding between us about marriage, Pussie & I having "sworn off" over a year ago, joined the "Order of Celibacy", & the "Order of the Holy Cross", & they are not to "want anything" of us, nor we of them, except true friendship, Oh! what a pleasure it is to have these two old friends look after us, & take us around! Oh, how thankful I am for it, Oh, my God, *may it continue always*, this Platonic & true friendship, & grow more & more true & confiding & charming, & strong *forever* & *ever*, until we four meet in the Celestial Court above.

FEBRUARY 28. I have been to church & Oh Oh what sermons! Mr. Camp seems inspired! when in the pulpit, but when out Oh! what a change, he is a "flirt" if ever I saw one, but the most innocent one! I have been riding with him to-day, over on North Haven, doing calls, on his parishoners, call it my 1st missionary tour, wonder if I will ever have another, I hope so, for although I *detest* his *continual* nonsense, still it is very pleasant to be talked to the way he talks. He is *so charming*, & I call him "mon cherr grandpere," et "mon cherr frere" et mon "tres cherr aime," & he calls me his "cherir", & son "libling", etc, pas tres souvent *though*, for I *won't allow* it.

MARCH 1. I have just returned from church, & communion, may God help me to keep near to him. I have yielded to the world this past quarter very much more than I realized, but now, God helping me, I start again with a clean page, & may God help me to keep it pure, not empty but full of good deeds, actions & thoughts.

MARCH 5. Mr. Camp has been here to-night playing chess with me until 11 o'clock, Papa says he must send me somewhere where I will have to "toe the mark," which means not have anything to do with man-kind, although there is never any reason for his being uneasy, still he always is when I have a fellow "look at me twice," which is a phenomena anyway, Mr. Camp was here last night also, he said to me to-night "Voudraiez vous aller a Paris avec moi?" Wonder what Papa would say to that.

MARCH 21. Saturday night, Mr. Camp just gone, played 6 games of chess, got mad & beaten 3 times, don't care if he didn't have a good time, am thoroughly disgusted with him, & myself too. I am an old *goose*, & he thinks so too, I've no doubt, he still thinks there is no seriousness to me, he is an old *"thing" anyhow*! etourdi, et charment. We talk literally nothing! The most giddy & light stuff & nonsense, I can't help it, I had a chance to speak of what was on my mind but I could not he is so etourdi, alas! & shall I ever?

APRIL 11. Oh dear! I am crying as hard as I can. How I long for some sympathetic soul with whom to commune, Oh, God, forgive me. I mean some earthy friend, *brave, true*, & *good*. Oh, why is it I cannot go to my father or mother, Oh! why is it, I cannot tell them every thing. They who are the most kind, most gentle, *best* of parents. Oh! wretch that I *am*! It is myself, my *own* detestible *self*. How I hate you for it. I despise you. I loath you. Oh, why can't I be like other girls, give vent to my loving, impulsive nature, air it, as it were. I have the kindest & dearest of parents & still I don't make them wholly happy I fear, I don't quite fill their hearts. Celia would be so much better, more satisfactory to them; why did not I be the one to get married & Celia the one to be a comfort to Papa & Mama. Papa is growing old. It pains me to watch it, Oh, why can I not talk to him of heaven, eternity, I desire to serve God faithfully in this way, for I believe that this is my calling for the present, I want to be a sweet, affectionate, fascinating, entertaining daughter.

APRIL 15. Mr. Cook has been here to-night, much to Papa's disgust, I don't see why Papa doesn't like to have either him or Mr. Camp call on me, & I can't understand why he should mind such old foggies as they are, he can't possibly think that I will fall in love with them. That would be too absurd!

APRIL 25. That old—goose is gone, I ought to be ashamed perhaps to speak of my pastor like this & of course I wouldn't for anything in the world to any one but you, my dear, diary, you & Pussie, are my busom friends on the subject. But what a old—what shall I say—fraud he is! Comes here & take tea, & flatter me just lays it on thick, & then flirt, & do all sorts of things that would be charming in any other man, but for a minister, — —! Well, I don't know! run on in the most nonsensical way to Papa when he *knows* that Papa is feeling *"blue"*, not a word of spiritual advice, or comfort, & then go to church the next day & preach the most magnificent & wonderful sermon, that I or any body ever heard, he put his whole soul in it too. He evidently does not put his soul to entertaining me, for it seems impossible that the same soul should work in such different channels, I have come to the conclusion that he tries to get all the lightness out of people & give vent to his buoyant spirits, so that it will rest him & better prepare him for his deep thought, & he thinks me capable of no higher or nobler or deeper thought than those with which he favors me. indeed—! & I resented his conduct to-night, I was actually ugly, I was *so sarcastic*, I could not help it, he rubs me the wrong way always. I don't think, in fact I am sure he will not come here again very soon, he did not enjoy two minutes of his time I'll warrant, I was insulted in the first place by him when he first came in the room, that set me off for the rest of the time he put his arm around——I mean I was fixing the string of the curtain, to pull it up, & it got fast, so I mounted the rocker & he came to steady it for me, but full of the mischief as he always is, he unsteaded it so that I *almost* fell into his "fond embrace",—of course I was indignant! I just guess I was! However I wish he could come here oftener, if he has a mind to make a goose of himself I don't care for myself but I hate to have Papa see him do so. & indeed he don't see half, through my management. I screen him as much as possible.

APRIL 26. Mr. Cook came down after church & made quite a long call much to my fathers disgust, after he left he actually threatened to tell him not to come again or have any thing more to do with me. Oh! Papa is too absurd! as if there could be any harm in Mr. Cook's coming to see me & taking me to ride &

sail! It amuses me so I almost split trying not to smile when he talks that way. Of course I don't want him to see that I am laughing, but I can't help it. Papa's in earnest, & I don't want to give up Mr. Cook's friendship.

MAY 15. How *can* I put on paper my thought! I am in a perfect whirl of confusion! Mad as a wet hen! Sorry as I can be! & Indignant, also? Mr. Camp & I have had a *terrible, terrible,* time, a real fight! He invited Puss & I to go up to the housewarming at Clara's & took us as far as the rendezvous & then went off with another girl, & left us to go with other gentlemen, now this didn't suit us at all, & we were mad! (as thunder!) & just let him see it too!!! & to-night he came down after prayer meeting & begged my pardon, & instead of treating him like a minister, just gave him a piece of my mind! (much to my mother's disgust & chagrin, thank goodness Papa had retired) He presented me with a lovely rose as a peace offering, & I did not even thank him & notice it, I was ugly! & looked ugly!! & Oh! dear, how I did give it to him. I wonder how it will be after this with us, he probably will *never* ask me to go any where again with him. & I wouldn't go! either! I *do hope* though, that it is in God's good providence to let this friendship continue, more true, more firm, more loving, & more intimate than it has ever been before. May it draw us closer together.

MAY 29. Oh! Day most beautiful & rare. How can I express myself, Mr. Camp & I have been riding, we went to the "Lovely Long Pond Spring" & drank its waters, & made a wish there above the spring. Mr. C. was so "sweet", you see dear diary, I don't want you to think that I am in love with him, my minister 30 or I mean 43 years old. A "vieux garcon". Oh! not at all! I *assure* you! I look upon him & he upon me in the light of true disinterested friends, it is pure *Platonic* Love that exists between us, nothing more or less. We converse about *love* freely, & we understand each other. But he is a great blessing to me, I thank God for his great kindness in giving me such a friend.

I dare not put on paper the soft sweet words he tells me, if I were his "sweetheart" he could not say or act much more, but he knows I understand, & match him in that.

MAY 31. "And their souls shall be like a well watered garden of the Lord" such was Mr. Camp's text this morning, Oh! what a sermon! Love, joy, peace, longsuffering, gentleness, humility, goodness, patience, & truth, are the fruits of the garden of the Lord. I love God, & his love fills me with a love to all his creatures & all Nature. What did Mr. Camp mean when he said in *soft sweet tones* while he found my hand & *pressed* it gently, "I warn you against love, beware of love"? When out riding in the woods he talks of love to fellow creatures, but not to *one* creature? When picking violets he takes his seat at my feet & holds my hand (when I allow it) & repeats poetry about love? when he takes my arm & looks into my face, *aye my eyes*, & says the sweetest *things imaginable*, sometimes in French & sometimes in English? Of course he *knows I know* it is purely *Platonic*, but then it *savors* of flirtation too. He is a real good man, any way, pure & high & noble in his impulses.

JUNE 2. I am just as quiet & "idealess" when I want to be lively & bright, & Puss is always witty, can always find something to say to people. I am not talented in music or singing or reading or talking. I could paint if I gave my time to it, but this hard to do when one is not taking lecons. & besides no one can amuse or rather entertain others by painting, it seems to me it is the most selfish talent there is, I love it though! Still I don't paint much.

I have taken music lessons all winter & still I can not play much. Why I have scarcely touched my brush since Xmas. & I am very discouraged about this also. Oh! dear, I can't talk "a perfect string"! either, I am so quiet, I have no "sparkling wit", I am not good looking, & although I *do* dress handsomely still it can not make me attractive—Oh! dear, I am way up one day & way down the next & I am way way down to-day.

JUNE 28. To-day, Sunday, I consecrate myself anew to Christ, & all my powers & energy, & I hencefourth leave Mr. Camp—I will *have nothing more to do with him accept as my* pastor, he has completely *disgusted me*, I shall not be "cosey" with him anymore. I feel hurt & pained to say so, but I *must!* So *here goes* good bye— — —*Adonis! good bye*!

JULY 30. [Brother] Charlie has been home, & Oh! dear! I feel so very sad over him, he has taken to reading Darwin & Herbert Spenser & others of the same order, he partly believes in "Evolution", & is investigating too far for his own good I am afraid. I must pray for him. I am going to read Darwin & H. S. myself to see what they are.

SEPTEMBER 27. Yesterday was an important day with me. I took a ride with Mr. Camp, & fought the whole time, he made a remark to the effect that all the girls were in love with him etc, which just set me off. & I stormed & stormed, my indignation knew no bounds, I was just wild. I told him—my pastor—"*that of all men I ever saw he* was the most *conceited.* I wanted to have nothing more to do with him", (which is a big he) I guess it is all up with us now, for sure, but I *hope* not.

OCTOBER 3. Mr. Camp spent this evening with me playing chess. I enjoyed it immensely, but do not understand how it is that he—a talented 44 yrs old bachelor, & a minister can want to spend so much time on me, a green innocent, country maiden.

◇ *1886* ◇

MAY 30. Mr. Camp, *my pastor, my friend, my companion, my brother, my "lover",* & my I don't know what else—has very much offended—nay *hurt* me. I am wounded to the heart's core. & have scarcely been civil to him since—nay I know I have been *very uncivil,* & I am sorry, & I was intending never to forgive him unless he apolizes, & to treat him coolly etc, & have until I feel that now he no longer is my *warm* friend, & I *am* sorry, for it is nice to be loved, & I *long* to be loved by everybody, & to be sought after also. But alas, I fear he has forever turned from me, & toward Puss who is all sweetness to him.

NOVEMBER 14. Have just returned from church, after having heard a splendid sermon, he is certainly a wonderful man! We shall miss him so much when he goes to Palestine, which will be about a month from now. Last week he did not come near me the whole week through, he evidently cares *no more* about me now than any one of "the flock", I am quite forgotten by him, do not even come into his thoughts I suppose, & if I do it is probably with unpleasantness. He need not pay me "duty calls" *any way*, I'd much rather he would not come at all, if he cannot "want" to come, he used once to "love" to come, alas! How did things get so! It is my fault I know but I could not seem to help it, I am real sorry now.

DECEMBER 11. To-day is my 'jour de naissance,' I am 22 years old! I can not realize it. It seems as though I could not have it so, why I am actually getting old, shall be on the down hill side of life before long! I wonder if I'll ever marry! I wonder if I shall live to grow old!

Dear diary! *He* is gone! Yes! *he* is gone, & I played my role of indifference & coolness to the last, he came down to say good bye in the morning, with his eyes full of tears & his voice unsteady, he could scarcely speak, he pressed my hand long & lovingly, I just let him hold it, but other wise I was: *Stony!* He probably thinks me the coldest & most ungrateful & uninteresting girl He ever saw, he little knew how I was longing to comfort him, & to unbend & be what I once was with him, but alas, I could not! I *hate myself*, I am a perfect goose! The most unsatisfactory piece of flesh God ever made it seems to me. I long so to be what I am not.

◇ *1887* ◇

APRIL 7. My dear diary, It seems to me that I can never tell you how & where the last three months have fled, but I must try at least—so here goes—Dec. 29th. 1886. I started for Brooklyn, to visit Annie Rhodes, & Feb. 25th. 1887 I returned home. Of course I had a charming time, & now it seems more like a delightful dream than a reality. I never had such a delightful winter or visit. Oh! It was glorious! I certainly did receive much favor, was invited out *all* the time nearly, & had lots of beaux. Mr. Nilsson was all attention & Mr. Boyd was very polite to me & I expect they will both be down here this summer, that is they *say* they shall come, but I shall not believe it until I see them. Men are such fickle things! I went to the theatre a good deal—for *that* is all *new* to me—Mr. Boyd seemed to me a clean pure minded man amid a lot of evil in men as I saw on the stage— Saw the best plays, & to lots of Art Collections. I took painting lessons of the Misses Cranbery on East 47th St, New York. Everyday for a month & worked real hard at it. I did enjoy it more than I *ever* can tell any one. Since my return I have painted quite a good deal, keeping up my practise, paint an hour or two every day if possible. I do hope that my kind Heavenly Father will prosper me in my chosen *profession* & beloved Art, for I do *love* it. & now what I want to do is to have a class in painting next fall & winter, & to sell my work, get orders etc. so that I may be able to help support myself & the family expenses to help bear. I am 22 years old, & I think that it is only right that I should be doing somethings, & I consecrate my work all to God's service.

APRIL. I must confess I find these fellows here *fearfully stupid*. they don't seem to know *beans*, & those that do, don't care for me. I suppose, at all events, I won't *stoop* for the sake of having a fellow, I don't care enough about it for that, I will bide my time, when I will have a fellow to wait upon me after my own heart. He must be *tall*, very *noble, manly, good, handsome*, dark quite, well educated, witty, smart, quick to sympathize, popular, sought after, learned, professional, *loving*, kind & true, there—when I meet *him* I shall indeed be happy, if he will only like me. This going out of an evening & having to come home alone with the girls is horrid I think. I am quite sick of it, I think it will be lovely to have a fellow at one's elbow ever ready to do one's bidding. I don't care to fall in love just yet, but I'd like to be loved by several first.

APRIL 29. Oh! How I *hate* myself! How I do *loathe* myself! How I do *long* to be good! I have been a wicked girl to-day, got provoked at Papa & spoke harshly to him, & Oh! How sorry I am now, how I long I could be to him the loving sweet daughter, that I *long* to be! God knows, I do *try*, but somehow, it all turns out wrong or crooked. I leave just the impression which I do not wish to leave. Oh! How I long to tell someone just how I feel, but there is not a soul in this whole world who seems to understand me. I am like my father very close mouthed, shutting up all my feelings & impulses for no eye to behold. I wish I could express myself. I *must* find my way to the interior of my father's heart. Oh! God,—do help me!

MAY 22. I'm very busy painting all the spare time I get, from nature. Our new pastor, Mr. C. Wilson was here and preached for us today. Do not know him much yet, guess there is no danger of his being at all like Mr. Camp. Guess he don't know how to *flirt*! It doesn't seem possible that our dear little "domonie" is forever gone from us. He will never have a substitute here, I fear, & at all event, not in my heart, not to me. Although false to me & I false to him, I shall always cherish his memory and association.

JULY 7. Mr. Boyd came this noon.

JULY 8. Mr. Boyd was called back again to the city to-day very unexpectedly. Do hope he is *sincere*. What pesky luck I've had! It could scarcely have been farther from my anticipation.

Never was more disappointed in my life! I looked like the Old Boy all the while Mr. B. was here. Everything went wrong almost. Never felt so flat over any thing in my life. Would not have believed Mr. B. so false & insincere, altho. I imagined him to be weak, (—but a *liar*.) I was the biggest fool. Can not imagine what got into me to do so! I have no faith in any *man*. I *long* to find one who could be true.

My teachers have gone, been here 3 weeks, which time, has been spent out of doors all day sketching. I have learned a good deal. Oh! Mr. Boyd, if *you* had only been satisfied & pleased I should have been perfectly satisfied with the summer. I wonder if he is thoroughly disgusted with me & I wonder if he'll notice me next winter, & I wonder if we will ever understand each other. Oh! I do hope so.

SEPTEMBER 21. Another ten cents invested, & my 6th Book commenced, I shall have quite a library if I keep on. Had no idea that I should ever become such an *author*, & can remember when I would have laughed at myself for keeping a diary, although this I commenced when I was 15 years old, with no thought of keeping it up, but I am so glad I have, as it has been a great source of pleasure to me, & an escape valve for my pent up feelings, beside being a valuable record for reference. I feel quite a responsibility at having so much *trash* in the house & would not have any one find it out for anything. I sometimes think I will *burn* them all up, then again I hate to do so. So I keep them, but I think if I were to be taken seriously ill, I would get someone to burn them all before my eyes. I would not like to die before these books go out of existence, they would be shocking revelations of my inner self, which I never wish to be revealed. I know that Papa thinks I am light & *frivorless* to a shameful degree, with never a thought deeper than *fun* & *goings*, but he's mistaken!

Annie Rhodes has spent 6 weeks with me again this summer. I go there in the winter of course she comes here in the summer. This to *my mind* is an *excellent* arrangement. I know I learn a great deal up there in the winter beside cultivating society manners & seeing how people of wealth & luxury live, & also by attending the places of amusement that I do, then there is so much to learn from observation. & the general rush & push of the crowds is inspiring to a country girl, besides this I form many pleasant relations, in friendships, which will be a life long blessing. I have lots of attention from nice young gentlemen there & here in winter I don't even see one except Chas Cook, who is the biggest "chestnut" out, & a perfect *bore*.

Mr. Boyd paid me a short visit. He found me "head over-heals" in paint. I appeared to him in a Mother Hubbard wrapper, all paint-paint-paint. The next day was hot as love & he did nothing but wipe off the perspiration & slap the mosquitos. In fact—I think he was quite disgusted with every *darn* thing he saw, & I feel *instinctively* he turned up his aristocratic nose at everything. He is very nice & handsome & the fool knows it, although I do like him very much, still I think he is just such a "snob". I am very sorry that circumstance should have happened as they did, but I can't help it. It is a good test to his sincerity & friendship, a fellow who can't stand a little paint &

mosquitoes is not worth noticing. But I *like* him—so much! I think we were congenial—he touched my nature.

The *Future* is blackness & darkness for me. I *dread* to face it, but I *must* & God helping me I *will* be *brave*. I can not bear to think of living without my kind earthly guardians, as I suppose some day I must, when they go Home. If it were not wrong I should want to go too. For what has this world to offer for me besides *them—nothing*. I must work for my living & go through life *alone*, & I *dread* it. Not that I am not willing to work for I *am*, if I only knew how to start myself. I feel so *useless*, & long for action. I ought to understand business affairs, & Papa's business affairs too, but I don't. I ought to be earning money *now*, instead of being a drain on Papa's purse, but I am *not*, & don't see how I can either, this is the worst of it. Once started I think I'd get along O.K. If I could only feel that I will always have a home here, in *this* home which my every thought & even fibre of my being *loves so well*, & which I *know* I could keep up. I'd work till my fingers were sore rather than see it *sold* or run down. I'd work the garden on a paying scale, not as a pastime or pleasure. I'd sell the fruit & rent the barn & hire the shop & keep a few nice quiet boarders rather than see an *inch* of it sold. I could keep a select school also. Oh—why can't life glide along just as it does now, forever this sweet, quiet, peaceful home life? Without rude & harsh awakenings & changes, cruel & bitter, Oh, I feel as if I should like to die when I think of the anguish which I know must await me. Why must there be a cruel end to all this? How can I ever live without my earthy parents? I've no husband, I'm not engaged even, I have no one else in the world to whom I can look for the love which they bear me. I don't suppose I can ever love any other man *half* what I love my father, be he *perfection*. I *do* want to be *independent* & *useful*, very much, to have the assurance that I am not dependent upon any one for existence, save God.

OCTOBER 12. Summer is over—yes—gone—& but for one thing—it has been *perfect*—one thing—& that means all—I can not tell *why* I care—I have all heart could wish & plenty of beaux—why would I give them all to recall those unfortunate days when I risked so much so thoughtlessly—but I never dreamed he would notice or care what I wore if he valued my friendship—I am not in love—only I liked him so—I understood him & I feel he understood me—It always made me so *mad* when the girls called him "fashion plate" & said "he would never look at a girl who did not dress well" Oh how indignant I would be—yes—somehow—I *believed* in Mr. B. as a pure honest, noble fellow. I like him better than all the other men I know—& while I am not in love with him—I would give the friendship of them all for his—& I can't tell *why*—he is not as handsome as some of my friends who are really devoted to me— he is not rich I know—for he is the son of a *baker* in *Greenpoint* & that can't mean wealth—but I don't care a *rap* about that—I had riches all my life—I don't measure my friends by riches— but by character—I am not thinking of *marrying* but if I were— I'd rather marry a man whom I could love & trust without a penny than a millionaire whom I did not love. I think I shall never marry now—I'll give my life to my aged parents. Mr. Wick talks of marriage—*bah*—why do I hate it so from *him*—Axel talks of marriage—no—no Axel—*I won't*—when other fellows talk of love to me—it is so absurd—but *his face* Mr. B's looms up & I *can't* help it. Oh—shall I wish I had never seen him—? Has he crossed my life to blight it—to knock from me my natural youth & joyous gaiety—somehow I feel I have lived years of trouble since he left here—Oh—May God spare the bitterness to know he is false to our friendship—& may God help me to behave & to be strong—for I feel I can never trust *any* man again—& I don't want to loose my faith in manhood— & may God forgive him the wrong he has done to a little country lass who was so trusting. I'll trust him yet—until I *know* he is false—he has a right to discard our friendship—but no gentleman of *honor* would do it without an honest cause & a fair understanding—I do not blame him in one sense for wanting a girl to look nice when she is with him—but I do blame him for condemming a girl just for her clothes if that is all—I wonder if it is all—can there be anything else?—no—I feel it was just that—I, who am so great a believer in neatness & sweetness

& simplicity in a girls house dress I—to think I should be con-
demned for the lack of it—I did it deliberately & to try him—
it is hard—& false & a *mistake*—but too late—I will trust him—
& see what he says this winter—I will try to be all I would like
him to *think* me—I will make of my self all I can for his sake—
not that I love him—but because I wish to be true to our
friendship—

Oh—Mr. B.—you have touched me from a girl into a *woman*,
give me back my *girlhood*—give me back the *something* I know
not what to call it—that is gone. P. S. so this is my secret—
the first I ever have had in my whole life—my secret to hide
& to bury & to tear out of my life if I can—no one must guess
it. His name never crosses my lips—People say to me sometimes Why Annie no girl in her senses would be so indifferent
to the attentions of fine men as you are—why *don't* you marry
some of them & I answer—I shall never marry—I am the one
to take care of my father & mother in their old age—

I see myself a foolish girl—full of high strung foolishness—
yet behind it all—& through it all I feel deeply seriously &
with great force. I am not a shallow girl though I am so full of
all kinds of feeling—& enjoy life so much that I am enthusiastic
but I feel that I am not a *fool*—but I shall be one if I allow such
a man as Mr. B—to ruin my joyous life—no I'll fight it down—
& live for my Father who needs me so much.

◇ *1888* ◇

JANUARY 11. Chas here to-night. Much to Papa's disgust
He *is* a bore sometimes, as well as *pesky* handy at others. What
an old codger he is! Lazy as the old scratch! Should think he'd
get tired of chasing up the girls & always getting left. Mr. Camp
seems to remember some of his old friends still. Madam Rumor
says that he is engaged to Pussie—well "mebee he is, but I
doubt it," at all events I think they are matched as far as flirting
goes.

JANUARY 13. I wonder why I am such a stupid gump! Papa
is smart & a thinker, Mama is all that is sweet, gentle & lovable

in woman, yet I—their child, am an old stupid blockhead about most things! Pshaw!!! I am way down in the mind compared to where I ought to be. I *hate* myself. I am a complete failure anyhow! I wonder for what I was born sometimes!

JANUARY 31. Does God not require us to use & increase our talents, great or small? May it not be possible that my Art is yet to help me fight the battle of life? & should I not prepare myself to meet the emergency? I never expect to marry, & if I *did* I had a thousand times rather toil for my own living than marrying for a *living*. It looks reasonable that in a country of 66000 more women than men, all women can not marry, unless they turn Mormons pretty rapidly! So should not the 66000 women be prepared to be independant and useful? is this *unwomanly*? No, *I* think not. I just *don't* care what the world thinks! If my one poor, wea, mite of a talent happens to be an artistic one; why I can't help it, I suppose its best. I'd much *rather* it had been music as I love both well, but I did not have the choosing!

I don't see what gets into me! I must be a *goose*! but I can't help it. When it comes to talking *trash*, meaningless nothings, *nonsense—then* I can beat the monkeys in Central Park I believe, & this is often so when I *really* am *thinking most* of serious things! I fairly *hate* myself! sometimes, I wonder if God has any respect for me when I live such a double life! Darn it. There! I feel better & there's no harm in it. Webster ought to be *hung* for not putting such an expressive & harmless slang word in the dictionary.

I wonder how much Papa is going to *shell out* for me to go to the city with? He is always very generous, it quite scares me when I think how much he "shelled" out for me last winter. Gum! I did spend a pile of money! Lots more than I am worth! I feel *meaner* than dirt to take any, when I know what a pile of bills he has to pay this month, & I *run up* most of them too, especially when I know it may be a long day before I can earn enough to pay him back. What an unsatisfactory thing it is to have *girls* for children any way! They are honestly more cost & bother than they are worth, & then how fearful it would be if I should not amount to any thing after all! Oh! Agony! Just to think of it! Suppose I should turn out a *fizzle*—God forbid! I certainly *am* not a *genius*! I feel not a *bit* like one! & If I ever *do* amount to any thing, it'll be through, hard work, perserverance & *push*, & the grace of God. I suppose I *am* frivolous, I'm young & naturally like life, & gaiety, & what is the harm any way? Isn't there a time for all things? & don't even the wisest people have to sow their oats sometime? & Isn't it better the soonest sowed? No— this isn't logical, I'll admit. I wish it didn't cost so much to educate a girl! Now a boy could work his way through life lots easier than a girl without a trade & are lots less bother to their parents! Oh dear! My senses alive!!! Pshaw!!! What a puzzle life is any way! Well, I must not use any more *such shocking bad* language! I am quite demoralizing!

APRIL. 6. "Home again, from a foreign shore" [Brooklyn], & indeed, there is no place like home. I have had many a good time since I have been away, & have had what would be called "an elegant time", but to be *frank*, there has been a *heartache* at the bottom of it all which has destroyed all of its gloss, *no one guesses* of this, it is safely hidden in my own breast, & no ear of mortal shall ever know it. It is all my own fault as usual, it always is, all due to a moment's reckless folly, impulsiveness! Oh! How I long to *undo*, to *correct*, roll away the clouds, to wipe out misunderstandings! I wonder if one who repents & who *mends* herself, who struggles to keep herself to the ideal, if she ever has opportunities to make *up*, to regain that which she has lost? Oh! why should it not be so? & yet how *can* it be. Are not *we* lost *forever* to *each other*? Is there any hope of reunion of sympathies? Any chance of mutual flow of soul again? Any possibility of again ascending the throne of perfection in *his* eyes? & yet it should be so. But I don't see how it can *ever possibly*. I am humilated beyond expression! I am filled with remorse, & yet—should I not be *glad* that I have escaped danger, that I have found out the true strength of character of the man, should I care about the friendship of a man who would throw over a girl for *one* fault, & when he was not *sure* of that either? Should character not demand *respect*, should friendship not require its courtesies? Should former delicious joys be for naught?

"I'm young and naturally like life." (*Courtesy of Richard Taylor*)

(Mr. Boyd is the man I refer to—he cut me dead this winter—
all because—(I suppose) the way I *looked* that day—paint &
mosquitoes—) Ah!——alas, how frail is man, & how weak is
woman. How uncertain & fickle is man. How false & unjust!
But I——*will* be *true* to *him*, even though he has played me
false! No world shall ever cross my lips against him! God grant
us an explanation! —My heart is lonely & sad—ah! How I long
for love. I have spent 9 weeks I guess in the city. I have studied
at the studio again very hard, & very faithfully have been studying from life & from caste.

Axel——ah! How can I say it, did just the other thing.
Yes—he offered me his "heart, soul, body & his all", he asked
me to be his wife. &—I refused him—why—said I did not love
him enough! Oh—don't I? How terrible if I should make a
mistake in this matter! He is good & true, & I honor, respect
& *like* him immensely, but I *don't* think I love him as he ought
to be loved. (I know in my heart I'd rather have one hour with
Mr. B—than a day with Axel) what does it mean?

MAY 1. Have just returned from the Young Peoples Lyceum
(litterary) where, being the chairman & leader of several committees I had to *push* the thing a good deal. We girls a lot of us
are off for a ride after May Flowers, a *"hen* party," this place is
mostly hens, I call it "she-town." I wish such a thing as a real
desirable good-looking man might pop in upon us here & cause
some little excitement, it would be such a variety & add a little
spice to S.H. It is so tame & quiet here, so devoid of any
sudjestion of romance or adventure & I must admit I've a failing
for *both*. I wish some nice young man, my ideal, as it were, would
drop his "hand, heart soul & his all" at my feet. Some one
whom the other girls are *"aching* for." But—what nonsense for
me a S. School *teacher*. I'm ashamed of myself, but its *true anyway*.

MAY 7. Pussie is engaged to marry Mr. Camp, three years
ago I little thought it, now I was prepared for it—well—Heaven
bless her—sweet girl, is what my heart says. I love her dearly
& am glad she is to be so happy. I expect my future to be
darkness. I have such a brilliantly happy Past. I have discarded
my lovers & now I have only my Art for the Future to look to

now. I may never marry, I have no feeling intense enough for matromony for any of my friends. & I am getting old I am 23 years old! Life has only one bright spot for the future after my present friends are all married, & my parents gone *Home*, & left alone in the world. Life has but one & I thank God for one, this is my *Art*.

JULY 5. The 4th is over——ah—how different this night from one year ago! —ah John B. why *did* you do so—ah, Annie B. why *did you* do so,—well the Past shall throw no shadow o'er the Present, except for the severe lesson it has taught me—oh If I had only been my *true* self, why did I so deceive him! Why was I permitted to so wrong my self & him. It *was* a wrong to him, for I liked him & he liked me, he might have proposed to me some day had he been favorably impressed.

Load of people here yesterday very festive times about, I was at Nell Adams tennis party,—darn poor time though.——no fellows here & no romances weaving. I am very busy & do not mind so much, my Art takes up my leasure, but I *do* long for some romantic affairs, some "tenderness by moonlight," some congenial soul.

JULY 10. Darn it all! there! I feel disatisfied with myself & every thing generally to-night. How I wish I had a beau, not that I want to get married, but he'd be so handy, & it would be so nice to have some one to fall back on when one wants to invite in a few friends or go off on a stroll or cruise to have some one to depend upon for an escort, Pshaw! what an inconvenience men are & yet what a convenience! Botheration!

JULY 20. Good grief! if I haven't had a pickle! Mr. Smith called on me this evening, his first call & I thought he never *would* go, what a sticking plaster!

I never saw anything to beat his stupidity! I thought I should have to ask him to go! half past ten! first call & such a quiet sober man! ginks!

SEPTEMBER 7. One thing which stands out most prominent & conspicious in the events of the summer, & which has cast a damper over everything, which I can scarcely realize is yet true, it—oh—how can I bear to write it, Mr. Camp, the friend of my girl-hood, the pastor of my first years of communion, the sunshine of the village when he was here, the betrothed of my dearest friend Pussie, whom he was to marry in October, has cut his throat and jumped into a cistern where he was found dead, Oh! It is so *terrible*! He left S.H. some 2 or 3 years ago, went to Palestine, returned & became engaged to Pussie, but he never came down to see her, she would see him in Brooklyn. For about six weeks he has been sick, with inflamatory rhumatism, & irresyplus. They suppose the disease must have struck into his brain & made him unresponsible for the act, but there are many strange things about it, many hard & harsh things said about his being forced into a marriage which he felt wholly improper & even worse things about reasons he dared not marry on account of another woman, & all sorts of scandal, which is simply terrible to hear. Poor Pussie! My heart aches for her!

SEPTEMBER 25. Mr. Wick has been my special "affair" this week, we went sailing, & such fun, I "stole off", in the sly, Mama knew not a thing of where I was going, or Papa. The novelty of being off with a young unmarried minister & indeed a—more than friend—a suitor—the thought that Papa knew nothing of it, & Mama ditto, & the responsibility of the boat in a wind & the romance of the whole thing was—delicious. I made the best of it, & oh—my—the things he said to me the things he sudjested & left unsaid the things I said to him, the— well—to be frank, he as good as told me that I am the girl he meant to marry. I have not meant to flirt with him, I have not meant to do him wrong & I told him I "am a celabate," & all that, I refused to continue the correspondence this winter. He is a good young fellow of promise, but I could no sooner think of marrying him that I could think of *flying*!

OCTOBER 18. Have just returned from a Republican meeting, I am a Democrat because my father is one, but I am determined to be something because of my own convictions so I go to hear both sides, Papa & I have the most animated discussions, I naturally am soaked in Democratic law, but I am trying to open my eyes to see unpredujiced both sides.

I *long—long*—for what? —What *is* this craving of my inmost soul, some thing which cries for satisfaction but has never had it. can it be a—congenial spirit?—a soul akin to mine.—a heart that feels for me, a pulse that beats with mine? Shall this craving never be satisfied!

◊ *1889* ◊

JANUARY 22. Have just returned from the "social", of the Christian Endeavor Society, I had to read. They gave me hearty applause. I did dread it, but the Lord carried me through. I played the organ last Wed. & Friday, & at one of the Union meetings, I seem to be developing in all quarters, never thought I'd be an organist, or eloqutionist. It takes *consecration & nerve, will*—especially if one inherits *diffidence* & bashfulness as I do.

SEPTEMBER 25. Axel came to see me several times & we walked & talked & oh—how he did *plead* again,—that is the fourth time he has proposed to me & four times he has been rejected.

NOVEMBER 2. My *Art*—how my soul throbs in response to its longings & aspiration—how I yearn to *do, well*—how I yearn to be a painter who can praise God with my work—who can paint to tell a moral! Yes—it is my great comfort— In my sorrow & remorse & trouble I usually can forget myself in my art. I want to be able to help Papa this winter by helping myself—I want to earn by my work. I do *hate* this *dependance*—& shall be glad when *woman* shall be as free to independance as man, & shall try harder than ever to earn money—not for it-self—but for *independance & helpfulness*.

NOVEMBER 9. John W. Boyd!—ah!—what a winter of joy— also another winter of pain—does that name call up—I never liked man so well—surely—even now after two years of cruel silence—I long to see his pure noble brow—I dislike his big- otted aristocratic notions, his snoberiness, & his pharisuical ac- counts of himself—but I love the memory of his sweet, blue eyes—so wistful & admiring—but of Axel—I certainly don't think I can engage myself to him feeling this way about an- other—yet I am not in *love* with either—J.B. hurt my pride—

& I long to conquer him & bring him to me again—not to marry him.

◇ *1893* ◇

MAY 28. Shall I or shall I not add another page to this my long neglected diary. I have given it up long ago, three years since I have written in it & why—partly because I began to feel it was a useless waste of time & eye sight & partly because I was so sick at heart that I no longer had any heart to write— but lately, it has been heavy upon me to cast one more page into the record—I only excuse myself for adding another page to it all—by the thought that I shall guard it from sight & since I have been so silly I may as well put in one more line to my history—to perhaps—complete a work unfinished—& then too—the old longing seems to be upon me to *tell* some one & that I *never do.* So I resort again as when a child to you my Diary—how can I tell it all—three years of my life has passed since I last looked upon this book—they have been years of prosperity, years of comforts, of *out ward* free heartedness & yet—to you *alone*, my Diary, I confess that they have been years of mute suffering, mute speechless pain, struggle—do I even to my self admit that I *love*—perhaps I do not—I will never admit it *any way*, until my love is asked for—but this I will admit—I do not understand it—but this I do know that some how this man holds a sway over me I cannot shake off—for seven long years I have *tried* to forget—oh—why did I ever meet him? why did I ever go to Brooklyn? The history of my life for the past seven years is really but the history of a new life, at first bright & beautiful—then crushed, hidden, stran- gled, tortured, always trying to smoother it, but never suc- ceeding, until now, at last, it burst out afresh—I met him 7 years ago—I believe I *touch* his spirit—but something happened six years ago which separated us—I believed he cared not— for it was his priviledge as a *man* to seek—not *mine*—he sought me not—I tried to forget—I had other lovers, manly noble men—whom I would have liked to marry if I *could* have loved them—but ever would come up before me those sweet deep blue eyes—& my whole woman's nature would recoil at the thought! *Never*, it sickened me—better live true to my better nature than sell my body to be the wife of a man who cannot win my heart. After six years of silence we are brought to-gether this winter at Euchre—(it was at Euchre I first met him). — we become friendly again—It seems to me I can recall every word we ever spoke & every gesture he ever made—He is little—I never like *little* men—he is not handsome—he is not witty—nor brilliant—he is of no more aristocratic birth than am I—He is only the son of a Baker in Greenpoint—the girls all tell me he is proud & selfish & fickle—I'll not believe it. I may never see him again—he does not care enough even for me to write. —he evidently cares for me only as a passing friendship— he probably has plenty of girls—city butter-flies—perhaps he even may consider me beneath him—because I am a country girl—but I can assure him he is wrong there.

These years have passed—neither of us have married—the tie of friendship is renewed—but what does it mean—some-times I ask myself am I the victim of a great passionate love, which can never die until I die—a love which shakes the very center of my being—? only to be the toy of a man of the world? for they tell me he is such—& is not a *pure* man—They *lie*— he *is* pure. Oh—why can I not read his heart—I sometimes think I do—but how can I dare to trust only my intuitions or my interpretations—He says he is coming here again—oh— unless he come *true* fair & honest—may God keep him away forever—for I fear to trust my self—I was willing to almost die for him the last time I saw him.—I ask from him no more than I can give—I can give much—my nature is deep & such as I love but once—but no—I dare not think he cares,—& so—I *will not* love him, never, until I have the *right*—no—I will tear it out by the roots—at least it shall *not grow*—I can keep my secret—& be true to it,—& as long as I feel this way—never shall think of marriage.

Why—when I consider how little I know of this man—& yet I feel that I *know* him—why I don't—he may be the very opposite from what I think—I do not even know or have any idea of what his business is, I never thought or cared to ask—He is not a religious man—I know I should be unhappy to marry a man with whom I could not make a Christian home. Could I expect that from a man brought up in the swim of city society, whose worldly tastes have been formed—who is far too old to be expected to be easily moved—& yet—this one thing I *must* have.

I know not but that I am only the victim of my own sentimental loving romantic nature—perhaps this is all only an ideal I am loving after all & did I come to know him more intimately perhaps I would not like him at all.

JUNE 7. No letter from Mr. B. yet—he liked me "well enough" for a passing friend—but I *can not* be in his thought as he is in mine else he could not refrain from sending me some token.

JULY 2. A letter from Mr. B.—he says he leaves for Shelter Island on Sat. next—& would like to "make his call" on the following Wed. now does he mean by that, that his vacation interests center in Shelter Island & he only proposes a call on me—? Why does he go to Shelter Island at all if he *cares* to be here? Does he care? Why does he come at all then?

JULY 4. I replied to-day to Mr. B's note—I begin to tremble—Oh—how I have prayed that if this is a *pure* thing I may be permitted to have it—if it be a love which is after gain, imaginary wealth, *anything*—but a pure love—that it may be taken away from me—& yet—how foolish I talk—for what right have I to suppose for a moment that it is anything but a passing friendship—oh—the agony of it!!!

JULY 12. Mr. B. came to-day—I took him to drive to the Park. To-night—I took him sailing—I think I am a trifle disappointed—altho—we have to-morrow yet in which to *really* get nearer to each other—& then I can better *tell*.

JULY 14. Rose at 5 A.M. to the gental sound of a peble & *him* seranade under my window—we went to the East Hampton Beach—it was *glorious*—we learned more & more of each other—got a good deal nearer— After dinner he came up &

we were alone & *talked*—& say good bye—until a week from to-morrow—when he calls on his way to the city—

JULY 16. Have been trying to consider about Mr. B—why don't I throw him up! I am not fascinated by any thing about him— Indeed I see no inducement for me to *allow* my self to fall in love with him, except that I love him with all his faults—

JULY 23. I am lead to believe that he is in *earnest*—but he *works slowly*—& *surely*—but I am not so sure about his sureness as I am about his slowness. I know Mr. Wick—with half his *chances* would have come to the point—but not so Mr. B. & I am glad—as I certainly had no answer ready for him—I am convinced but he wishes to woo me little by little, giving both himself & me a chance to realize what we are doing—each step is accompanied by a pause between—a time for reflection as it were—sometimes I wonder if this *really is* the man I have *longed* & suffered for so long—for now that his friendship is mine I begin to fear lest I may have been hugging an *ideal* Mr. B. May God solve the riddle & prevent me from making a mistake—

DECEMBER 28. I have been to Brooklyn, with its delights in the social way. Mr. B. was very polite to me in the city— yet it is absolutely certain to me that he does not *care* for me— no man who cared would let the woman he cared for go away with no more manifestation of right, no seeking for her company in the future, no request to write, etc—Surely he does not think I could be satisfied with that cold, easy passive sort & call it *love*—*never*, I am capable of a grand passion— The night of my birthday eve, I cried, & sobbed until I was weak—I struggled & agonized with this thing—& finally after hours of torture I took away his portrait locked it away in my private draw with all his things—& resolved to *forget*—to strangle & drown this *fearful fearful* grip he has had upon me—I will bury him from my life—*forever*—I have kissed his photo—*once*—& for the *last*—& hid it from my sight—& now it only remains for me to be brave—& forget—God help me—for I feel my weakness—I am at best only a woman—I leave the problem of my life in His Hands to solve.

NEW YEARS EVE. The family have gone to service—I felt

like staying home with my thoughts, I wanted to be alone a few moments & 'ere the old beloved year died I wanted to *hug* it a little—it has been so sweet—but only a little for I dare not trust myself—Six years ago to-night I met him— One year ago & I had no hope of ever seeing him to speak to again—to-night I am full of enjoyment of his friendship—& yet I am fighting the old fight to forget him— If he knew—I wonder would he pity me—I could not bear that—no he must never know—cut out my tongue first! He sent me a magazine—how I sulked off by my self on the shore & found a big rock & there greedily devoured it—& gloated over the marked places as if trying to make them tell me his thought. I am sure he cares not—his cold calm passionless friendship is the most deadly thing he can give me—& yet I want it—& I wish him well.

◇ 1894 ◇

JANUARY 21. Just returned from morning service. Mr. Wilson preached about "letting up" on the cares & strain of life & living easier, enjoying life more—I mean to do so—it is my message from God to me to-day.

FEBRUARY 5. Mr. Boyd came again to S.H. to-day. We have been sleighriding all the after-noon—I wonder if I am liking him *less*—I almost hope so—& yet—if I but knew *him* better—he certainly impressed me less to-day—I think—I don't think he has a fine face—nor good *indications* of many of the traits of character I like best—but I may be mistaken—I want to get at Mr. B.'s *religious* views—& I must to-morrow—

On Friday morning—I was convinced he was pleased with his visit but was not in any sense in love—or particularly interested—but at night I received a letter written from the hotel—in which he strikes a higher note than he has ever put in words—I am a little doubtful now as to his position of indifference, but I—am I becoming indifferent—to be sure his coolness has driven me to the verge of rebellion & I wonder if I am finding out that I have been mistaken that I am not in love with him—only with an ideal J.B. I *must* find out—for I

would not hurt him—& I must be careful now what I do to
encourage or discourage— Oh that Mr. Wick would come upon
the scene that I might compare them & know *finally* which is
the man— Do I approve of him—his aims in life? What are
they? I cannot marry a man whose aim is *"social success"*—that
may be all right for some—but not for me—

FEBRUARY 14. Such a lovely valentine came to-day from
Mr. B——so sweet & tender of him—but Oh,—What shall I
do about it—I feel I must be making up my mind—I feel as
though I should choke when I consider it—it appauls me so—
& yet—oh—what a queer girl I am. If he does succeed—he
succeeds absolutely— All doubts & querries go forever.

Where & what is J.B. doing to-day I wonder? Can see his fair
forehead & bushy hair now as he sits in his father's pew—I
always have to bob my own to get a glimpse of him from Annie
R's pew—how my heart is in my mouth when I sit with Mrs.
C—who sits directly back of him. She has been *so* good—so
kind to me—to *us*—forget she told me not to think of *him* as
any but a friend—she said one day "Annie don't you marry
him—he is nice enough & all that—but he is not half good
enough for you—his father is poor—he has broken one girls
heart by jilting her—don't you marry *him*, Annie—" in fun of
course this was said—yet in earnest—I care not for his poverty
or his father's—I care not that he may have been engaged
once—but I do care if he *deliberately* threw over a good girl—
& killed her by it—but I *won't* believe that— Many an engagement has been entered into unwisely—where a man is
young & unsettled in his views—I will not believe evil of him
unless I *know* from his own lips if it is so—even then I'd forgive
if he tell me frankly—

FEBRUARY 27. Gardie was down to tea last night with his
girl Maud—& two such happy mortals you never saw! He positively couldn't keep his hands off of her. I think they were
absolutely ridiculous. I *like demonstration*—I like affection—&
affectionate people—but I *don't* like to see the thing made *too*
common for vulgar curiosity to laugh at, for the world to jeer
at—& Gardie is certainly a bit *too much* for good taste—I have

been wondering if with all their *show* of devotion if the *love* was any deeper than mine would be—for I know I should not act like that before people—nor behind them either for that matter—I wonder if ever the time will come when J.B. will feel the right to place his *hands* on *me* as Gardie does on Maud——I feel as if I should choke to think of it—why I feel as if I should die of—what—the pain of it or the bliss of it, which is it— Is bliss akin to pain? —oh—goodness—It makes me breathe hard for I feel as if I was going to smoother—at the very thought—for he *never* has laid so much as his little finger on me—& even a shake hands makes me all *creepers*—I don't see how I should ever stand a *caress*—& yet I could have even longed to lay a cool gentle kiss upon his fair open forehead— What a queer mixture of passion & mood & hopes we are—!

I don't suppose he ever thinks of these things—& yet I bet he has kissed many other girls—& hugged them too—but not a shadow of familarity has he even offered me—I respect him for that—& yet at times his coldness drives me wild. —I wonder if there is any other girl in town who has had the lovers I have had—who have *kept* sacred their lips & their *person*—for the one who at last may succeed—? Whenever they have begged for favors always—his blue eyes—& pure brow would rise up—& although I knew I might never see him again—yet I couldn't let them place their lips upon mine—I may be silly—no doubt I am. Most girls take those things naturally & all they can get—*but I can't*—it seems like being false to my womanliness—I know Puss would think me a *fool*—she says a man does not appreciate those things from a girl—but I can't help it—I shall let no man but *one* give me my first *lip* kiss—& if not he—then *no man*—

MARCH 18. One year ago this week—*we met*—what a joyous year—! how I have enjoyed his friendship! Clouds seem to be trying to gather, letters from Mrs. Conklin & Annie R. saying—Oh Annie—drop him—he is not worthy—! they like him for me as a *friend*—but they hear rumors—they hear that *his* Mother is *talking* & that she thinks I am rich—(I know he doesn't for I have told him so—& I don't care what she thinks)—I have

a very very small opinion of *her*—a proud—haughty—extravagant, vain, woman! a woman who lacks the inate refinement
of a lady born—she savors of the *new rich* kind—of *pork &
pomposity*—Oh—I wish he was not *her* son.

MARCH 24. I wonder if *he* will send me an Easter Greeting—
why should he—& yet if he *cares*—as I do he will—I *must not*
send him anything—it must come *only* from him—he is a *man*—
I only a woman & must wait—I *cannot & will not ever* put him
under the slightest necessity to do me a courtesy— He must
woo—if he *wants* to win—he will—

MAY 26. He never seems to *care* enough for me to put himself
out in the least—he takes things as they *happen*—not *seeks* or
make an *effort* to get to me—now he came here last summer—
but *only* when it was his vacation—he came here last winter—
but on his vacation—not a Sunday since or before—he says he
is coming this summer—*on his vacation*—now I am tired of this
sort of thing—I am not a *vacation* girl—if he does not care
enough to come down for a Sunday—I think he cares very little.
I had best quite drop him *entirely*—& try once more to forever
shake him from my thoughts & life— But I do love Mr. B—
oh—my Diary—how I would scorn to own it to *any* human
being—*never*—*never* will I reveal it not even to my mother—a
girl should never reveal her love until it has been asked for. For
his sake I try to keep my mind & thoughts clean & pure—I try
to *be* what I think he would have me—& oh—*how* can I write
it, the foul charge A.R. made against him—that he keeps a bad
woman in N.Y.—& that he is a man of the world *entirely*—&
also that he laughs to people about me & says he can marry me
for the asking! No. I don't believe he said it.

JUNE 2. Have received a letter from him—in which he
says—he wants to be considered my truest & best friend—&
I must not murmur if he desires to devote all his time to me—
Oh—what joy & peace that letter has brought—how my soul
leapt for joy—! He wants me to assure him that he may come
& will be welcomed—else he will not feel justified in coming—
I shall *not* do that—it is unwomanly for me to write him to come
in that way—he should *dare*—he should be bold to win his

way—I cannot lay my self in his path that way—he must find
me—seek me—

SEPTEMBER 5. Words—words—words—what vain things
when the heart is on *fire to express* a world of meaning— I have
so much to say I cannot say it—this is the most eventful summer
of my life—at once the most anxious & the happiest—I have
so many events to record I scarcely know where to begin—Papa
ill—unutterably sad—this passing away of the aged—dear dear
Papa—how I yearn to make him young—then underneath, it
all—there has risen a great & holy joy a deep sublime sweetness—a *wonderful, unexpected,—unspeakable* joy—for on my
third finger of my left hand flashes a *beautiful* diamond pledge
of my own true lover's love—what is it I am writing? It sounds
like a myth!!! I scarce know how it has all come about, I only
know, he came, he saw, he conquered—it happened on Mon-
tauk Pt.—on a glorious day—the 19th of July. & strange to
say—(what a puzzle I am any way)—I had *truely no answer
ready—after all my years of love & anguish I had no answer ready—
I was troubled with doubts, doubts lest I did not really love him—
only the ideal*—doubts lest I should find myself disappointed if
I were engaged to him, doubts lest I really loved Mr. Wick with
a calmer but more *right kind* of love—but oh—I am so glad to
say—they have gone—*he stole* them away—by his sweet love
making—he taught me my own heart—he *won* me at the critical
moment—I love—deep—*surely* & oh so tenderly—& with him
I am at *rest,* happy—I *question* not—surely this is perfect love—
I know he is not what I thought I was looking for—he is not
rich, he is not handsome, he is not witty—nor yet brilliant—
he is not a man of position in the eyes of the world   he is
simply & only John Boyd—a man from *Greenpoint*—a wage-
winner—a good—honest—noble *man.*

◇   ◇

Afterword

Annie Cooper and John Boyd were married on February 20, 1895. It was a wedding tinged with sadness, for her father had died the previous October.

The marriage was remarkably "modern" in some respects. In a letter to John on November 12, 1894, during their engagement, Annie set the stage:

"One thing I am ready to accept of you—& you must be of me— that is, your own individuality. It is *your own & as such* I will try to keep it & study it & adapt myself to it, but not try to make it like someone else's or my own ideal. Will you be that liberal with me dear?"

She described the success of this approach in her journal two years later: "In taking for our rule for each 'freedom of opinion yet with mutual respect' we do not grow into a narrow groove, the stultifying of one to satisfy the other, but we establish a broader base & agree sometimes to disagree & yet cemented by our common love we are at peace." This happy arrangement lasted for over forty years, until John Boyd's death in 1939.

Annie's diaries, as they had been, ended with her engagement. During the months just before her marriage she poured her feelings into letters to John, writing him in the frank, open manner she had previously reserved only for the journals.

After her marriage, Annie began to keep a simple record of daily events. The urge to write more sometimes overcame her and she yielded, then regretted it, as she noted in August of 1897: 'My feelings get the best of me if I attempt to write; therefore, as I did not intend this book for a record of my heart's experiences, I dare not often write in it. I mean only to record events & am frightened sometimes by what I write."

The precise nature of these fears is detailed in a postscript to her youthful diary, written when Annie was 33: "Aunt Hattie no doubt meant well in starting me upon this set of book keeping, but it seems to me today a great mistake. I am tormented now with fear lest it fall

The Long Island Herald House (*Courtesy of Joan Baren*)

into other hands & yet have a kind of dread to burn it up. I feel I must & ought & yet I hate to do it today & so it goes, from week to week, & I wonder when my strength will be sufficient to the task. It is like burning myself up & yet far better to burn than have it fall into other hands to be laughed at or to hurt.

"I have laughed until I ached over the first books. The others are written in *blood*, so vitally real they are to me. Yet I cannot realize that I am the foolish child, so full of human passions of all kinds that it reveals. May God guard these books—& burn them when it is time."

Annie and John Boyd were the parents of a son, Cooper, born in 1898; and a daughter, Nancy, born in 1902. Mother and children spent their summers in Sag Harbor, with John joining them from Brooklyn on his vacations. The large house on Main Street where Annie had grown up was rented out after Mrs. Cooper's death, and Annie took a small eighteenth-century cottage on the property for her summer home, adding a porch and dormers. This house, known today as the "Long Island Herald House," is one of the oldest surviving buildings in the village. Both Cooper houses are today protected as part of Sag Harbor's National Historic District.

Annie Cooper Boyd continued to paint throughout her life; she produced a large body of work testifying to her deep love of Long Island's history and landscape. During the Depression she showed and sold her paintings from the Sag Harbor cottage. This evolved into a museum, successfully anticipating the interest in Sag Harbor's history that would become the basis for its renewed prosperity some thirty years later. Annie's affection for her hometown was amply reciprocated; this local news item is typical:

"All the fortunate persons who so far were able to attend the exhibition of paintings held in the Cooper House were astonished at the versatility of the artist . . . The history of Sag Harbor from the first ferry boat to the present day was depicted in color. Sag Harbor is to be congratulated in having such a talented person in its village."

Both of Annie's children were artistic. Her son Cooper developed into a gifted violinist who established his own music school. Her daughter Nancy has had a long and fascinating life: education at Barnard College in the 1920's, a time of new ideas which shocked her parents (Margaret Mead was a classmate); marriage and life in Minnesota in a house designed by Frank Lloyd Wright; analysis in Paris by Otto Rank and the study of writing with Meridel LeSeur. Nancy Boyd Willey lives today in Sag Harbor and is active in the environmental and historic preservation movements. After her mother's death in 1941, she discovered the early diaries—in an old sea chest where Annie had stored them—and prepared them for publication with the collaboration of Jean Detre.

THE DIARY OF

Martha Lavell

Minneapolis, Minnesota
1926–1938

Martha Lavell (*Courtesy of Martha Lavell*)

◇   ◇

Introduction

Martha Lavell began her "Book of Thoughts," as she called this journal, at the beginning of her freshman year at Mills College in Oakland, California. It was an important year for her; she was away from home for the first time. Home was in Minneapolis, Minnesota, seemingly in another world. "When I first saw palm trees," she wrote, "something inside of me turned upside down, and I couldn't bear to look at one."

Something had indeed turned upside down, and her journals record the results: what she termed "beginning to think," and the emotional and social changes this sparked.

Martha had been born in Minneapolis in 1909. Her father, a librarian, had died when she was four, and her mother raised Martha and a younger daughter, Virginia (Ginny), by herself, supporting them with various endeavors including a business that produced painted wrought-iron bookends and candlesticks. Martha was a shy and lonely child, as she later described it, "terribly repressed, with such an inferiority complex," which she attributed, in part, to the lack of a father.

Martha's father had been an agnostic, and through his influence her mother had rejected organized religion. Because of the family's radical religious and political views, they had few friends; not until joining the Unitarian Church in 1929 did they begin to meet congenial people who shared their values.

It was perhaps her concern with this isolation that brought Martha back from California to spend her remaining three years of college at the University of Minnesota. Her mother, she said, was too lonely without her, but clearly Lavell herself missed the protective cocoon of her family. She would return to this sheltered environment after graduate school and a brief stint as a social worker in Milwaukee. By this time, 1933, the Depression had forced her uncle, aunt and cousins Ann and Arthur to share their six-room house.

Family life versus independence is a recurring theme in the journals. Marriage is another; Martha planned to marry a "prince" and have children and an "'experimental home' where I can bring up orphans

189

and experiment on problem children." Lavell addressed her diary to "Tusitala," the future husband whom she had never met. (She admired Robert Louis Stevenson and so borrowed "Tusitala," Stevenson's Samoan name).

Although the "prince" was very much a part of her future plans, Martha had no idea how to meet him. The romantic literature she'd read in her teens had convinced her that if she simply waited for him, he would arrive. By the time she was 21, she had realized her mistake—but the "pattern of hoping and dreaming," as she later described it, was set. Despite her frequent resolutions in the journal to "sit on my repressions, fling reserve to the winds, and become aggressive," she clearly didn't know how to do this.

In addition to the "Books of Thoughts" from which these excerpts were taken, Lavell kept "Line a Day" diaries in which she recorded details of her everyday life. The "Books of Thoughts," along with a "Family Record" she kept in later years, are now in the Sophia Smith Collection at Smith College.

◇ *1926* ◇

Oakland, California. SEPTEMBER 26. Mills College is a beautiful place. I know I would love every nook in it, if I could find them all. I wish you could see my new home.

So far the days have been very happy, and cram-full of fun and study. Last night the Baby Party was given, at which the Sophomores were dressed as boys, and the Freshmen as little girls. The Juniors were not there, but the Seniors came dressed in outlandish old-fashioned costumes, and entertained us. We played children's games.

Yesterday, I had just oodles to study, but I went to the library and found a book to read. I promised myself that I wouldn't read it until today but after a while I got rather disgusted with my English, and decided to read the first chapter. And I read the whole book!

I am happy! There was a girl at our table the other day who certainly was a pessimist. She declared that "it wasn't right to bring children into the world only to suffer. That it was better for the race to die out than to compell children to live and be unhappy. That of course they'd be unhappy. She was unhappy. Everyone was." Did you ever hear anything like that? She's cuckoo.

College life is so different from a home life. But we do have loads of fun. Sunday night, while Alice and I were studying, we heard the awfullest noise in the hall and rushed out to investigate. Beryl Pear (since elected Hall pres.) was trying to play a violin, and she didn't know much about it. Another girl had a cello, and a third a tin horn. I joined in with my harmonica and you would have thought some one was being murdered. But it was so much fun. I love to make noise, but I don't have a chance very often.

OCTOBER 17. Mother sent me a bridge case yesterday, rose leather, with two packs of cards and a score pad. So, of course, we played bridge last night. We had a grand time, played until about nine, and then went up on the hill for some ice cream. I didn't get to bed until eleven.

NOVEMBER 4. We had an oral quiz in Botany lab, and much to my delight I knew just about everything he asked. It seemed like the old times again, when I always knew the answers, and when it seemed only natural that I should. That was the first time I've felt that way since I came here to Mills.

NOVEMBER 7. Last night was the Hall dance, but several of us couldn't go since we couldn't get blind dates. However we formed the Old Maids' Club and had one grand scandalized meeting about what the young people were coming to. We went up on the hill to have some ice cream and decided it was our duty to reform the boys and girls. Just think, they bobbed their hair (the girls I mean) and wore stockings that could be seen through! Shocking!

◇ *1927* ◇

[Minneapolis, Minnesota] OCTOBER 3. I certainly did enjoy reading this over the other day. I only wish I had kept on writing the rest of the college year, for my impressions are recorded so completely that someday they would have been ever so interesting to read. I've noticed that there are not many of my thoughts for those four months, and I believe that I began to think only a few months ago. I was discovering myself, I think, in those five last months of school, first my mind and then one day my body. And it was my friendship with Jane Secrest which started the first, I believe. She's a very introspective person and I was taking Psychology besides; we differed greatly on several subjects and would argue for hours, though we never reached a conclusion. I never had cared much about arguing before, except with my teachers. I have found just about four to whom I could tell just what I thought and who would do the same to me, and I got the most out of those four that I never got from any teacher. But I had never yet met a girl my own age who affected me that way, as a sort of challenge. Jane was that kind. We were both studying History and there were a good many points of argument in that. I think History was one of the things which woke me up. I got some decided views about reli-

gion and war and Jane and I discussed them. Our talks weren't always arguments; often they were ponderings on the whys and wherefores of life. Jane used to say that she wouldn't mind being a reincarnationist, but I thought it would be dreadful to believe in such a thing. We had been reading some of Dorothy Canfield Fisher's books which are full of queer ideas, and we had big arguments over them. One was whether a man should always be the wagearner and the woman the homemaker. Then we had inumerable theories on the art of bringing up children. When Jane got going, it was hard to stop. I guess the only thing we never argued over was the existence of such a thing as love. We took it for granted.

So that was what started my mind awaking and its been diligent ever since. For want of an outlet, I've become rather moody and at times I see no good in life whatever. Back [in September] I recounted the opinions of a certain girl about happiness, and added that she was cuckoo. Now I wonder if she wasn't right. I miss Jane so much and I don't believe I'll ever find another girl who's as much an "arguer" as she was. Aunt Julie used to say that I needed someone to draw me out. I'm beginning to wonder if Jane wasn't that person.

When I think of the kind of books I read in High School, I just groan. Such a lot of time wasted. Mother used to tell me so but I could never see it her way. If I had only had an older sister or brother to interest me in other things. Believe me, Gin is going to lead quite a different life from mine, if I ever discover a way to get her started in the right channel. I read sixty books the first semester at Mills, and each one a light, worthless novel. Well, English informed me that there was such a thing as criticism, and an American Literature which was just now going through a very interesting crisis. Those horrid dry, useless books which I had hated so I learned to see in another light and since then I have been following up the new ones with great interest.

When I read over the things I wrote here during those three months, I thought that sometimes my way of expressing things is a little stilted. I can't figure out why, or how to remedy it. Somehow all my life I have wanted to be a writer and in school

I always got A in my themes. But last year I just couldn't write anything that seemed worthwhile to the teachers until I wrote about my Crooked Man. So it seems to me that I'm cut out for crazy, fanciful stuff, but where will that get me?

Another thing. How come I, at my age, still can devour the Oz books with utmost delight, in short, go wild over them? I should have given up such childish performances long ago, but I didn't. So what's wrong? I've puzzled over it so much. Perhaps I really am a Freak, as I've called myself so many times in fun.

Is there any special thing that a person who is crazy over Maps and making them is cut out for? I took such delight in making a map of the Land of Oz complete in every detail. And I love to pore over old maps and new ones too if they're intricate enough. But I'm not at all interested in the people who live in those faraway places, don't care a hang about how they live or what they think. It's very queer.

I've often wondered why I don't care much for nature. Trees and mountains and flowers don't thrill me at all. But I couldn't live without blue skies and the clouds and the wind. The wind is absolutely essential to my being. It's not the looks of things that I like, it's their feeling.

DECEMBER. I've been having several arguments with Grammy over religion and it has just astounded me how little she knows how to reason. We don't agree at all and when I fire some shot at her like: "You say your God is a God of Love. Then why does he condemn all the heathens to everlasting punishment, as you say he does, just because they don't know him? It isn't their fault!" she merely replies fervently "God is just. We don't understand his ways, but he is wise, oh, so wise, and we must love him." Now do you call that an answer to my question? Glory be, when I think of people being brought up to believe as she does, blindly and with no reasoning power whatever, it makes me gnash my teeth with rage!

I couldn't believe in her God. All bunk. Grandmother shudders at our disbelief for Mother has about the same ideas as I have and Gin thinks she has too. It worries Grammy a great deal. I think she considers us atheists. But I'm not. I believe there is some great power behind everything and that this world is destined for something truly great. Gram thinks the world will end any minute. This world is too far from perfection still; it's too unjust, and too cruel to end now. That seems a queer thing for a girl of eighteen to be saying, doesn't it?

Civilization has been all wrong through all these ages. Of course, it is evolving from something worse to something better all the time, but I sometimes wonder, why did it start out the way it did? Why didn't men and women live on an equal basis, in the first place? I'm glad I'm living in this age; people are beginning to wake up. There was a time when I thought woman suffrage was "insufferable," and when I was very indignant at seeing a man sitting down in a streetcar with a woman standing. I've changed my mind in the last year. I don't know how it happened.

I don't think I have much pity in me; I hate lots of people; I get mad very easily, though only inside, but I must live my life on a square basis. I am beginning to see the other side of the question. It isn't just that women want their rights; it's that they want men to have theirs, after all these years. I figure a man has just as much right to a seat as I have. He shouldn't have to spend his money on a woman when she spends none on him. He shouldn't have to earn the family's living any more than she. But neither should she have to bring the children up any more than he. I think God made us to go hand in hand through life together, sharing burdens and joys equally. And how many thousands of years it has taken us to realize it! We're not there yet; there are many people in this world who haven't learned how to *think*.

I must share my ideas and ponderings, if only with a notebook. Perhaps someday I shall find someone who will understand.

◇ 1928 ◇

JANUARY 8. I've been thinking that I'd like to write a book about my ideas. They're so different from most people's, at least I think they are. I get to day-dreaming and imagining what a furor the book would create, how critics would say it was the book of the year, etc. It would be about a man and a woman who would discover together the true plan of life and would live it to the utmost of their ability. Life can be so wonderful, it seems to me, if we can believe and discover it. I wonder if other boys and girls dream as I do, of a perfect life. I do believe that a man can be perfect, if his parents are wise enough. That's why I want to know everything, so that I can teach it to my children. There are so many things I might have known if there had been someone to teach me. I've wondered often how different a person I would have been if my father had lived. But it does no good to wonder. My children are going to be as perfect in mind and body as I can make them.

It thrills me so to be able to write these things. I'm finding that I can express myself better and better as the months go by, and I'm so glad. I used to get rather worried because I was more interested in book people than in real people. I knew there was something wrong, but just didn't care about the people around me at all. Now I want to know what everyone thinks about things. I want to know why they think and act as they do. I never used to care how the people lived in Asia or the South Pole or Japan. But now I want to know what they think about death and war and marriage. I wonder if that isn't why I've liked languages so. Sort of an unconscious preparation for contacts with faraway people, perhaps. I've always liked to ponder maps so, maybe that means that someday I'll see those places.

All [cousin] Ann thinks about nowadays is dying for her country. She "wouldn't care if all Europe should sink." She's 100 percent American. It would be glorious to go to war for America and die for her country's cause. Gin's the same way, I think, though she doesn't talk about it so much. They're both going to marry a soldier and they wouldn't think of liking a boy who doesn't intend to go to West Point. I can't understand it. Heaven knows, I never felt that way. Is it natural to most girls?

[Ann] got to talking about musicians the other day; said it

was sissified for a man to write music or paint pictures. Aunt Marguerite thought so too so I kept silent. Sometimes it does no good whatever to argue. But oh, how can they think that only women can appreciate beauty? If I felt that I never will find the man who will love the wind and clouds and sunset as much as I do, I'd think that life isn't worth living.

Oh, how I love to sing. I'm beginning to know how to let my voice out now and when it's working right, I can sing and sing for the longest time. How lovely it would be if Tusitala should know me by my song.

Is it so terrible for me to dream such things? I most always keep them way back in my head and let them out only for a little peek once in a while. They're not my whole life. If they were it might be serious. I suppose to some people I'd seem a silly foolish girl full of "slush." But it isn't that. Surely every girl has her dreams. If I only don't let my dreams become everything, and I'll never do that. I'm too full of other things. I think that life will hold a great deal for me if I will *let* it.

Ginny gets so worried over the youth of today. She says everyone at school puts on lipstick and rouge and smokes and "pets" and everything. She thinks flappers are terrible. She was horrified at my ideas that the modern youth is better than it ever was. I'm an enthusiastic champion of modern ideas. At last we have reached the conclusion that though there will be girls and boys who are coarse enough to smoke, drink and pet, still we can be modern without copying them. She seems to be satisfied with that, though she does refuse to read a story in which a woman smokes.

Jane and I used to wonder if there are any boys in this world who wouldn't insist on a girl's petting, real boys, that is, not saps. Goodness knows, I've known plenty of nice old-fashioned boys who wouldn't think of petting, but the kind I'd like to know is an up-to-date one with advanced ideas. I consider myself a free-thinker, a reactionist and a radical. I'm a one-man person, of which there are few today. *And* the reason that I'm a one-man person is that I believe that's what Nature intended us to be. I'm not that because I'm old-fashioned or because I believe in modesty and purity for women. I do believe that Nature intended "free love," [(crossed out) we're only animals anyway] but *also* at the same time the "one-mate" idea. There, is that old-fashioned?

If I ever get married, it won't be by a minister. Of course, there'd have to be a representative of the law present, but I wouldn't have even that if I could have my way. In my mind, a marriage is made by two people when they declare their love for each other, and that's all there is to it.

Sometimes I think that it's awful to live in a city. I'd like to have more space around me, more woods and meadows. When I think of the happy times I had as a child, playing fairies in the swamps and woods around here, I wonder where my children will find a fairyland. Certainly not in these crowded streets.

JANUARY 14. Yesterday was Friday the thirteenth. I'm not at all superstitious, thank goodness. Gin thinks that if she thinks about her tooth it will start aching, or if she says she's glad she hasn't a cold, then she'll get one. I wonder if I thought those things when I was her age. How I wish that she'd write down her ideas, as I'm doing now. How far away I am from myself at fourteen; I don't remember that little girl very well.

Ever since I learned last June at the commencement exercises that a Ph.D. is the highest degree given by a college, I've been wild to get one myself. Lately I've wondered if I'll ever know enough or have enough understanding to obtain one. Somehow I just can't think of facing life without a Ph.D. That seems rather silly, doesn't it, but that's the way I feel about it.

JANUARY 18. I hereby solemnly promise myself that I shall never go out with a boy and let him pay for me.

My children are never going to believe in Santa Claus. Nor the Easter Rabbit. Nor fairies. Nor ghosts. Nor anything. I don't think it's good for them. They're going to know all about them, of course, and love them as legends, but that's *all*. I have a good many ideas on how children should be brought up. I've been wondering lately if it wouldn't be possible to make a child perfect with only one ideal or teaching—"Be kind." How different most people would be if they had had that motto from their childhood up.

FEBRUARY 13. I seem to have exhausted my mind, for I haven't had any very definite thoughts or ideas for some time. No one *knows* how I miss D. Orr [Mills College English teacher]. It may be that distance lends enchantment, but sometimes I feel as if I can't live without her. Silly perhaps, for I never really knew her, but I've always felt that if I could know her I'd worship her. How I'd love to have her for a friend. And I'll probably never see her again. Oh, why did I ever meet her? But I am glad I did, for I never knew before that girls could be so dear.

There were three girls out at Mills whom I worshipped from a distance, counting D. Orr. I wonder if it is natural for girls to like an older girl very much at some time in their life. I had missed it till then, and although I acknowledged to myself that I would like to know them, I didn't think my state could be called a crush. It wasn't at all violent, only a wistful longing for their liking. They were the first girls I had known whom it seemed to me natural for a man to fall in love with. I wonder if ever a younger girl will want to know me, because I seem to her the embodiment of her ideal. That would be wonderful. If I only had D. Orr's smile.

FEBRUARY 20. Here's something which I wrote last November, and I want it in here with my other thoughts.

"I love to laugh at people. Inside of me, of course, for I wouldn't want to hurt their feelings, but they are so absurd! My sleeves happen to be too short; everybody stares, and I can imagine their thoughts. It's such a joke that people should be so concerned with anything so unimportant as sleeves. And they are so proper and conventional. How I would love to go along the street singing, or sit on one foot in the streetcar, or talk to any boy I wanted to. But I'm not quite that independent yet; too much depends on my conforming. Nevertheless, I intend to be absolutely myself, someday, no matter what anyone thinks. There are very few people who really know *me*, they just see and like the outside. I don't amount to much on the outside—only pretty; it's the thoughts that are never expressed that are interesting. And it's these people who won't hear them who keep them from being expressed. They don't know that there's someone here who amounts to something. That's why I laugh at them; it's such a joke to think of what they're missing."

FEBRUARY 29. There's a conflict going on inside of me. I would love to believe, and I can't help thinking, that clothes shouldn't matter; but I can't keep them from mattering, and it bothers me so. I hate the idea of associating with girls who aren't dressed cleverly and well. What shall I do about it?

MARCH 14. It seems so queer to think that my children will have new ideas quite different from my own. Mine seem the best possible to me now, but I suppose that there will be better ones thirty years from now. And I do hope, Oh how I hope that I will be broad enough to accept them.

APRIL 2. It seems to me that my life now is a reaching out for new ideas. I don't seem to miss the social life I would have had if I had joined a sorority. I don't long for dances and boys to go out with, though I'd love to know them, just to know their ideas. Aunt Lena can't understand why I don't powder my nose and put on rouge and get some boy friends and gad around. I guess I've passed through the powder and rouge stage; they don't seem to matter. But I'm not indifferent about my looks; I love pretty clothes, and oh how happy my beauty makes me. But I don't care for jewels and I'd never spend all a man's money on my clothes. I don't want a man to spend money on me ever; I want to make my own living.

I was reading something Dorothy Dix wrote yesterday. She said that the girl who is merely average gets along best in this world. That may be so, but aren't there superior men to like the superior women? She spoke as if men don't like the superior girl, superior in wisdom, beauty, accomplishments, intelligence and the like. But heavens, it seems to me that there must be men that are above average in the same way, and that they would be interested in only people like them. Also Miss Dix said that a girl should not be a good talker, but a good listener and that she should know just a little less than her husband so that he can feel his superiority. That's all wrong. How are we going to have absolute equality in this world if men are to feel superior to women? Surely there must be men who feel the same way.

There has always been something inside of me that was afraid to express itself. I always used to be afraid of doing things because of what other people would think. Lately I've been trying to make myself do things. For instance, one night in the streetcar it was very hot and I wanted to open the window. But something wouldn't let me. So I said "Don't be dumb. What does it matter what people think? You open that window!" And I did. Now that sounds awfully foolish, but it's so.

APRIL 9. Easter passed by without our dressing up or going to church. We had boiled potatoes and fried eggs for dinner. What would most people say to that?

There is nothing for which I am more thankful to my mother than for her having brought me up without religion.

I have decided that I shan't go to any more pictures or read any more books unless I am sure I will get something out of them besides pleasure.

APRIL 14. I discovered a book that belonged to my father packed away upstairs the other day. It's all filled with margin comments written by him and I loved reading them over. It seems so strange that he believed in evolution and that so many years later I should reach the same conclusion.

APRIL 15. I think it is just terrible the way boys and girls are brought up. All they think about is sex. It seems to me that Gin and her friends never get together but they talk about boys and whether so-and-so is boy crazy. If there's a boy anywhere in Jefferson High who doesn't like girls, we're sure to hear about it. Gin followed one home from school to see where he lived and went into raptures when she discovered he lived across the street.

There never were any attractive boys in my classes; maybe that's why I escaped that sillyness. It's just a shame that even the littlest children have "sweethearts." I don't think it's normal, even if it is average. I just hope I have a dozen children who will grow up so used to having other boys and girls around them that they'll "think nothing of it." And they will be used to seeing each other with no clothes on, and there will be pictures and statues of the nude around so that when they reach the adolescent age they won't be embarrassed at seeing a woman's body. They will be told how life begins as soon as they ask about it, the whole, unvarnished *truth*. They'll never have to whisper in the dark about unknown things, as most little girls do. I want my children to have as natural and frank a life as possible.

APRIL 30. All the people who really think are wondering what good there is in life. They seem so bitter and discouraged. Either they don't think deep enough, or I don't, for I can see something to live for. "Oh beautiful for patriots' dream, that sees beyond the years, thine alabaster cities gleam, undimmed by human tears!"

MAY 4. It's queer what little things can make me happy. A scene or a phrase which recalls some book will just tickle me inside. There was a man on the [street-] car yesterday who looked just like an elf and I had the most fun watching him. Yes, I can get along without other people very well, though I'd rather not.

This year has been so different from last. At Mills I was always with someone, talking and musing. I had such happy times. Here I have no friends at all. But this notebook seems to make up for them, for I believe I've had more ideas because of writing them down. There don't seem to be any people who think as I do, here in college. Mother is afraid I'll have to go through life alone. But there must be men and women who are interested in serious things. The biggest thing that separates me from the rest is my "one-man" idea. Sometimes I do think I'm a generation ahead of my time.

MAY 16. John Fiske suggests that there would be no point in trying to make all people happy. There must be sorrow in the world for us to appreciate the happiness. That sounds logical, but if happiness isn't the end toward which we're evolving, then what on *earth is* the purpose? Fiske prefers the perfecting of human character but it seems to me that would be the same as happiness. I don't think I believe in a future life; there'd be no point to one.

JUNE 5. Do you remember, Tusitala, how I wrote in here, months ago, that I was beginning to be interested in people and their ideas? Now my thoughts are all with this world in which I'm living, what it has been and what it can be.

JUNE 23. I think I'm beginning to see the difference between sentiment and sentimentality. All those books which a year ago I thought "sweet" and "darling" seem so silly and worthless now. But I was wrong when I said I would never read another book unless I got something out of it besides pleasure. For I see now that no matter what book I read, I get something out of it, if only hatred for its ideas and characters. Life in those books isn't real. The people are too perfect, their environment too perfect and their lives too trivial.

JULY 7. Isn't it queer that so many people have world peace in their vision. A few hundred years ago no one thought about such a thing, at least not the average person. You can't tell me that the world isn't better today than it was in the last generation.

I have cut out and put away the two key-note speeches of the conventions, Democratic and Republican. They are almost opposite in viewpoint, the former accusing the latter of insincerity and everything else under the sun. I do not know enough yet to decide which is true and sincere, but I hope that someday I will.

I have so many boxes and envelopes full of things which I have collected in the past three years. I enjoy looking them over so much. I wish I had thought of collecting my *ideas* too, long before this.

I just can't figure out a way by which a man and a woman could bring up their children together, without the man's being away all day. Children never get to know the parent who is not home during the day and feel at ease with him when he is at home on unusual occasions.

I'd give anything if I could wear trousers. It's perfectly terrible to have to sit with one's knees together for fear someone might see up, and to be in constant danger of having one's skirt blow up to one's waist. *Darn*. Why can't we women be treated the same as men? My children are not going to be brought up with a single distinction between boys and girls. I realize the fact that there has to be some difference. Girls might wear silk trousers and such. And why should they have longer hair than men?

If I were a man, it seems to me that women wouldn't seem human to me. They'd seem so unnatural and *stilted*.

Mother says I'll never find a man who will have all the same ideas as I have. I suppose that's logical but I don't quite see why it is. My ideas seem to me right, so how could anyone who has a *brain*, have different ones? It's all a mixup, and I suppose my ideas aren't right, but they seem so now.

I'm not one bit fatter than I was a year ago. I do so want to have a perfect body, but I don't know how. I wish I were *strong*. I wonder if on my twentieth birthday I'll still be weak and thin. On the last night of my 18th year I stood looking at the stars through my window and I thought, "What a wonderful world this is! Will I ever be worthy of it?" Knowledge and health, those are my aims this year.

JULY 26. I found the most wonderful thing the other day. Tears came to my eyes when I read it, it thrilled me so. It was in Philip Gibb's "Day After Tomorrow." He was describing his vision of the world-to-be: "There is no outer difference between men and women." To think that other people have dreamed of such a thing! Nothing could make me more happy.

It is so wonderful to think that somewhere there are men and women who have the same dreams and ideals as I have! Will I ever meet them?

AUGUST 5. We discovered Fairyland today. We rode through the loveliest place. It was a winding road through tall twisty sumac trees, twice as large as a man. It was so enchanting that I was quite thrilled for a few minutes. But somehow I have drifted away from my old delight in such things. They will always interest me, I know, but something's missing now. It makes me so sorry.

AUGUST 7. I have been reading Ella Cabot's "Seven Ages of Childhood." It gave me a lot of new ideas about children. She said that she read her girlhood diary with something between laughter and shame. I wonder if that will be the way with me. It does seem horrid, that someday I shall laugh at all these precious thoughts. Well, it remains to be seen.

SEPTEMBER 3. We took a trip out to Valley Forge. It was quite exciting and it made me *think* a great deal. There is a lovely cathedral there, and monuments, in memory of the heroes of the Revolutionary War. They represent millions of dollars. Now what good are they doing anyone? Bolstering up American patriotism. Think of what suffering that money might relieve, and what happiness it could bring to millions. It's a mistake, raising monuments to the memory of dead people. Too much nationalism, with the interests of nations at heart, not the interest of human happiness.

NOVEMBER 6. A great step forward to the equality of men and women has been taken by the men of this University. They have formed a club whose purpose is to further the custom of the woman's paying for herself on all dates. I was beginning to think that I would have to forget my vow of January 18, until I should find a man with the same idea. Jane Secrest wrote in great protest that such a stand would outrage a man's vanity. However such doesn't seem to be the case with the Dutch Date Club. I'm so tickled over it!

◇ *1929* ◇

FEBRUARY 17. Mr. Bird [psychology professor] has been discussing the possibility of the existence of a fighting instinct. He believes that war and the acceptance of war are founded on a great many more things than a fighting instinct. The attitude toward war is mostly habit, he says. Even if the whole thing is habit, I dispair of ever educating man differently. But it does seem to me that the many men and women who abhor the thought of war could refuse to fight.

That old story about the man without a country is all bunk. If the United States ever again enters a war I'll desert it, without any compunctions. *I swear it*!

I have been reading the poems of Rupert Brooke lately. He seems to have been the kind of man I've always dreamed of. How he appreciated little things! "Sleep, and high places." Reading his poems makes me realize how little I am worthy of such a man, if ever such a one should come.

It is getting harder and harder to express myself in writing. Perhaps I shall not write much more in here. My thoughts now do not seem the kind that I just have to put down. Perhaps it was just a phase of my development and won't appear again. But how I have loved it and how I have loved reading them over, all those wonderful thoughts. What a different person I am now from the one I was two years ago! Life is so much richer. This book is indeed a treasure and I shall keep it always. Perhaps some day I shall be able to show it to someone, to the Tusitala to whom I have addressed it and who has been always in my dreams. Will you laugh at all those schoolgirl thoughts, or will you love them as I do, Tusitala?

APRIL 13. In reading this over today I noticed what I wrote a year ago about the importance of clothes. I think my attitude has changed. Somehow I sort of hate to wear nice clothes, because there are so many girls who can't. I feel rather guilty and quite uncomfortable when I wear my blue coat and my lovely fur. My friends' clothes aren't half so pretty and I wish mine weren't. There's so much injustice in this world. It makes me so sorry.

MAY 24. I have been so happy these last five months, happier than I ever expected to be, for I have found people who have the same ideas about religion as I have—the Unitarians. Dr. Dietrich, their minister, has said things I never expected to hear anyone say. How much we have enjoyed his talks on Sundays. And to think that there are so many people who believe as we do—that there is no need of a God to live a good life. We feel more at home in this world now!

AUGUST 16. I'm beginning to believe I'm rather abnormal in regards to liking boys. I don't seem to mind the fact that I haven't any dates. I wonder if I'm undersexed. If so, I ought to do something to get over it. I couldn't do it alone though, since I don't know any boys. However it may be just a matter of my state of mind; if I could just persuade myself to think more of the physical side, things might be remedied. But it's the interests, aims and ideals of a man that interest me and not the fact that he is a man. I have a pet idea that physical love is merely a matter of volition. Of course, I know nothing about it, but I'll swear I could have fallen in love with Mr. Bird last winter if I had kept on thinking about what a splendid face he had.

SEPTEMBER 6. What a child I was when I went out to Mills. There were many Freshmen there who were undoubtedly as far developed as I am now. And it makes me wonder if those same girls are still three years ahead of me. What a queer thing life is. What a queer situation—so very many girls gathered together, with as many environments behind them, and with what different futures ahead of them. It sort of seems unfair; that some should still be little children, living only for pleasure, and some are reaching out, grasping ideas and thinking on a level with maturer minds. How much more the latter are getting out of life. When I associated with them, I felt myself inferior and looked down upon, and I did not understand it. I could not see that I was still a child who had not "finished playing," and who had not begun to think.

How much I regret now that I went out to Mills that year. I wish I could have waited until my mind had matured. But I'm not certain that it would have matured if it had been idle here at home or working away at some position. Perhaps it was the steady piling up of different stimuli that changed me from a child into a woman. Perhaps in a few years I'll look back upon myself at twenty as very young and inexperienced. However, I think not.

All through school there were children who were older mentally than I; I was possessed by a terrible inferiority complex,
probably caused by that one fact. But why was I younger mentally in the first place? It may have been the absence of a father
and mother to guide my mind into the right channels. And yet
one might think that a child without a father would be older
because of more responsibility than other children. It's very hard
to do my developing all by myself. I think my father would
have understood. There is no one to whom I can talk about
these things; only in books do I find friends who believe as I
do, who sympathize with me, and who inspire me to better
things.

OCTOBER 16. Again I am starting a new book of thoughts,
for I find I can't get along without writing things down. So here
is this book, dedicated as before to "Tusitala."

And what a lot there is to begin with. Sociology—a science
which, as I know now, is the only subject I should be majoring
in; in which I have been vitally interested for more than two
years. I did not realize I was; but I see now that it was not the
individual's behavior, but the institutions of the group which
meant the most to me.

OCTOBER 22. I wish I knew of something I could do to
promote the cause of peace. I myself believe that pacts, world
courts and disarmament will do little; that it is only by educating
the children to be peace-minded that we will make any progress.
The 100 per cent Americanism, the anthem singing, the scorn
for all other nations, the flag worship which are being drilled
into the coming generation will lead inevitably to another war.

OCTOBER 24. I was very pleased the other day in French
class (18th century) when the prof. quoted Pierre Boyle as saying
that atheists are no more immoral than theists and that Christians make virtues of what were sins to Jesus, i.e., war. Whereupon, Mr. Sirich launched out on a wholesale condemnation of
the attitude of the ministers toward the last War. Quite apparent
that he's an agnostic and a pacifist. Oh, I'm getting a big kick
out of French this year.

We're studying sex differences in Psych. just now. At first I didn't think I'd like Mr. Paterson as a prof. (he's not at all like Mr. Bird). However the other day he said he believed that all sex differences could be attributed to differential training, and I am completely won over. Any man who recognizes no inherent difference between the sexes receives my vehement blessing.

NOVEMBER 5. A topic which interests me a good deal is the problem of femininity. Do all women develop it? If so, at what time and for what reason? You might think that it would depend on the factor of adolescence, yet some girls reach that stage without acquiring any femininity. Is it possible to be "feminine" and not be interested in boys? Do girls who develop their femininity relatively late in adolescence (around 20) get a worse dose? A very puzzling problem and to me a vital one.

I can't analyse what I mean by femininity. There seems to be some little manner of walking, of dress, of movement, and of speech which cuts some girls off from others. Are the ones who haven't this characteristic at a disadvantage with the opposite sex? It seems plausible. Yet some of the nicest people haven't it. Is it because they have associated more with boys or because they don't know any boys? And most important of all, is it natural or acquired? I don't wish to seem to men different from them, yet I wonder if I can help it. Can one have "consciousness of sex" without being feminine? I'm not sure that term is appropriate; I coined it myself. Do all women acquire this "consciousness"? Does it come upon them in college, or was I just sexually retarded?

NOVEMBER 11. I am going to write down what seems to me to be the only original idea I have ever had, one which "blossomed in my own mind" not long ago—most orthodox Christians would never stand for a king or government as tyrannical and cruel as their God.

NOVEMBER 24. Here's something I thought of the other night and which puzzles me a great deal. In every animal under the sun below man (as far as I know) it is the male who has to please the female. Yet among men, it is the opposite.

DECEMBER 30. Isn't it too bad that as children grow up they lose their habit of playing outdoors. Except for skating, I am never outside for pure amusement. And the way we used to roam around everywhere, even in winter, just for the fun of it. No more cries of "Let's go out and play."

◇ *1930* ◇

JANUARY 2. I wonder how much I've changed in the last year and whether I am any more worthy of a "thinker." Looking back I find that it has been a much richer year. Greatest influence of all, Mr. Dietrich. It is hard to phrase just what he has done for me. Given me a different outlook on life, I think.

I wonder what new heights I shall reach in the coming year. I seem to know that I'll keep on growing, don't I? A self-confidence that I never possessed in high school. I regret so much that I took all those crazy languages (though I do fancy sometimes that they make me more of an internationalist, perhaps). I've wasted so much time! I'd like to take another year here. Geology, anthropology, child guidance, chemistry, more sociology—all of these I'd like to take. And most of all, I wish I had more time to read! My book list grows longer and longer; I read only one book a month.

FEBRUARY 12. My mind has been occupied lately with thoughts of next year and what I'll be doing. I think I'd like to take psychiatric social work at Smith. It's a 13 month course and would mean my being away from home at least a year. Maybe I have an exaggerated sense of my own importance but I don't see how the family would get along without me. We're so isolated; and not having any friends is a great strain on Mother. With Gin beginning to go out nights we're left alone sometimes and what she'd do without me here I can't imagine. And Gin needs someone who can guide her over the "rough spots" of her adolescence. She has friends who have some wrong ideas, I think, and I'm so afraid she won't be able to resist them. She came home today with the statement that she didn't see why one shouldn't kiss boys as well as girls. I wasn't of much help because the only reason I could give was that kisses are sexual (and why have sexual relationships at her age?) but she thought that was silly. She's influenced too much by what the crowd thinks and of course won't listen to anything her mother says. It may be that she'd be better off without me, but how is one to tell? I can give her a slightly scientific view on a few questions but she may not continue to value my opinions. And anyhow, what am I that I should know the right answers to her moral problems? *I'm* not sure for instance, that one ought not to kiss boys (I know only that I've never had the inclination and that's not going to help her any). For all I know, it might be the best way to keep her free of repressions, yet what's to prevent her carrying it to extremes? And I *do know* that one can't live a full and fine life if one does carry it to extremes.

And so I don't know whether I ought to go away or not. Gin plainly does not think Mother is modern enough, and I'm afraid she's beginning to think I'm rather old fashioned. With all her love for fun and dancing, and my interest in serious things more than enjoyment, perhaps we'll draw apart.

FEBRUARY 20. One thing which annoys me greatly is the fact that our Child Training class is made up entirely of women. Why *is* it that men aren't interested in children? If I ever choose a husband it will be one who's vitally interested. It is the thing to which I look forward most, I cannot imagine living without children.

MARCH 2. It is really quite surprising, how different my college life is this year from that first lonely year [at the University]. Day after day of solitary lunches, then, of walking across campus meeting no familiar face. Now I am hardly ever alone; friends in all my classes, companions for lunch, greetings from passing friends wherever I go. I think that my attitude has changed; I am more ready to go half-way. And it makes me rage that a girl could grow up like that, so terribly repressed, with such an inferiority complex. I do not understand how it ever happened.

MARCH 22. Cosette Morse, whom I met in my French class, is the easiest girl to talk to whom I've yet come across. We eat lunch together about once a week. Last time I remarked that I wished there was some way people could get together for a good time without playing bridge. She agreed and said she wished someone would revive the "salon" idea where people got together and discussed philosophical questions. We have decided to try it out and I am going to invite a half dozen girls over and see if it'll work. Perhaps later on, if it's a success, someone will introduce some men which would make it a great deal more interesting. I long so to know what men think about various things.

I'd like someone to tell me whether I'm too dependant on my family. I hate the idea of not being able to enjoy Gin's last year in high school with her. Seems to me that's a desirable attitude, but it may be that I'm old enough now to break away from those ties and strike out for myself. Yet I'd hate so to grow away from Gin, and develop new interests apart from hers. Wish I knew whether that's a normal situation or a sister-fixation.

MAY 17. I have decided to go to Smith next year. I can hardly bear to think of not seeing Virginia for a whole year.

One of my favorite fancies is that during my college years I have been training for parenthood. Not as much as I should have, I know that well. But even so, my psychology and sociology ought to help a little. My idea of marriage is a union primarily for the purpose of having children. Any other relation should be sanctioned *outside* of marriage, but only the physically and mentally fit, with a definite wish for children should be allowed to marry.

[Smith College] JULY 12. Certainly haven't run out of ideas, too many new experiences for that, but not enough time to write them down. Smith is a beautiful place and I love living here. There is a great deal of work to be done, no free time at all. The lectures, most of them, are fascinating.

It is no longer hard to make friends. No more of that crushing feeling of inferiority that [once] handicapped me in the presence of any girl. Wonder how I ever happened to conquer it.

JULY 14. Real living has actually begun. I have taken part in two discussions. The first was carried on under the auspices of bridge, up in Janet's room. Four of us from the Minn. U. had gathered. We played four hands of bridge and then got started conversing. It was mostly Catholicism and birth control.

Connie is a Catholic and for the first time found herself searching her mind to see what she really did believe. She was astounded to discover that she didn't believe any of the Catholic dogma which she'd been brought up on. The rest of us were avowedly agnostics. Then we got into a discussion of bearing children, and of birth control, such as any four young girls would get into, I suppose, at eleven o'clock P.M. I enjoyed it immensely (naturally).

JULY 23. I am having my first introduction to Psychoanalysis. It seems to me the most preposterous illogical stuff that anyone could think up. Yet my reaction merely proves their point. I probably have Oedipus complexes and castration complexes and everything else Freud mentions in my Unconscious which are so repellant to me that my conscious ego won't accept them.

AUGUST 6. Our Health and Disease teacher is a wonderful young woman. I respect and admire her very much. She has been lecturing to us on reproduction and I've found there was a great deal I didn't know. Queer how one is always learning things. My sophomore year in college, after I had discovered the man's part in procreation, I was very disturbed and surprised to see a statement in my psychology book about the individual being formed by the union of two cells—one from the father and one from the mother. Think of it! A statement like that— right in a book! Then I started majoring in psychology and my professors brought up sex a great deal and discussed its emotions and perversions. Think of it! Right out in a mixed class! Then I came here and started reading psychoanalysis where the word penis is mentioned on almost every page. Would I ever be able to use the word penis in conversation without embarrassment? And now—not only has that time come—but I can discuss any phase of intercourse with a girl whom I've known only four weeks. Alas—what am I coming to! But it's rather amusing: probably in a few weeks or months I shall know and be used to even more.

AUGUST 11. Sometimes I am assailed with doubts as to whether I have enough ability and backbone to ever succeed in this work. I am greatly interested in everything I read but

I'm rather afraid that perhaps I haven't the stamina for it. I don't spend as much time studying as do the rest—it seems as if I just *must* have eight hours of sleep. Am I pampering myself? I *don't* see how I can do it.

I *hate* to be busy all the time. I like to have time to write letters, to write in my diary and to express all my ideas in here. Does that mean I'm too egocentric? I wish there were someone with whom I could talk this all over. I suppose I'd start in weeping, as I almost am now. Oh, dear, I must be a very weak individual. I suppose I'll go ahead and sit up till all hours of the night just to get through but I *don't see* how I'll ever survive.

AUGUST 28. The two months [of classes at the Smith campus] are over. I've learned a great deal, especially about medicine and psychoanalysis. Have made new friends and had a rather happy time. But I don't think my viewpoint is much different. Everyone talks about the psychiatric point-of-view being acquired here, but I think I had it before I came.

[Chicago] SEPTEMBER 23. Over two weeks have gone by and I feel like an experienced worker already. Have been out on three cases and have taken one history, and have attended numerous staff meetings. I do enjoy the latter. I feel as if I were really in the professional world at last, among people who are doing things.

So far I've felt rather pessimistic about the work that is being done. I suppose this is the period of depression we're supposed to go through. Jean and I had a long talk one night concerning the philosophy of social work. I had been puzzling a great deal, as she had, over the fact that many of our fellow-students do not seem to have the right sense of values. And .ve debated whether they can be as good social workers without it.

I've come to the conclusion that I cannot endure another year with no men companions. Something will have to be done. Evidently I shall have to sit on my repressions, fling reserve to the winds, and become aggressive. When a girl can't look at a man without seeing him as a possible husband, there's something pretty wrong somewhere. Here I've sat for the last six years with my mantle before me, placidly waiting for the prince to arrive. It was rather a rude jolt to discover that nothing happened, and that the only way to have that prince is to go out and get him. It'll probably take ages now to make up for all that practice I should have been getting in the last eight years. Here am I, at the age of 21, so self-conscious at the thought of talking with a man that I cannot even feature smiling at one. Very easy to foresee the result: I'll turn out an old maid.

And I don't want to be an old maid! I want a husband and children and an "experimental home" where I can bring up orphans and experiment on problem children. I've so many things planned for my life, I don't want to have to give them *all* up. (I realize most of them are wild and impractical, perhaps impossible, but at least the husband and children aren't.) If none of them work out, then I will have wasted a great many hours day-dreaming about them. I don't mean that I couldn't live just as useful a life, single, but I know I wouldn't be as happy. And when one has the interest and training that I've received, it doesn't seem exactly fair.

One of the girls I met this summer I was especially attracted to. I believe maybe it was her liking for introspection and discussion. Yet Janet and I were as far apart as the two poles in experience and in ideals. She had gone with many men and had "necked" with them. And she didn't believe that it is possible in this age to ever find a man (whom you'd care to marry) who hadn't had intercourse with other women. I don't want to accept that! And she was willing to marry a man who had kissed other women. Perhaps someday I will have to give up my ideal in regard to that, but oh I don't want to! I have such a beautiful ideal in my dreams of the future: a man and woman starting out on the adventure of marriage together and discovering all its experiences together. Is is such an impossible thing? Perhaps I ask too much.

OCTOBER 23. It is now over a year ago that I began this book. I don't have quite the feeling of confidence I had when I began it. There was a definite feeling of self-satisfaction which now seems to be rather dimmed. I have been reading Beatrice Webb's "My Apprenticeship," which filled me with doubts as to my own abilities and character. I am beginning to realize my social and intellectual immaturity and my tremendous ignorance of what is going on in the world. Beatrice Webb at 15 seems far above me at 21. I only hope it doesn't take too long to make up for those years of stagnation.

I feel very insecure these days as to my future. Sometimes I am overwhelmed by a dull pessimism; I don't seem to have the driving power and the zest for living that I had last year. Is it because I am meeting the serious problems of life this year, or because I miss the stimulation of Mr. Dietrich and those friends "whose hearts beat with mine" or because I can no longer go ahead without the normal companionship with men? At times I catch myself being almost apathetic.

I know now that I haven't the independence I thought I had. There is nothing I would like better than to go back to my precious home and live the sheltered happy life which I led last year. But I know I must break away, must make new friends, find new interests, enjoy other comradeship. But I'm having a very lonely time of it.

NOVEMBER 10. I am filled with the desire to express myself in some way. I can't sew and I can't paint so this is about the only avenue of creative work open to me. How I wish that I had been taught to do things like painting and sculpturing and writing, etc. My leisure time would be much richer now.

◇ *1931* ◇

JANUARY 1. Why can't people see that our whole social order is a mess? Look at the financial depression. The country seems to be in an awful condition. The United Charities are receiving a hundred new cases every day. From what we hear of the work of the social agencies it seems to be an emergency situation. Someone was saying today that she had heard it said that there is a secret agreement between the few in control in each city to hold onto the money. It may not be true, of course, but the idea is monstrous. Gin has turned communist and I don't blame her. I'm not at all sure communism or socialism would work, but I'm willing to give them a chance. Anything is better than an economic system based on greed and disregard of human life.

The upper classes know so little of what's going on among their less-fortunate brothers. One has only to walk through the streets where I've walked and enter the homes I've visited, talk to the people I've come in contact with and read the books I've read, to know that there is nothing beautiful in the lives of those who have to struggle for a living.

JANUARY 18. This eight-hour day idea doesn't suit me. I've always had so much more leisure than I have now, because of being in school. I don't see how people can enjoy life when they hardly have time to *think*, they're so busy. My Saturdays and Sundays are scheduled for weeks ahead and there are always conflicting events. I want some time to just loaf; there's an advantage in leisure. It makes for tranquility of spirit and vitality of mind.

FEBRUARY 9. Mother was here for a week. It seemed queer to have her here in this place, the associations of which are connected with the Institute and my work. I never happened to realize before how little I really know my mother. I am acquainted with most of her ideas, but of her attitude toward her own life, I know little. How queer it would feel to be her age, to have one's life behind one as she has and to be living only for one's children. My imagination doesn't work that far ahead. I look forward to marriage and children, to companionship with a husband which will last many years. But after the children are grown and scattered there's a blank wall. And if one's husband died, it seems to me the flame of living would go out. Mother has little to look forward to, except the happiness of Gin and me. Wonder if something like that will happen to me. Perhaps I'll never marry, and go through the years as a lonesome, loveless spinster. Or maybe I'll marry a bond salesman, live in an apartment, have two problem children, forget my mental hygiene, and lose interest in my ideals and in humanity. How could I bear it! I can see myself at fifty, looking back upon that hopeful, earnest, exultant, wondering girl of twenty-one, and saying bitterly, like the character in "The Great Divide" "I held my life so dear!" Oh, youth! How confident and idealistic it is.

FEBRUARY 22. Don't think I'd miss writing down my thoughts in here at all, only I like to have them recorded, if only for future pleasure in remembering them. I've been changing a great deal, I think. I'm greatly interested in socialism. Have heard Norman Thomas twice and quite worship him. (No other outlet for my sex urge.) The things he says thrill me and his personality is charming. (Darn, why can't I meet men like that?) These nine months are giving me an experience with people, an actual acquaintance with their ways of life and their problems which I should have had to some extent at least, years ago. I'm gaining confidence in myself bit by bit, though that old inferiority feeling isn't as dead as I thought it was. I have periods of discontent, feelings of insecurity that at times are overwhelming. Sometimes I can't see any point about myself to be proud of. Certainly not my intelligence. Beauty is nothing. As for my religion and my interest in social affairs, sometimes I'm seized with the doubt that it's only superficial.

Perhaps the greatest change in my character has been that of my attitude toward sex. It is much more wholesome and natural. Maybe it is due to the free and open discussion of sex problems with which we students come in contact. A great deal of the shyness and embarrassment has gone, I think.

Those feelings of discontent aren't quite the same as I described last October. The driving power doesn't seem lacking any more, perhaps because I've been having better times and perhaps because I'm beginning to have a little success in my work.

MARCH 3. One of the social workers told me how much a psychiatrist had liked my history on a case that was examined today—that he had said, "Who took this—this is fine," etc. I was greatly flattered. Then we had such fun at the French table tonight and I discovered that my French is better than most. How sweet to have one's ego bolstered up! Ha! Well, mine needs it. Probably next week I'll be in the dumps because of some shortcoming or other.

So many people seem to agree that another world war is imminent. The youth of Europe is being prepared for it, they say. And there's certainly no trend toward peace in America! And when one thinks of what the United States might do if she wanted to. Through our strength we could create world-wide peace.

APRIL 24. Somehow I feel that this book of thoughts will not survive much longer. It is becoming too mechanical a thing. And I am beginning to realize that it's rather bad for one's character. I have lately been accused of being ego-centric. Perhaps writing my thoughts is one proof of it.

APRIL 29. I'm beginning to think I don't know *what* I want to do with my life. I'm rather losing interest in Child Guidance. Bit by bit I am getting reconciled to the unpleasant fact that I'll never be able to carry out that day-dream of mine about an experimental home. So I've been trying to find something to put in its place, and I haven't succeeded very well. I do know this: I want to do something that's worthwhile, that in some way or other is helping someone. Perhaps I am cut out for social reform, rather than for social case work.

This thing I am beginning to see: that it won't matter much what kind of a position I get next year. If it isn't exactly to my liking it needn't matter much; I can probably profit from it in some way. Whatever I go into won't necessarily be my life work. My interests may keep on changing, for many years.

MAY 1. Evidently my emotional development has never reached the hetero-sexual stage. My physical development has, surely, for I am easily stimulated sexually. But it is more a psychic stimulation, I think. For some reason, I see more in women to adore than in men. The admiration I have felt for various men has been more an intellectual one, it seems to me. Anyway, I've never met a young man who attracted me as much as Haydon & Reese & Mr. Sirich & Mr. Bird & Prof. Thiel.*

---

* The latter three had been M.L.'s teachers. Haydon was a philosophy professor at the University of Chicago; Reese, a Unitarian minister who ran a Chicago settlement house.

I suppose that's easily explainable in psychoanalytic terms. The transfer from the homo-sexual to the hetero-sexual stage is most easily secured by an attachment for a parent of the opposite sex, as a half-way point. And since I have no father, these older men are taking his place in my emotional life. But even my transfer to them is not completely effected, evidently, for I am *so* greatly susceptible to an attraction for women. It seems to be women of a certain type too, which is rather puzzling. The women I've had crushes on (for they answer to that description I suppose, though I do hate the word), have all had something in common, though I can't analyse it. I've wondered if it's a tendency toward masculinity. But I don't know in what *way* they're masculine, if so. It bothers me, this queer moved feeling which comes over me at times, in the presence of these women and even at the thought of them. It *isn't* normal, I know; but what is one to do about it? Especially when one knows no men to transfer the feeling to? Sometimes when I've caught myself dwelling on the thought of some woman, I've stamped my foot in anger & tried to turn my mind toward other things, for I realize the danger of going to an extreme. For it's just a facial expression, a smile, or even the look in their eyes, which occasions that thrilled feeling. And no matter how much I fight against it, dismiss it from my mind immediately, that feeling returns again & again.

[*On vacation in Minnesota*] *JUNE 26.* Such utter peace & calm, here at the Lakes. One could completely forget the existence of any other world, of man-made ugliness, of unhappiness.

The nine months are over. The year is one jumble of impressions, the evaluation of which I have hardly begun.

Funny how easy it is to drop that "Smith" personality, to return again to the old familiar life. I find it an effort to recall my work at the Institute, even to think of my life at the Y.[W.C.A.] My personality has changed in the last year, I think, but it does not show the new characteristics to the people "back home."

[*Smith College*] *JULY 12.* One of the girls whom I knew last year at Smith has told me that I seem more "friendly" this summer. Wonder if I've always been more reserved than I thought I was; if that is the reason some people haven't seemed very interested in me.

JULY 29. I was quite astounded today when I picked up my book of poetry and noticed what a change there has been in my handwriting since 1926. The letters were so tiny and unformed then. Someone told me lately that she considers my handwriting indicative of my emotional development; it is rather immature, in other words. It is a queer idea to suppose that character comes out in one's writing.

Have been working quite steadily on thesis. I am not at all satisfied with it; seems as if I haven't done half enough work on it. What's occupying my mind most is plans for next year. Can't decide whether I should accept any job I'm offered (there's a vacancy in Milwaukee for which I've applied) or go home without one and hope for one there. The prospect of going to a new city and working out my future there is rather alluring; still the idea of being at home next year, with Gin going to the U, and having good times with family and old friends also attracts me. I do feel as if I'm needed at home; Mother has little recreation and less companionship, without me there. On the other hand, perhaps I should forget my family and go away and "lead my own life." I'm getting rather tired of hearing that latter doctrine harped upon; that doesn't prove it isn't valid, however.

AUGUST 3. I was down in the dumps, a few minutes ago, disgusted with myself and life in general. Then I suddenly thought of something I wanted to write in here, and I have become all animated and pleasant. Now just what does that indicate? An underlying drive for writing or an egocentric pleasure in thinking about myself?

Lately I have begun to suspect myself of being shamefully neurotic. Seems as though I've had aches and pains in every part of my body in the last year. Perhaps a reaction to too sudden an uprooting from family life and to the pressure of responsibilities and independence. It occurred to me the other day that my lack of interest in smoking and drinking coffee are probably due to the reluctance at growing up (also my preference to let Mother drive the car).

When I went away to college, I was perhaps carried away by the new independence, and wishing to be as sophisticated as my companions, let my hair grow. Upon reaching home, I found that my new appearance was not at all acceptable. My mother didn't like to see her little girl growing away from her. However, she stood it, wishing me to be happy, until grandmother died, when she suddenly demanded that I cut my hair. Having had one dependent taken away, she wasn't going to let another slip away and grow up. Figuratively speaking then, I regressed into childhood ways. My hair remained short for almost two years. Then Gin and Mother began coaxing me to let it grow; Gin's was becoming long. And I suppose Mother was now reconciled to having her daughters grow up, since the youngest showed unmistakable evidences of intending to do so, anyway. I fought against the idea, but finally succumbed. Now isn't that a nice little triumph for psychoanalytic doctrine? Preposterous, perhaps, but very amusing.

I've just decided that my hopes have been too high and it's time I came down to earth. There's such a thing as being too darned particular, both about ambitions and husbands. If there's anything that was missing in my childhood training, it was the admonition, "Stop daydreaming." It'll be a wonder if the absence of that principle doesn't ruin my whole life.

[Minneapolis] SEPTEMBER 3. Well it seems that my work at Smith was not satisfactory in one course, and I shall have to do some extra work before receiving my diploma. It certainly is a hard thing to face: mediocrity in every line of work I have so far tried.

SEPTEMBER 25. There seems to be little likelihood of an interesting job, and life seems to be a mixup. Business is terrible; Mother may have to get some kind of a job. That would mean Chicago or New York. And here I'd be in Minneapolis, tied to a job in which I wasn't a bit interested. And if I don't get a job here, I'll have to go elsewhere. I'd hate giving up all the enthusiastic plans I have made: to take geology in night school from Mr. Thiel, fun with Cosette and Lucille, pleasant evenings with the family, etc. I wonder how it will all turn out.

OCTOBER 8. Well, it's to be Milwaukee this year. I'm leaving behind many good times, but I'm going out into the world to seek my fortune, and I have hopes that I will meet with pleasant and broadening experiences. The new life will perhaps be hard to adjust to, but it will be good for me, that's certain.

[Milwaukee] OCTOBER 18. I think I'm going to be quite satisfied with my work. The other workers are congenial, and I am greatly attracted to the supervisor, Mrs. Newbold. Have a feeling that I may learn a lot from her. She has poise, and yet she is vivid. She's one of the few persons I know who are attractive without rouge.

I'm enjoying getting acquainted with Milwaukee. I never have any trouble finding my way around in a strange city; it's fun to learn the streets and directions. Have visited two art museums, and had a lovely walk over to the lake. A year ago I wouldn't have done things like that; I've learned a little aggressiveness.

DECEMBER 6. Well, I'm beginning to feel as if I know what everything is all about, and I'm nicely settled in my room, and I have a budget going nicely, and I have interesting books to read, and I'm quite contented. The next thing on the program is some intellectual companionship, particularly masculine, and where I am going to find it? The girls at the office are not exactly my type; their idea of a good time consists of a date with a wise-cracking man and plenty of liquor and cigarettes.

My idea of recreation is discussions & reading and music and contact with nature. Their type of recreation is so dependent on sex differences. And my whole purpose in life is to minimize those differences. There surely must be men who are sympathetic to those principles. They are the only sound basis of a satisfactory sex life as I see it. And of life in general too.

I don't believe I've been taught to do my own thinking much, for I have a tendency to agree entirely with people whose ideas I like. If I have respect for a person, I seem to think that he ought to be right in all his ideas. Jane Addams, for instance, or

Bertrand Russell. I forget that one person cannot judge correctly on all subjects. I'm quite inclined to hero-worship, I guess, probably because I have no God to waste my worship on.

◇ *1932* ◇

JANUARY 8. Why must my personality continue to be immature and shallow? I feel so inferior to many women I have known. Of course they have been older than I, but still I think I seem younger than I should. I yearn so for knowledge that is worth something, real factual knowledge of the world.

JANUARY 17. It's funny how I've always looked forward to having children of my own. I don't know when my fancying concerning them began, but in high school it was at its height. I thought of my future children as being aged 14, 12, 10, & 8. Their names, their appearance, their personalities, their interests were firmly fixed. Even the color of their bedrooms and their favorite pets entered into my fancies.

It's rather a shame for a girl to grow up with ideas and interests like those. For it's apt to be a difficult adjustment if she has to lead a single life. I've no special abilities in the way of a profession; I don't really expect to make a good social worker and there's nothing else I'm fitted for. I don't know what I'll do with my life if I don't marry. The possibility just hasn't entered into my plans.

FEBRUARY 25. During a week-end visit at home recently we launched a discussion of sex and love which was very satisfying. In how many families can mother and daughters disclose their frank views on such a subject? It hasn't always been so, in ours, but mother has gradually grown accustomed to the conversation of the younger generation and can now enter into it.

MARCH 19. I am a person who seldom gets angry. That is a logical characteristic of one who does not believe in free will. Then too, I am becoming able to check somewhat my daydreaming tendencies—the ones which have to do with self-aggrandizement, at least. I don't believe I have ever tried much to analyse my character. I have done considerable thinking in regard to my personality and beliefs and attitudes, but I really have little conception of my strengths and weaknesses.

MARCH 27. I am celebrating today the birth of an ambition. Up to date I have never had any kind of an ambition unconnected with marriage and children. I was reading Randall's "A World Community" today, and I was seized by the idea that perhaps I could do something to further his cause. If I really have any ability in public speaking I might be able to put across to people the ideals of internationalism. I am going to keep this in mind, continue with my reading on the subject, and plan to take several courses in night school. It is a good idea, I think.

JUNE 26. I wish someone would tell me whether it is a good idea to start another book of thoughts. I enjoy the attempt at expressing what's in my mind, and no doubt it helps to clarify my ideas. However, it may be that expression serves to focus my attention on myself, thereby fostering too large a sense of my own importance. It's hard to tell.

I wonder if the practice of self-examination can go too far. Not to take oneself too seriously—that is a good maxim to keep in mind. But to take the world seriously, how can one help that?

JULY 4. I am beginning to believe I don't want to be a social worker any longer than I can help. In the first place, I haven't enough skill in handling people. Besides, I don't think our present state of knowledge regarding human behavior is enough advanced to enable us to work with people at all safely. At least mine isn't, in spite of the training I've had. I feel a great reluctance at the idea of my working with unmarried mothers; I'm afraid I'd bungle things horribly.

However, the suspicion comes to me at times that perhaps I'll never be contented with any field, but turn to another as soon as I'm settled in one. How could one conquer such a characteristic?

JULY 10. I had my first interview last week with an alleged father of an illegitimate child. The prospect was none too pleasing; I was sure to be somewhat embarrassed and I had no practice in being hard-boiled—should it be necessary. But everything went off all right. I think experiences like that may make it easier for me to become acquainted with men, if ever the opportunity arrives. To have talked to a number of men about their relations with women ought to take away some of my old reserve and help me to be less of an automaton.

JULY 19. It begins to look as if my career in social work is to be cut short. And all on account of the fact that I can't make decisions. Mrs. Newbold is kind enough to put it thus: I have such a mania for being fair to people and for seeing the other side of things that I'll never make the dominating, self-assertive person a social worker has to be. I'm too considerate of other people. Imagine those qualities being drawbacks. Mrs. N. is of the opinion that I've carried them to an extreme. Well, I have been consciously trying to acquire them but I wouldn't have said I was near approaching the point of perfection. I can't help thinking that the more people who go to extremes in consideration and fairness and understanding, the better off the rest would be.

What am I to do? Social work has been my only training. My interests lie along the lines of social research, but I fully expect that field to turn up its nose at my qualifications. Funny thing: I never was very good in statistics in psychology classes, but perhaps a latent ability along statistical lines is coming out.

Statistical work would remove me from the necessity of handling people. That would be to the good (not of my character, perhaps, but of my professional success), and yet I'd hate to be removed from people altogether. I really wish that I might in some way take advantage of my intense interest in children.

[Minneapolis] AUGUST 19. Out of various discussions, books, and college courses, I have formulated a collection of ideas which might be called my sex code. In spite of being rather mixed up, it has clarified my mind, and it will be a convenient aid in case of need. Here 'tis.

1. In the first place, I believe that sex life without companionship and mutual respect is not worth having.

2. Since sex desires can be controlled temporarily, this should be done until one can find the companionship and respect along with sex gratification.

3. The natural course of things is for physical caresses to lead inevitably to sex relations. If this course is repeatedly interrupted, the result may be physical or emotional maladjustment. Therefore, why begin it at all?

4. The sex life means most when associated with one individual through a life-time. Therefore the best way is to not indulge sex desires until one finds the individual who can be a life companion.

AUGUST 22. Queer how my ideals regarding a husband have lately been crystalizing. The character taken by Lionel Barrymore in "Grand Hotel" made a great impression upon me and has become one of the definite points in my picture of a fine and good man.

I'm afraid that I'm in the state now which would lead me to go too far if I should meet any man who even approximated my ideal. I want to know many men before *the* one comes along. Dear me, here I am in just the same state as I was two years ago, when I wrote down a long & vehement harangue about myself in relation to men. I thought then that I was desperate, but it didn't do any good. Will this keep up the rest of my life?

If I could only forget the years-old plan of marriage, and take a vivid interest in some other life-work, my future happiness might be more probable. If there were only some way of discovering one's abilities!

OCTOBER 12. Besides being on the lookout for a job, I've joined the Socialist Party. In four weeks I've met more people and had more excitement than I ever thought possible. It's good to feel oneself a part of the group working for a better social order and to be among people who have the same social ideals. Mother feels it especially, as she has been up to now something of an outcast among her friends because of her political beliefs.

NOVEMBER 9. One year ago I gave vent to some of my doubts and hopes concerning my sister's future development. The fears were unsubstantiated in the months that followed. Virginia has turned out to be a broad-minded individual, actively interested in social problems. She has a keen insight into her own character and into the behavior and thinking of other people. I have been greatly surprised by her knowledge of psychology.

Gin and I are together quite a bit, these days. We are very companionable. We enjoy the same kinds of things, and react alike to most every situation. Recently she declared that I am her best friend. That certainly pleased me.

◇ *1933* ◇

FEBRUARY 5. I'm starting in at a new job, this time social research. The work so far has been rather routine. At any rate it doesn't require much ingenuity, which is lucky for me. And there'll be no more of those puzzling, trying situations which involved handling other people. That will be a relief, but perhaps not to my ultimate benefit. I mean to put my whole self into this work, however monotonous I may find it, in order to make a success of it. For I feel that I haven't the ability for work I'd enjoy more, and I'm afraid I'll never do anything especially notable in this world, anyhow. So I may as well learn to be content with relatively mediocre achievements. They must be, however, in some field of service to society, to justify my living.

Oddly enough, that was not written in a spirit at all pessimistic or bitter. I'm becoming reconciled at least to my shortcomings. Incidentally though, it seems that my native endowment is greater than supposed, for in an analogies test recently my grade was in the 90th percentile for graduates. Evidently that implies too little effort on my part or else some emotional maladjustment. It's beyond me which.

MAY 30. The condition of the country at this time is certainly puzzling. The papers are full of items proving prosperity is on its way; and Roosevelt has become the people's idol. It's hard to tell just what he's about; quite a bit of liberal legislation has been talked about in the headlines. How far his policies really go is hard to tell.

JULY 29. I have recently had an experience which came

rather late in life to me. I met the only person (my age) of the opposite sex whom I've so far been at all attracted to, and he wasn't attracted to me. Why couldn't it have happened earlier and oftener? It may be dumb of me, but I can't help wondering what effect my not knowing this person will have on my future life.

OCTOBER 8. This book of thoughts is becoming more & more neglected. It isn't that I haven't the ideas but I'm always too busy or too indifferent at the moment to write them. Inertia is troubling me this days, for the same old reasons—no male companionship and no vocational success. The Depression hasn't bothered me half as much as those two. I've felt it, I think, only through Mother's worrying and fretting. Money is not at all necessary to my contentment. If only the necessary bills could be paid, I could forget all about money. I've applied for a research job, and I have misgivings about my interest in even research work, but at times I reassure myself by thinking that, if I could have the normal relationships with men, I would probably make a success of the work and really like it.

NOVEMBER 26. Actually I've landed a permanent job, research work in the Students' Health Service at the University. I think I don't really realize my good fortune yet; it's coming over me by degrees, just what this will mean. In the first place it's another chance at making good; I think I'm capable of doing the work satisfactorily. If my personal problems can get straightened somehow, I ought to be content even without an absorbing job. But by leaving temporarily the field of my true interests, the social sciences, I am perhaps turning my back on many possible contacts, congenial friends of both sexes.

I fear I am a most self-centered person. My thoughts are usually of myself and my future; the years-old day-dreaming habit has not abated, and its influence is not broadening. One of the advantages of writing my thoughts, I believe, is that it helps me to think an idea through, further than I would otherwise.

◇ *1934* ◇

FEBRUARY 22. As I look back on my social work career, I think the way I profited from it most was in my relationship with other people. Absolutely disappeared is any trace of reserve in meeting people. Most of the girls in the office I have little in common with, except for one who likes to discuss books. The rest move in a world of clothes and bridge, largely. Weddings are a popular topic of conversation, and most of the girls are concerned with the conventional trappings. In fact they're conventional in every way.

I have just joined the Minneapolis Civic Opera group; it promises to be much fun. I get the greatest enjoyment out of reading vocal music. Also I hope I'll make new acquaintances through this contact. If not, I'll just have to get away from this town, for I will have exhausted its possibilities for companionship. If the Depression is over in two years, and civilization miraculously intact, I shall try for a job in New York. In such a large place there ought to be congenial people.

I still have my beautiful philosophy of humanism to comfort me. Wonder how hard I could lean on it if things got too bad— if precious life were confronted with extinction in the imminent damfool war. And why do I write "if"—what else *can* happen? Heavens, for a gloomy future. (No wonder Gin can take little interest in the choice of her lifework, but prefers to enjoy the present.)

But however dubious the future appears, I can't stop thinking about my own, it seems. The truth is, I don't really enjoy my work, and I want to get away where I'll meet people. But I feel obligated to stay here another year, and I wonder what kind of a disposition I'll have by the time it's up.

I had a rather interesting thought recently. I was considering the effect on me of all the sex information and attitudes poured into the Smith students. When we left the school, our knowledge of the normal & abnormal sex life were pretty complete. I was analysing the difference between my reaction to this and the reactions of several girls I knew. They went to the extreme in their own behavior, leaving the accepted moral standards behind. [But I am] an open-minded individual, so aware of biological conditions as to be "unshockable," so used to their existence as to be unembarrassed by them, so oriented to them as to accept them gladly, and yet conditioned in such a way as to prefer to put off heterosexual fulfillment until it can mean also a beautiful human relationship. Although such a combination creates special problems, it has advantages.

AUGUST 19. Back to work [after vacation] on the morrow. To me it's rather a serious, sad thing. Back to a work I'm not supremely interested in, to associates I don't care for, to a year in a "desert of waiting." I do know I'll have many happy times, for there are one or two fine friends, and the opera chorus singing, and the excitement of the coming election. But taken as a whole, it's just another year of existing. The life I day-dream about is one spent in a congenial occupation (heaven knows what!) among friends, a dozen at least, of intellectual interests, one of whom would someday prove the finest friend of all. I've got to have him, at least—I'll never be reconciled to giving up that precious vision.

DECEMBER 29. Cecil Lavell, our most congenial uncle, whom we met last summer, sent us a copy of a book he wrote— *A Biography of the Greek People*. It promises to be most interesting and instructive.

My fantasy-life is increasing at a great rate, darn it all. Worst of it is, it's so irrational. All about the wonderful people I *might* meet, in New York next year. If I should never meet any like them, or never even get to New York, it certainly would mean a difficult adjustment. Why do I have to be a person who yearns for the impossible?

◇ *1935* ◇

JUNE 28. I'm quite sure my personality is more spontaneous; no one would take me for the reserved creature I was in college. Maybe the dancing I've been doing about the house contributed to that. Could anyone with free, limber muscles be reserved?

As for the ease with men, my contacts with doctors at my office have helped some, I believe. One or two of them are so informal that I've learned to treat them as naturally as I do girls, and I'm grateful to them. But that may not carry over when (and if) I meet men of possible "eligibility."

Well, as for the coming year, the only goal in my mind is to find a mate. How and where are the heartbreaking questions. Wish there were matrimonial agencies for such as me. Or at least someone with infinite wisdom to give advice.

Definite goals for the meantime are taking shape in my mind. More outdoor life; I'd like to spend Sundays out-of-doors entirely. The study of harmony in earnest and thence to a deeper appreciation of music. Close following of world events, through the interpretation of the *New Republic* and others.

◇ *1937* ◇

APRIL 11. Lately I've had no use for a book of thoughts, for I've been expressing myself very satisfyingly to Uncle Cecil. Such a relationship as I have never had—it makes me sing inside whenever I think of it and especially when I get a letter from him. It ought to do me much good, and indeed I think it has given me a little more poise and confidence.

◇ *1938* ◇

JANUARY 23. This thing seems to be petering out, and maybe it's just as well. Reading it over gives me a dissatisfied feeling of amateurish thinking and naiveté. Anyhow the need for it has disappeared. Cecil has taken the place of the long-wished-for confidante, and though he isn't what I imagined eleven years ago in Tusitala, he's next best, and probably the best I'll ever have.

◇   ◇

Afterword

Uncle Cecil's interest was a valuable boost to Lavell's self-esteem. (He was about the age her father would have been.) She lost some of her shyness and began to enjoy dating; but the man she was looking for, one who would view her as an equal, continued to be elusive.

She continued to live with her mother and sister until 1943, when Virginia went to graduate school at the University of Chicago. Two years later Martha moved to New York to pursue a career as an editor; she later spent six years in Toronto on the editorial staff of a psychiatric journal, and eventually settled in Philadelphia. The family was reunited in 1954 when Virginia and her mother joined Martha there, and the two sisters have continued to live together since their mother's death.

In an article entitled "Some Reflections of a Renegade Social Worker,"* Martha Lavell, then working at the Human Resources Center of the University of Pennsylvania, looked back over the course of her career.

"If it had occurred to me to work for a few years between college and graduate school, I might never have chosen the field of social work," she wrote. "[But] the Smith experience provided some much-needed self-knowledge, although corresponding behavioral change was slow to develop. One reason for this, I suspect, was the doubts I had about the place of women in the world. I do not recall receiving either denial or corroboration of these doubts [at] Smith, which was long before the days of women's liberation.

"Through the experiences of fieldwork days [in Chicago] the suspicion grew that rather than helping people to adjust to the world, I desired to 'make the world more adjustable *to*.' I had no idea how this could be done, and the ambition was an incongruous one for a very retiring person.

"After many years and through many byways, I have come back to

---

* *Smith College School for Social Work Journal,* Winter 1977

my student ambition to make the world more adjustable to. Social research, broadly defined, became my final career. [The Human Resources Center was teaching varied groups of people ways of working for change in their communities.] My special interest has been suburban women, many of whom have become, after our training, activists for constructive social change.

"This concern with women's power to change their society has led me to . . . the history of women as social reformers. Everything I learn about the 19th century American women who rose above repressive social influences to bring about incredible changes, reinforces my belief that human beings have infinite capacity to create a better world."

Martha Lavell is still actively involved in putting these beliefs into practice. In 1976, she helped found the Women's Rights Centennial Committee, which on July 4 of that year presented an historic series of events in Philadelphia to commemorate the 1876 Declaration of Women's Rights.

◇　　◇

THE DIARY OF

Azalia Emma Peet

West Webster, New York
1913–1916

◇　　◇

Azalia Emma Peet (*Courtesy of Sophia Smith Collection, Smith College*)

◇　◇

Introduction

Azalia Emma Peet was born in Rochester, New York in 1887. "My father owned the family farm, 10 miles east of Rochester," in West Webster, New York, she later told an interviewer. "As a child my vacations were spent there. During my freshman year at college my father and mother moved there and 'Peet Acres' became my year round home.

"My parents were very interested in education," she said, "my mother was a teacher prior to her marriage . . . I was an only daughter, and my older brother went to the University of Rochester and my younger [one] to Cornell. When I was ready for college (Rochester University opened its doors to women that year) my father and my brother both absolutely refused to have me go to a college where there were men, so I was sent immediately to a woman's college."

At Smith College, Peet majored in history and philosophy. After graduation, unsure where her duty lay, she returned to her family in West Webster. She had always been religious and now she became active in Methodist youth work.

"At that time," she later explained, "there were in the churches very few organizations that appealed to girls, especially in the rural areas. The missionary group in the local church [had] organized them into girls' mission study groups . . . called the Standard Bearers." Azalia became Secretary of Youth Work in Rochester District and Superintendent of Young People's Work in the Genesee Conference. Despite her interest in missions she had no intention of going abroad herself: "Although my mother was interested in missionary work it was the one thing I told her I was never going to do. . . . I wanted to be married and have a family."

Azalia Peet at 24 was searching for a direction in life. On March 7, 1912, she wrote in her journal, "For more than eighteen months I have lived in the country since graduation from college and the problems of the country do interest me greatly. The people need much that the college educated woman has to give. The question is, how is she to give it?" By the following year her need for an answer was becoming more acute.

◇ *1913* ◇

APRIL 6. What is it that Azalia Emma is really striving for? What is her life's goal? What is the all embracing ideal which figures large whenever she takes time to really consider life and her relation to it? These are some of the many questions which she faced as she walked with Mac (her Scotch collie) toward the north to-day after a discouraging time in Sunday School class and after reading a new story in the Ladies Home Journal by Mrs. Jeanette Lee.

Is a life devoted to *mere* helpfulness to others, disregarding self, the real goal, the summum bonum of existence? Is this not a narrow view?

Is the well rounded development of the artistic nature not a bigger, broader more comprehensive ideal?

Is it wrong to even suggest this? I know not. One thing I do know—I did not give my girls in S.S. a single practical suggestion on the Jacob and Esau lesson and it was such an opportunity! Eleven girls out and two of them were ones whom I was especially anxious to help or at least to hold. I was blue about it all as I always am after being conscious of a failure.

Have been reading Effey's Journal for the past two years and it has inspired me to try to write now and then in mine. What a wonderful child she is! I would give a great deal for much of Effey which she values lightly.

I think I never felt my lack of something to give to anyone more than I felt it yesterday when that child ran in for an hour. Some way of late I have been drained to the very depths without getting a fresh supply of ideas, of helpful thoughts, of beautiful music or poetry or prose. She felt the lack too. It hurts when one falls in the estimation of one's friends. I must grow faster, develop more quickly if I am to long be esteemed by some of my young friends. I must find time for the daily news, for poetry, for worth while books, for music, for art, for lectures. Meanwhile my spirit life must not suffer for I still must be happy.

But enough—Azalia Emma is sleepy. One more query. Is the prince on his way?

APRIL 12. This week has brought me much in the way of inspiring food for thought—at least it has seen Azalia Emma at gatherings where inspiration ought to be gained. However the only helpful suggestion given me by Mrs. Kitchelt at The College Woman's Club was a quotation which she gave on Culture which as near as I can remember ran as follows. "True culture is not to be gained from much learning but is best expressed by *a sense of kinship* with one's fellow man." Her talk was on the immigrant. A sense of kinship is the essential quality needed by the city girl who takes up her abode in the country.

Wednesday last found me very tired but the Child's Welfare Exhibit was worth it. There are a lot of people in this old world whose sole end and aim is the betterment of mankind. After all are they not the people one would choose to live with in preference to the true artists? Maybe they are artists in their own sphere—if so the foregoing sentence is redundant. (I think that is the right word.)

And yesterday a missionary meeting. The children and girls were an inspiration. I do like the children and—I like them to love me. I wonder if everyone craves affection. If so why is it wrong or at least unwise to show ones affection too strongly? I do not question that it is unwise but the why of it all puzzles me.

To-day I saw a piece of faeryland. Pink and lavender and white in the dainty flowers broadcast in the woods. Hepaticas are in full bloom!

Effey is going to Cornell! Yes I am glad. It is a wonderful opportunity. Why Oh why is it that I am having to persuade myself that I am glad? I guess it is simply a personal preference for a woman's college and a certain particular woman's college [Smith] at that, which makes me a trifle doubtful in my mind. Effey has so much in her that she ought to make a remarkable woman. May she meet and learn to know the right people!!

I shall miss Effey next year!

The prince does not come. I wonder whether he ever will and if he does not is it my fault?

This night I need a blessing.

To-morrow another opportunity for service awaits. May I measure up to the need!

APRIL 23. I sat down with the intention of answering one or two letters before retiring but I value my friends too much to inflict upon them the mood which is now upon me.

What a joy to have a somewhere to vent ones feelings without having to count the cost. Is this legitimate, I wonder.

Our busy [farming] season is on and I am overwhelmed with the query—Does it pay? does it pay? Last night father was so nearly ill from over work that I was actually alarmed. Mother was so nervous from fretting about him that she lay awake long hours in the night. Nelson [brother] and father worked until almost eight P.M. before eating supper last night then Nelson got off at day break to-day. He has only just returned, minus supper and it is past bed-time. He is "All in"—poor fellow. Father and mother are in Rochester—Aunt Libbie's affairs need straightening—and Grand mother is very ill. And so it goes.

It is really not hard for me this Spring. Indeed I have never had it easier. Bertha is able to do practically all the work so that when the planning is done I am quite free to sew or read or write. But I almost wish I might suffer some of the over work— it would be easier than watching others suffer.

All this turmoil, this hustling, this fretting, this overdoing— and what does it amount to? A yearly income which hardly pays our running expenses and that is all. Ought not ones employment to bring in something beside money and gray hairs? Ought it not to offer some other and more attractive features? But it does—I guess—only they are not overly apparent just now.

Farming does have a seamy side just like all other occupations but it has its happy aspects as well. Cheer up.

I went to prayer meeting to-night and was glad I went. Mr. Connal is surely sincere and I admire him. I sincerely hope it is not wrong in the eyes of Almighty God to differ with both him and Uncle Wilbur on certain religious views. I trust that my surrender is complete—I want it to be—and I am hoping someday to know more fully the ground on which I stand. How to reconcile my interest in Missions in the church and in the community with the interest in the home, becomes more of a problem each day. One time I feel the *awful* need of the wider field, the next, the all absorbing need of the world lying right at hand. When I plead for the former and feel as I do to-night about my home—it almost becomes a sacrilege. I doubt very much whether I could successfully talk to girls about the need of the foreign field, to-night. I am glad I don't have to.

Mother and father have just returned. They seem not so tired as I feared.

APRIL 27. "No one but God and I knows what is in my heart." Sometimes I think no one but God knows.

Am I sincere in my anxiety for the soul welfare of others? Am I a fit person to deal with another's soul? Even am I worthy of being divinely used? No. Moreover is it not often for the glory of Azalia Emma! *Yes.*

SEPTEMBER 21. My little mother is no longer with us. On August 9th while seated with Annie and me about the evening lamp she suddenly "was not for God took her." She went with her knitting in her hands. My mother was always busy. Slowly I am coming to realize that she is gone—at first it was impossible. This very minute it seems as if she must be peacefully sleeping across the hall. I have a wonderful memory of my little mother. Always frail since I can remember, yet she was ever giving—giving of herself to all. Hers was a life dedicated to rich self sacrifice and in this she found great delight. I shall probably never know the trials, the small economies and the unselfish sacrifice which my mother cheerfully and silently suffered that my college course could be a reality. I shall always prize these three years with her since college when in a small measure I have lightened her burdens and perhaps smoothed her pathway. One day last winter when she was very ill she grasped my hand and told me over and over how much she appreciated all that I did for her. Yes often she used to say no other daughter could be so good. I say this not boastfully but I simply want to re-

member it. On the same occasion she said—"You will be very
good to father won't you, dear." Yes—that is my task now. Not
that it is arduous in any sense nor do I know what I should do
or what I would want to do were this not my duty, still it keeps
me here in West Webster when perhaps I should otherwise be
perfecting myself along some line which would offer me a living
wage when it becomes necessary for me to earn one. Meanwhile
I am growing older each day but "the Lord will provide." He
always has.

One of the awful things about mother's leaving us and yet it
is all as it should be, I suppose, is the fact that everything moves
on just the same. We eat, drink and are merry, we entertain
and are entertained, we enjoy our friends even more because
our loss has loosened up their heartstrings and ours and allowed
us a closer companionship. Even God, whom I have always
thought of as *the only* solace at such a time, did not seem quite
so necessary because of the goodness, the love and the sympathy
of my friends. It seems sometimes as if my Heavenly Father
in making my sorrow so easy to bear because of the goodness
of my friends was giving me too easy a cushion, was lightening
my burden too much for my own good.

I sincerely hope not. I do feel my need of Divine guidance
and love very much.

I am jealous. I am not willing to share my friends. This is
not the first time I have encountered this stone wall. This time
it is Effey and Nannie. With shame do I confess it. I love them
both and I think I know almost all of their faults. But even you,
Old Journal, are not to see them set down in order. Doubtless
they in turn are quite well acquainted with my faults.

Bertha G. came on the first of this month. I was again disappointed. Why cannot I pass over Bertha's faults as I used to
do? Why don't she love me as she did? I am disappointed and
I think she is decidedly so in me if she thinks seriously about
me at all.

My [Sunday School] girls are my joy and my pride, also my
inspiration. What I should do without them is beyond my ken.

Does God wish me to be willing to make a failure of my life?

Does He demand this ultimate consecration? God wishes to live thru Azalia Emma and He does not create failures in his own eyes. Sometimes in the eyes of the world such lives seem failures.

SEPTEMBER 23. "It is a great thing to sacrifice but it is a greater to consent not to sacrifice in one's own way."

SEPTEMBER 26. A successful meeting just over and the girls are gone. Was it a success? God only knows. The world—yes the girls thought it interesting but someway I am so disappointed. Sara had promised to stay all night and then didn't. She had good reasons doubtless but I am blue and I did want her so much. I must go to bed. There has been too much nerve racking work this week and I must rest up. This doubtless accounts for my blueness. Two missionary meetings to say nothing of three missionary committee meetings within one week.

The more we like people the keener our disappointment when they fail us.

NOVEMBER 9. The first Sunday that father and I have spent alone since mother left us thirteen weeks ago yesterday. It was hard to stand it at times but I must be brave. Father is getting older and is erratic on certain subjects. May I be given grace and wisdom, yes and tact to cope with the situation here and to indeed carry out mother's wish that I "be good to father." He is always kind to me and just. Why is he so unjust at times to the boys?

I have been away on a glorious vacation but it is good to be at home once more and busy.

NOVEMBER 23. The most peculiar kind of a temptation has assailed me to-day. Why, Oh why is it that I have such a well-defined sense of the "ought." It is all about a party too and probably a stupid one at that. Here are the facts. I sincerely hope that in setting them down here I will get them out of my system and be ready for something more worth while.

Martha is giving a dinner party for a number of college men and girls on Friday next at Spencerport, the occasion being the christening of the new piano at the Ranch. Nelson, Gertrude [sister-in-law] and I are invited. Autos are to carry us to and from Rochester. The evening will be partly spent in dancing.

Next Friday is Standard Bearers [missionary society] night in W. Webster and there is a big dance on hand at Webster which will take a number of my girls. There is a Basket Ball game which will take some more. There was some talk of postponing the S.B. meeting but I said that I never had postponed it for a dance and I didn't think I should begin now. I had it all planned that I would quietly send my regrets and on the whole I was not sorry for I don't dance with men, when to-night Gertrude and Nelson fairly "lit into" me and insisted that I should go. It is true that since college I have not been to a single party of this kind where I would meet college men but—think of the example I would set before my girls of loyalty to a cause should I cut the missionary meeting and go to the "Dance."

I am afraid strenuous efforts may be made to change the date even now in which case I don't know what I shall do. I sincerely hope I will do what is right in the case—that is not what I started out to write—I hope that I will be let alone in this matter and allowed to do as my conscience dictates. I must say in justice to all concerned that I would like to meet and know the men who will be at Martha's party for I do need to know young men.

And still the "prince" waits. Must all my "mothering" be expended on my "girls"? I love them dearly. Am I getting too interested in them to become a well-rounded individual? I want with God's help to make my life one of "good success" and I feel that this means an artistically lived life. Am I viewing life thru the eyes of the artist or the artisan?

For the last two Sundays I have thoroughly enjoyed my S.S. teaching but I doubt whether I have accomplished anything aside from keeping the attention of the class. In this I have succeeded fairly well. It is easy for me to meet and talk with girls but when it comes to talking *to* them I am not sure that I have any degree of success. To be sure they almost invariably give me their undivided attention, someway I cannot talk until I have that, but whether I really say anything to command the respect of the minds of my hearers is another question. I try to do so but—my efforts are so poor.

After talking for a half hour on some subject intended to inspire to greater endeavor there usually follows in my own heart a fit of despondency as if the inspiration I had given out had in some way robbed me of something essential. Because of this I wonder if my inspiration is from God—His supply ought to be exhaustless and to multiply by being used. I guess in reality it does increase, only the fatigue which accompanies the talk makes me despondent. The thought in the above is rather mixed. I am too tired to straighten it out but will leave it as an illustration of the way my mind jumps to conclusions, leaving many steps untrod. Sometimes I myself cannot locate the missing steps and so maybe they are not there. I don't wonder that people do not find what I have to say really worth listening to.

I must to bed. My mind ought to rest easier after having rid itself of all the above.

NOVEMBER 30. I went to Martha's party. The S.B. meeting was changed, not on my account alone however. I had a good time but there was in it all a bit of lonesomeness after all. I did enjoy meeting the people, many of them old friends.

I had a wretched time in S.S. to-day. Many girls—poor attention—inadequate preparation on my part. I am at a loss to know just what to do. I am not accomplishing results.

DECEMBER 14. A nice day—but a horrid headache.

My girls mean so much to me. Effey was here yesterday. She startled me by saying she did not know me anymore. I managed to find out that she was jealous—jealous of Faith and Florence I guess. Why! Oh why is it, we have to be jealous? When did this old journal record jealousy before? Not many pages back and it was I who was jealous of Effey. The regulation of ones friendships do surely require much tact, much patience, a good deal of love.

I do love Effey but I don't want to confine my love to her. I love Faith but this ought not to interfere with my loving some other girl just as much.

And still the prince lingers. I guess he is lost and will never come. Meanwhile I am enjoying the passing moments. My days are full of happiness and my nights of peace. What more could I desire? There is one thing. This order will not always last. What next, what next is the insistent cry. It is my fervent prayer that whatever be the next thing, I may be prepared for it and may be found ready.

I want the prince but maybe a career would do. But the career must be in the world of people—not of things. I love things—in a way—I am fond of my books, my pictures, my room, my desk because of happy associations. But—I love people just because they are alive—because I can learn from them, yes—and because I am permitted sometimes to help a little. But the prince, I want him.

DECEMBER 26. It was a happy Christmas even though it was the first without Mother. Mortimer and Annie did all in their power to give us a nice time. The baby was *dear*. I never imagined that a little tot could enjoy a Christmas so much.

◇ *1914* ◇

JANUARY 4. We were talking about atmosphere, last evening, Winifred, Effey and I. Winnie said that she liked the atmosphere of our house. What constitutes atmosphere anyway and why was I relieved to get away from the atmosphere of Mortimer's and Annie's house?

Now I thoroughly enjoyed the literary surroundings there, and the browsing was great. So was the late breakfast and the luxury of having it served in bed. But yet—it lacked some essentials. Was it cynical, was it wholehearted sincere? Is it polite or necessary or kind to force one's own opinions on another? Is it a sign of liberality to recognize in another's opinions, however they may differ from ones own, a certain degree of "reason for being?"

Last evening Faith, Florence, Effy and Winnie were here to dinner and remained all night. What a happy house party we did have!

Still no prince!

JANUARY 5. A happy day spent in Rochester. I have been working on the paper which I am expected to give before the College Woman's Club of Rochester next Monday and so spent several hours in the University of Rochester library. This afternoon I heard Ethel Curtiss talk most enthusiastically on her rural missionary work in Vermont. For almost a year she devoted her entire time to this kind of work and her tales were so much like my own experiences here in W. Webster. She seemed to accomplish so much that I found myself questioning at every turn why haven't you done something big like this, Azalia Emma. Have you perchance learned something in the last three years which Ethel Curtiss has not which in a way balances up? Maybe—I know not.

JANUARY 8. Did you ever do some "fool stunt" just because you wanted to—you, yourself, wanted to? For instance—I came up-stairs to bed just now—it is late—father must take an early car—breakfast must be on time to avoid a repetition of the fracas of this morning and yet—I took a notion that I wanted to put on my new boudoir cap—a fetching piece of frilliness.

No one would see it but just myself but I took a good deal of delight in humoring myself to that extent when my more practical nature requested a hasty preparation for bed. Another instance—I caught sight of a snap shot of Faith, decided that I was tired of that particular pose, remembered that in an envelope tucked away in the left hand corner, backside of the lowest drawer in my desk, there were other snaps of her and proceeded to look them up.

Isn't it queer!

Yesterday I learned that the prince (was he *the* prince?) is married.

APRIL 19. After all is said and done—this is a lonely world. Maybe it is just the natural unrest due to a Sunday alone with father. At any rate—the joy of living has not been very conspicuous this afternoon.

Patty [friend] is here—has been with me two weeks and I enjoy having her here. We are very congenial at times. To-night she disappointed me a little by going to Rochester when I felt she ought to go to bed. She has been ill a couple of weeks.

Sara came and brought me her photograph this afternoon. It is very like her and I shall enjoy having it in sight.

Sara is a dear and I love her much.

A good deal more than she does me. However, there is something wrong with Azalia Emma that she cannot make her religion attractive enough to be desired by such girls as she is. So attractive, so gifted, so talented, a born leader and having a well defined sense of the artistic, why is it that she will not welcome the opportunity to *live* artistically.

Patty has a very sensitive nature and is musical to the back bone. I wish a little real stability might be injected into her being. It will be such fun to see what kind of women all my girls develop into.

I live in my girls—I wonder whether I am neglecting father. To-night had I consulted my own feelings only, I should have gone to hear the Easter music repeated at the Central church but it left father alone and besides he didn't approve of Patty's going so I stayed at home. It is just as well. I am not stagnating for places to go. In reality I go too much for the good of my household.

I haven't felt like writing in this journal for months and I don't to-night. Patty kept her journal in German for two yrs. Maybe such a method of keeping one would be worth while.

My S.S. class bothers me and I am glad it does. I need to be bothered. I need to be pricked and pressed to the wall and made to work hard and really accomplish something worth while.

To-night the sundown was glorious and the birds and tree frogs enjoyed it to the full. I wanted the prince as I walked home from one of the neighbors alone to an empty house—no it was not empty—father and George were here.

MAY 24. Apple blossom Sunday and the country is *glorious*. I slept with Patty last night in my old room. It was so nice— in more ways than one. Patty has been away a part of a week and I missed her so much. Fine to have her back *home*. I ran away from home last Monday and went down to see Sara at Clifton Springs.

The past five weeks have been hard ones and so the two days among such different surroundings was greatly appreciated. I must have a [hired] girl soon. Esca has been under quarantine for Scarlet Fever but hopes to come back soon.

Not the man who does not have passions but the one who controls them is the good and great.

Ideals for ourselves give the impetus to conduct—not ideals for the other fellow.

The criterion by which to judge a friend is not how nearly he has achieved our ideal but rather what his own ideals are and how his ideals correspond to ours.

JUNE 7. Yesterday was a queer day, so happy, so disappointing, and withal so much worth while. It was the annual picnic of the Standard Bearers. It was a beautiful warm June day and everything looked its best. Mrs. Spaeth was the speaker and she surely did make an impression on my girls. She talked not on missions but on Whispering Voices using as a beginning the story of the maid of Orleans, Joan d'Arc. The modern day whispering voices were Ambition, Love, Opportunity, Duty and others, making a strong plea for workers on the foreign field. She said that no girl ought to go without a definite call. But this was what to her constituted a definite call. When one has searched out every reason why one *shouldn't* go and can find no definite reason, one may be pretty sure that one *ought* to go.

Edith came home with me and we had a fine talk—some time was spent in the moonlight by my west window. The disappointing time came at the meeting. Why is it that the more one loves a person the more it hurts when that person disappoints.

Patty—but then she knows she hurt just cruelly—not only me but her invited guest Laura—I think she will not do it again right away.

AUGUST 3. Baby Samuel is sick for the first time and we are all worried. Gertrude just said to Aunt Jennie, "Do you suppose I will ever get over having that *awful* sinking feeling inside of me?" And Aunt Jennie said "No—you will never get over having it even when the children grow up." I came home and wondered whether I really wanted children of my own. Selfishly speaking I am happier thus as I sit by an open west window in my old room enjoying to the full a marvelous sunset. All is so peaceful and quiet here—no one to disturb me or to demand attention. But Oh! I do want the other life—the right prince and the dear babies. Are they ever to be mine, I wonder? If it is for the best, they too will come. My life is given me day by day and all will be well.

The summer has been so happy but withal so selfish. I have been to Silver Bay for ten days at great expense to father but I did have such a lovely time.

Being with Grace Travis who was so radiantly happy in her engagement to Wendell Cleland meant much to me and convinced me of the necessity of waiting for just the right man. Grace and I are so congenial—we like the same things and—we bring out the best in each other. I went to Silver Bay with one big question unsettled. I have been struggling with it for many months, yes several years—I hope I have with the help of my God settled it, once and for all but I am not going to say that I will never change my mind because I cannot say what the future may make of me. The question was this—"Are you Azalia Emma, willing to let Jesus absolutely direct your life; are you willing, if it be his will, to let your life be a failure in the eyes of the world—in other words are you willing to make the supreme sacrifice." Now I had a pretty good idea of what an artistically developed life might be and it was harder than anything I ever did to give up my will and say *Thy* will be done, especially if *Thy* will might happen to mean the Orient at some future date. On Sunday July 19th I talked with God about it a long time in my room at Silver Bay, then taking Bible and writing materials I went out to seek a sheltered nook out-of-doors when I met Grace. Together we walked to a beautiful spot high up in the pine grove which looked down on beautiful Lake George. In vain did I try to write letters. Words would not come and finally in desperation I said to Grace—"I hate to have conclusions forced upon me." And then we talked it out together as she put her arms around me and kissed me. I had really decided when on my knees before God but it was *so* hard to tell anyone about it. As we finished talking—there was not much to say—both of us felt the seriousness of the occasion—we talked with God about it and then went down the hillside together. That night I gave my name to Mr. Meyer as a Volunteer if it be God's will. There is absolutely no opening for me to go thru just now and none in sight so for the time being Azalia Emma will stay at Peet Acres. One thing troubles me. Ought I to tell father? I dislike to do it very much but I would do it if I really thought it was the right thing. Just now it is my duty to stay and make a home for him. It is one year this week since mother left us. If I tell him he will think I am unhappy here and that he is standing in the way of my chosen career. What to do I know not. It seems cowardly not to tell him.

Faith has been here for ten days and we were so happy together. She is developing into a beautiful girl. I love her voice and her manner and her beautiful unselfish character. She is unconsciously just plain good all the time and so thoughtful in every little detail. While she was here I had one of the unhappiest days I have ever spent and her intuition and silent sympathy were perfectly wonderful. It more than half took away the sting of the pain. I have since learned that my sorrow was groundless and am *much happier*.

AUGUST 16. Patty's birthday. A day begun in sunshine and ended in showers. A beautiful day in many ways. Last evening the Standard Bearers gave a farewell party for Patty in the form of a Corn and Sausage Roast. The setting was perfect. The old orchard with its soft carpet of grass furnished a splendid place for a fire. I hope I'll not soon forget the picture of "my" girls as they rollicked around the dying embers in a happy game of Drop the Handkerchief. Then the hymns—well there was something to be desired in the music but I think almost every girl there felt the beauty of it all. As my guest there came Nobe Amagasu, a Vassar girl whom I met three years ago. She will return to Japan when she finishes college and she wants to work with the factory girls. Never before has any girl so interested "my" girls as did Nobe. She came home and stayed with me all night. Patty and her Twinnie slept together on the porch. Quite a house party. I think Patty likes me a little. I love her so much and am so anxious that she shall do herself justice.

I am wondering to-night just when I shall have the privilege and the pleasure of having her here again. As I write this, father, Patty, Mattie [hired woman] and I are sitting about a cosy fire in the dining room. Mattie is so nice, so competent and so neat. I hope she stays. I am having a fine rest up while she is here.

I have been allowed to read Patty's diary for this year. It has told me three distinct things about her which I sincerely hope she will let me talk with her about. I wonder if I can set them down in order. First she plainly shows her attitude of freedom, absolute and unrestrained, with men. Secondly she voices a very deep feeling when she says in quoting Vina—"I would trust you anywhere" and couples it with her own mother's statement that she too trusts her Patty.

Patty appreciated this trust.

And lastly Patty showed me in her letters this summer as well as her diary her personal nearness to her God and her desire to give the peace of God to those unhappy. Dear Patty—why will she hold me at arm's length when I want to love her and to talk with her about the things nearest to her heart.

As I told Aunt Jennie to-day—I have *just the nicest crowd of girl friends*. It is a responsibility but I *must measure up to it*.

AUGUST 17. Gertrude gave a luncheon to-day for Mabel, Charlotte, Martha, Sue and myself. We had such fun. Martha, Charlotte, Sue and I belong to the S.O.S. or the Sacred Order of Spinsters—the watchword of which organization is Save our Souls! With two men working for Charlotte, and Martha not able to live without her mail this summer and Sue fussing too, it looks to me as if I would be the one and only member of this august body after a very short time. Martha has something on her mind—she was not herself to-day. She acted bored—I wonder what it is or *who* he is.

AUGUST 23. It never rained harder, thundered longer or

lightened with more vividness than it does this minute. I am ready for bed but think I will write awhile. Mac lies at my feet. Strange how he has taken a notion to coming upstairs during a thunder-storm.

I am a wee bit lonely to-night. A week ago Patty was here and she played for us in the dark. I can almost read Patty's thoughts as she plays. She is a dear and I do love her a lot. I hope she is not too lonely to-night. Artistically we are very congenial but practically I [cannot] wholly fit in with Patty's irresponsible nature.

I sat down to write a treatise on the feminist question—the magazines are full of it—and in a way it disgusts me. Now *I* am anxious to really do something worth while as an individual even if I should marry and I guess I wouldn't want my individuality swallowed up by my husband but—there are mighty more tactful ways of having one's own way than by preaching about it or heralding the idea abroad until everyone is tired of the subject before you have begun to reach after your end. And so I guess I am a feminist at heart—but I am enough of the old-fashioned woman to love to be loved, to be cared for and yes, at times, to be ruled. I sometimes wonder whether after a year or two of such life it would pall upon me and I should demand my freedom. I maintain that marriage can and ought to be a partnership deal between individuals of equal personality and that at various times each partner can rule and at various times each partner must concede a point and grant a request.

OCTOBER 3. A busy day and I ought to be studying my S.S. lesson and sewing and telephoning but instead I want to write in my journal. I had a good talk with Ruth Metzger today, the first really true heart to heart talk I ever had with her. Ruth down deep in her heart of hearts wants to come into the church tomorrow but will she take the step is the question. She distrusts herself—poor child—and wonders whether if she wants to do a thing today whether she will want to do the same tomorrow. She is interested in the church and what it stands for and I think she appreciates the heart interest of other people. We talked together about it with God. Oh! it was hard for me to do it—

but in a very broken fashion I did it and my heart has been singing ever since. Why Oh! why is it so difficult for me to do the very thing which brings the greatest happiness, why is it so hard for me to talk about the things which lie closest to my heart? Patty wants to read my journal. Shall I let her? Maybe just a little part. Patty is a dear big Sister and I hope I am thankful enough to the dear Father for sending her back to me for the winter. Everyone is so good to Azalia Emma. Why is she having such a fine time in this old world!

Later—Ruth did not join the church.

OCTOBER 18. A sermon meant for me was preached today. Mr. Connal used as his text that well-known text from Phillippians about leaving the things which are past and pressing on toward the prize, and in telling about certain things which we must leave behind he mentioned our past attainments. My! but he struck the nail on the head. I just wonder if he knew how hard it hit. With the help of an all-wise Father I am going to try to forget all past glories and to press forever onward towards the high calling which is in Christ.

I want to state here and now that you Azalia Emma are and have been very conceited, that you have nothing to be conceited over and that all that you have done has been because God worked in you.

NOVEMBER 18. Jessie Coit is here. Never in all my life have I been so dependent upon some power outside my own. Jessie is a dear and I love her much, admire her a great deal and am intensely sorry for her. I think I never had a more sincere heartache for anyone. I feel certain that in some way she is misinformed and I want to help her but she is so happy seemingly in her present religious views—and they are those of the Christian Science church—that I seem to have nothing to offer her. I am glad she is so happy but—I covet for her the real truth. If what she believes is the real truth for her I trust that she may continue to believe it but—I cannot now believe that this is so. She has absolutely the right idea on sacrifice of self—she has an abiding faith, she questions not as I do, but she has such queer notions about sin, suffering and death. They are beautiful to her but I cannot accept them. She says what of religious experience I have to offer could not satisfy her and she considers me very radical. I guess I am.

This is surely a wonderful experience which I am having, an experience which will not come to me often. It has driven me to my Father more frequently than any other experience and I am so thankful. It has brought up discussions with which I am unable to cope, it has brought me nearer to Jessie than any other thing could, and it has shown me my weakness. To-day Jessie talked to my class on sacrifice of self. I just wish Grace Travis might have heard her. It was the one thing which Grace and I decided was wholly lacking in Jessie.

Ought Jessie to keep the work in N.Y. Branch with her present religious views? I have advised her to do both this year although if she is to be a Scientist she cannot do so indefinitely. I cannot help but hope since this faith which she now holds is not well grounded that she may be led by God to see wherein it is wrong.

DECEMBER 6. Mother's Birthday—I am thinking of that other birthday four years ago when we had a cake with one candle on it in honor of the occasion and mother came out to the table for the first time after quite an illness. My little mother—how I should enjoy having her spend the evening with us this evening. It is sixteen months since she left us. Does she see me now as I write and would she approve of what I am doing?

Joe has been quite in evidence again and I refused last night to go with him to the Rochester Glee Club Concert. The prince doesn't come. Now and then I think I catch a glimpse of him but I soon find out my mistake.

◇ *1915* ◇

JANUARY 5. A very remarkable day.

The morning was a bit prosey but only made a better background for what followed. It was butchering time, a time that I despise because of the work it entails. This afternoon I had my long-planned for talk with Mrs. Spaeth on two subjects, Christian Science and myself. Not in connection with each other however.

It was a cosy tea party. Mrs. Spaeth I think, feels that my place is still here with father even though the boys seem to think I ought to try my wings.

JANUARY 17. It is again Sunday night and I really want to write. Patty is playing and I am going to sleep with her and I am glad. I wanted to to-night.

Sara is wearing an engagement ring. Gertrude noticed it last night when she was there at a party.

I hope with all my heart that she is doing just the best thing for herself and I guess she is. She will enjoy a home of her own. And so they go—my girls. I am so thankful for a little bit of their lives. Whatever would I do without them. Just this week the wonderful, wonderful opportunity which I have has been pressed home to me as I thought of the dozens of girls with whom I correspond or who come here to see me. I can scarcely believe my eyes when I get their letters breathing as they do a sincere admiration, a deep affection and an opportunity for helpfulness. It is wonderful to be the instrument used in helping to make girls grow. It is one of the things which makes my life in West Webster worth while.

The whole question about my going or staying has insisted on making itself known. The more I think about it the more confident I am that it is up to me to stay. Besides I really want to, maybe that influences me but anyway I am happy and I have quite a big niche here and I know of no opening elsewhere.

FEBRUARY 28. I am unhappy to-night.

It is hard to come up to this in one's life—where you love with a whole-souled love a certain individual and find that she does not love you or the ideals you stand for. Patty is a dear and I love her much but Oh! she disappoints so cruelly at times and after all why is it that she disappoints. Is it because she does not agree with me? Maybe but *I hope* I am not such a conceited person. Surely she has just as much right to her opinion as I have to mine and if she is "tired of Missions" she has

a right to jot it down in her diary if she wants to. Azalia Emma—
you don't have to read Patty's diary and I advise you not to do
so from now on. Was it that remark of hers which hurt? No—
not just that but it was the state of mind of which it was indicative, a state of mind which for two days has distressed and
perplexed me and which I think I can now decipher. It is the
natural reaction due to too much "religiousity" to coin a word,
coupled with a growing unrest. But Oh! my Father, it does make
it so difficult to work for Thee. What can I do? Show me the
way. Patty has no idea how difficult it is for me to live the Christ-
like life in its fullness with her critical eyes looking on. Dear
Father—show me how to do it. I am glad for the perplexing
situation, I realize it is only thus that I grow but well—I guess
I better go to bed. The world of to-morrow will demand a rested
Azalia Emma. Father let me know the true meaning of that
word Love, about which we talked in S.S. to-day. Let me see
it in the patience, the kindness, the generosity, the humility,
the courtesy, unselfishness, the guilelessness and the sincerity
of my friends.

And when the prince does come, let him show me the true
meaning too. Oh! may he come soon. I am so very much alone,
after all.

"The most perilous thing in friendship is to let a friend know
that we want to reform him."

MARCH 13. Sue announced her engagement to Dr. Towsey
to-day.

She is the first to break the charm of the S.O.S.'s. I wonder
who will be the next? Martha or Charlotte. Of one thing I am
sure. It will not be Azalia Emma however much I might desire
it. With Margery Taylor I can say—"We have hopes but no
prospects."

Patty—well what shall I say? Last Sunday we had a long,
long talk which I think we both enjoyed but it showed me a
side of Patty which disappoints and which I cannot help but
condemn. Doubtless Patty is far oftener disappointed in Azalia
Emma's lack of sympathy and understanding than A.E. is dis-

appointed in Patty's disregard of the decrees of custom and her seeming selfishness. I wonder if Patty really cares for me.

I have had an experience in the last two weeks—and experience in nursing. Marshall Murray, our new [hired] man, has been very ill with Blood Poisoning. It meant 24 hour duty some of the time. Taking care of a man was a new experience.

I sleep with Patty to-night.

APRIL 8. Why is it that the times when P.C.B. disappoints are invariably connected with Lewis? Is it because I cannot sympathize with the side of Patty which he brings out.

There was a party to-night. I wanted Patty to go. She had a severe headache and didn't want to go out, would not come to supper and I gave her headache medicine. I cancelled my own acceptance to the party partly because she was ill, partly because I was over tired anyway, and didn't feel like going—but I should have gone had Patty gone with me.

Along comes Lewis and the auto and they are both away and gone.

Now for Azalia Emma it would be absolutely wrong to accept one invitation, then refuse on the ground of health and turn around in the next breath and accept another invitation. However—maybe it is all for the best. I know not. But Patty's conduct would have been wrong for me—of this I am certain. I am tired to-night. I know I have been living on my nerves of late. I feel so upset away down deep and I do need some guidance.

APRIL 15. There is one thing which I have waited for for a long, long time and this week it came. I guess maybe Patty loves me a little, at any rate she loved me a little.

Mr. and Mrs. Spaeth were here and we all went to the woods. It was a joke about their wanting to be official Go-betweens. I think it is so amusing to have people literally marry me off. And yet—the prince—where is he?

I need something very much—I guess it is a bigger portion of "Thy" Spirit. I am sleeping with Patty. She begged me to.

JUNE 19. I am lonesome to-night. All day the house has fairly teemed with ghosts of memories of my Patty. She is in Kansas

City this very hour I suppose. Why! even my yellow toothbrush is lonely without its orange colored mate.

I think I'll close Patty's door and then every time I pass her room I'll not be expecting to see her.

JUNE 20. I have missed Patty at every turn. No disordered stack of music on the piano, no one with whom to enjoy the sunset, no one at her place at table. No Sunday night music in the dark and Oh! it is so lonesome.

I want her to say right now in her funny abrupt fashion, "Sleep with me to-night, Azalia Emma." Life is one series of changes and endeavors to get used to different conditions.

JULY 1. Standard Bearers Meeting is over and I am not sleepy. Again I missed Patty. Wonder what she would have thought about the meeting. Patty was always my interest thermometer. If a meeting interested her it was all right. I wonder if we are not all of us thermometers for someone!

It was good to be there. I really do feel that if I should not remain in W. Webster longer a spark of real vital missionary interest has been kindled which will not soon be smothered. The society might go to pieces, doubtless would in time as the girls scatter, but the girls themselves may say in after years— "Oh! yes—I have been interested in the cause of Missions since I was a girl."

AUGUST 3. The Rebeccas [club] elected me President—of course I withdrew. It is lovely to have so many friends and to be asked to assume so many responsible positions but there is a limit. For two years the Rebeccas have elected me Pres. and the Ladies Aid did so also this year or practically so.

It is not good for me to be so early pushed to the front.

I am lonely to-night. I wonder if it is the prince I'm wanting! Maybe it's a definite program for the next few years. It is hard to live in the dark and keep one's faith burning brightly—and it is not possible *alone*. For the host of loyal friends I am so thankful, for the joy of being very much needed I am thankful and for abounding health.

AUGUST 6. I believe I am growing up. I do so thoroughly enjoy reading things which used to be a task. I have been having such a pleasant time with a Biography of John Millington Synge. This statement startled me—

"He was an artist before he was a Nationalist and a very long way before." It aroused all those old questionings of mine.

I trust that the surrendered A.E.P. will be content with the artistic achievements which are possible through her great Teacher.

AUGUST 15. I must write it all down—at least as much as I can remember. Nannie hurt me horribly when she said that I didn't work hard, that I had a comparatively easy time, that I talked so much about my work that I gave all with whom I came in contact a terrible idea of my over worked condition. However I realize now that it was but an attempt on her part to gain from me a little appreciation of her own working ability which she thinks I horribly underestimate. Oh! dear—everything is in such a whirl. Maybe it isn't hard here—but I would hardly wish for Nannie anything harder than to exchange places with me. And yet the real sting of her criticism came in the fact that I am so conscious of its truth. I do not impress people with that calmness and peace of the Christ, that quiet acquiescence with an established order that bespeaks strength of character and depth. Instead I seem to beg from those about me a sympathy which they seem to love to give but which in Nannie's estimation I no more deserve than does she. Now I do not need or covet this—I do love to be appreciated that is human but I am sorry I do assume this attitude of soliciting sympathy for my position here on the farm when in fact my life here is an enviable one.

Then later we talked of aesthetic values, their presence in people—and their lack. On such questions we meet on common ground and I do believe that it is my appreciation for such things that makes Nannie like me a little. I cannot sympathize with all of Nannie's views—but Nannie changes her ideas as she grows. I have never been so conscious of this as I have been since she came this time. And she is more tolerant. She seems to be trying to understand.

I want the prince to come. No I am not lonely but I feel as if there was a big something in life that has as yet been denied me. When will he come? Never?

SEPTEMBER 5. Another milestone passed but I don't feel any older. And I am so well.

Patty is back and it is good to have her. To-night she is "on a tear" but I ran off upstairs so that it didn't annoy me. One thing I am going to try to do this week. I am going to stop uttering my criticisms of people and of things. I would give much to unsay some things I said to Patty this afternoon concerning Nannie. I must be more thoughtful of my friends and more loyal.

SEPTEMBER 17. The threshers have gone—so has the hottest and one of the busiest weeks of my life. I am sure it has been the hottest.

Two terrible experiences have been mine since last I wrote and I am loathe to even mention them here. First, foremost and all important—I think that my father is planning to marry again. Words fail me when I try to talk about it so I've said not a word to anyone except Patty and it was very hard to tell her even when I knew she of all people could truly sympathize, for her own father is shortly to be married. In a way I suppose father thinks it is for the best for me—this remarriage. It will leave me free to do as I please—(And what is that? As God pleases, I trust.)

However I cannot think of the young woman whom father is paying attention to as taking my little mother's place in our home and I sincerely hope I need not witness it if come it does. Father never in his life hurt me so cruelly as he did a week ago when he showed me quite plainly that he did not wish to take me places in the evening. Father has been unfair at times with the boys but I have always managed to escape from his anger. Last week he was beside himself because I wanted to go to Prayer Meeting. I don't think I'll ever mention going out with him in the evening when I know a certain young woman is to be there. And now I wonder when it is all going to be changed.

I am trying not to worry but just trust that "my God will provide" as He always has.

The other tragedy was a keen disappointment in my Patty. She is so different at different times. Last Sunday night I slept very little after knowing that she had smoked a cigar with Bob Connal. What is that streak in her? the self that certain of the boys seem to arouse in her? Bob must have an awful opinion of her now whereas Patty is at heart as pure and holy as a little child and oversensitive to everything. Will she never gain a little poise? Oh yes she will but I am fearful of what may happen to her in the meantime.

Patty is a dear. I shall long remember how she hugged me up tight last night when I asked her how long it took her to get used to Virginia. She never did it before. How good it is that a Divine Providence saves until we need it the thing we so much desire. All last year I craved Patty's demonstrative love and only once or twice did I receive it. I need it more now. I wonder if the Prince is waiting to be so very much needed. I wish he would come. I am twenty-eight years old and I feel as if I had been a wee bit robbed because this experience has been denied me.

However *I know* it is for the best someway.

SEPTEMBER 18. Father called me into the living room this morning and I knew by his manner that a trying scene would ensue. And it did. I have avoided it as much as I could, to-day he insisted on gaining my opinion of Mabel. He wanted to know whether I thought she would go with him fishing to-day. He also wanted to ascertain my feelings on the subject. Father is lonely—so are we all—but Father especially. But Oh! I fear he will never be happy with Mabel and I do pity the girl. My father is generous to a fault but there are many of his ways which are vexing.

Patty and I gathered Bittersweet to-day, a nice ride but Patty was blue when we got home. I wish I knew why. Everyone is telling her she ought to stay in town [Rochester] until I almost think they will persuade her to do so. Oh! I do hope not for I need her *so much*.

NOVEMBER 14. The diamond ring appeared on Mabel's hand to-day. Patty saw it. I told her to look for it. I simply could not.

What is to be my attitude toward this whole affair? Is it my duty to congratulate her and what about the wedding? When is it to be and where? Must I be present?

What am I to do with my life? I want to put it where it will mean the most in the Master's service but where that is I do not know.

I am willing to go to the Foreign Field if it is God's will. I am not sure that I would qualify there. Aunt Lola has invited me to go to Portland to live with her. I am considering entering the Y.W.C.A. Training School, I am so interested in the girls' work.

But aside from all this I do want to live the Christ life in its fullest sense. I sincerely hope at this critical turn I may not do the wrong thing.

I am so lonesome sometimes, so perplexed and so worried. It will all turn out for the best someway I feel sure.

DECEMBER 7. Mabel came here for the first time as Father's fiancée. I thought it would be worse than it was. I think it is nothing short of remarkable how all W. Webster refrains from talking with me about Father's approaching marriage. I never guessed they would be so considerate of my feelings. More each day do I realize that I *must* call on Mabel.

DECEMBER 25. It has been a happy day—and yet in spots a wee bit lonely. I guess it has been too plain sailing for me of late for I thrive and am happy in adversity. There were twelve of us at Mary's for dinner and we had a beautiful tree.

Mary has a nice home, a good husband, two darling babies and—is very much tied down. I have none of the aforesaid and am quite free—yet I would exchange with her in a minute if the "right prince" asked me.

I am sleeping in Patty's room alone. It seems strange. Patty is away. Where will I be next Christmas?

◇ *1916* ◇

JANUARY 23. Another Sunday and such a failure as far as I am concerned. Physically I have been overtired and that partially accounts for it. Sunday School was not all that could be desired.

Last week received a long letter from Olive Pye urging me to take up Bible Training and come to Korea. I say—urging, but I am not strictly accurate for she simply stated that there was an opening there at that time and that she would like me there. A note from Mrs. Spaeth telling me of two important sessions that she had in N.Y. concerning my [missionary] appointment. Miss Lewis wants my papers at once.

I want to state here that I want to find just *the* place where the Father would place me. Surely somewhere there is a definite plan for my life and if I but wait and work I feel sure the Good Father will lead my steps into it. I hope with all my heart that I will be entirely willing to say "Thy will not mine be done," no matter what the task.

FEBRUARY 26. I think it is quite time I wrote up my inner self—Seems as if she had been so unstable of late that it was hardly safe. This morning I woke up really happy and with a settled feeling—Why—Because I really enjoyed the sensation of considering myself a foreign missionary. The past months have seen Azalia Emma fluttering from one kind of life work to another in a blind fashion, trying to feel my way as I planned the next period of my life. I think I am ready to say that I want to do foreign work and that I do not think I'll be contented until I do it. Y.W.C.A. or Settlement would be only temporary. But all the family oppose.

But the queerest thing has happened. Patty with all her aversion to the foreign mission enterprise, with her many shortcomings—Bless her heart—thinks it is the only thing for me to do and was quite glad when I told her last evening that I had sent for my application papers from our Board. Will wonders never cease!

I had a nice talk with Miss Hughes yesterday. She told me that she thought when I once settled the question for myself— that the family would gradually acquiesce. I am hoping so.

MARCH 19. I am still happy about the thought of going abroad. Father is gradually becoming reconciled, the boys are great about it and so are Nannie and Gertrude. Even Aunt Jennie and Uncle Wilbur approve if I think it is really my task. I will not know whether the Board accepts me until May. Meanwhile I am devouring the Mission training school catalog.

I am lonely to-night, locked into my room. The family are all away and there is a strange new hired man in the house. If I am to be a Foreign Missionary I must learn to trust the Master for *everything*.

I really wanted Patty to stay with me to-night but she felt she must go.

Several times of late I have caught myself picturing Patty teaching in the Orient. And really I suppose stranger things than this have happened. Wouldn't it be lovely if we could be over there together.

Hartford, Connecticut. APRIL 3. I am in the Kennedy School of Missions and having a lovely time. It is a rest and recreation even though I do get so tired as to my head.

I am trusting that I may indeed find myself while here. I want to face every doubt be it concerning my Master or concerning my work, for Oh! I do so want to be just what my Heavenly Father wants me to be and I am eager to serve.

APRIL 22. Tomorrow is Easter and tonight while all is quiet and I am alone I want to think about the meaning of the day and to write down my thoughts on the subject. The question of the physical resurrection still remains open. It is one of the things which has been hung up in my brain room for some time awaiting a happy and satisfying solution. I had hoped to arrive at some conclusion e'er this but have not. Meanwhile what does Easter mean to me? It means joy and happiness and peace because it bespeaks the risen Lord in my heart. How can this be if he never rose from the dead! Ah but he did rise, spiritually. How do we know? By the testimony of his friends. But his friends testified to a bodily resurrection. Yes but does God ever work in any but Nature's ordained ways? He is able to—for God is all powerful—but we have no reason to believe that he does now and why should he [have] then? And after all is it any more wonderful for him to work outside of an ordained plan than to create the plan and adhere to it?

I am happy up here at Hartford but in a way I am downhearted too. I feel the utter lack of knowledge which I suppose must come. I feel the need of a much more constant companionship with the Master and a closer heart Knowledge of Him, I need the open eye to detect an opportunity for service and a tact that will make that service acceptable to the one who needs it.

Clifton Springs Sanatarium. JUNE 19. Here I am laid up for repairs, a hale and hearty looking individual. I am hoping a couple of weeks here will make the Board say that I may sail for Japan September 7.

I want to whisper into these pages while the memory of the day is very vivid, some impressions of yesterday [at home] which I suppose may be the last glimpse of Patty which will be mine for five long years. It was Sunday and a busy day made Patty hysterical then quiet in the afternoon but as we talked upstairs after dinner while she rested we decided that maybe life was and always would be just one change after another with the necessary heartbreaking partings. Tears came in Patty's eyes. Poor dear. It was as hard for her as for Azalia Emma for that very noon Mabel had in a rather cool manner told her that she didn't know whether she could have Patty come back for a week or two in the Fall or not.

At supper time Ella came. She stayed until the eight fifteen and Patty played. It was the only chance I had to talk with Ella about herself and I knew Patty could not help but be disturbed. She finally gave up playing—I knew why—she says she didn't.

After Ella went we undressed and lay out a long time looking up into the evergreen trees. It was glorious! Then we crept into bed upstairs. Oh but I forgot the happiest time of all. It came when Patty played just to Azalia Emma—I wonder if I can remember the things she played. "Lord for to-morrow and its needs" was so appropriate and brought the tears welling up, they splashed over while she played one verse of *my* hymn. I could hardly keep back the sobs at Home Sweet Home. I think it was O Perfect Day with which she closed. Dear Patty—I *hope* she knows how very very dear to me that music was.

I was so distressed when Patty said to me as we lay looking up into the evergreens "Don't you go and get any other sister while you are away." I tried to tell her that we all had to learn to share our friends.

Later I told her that I wanted *her* to find another sister—but Oh! do I? In my heart of hearts I fear I covet her love and *all* of it. I do know what she has done for me in the past two and a quarter years. She has made me far more sympathetic with girls, she has made me appreciative of music and of the artistic in many things and she has been a friend when I sorely needed friendship. And too she has intuitively denied me the physical part of friendship which in the past has been disastrous. She has made me keenly sensitive in so many ways. Father I thank thee for our friendship. It has been good.

I really said goodbye when we kissed each other good night and while she was all cuddled in my arms we asked the Good Father to keep us very close to Him on every step of our ways. Will Patty ever come to Japan? And will I ever get there myself?

Aoyama Jo Gakuin—Tokyo, Japan. OCTOBER 4. Is that not an imposing address! Indeed I am in Japan, have been here more than two weeks but in reality they seem at least two months. I am well and strong—yes and happy. At last I have broken all ties of friendship and home and come over here for what? Do you know Azalia Emma? Yes—I think I do. I have come here because I believe that there is a big untilled field here among the girls of fair Japan and because I have now no serious home ties and it seemed as if God wanted me to learn to know and love these girls. At first I wanted very much to keep on loving the American girls. That was so easy. But it did not satisfy that big hungry feeling in my heart and while doing it I could not

"Indeed I am in Japan." (*Courtesy of Sophia Smith Collection, Smith College*)

feel that I had truly dedicated my heart and life to the Master. And so I am here. I do not know for how long or for what kind of work but I am trying to live one day at a time trusting that the whole of God's plan will one day be revealed. The language is hard and I am very timid. The city is unsanitary and at present there is much Cholera here. The people with whom I am living are lovely to me but *so* different from the friends at home. It is so strange to begin in the kindergarten at twenty-nine and even learn to bow all over again. But the experience will be good for Azalia Emma. It was only yesterday she was complaining that everyone was *too good* to her. It is well to remember some of those wonderful times now. The times when everyone loved you and praised and gave gifts. Memories are happy things to have and of especial value to the traveler in Japan for they are neither heavy nor bulky, are not subject to duty nor inspected at the customs. They are of especial worth in times of homesickness and loneliness, and they never wear out with use.

◇   ◇

Afterword

Azalia Peet's life in Japan is richly documented in almost forty years' worth of diaries and letters now in the Sophia Smith Collection at Smith College.

As a missionary she concentrated on social welfare, especially where women were concerned. As she later remembered, "My interests were always in the women who worked in hospitals, in the mines, in offices, as teachers and those who graduated and married right away and went into homes. The Japanese girls were looking for a vision of something to do. Something more than just being shut away in a home with a baby a year." On furlough in 1923, she wrote her Master's Thesis for Boston University on women in Japanese factories.

In her missionary work Peet's interest in liberal interpretations of the Bible was not always approved of by her superiors, but "this was of great service to me in dealing with Japanese intellectual students," and such open-mindedness led to friendly working relationships with local Buddhist and Shinto priests.

During her 37 years in Japan, Azalia Peet established and ran day care centers, health clinics, social centers and schools. Her innovative approach extended to actually living among her Japanese colleagues, sharing whatever was available in the way of food and shelter—a radical idea at the time.

As World War II approached, Peet was working in a fishing village where she was the only American. The U.S. Embassy insisted that she leave; she was sent home against her will, one of the last Americans to leave Japan in 1941.

Instead of going back to Rochester as she had planned, Azalia found an acute need for her services on the West Coast of the U.S. The evacuation and internment of Japanese-Americans was causing great hardship and confusion, and with her knowledge of Japanese she was able to help people cope. She stayed in the camps of Oregon and Washington for four and a half years, living as the internees did under extremely difficult conditions.

270

After the war Azalia Peet was on one of the first boats going back to Japan. Her home had been destroyed by bombs but she started anew, establishing a community center in another village. She remained in Japan until her retirement in 1953, when she was awarded the Fifth Order of the Sacred Treasure by the Japanese government for her valued work.

Azalia Peet retained her intense interest in social problems until the end of her life. In an interview a few months before her death, she said, "I look at things from this standpoint—the survival of the worker that hasn't enough to eat, . . . that doesn't have any education and was deliberately uneducated for his servitude. So I'm interested in my own government and its attitude toward uneducated, troubled, sick people."

Azalia Emma Peet died on September 21, 1973 in a church retirement home in Asheville, North Carolina. All quotes in this Introduction and Afterword are from an interview conducted by Jacqueline Van Voris in January of 1973 for the Smith College Centennial Study.

THE DIARY OF

Winifred Willis

Ogunquit, Maine;
New York, New York
1923–1924

Winifred Willis (*The Schlesinger Library, Radcliffe College*)

◇　　◇

Introduction

Winifred Willis was already an accomplished writer by the age of twenty-one, when she began this, the thirty-sixth volume of her diary (the earlier volumes have, unfortunately, been lost).

Writing ability ran in the family; her father was a successful New York journalist. Willis herself nurtured her talent in her early years through an extensive self-imposed course of reading. Illness in early childhood had caused her to fall behind her classmates, and she left school permanently in the fifth grade. Although she later came to regret this lack of formal schooling, her knowledge of literature and philosophy was extensive.

Willis was born in Brooklyn in 1902, and grew up with her sister Harriet, two years her senior, in and near New York City. Their parents separated when Winifred was sixteen. Harriet continued to live with their father; Winifred took an apartment with her mother, supplementing their meager income by turning out "potboilers" which she sold to popular magazines, and poetry for such newspapers as the *New York Herald*.

The diary begins in Ogunquit, Maine, an artists' colony where Willis was spending the summer with friends, doing a great deal of writing, and pondering both her future and her secret romance with Bill, an old family friend.

◇ *1923* ◇

JULY 10. Ogunquit, Maine. Torn about as I was in my heart these past days I have had the misery of not hearing from Bill, when everything in me was crying out to him as never before. When finally his letter came it was short—he was terribly busy. . . .

I didn't write to Bill for several days, then last night I felt that I must. I wrote out my tortured heart to him. I didn't care how he might react to it—I just let go, and told him my longing for freedom, my loathing of the conventional New York life I have been living, my new, intense desire to be myself, complete, unfettered. I did not in any way appeal to him—I just *told* him as though we were talking, for I have talked to him just as freely many times. But just the fact that it was a letter made it far more personal, of course. A written word carries a certain destiny; a spoken word drops into silence and is no more. I explained to him how much I want to come home [to New York City] (though not why) but how torn I am about it, how I dread the old life of living other people's lives, of not being myself. I poured out my desire to write, and the impossibility of doing it seriously at home. All the time I felt, as I have felt through the whole business, that there was no real reason for it, no *grounds* for all I feel, no decent explanation.

It was midnight when I finished the letter, and I wrote at the bottom that I would walk the mile and a half to town and mail it immediately, for otherwise I would tear it up in the morning. When the letter was mailed I felt a weight lifted from my heart—I stumbled wearily home and lay down thinking "never mind, its gone, I don't care what he thinks of it or if he reads out of it what I am really trying to tell him. Nothing matters." And so I slept like the dead till almost eleven o'clock this morning. I will try not to give him a thought till I get his answer. But how frightened I shall be when it comes! I told him that I wanted to be free to live, to write, to love—will he understand why I so want to be free?

Sometimes I get by myself and admire the beauty around me,

but when I am around with the others it is nonexistent, forgotten. I used to long to travel, and feel that my life was wasted in one place, but I know now that time and place do not matter. So death cannot be very terrible, since we cannot take time and place into it. But one's inside being matters so! And who knows but that goes into death? One believes it at times.

Such strange things depress me! I remember when I was very little that certain faces, certain scenes, used to overwhelm me with an unbearable pain and sadness. I remember walking in Brooklyn with Mother when I was only about eight or nine years old, and we came to a big, dark, clanging street—it was raining, I think, and I know that a Salvation Army band was playing. Suddenly I was crying. A terrible, empty horror seemed to be reaching out of things at me, I could not imagine that I had ever been happy and gay, or that I had ever looked forward to anything with hope and delight. There was something as cold and final as death lying on my heart. A few times since I have had the same overwhelming sensation—in the dark of that hopelessness I could die without a regret. There are faces that give it to me—Margaret's face gives it to me. She is an old maid of thirty-eight, she is pale and thin and has always been sickly and nervous and dissatisfied. There is a young boy she knows in her town, Cambridge—he is a Harvard student and lives winters with her family. She talks constantly of "Ralph" and I know that she loves him, and does not even know it herself. When she speaks of him I could kill her—I hate the hopelessness of her—she sickens me with the drab possibilities of life. A weak, nervous woman, fading away because there is no man to feed her, and keep her from starving to death! When I see such things life towers up like a black, black cloud over and around me—there is no escape. Yes—Bill is the escape. In his arms, hot with his nearness, the black cloud couldn't touch me. I feel that I shall never be alone with him again. That would be a living death to me.

JULY 11. Last night was strange—I could not sleep. When the first streak of rose came through the sky I sat up in the window, watching. The land was inky black, a narrow darkness thrusting its points out into the green blue sea and sky. The horizon was dark, with the rose flushing it and gradually lifting it up and back. I wanted to wait for the sun to burst through but was too tired so went back to bed after pulling the window shade down to keep the glory out of my eyes.

JULY 13. No letter from Bill yet. I await his letter in a state between fear and longing, the tensity of which makes me feel half ill. If he understands the stormy heart that dictated my letter to him, it seems as though his reply must give some hint of it.

I am more unsettled than ever. A letter arrived from Anna Hedrick urging me to come down to Virginia for a while. And yet I have written Mother I want to come home, and I do with all my heart.

If Bill's letter discourages me I shall not return however, but go on down to Virginia. My only reason for returning to New York is Bill, and unless he understands that there is no use in my going at all. I have some vague idea of getting some sort of a job in a strange city, and living there alone. Washington might be a good place. I could get along with an allowance and what I could earn. I have three short stories here in my room that I have written—and finished!—since I have been here. "The Mirth of the Gods" I have at *Brief Stories*, and "The Wheel of the Wagon" I shall send to *Double Dealer* when Bill returns it. My poems are selling better than might have been expected, and in every way my writing is improving, as I well know.

Ah well, the gods or something take care of things. Whatever I do there is some destiny shaping my end, roughhew it how I will. I have had that sense of destiny too long, too heavily, not to believe in it more or less.

JULY 15. A letter Saturday morning addressed in Bill's handwriting made my heart leap. Imagine how flat it fell when I found only the carbon copies of some poems he had sent out to the Herald for me. No word of any kind in answer to my letter! I hated him, *hated* him. . . . I can reach no decision about going home until I hear from him.

All day the land and sea have lain shrouded in mist, and this afternoon the rain thundered down as tho bent on wrecking our little bungalow, while Bet, A. and D. (two artists, a man and a girl, who are spending a month here together) and myself played bridge within. I have come to my room and can hear the thundering of the sea against the rocks, and the soft patter of a gentler rain-fall which has come on. I have been thinking how wonderful, how perfect, it would be if Bill and I could have a week, or a month somewhere together. . . . It seems to me the world would never be meaningless again if we could have that, he and I. Dark life must always be at times, and even dull, but the uselessness would go out of things I know if we could have a little of the best of life for a while, however brief, together. Sometimes now, because of the reserve that he cannot keep out of his letters, I wonder if I have ever really made him kiss me, or only dreamed it. His letters are so like the outer crust of him, and that crust was all I, or anyone, ever saw of him thru all the years of casual intercourse.

JULY 17. When at last a letter came from Bill today I decided to put off my home-going no longer, and have made all arrangements to leave on the 9.31 from Kennebunk tomorrow evening. He said: "Your letter of rebellion was read carefully. Don't my dear make this mistake of many and confuse liberty with license. And don't ever forget that conventions and the so-called old fashioned ideas are the lubricants of every day life, and are the result of years of experience. Each must live the way that has been learned is best for all, and it is selfish for one to 'fling' convention to the winds. . . . You can live your own life and seek and strive for your ideals. But it all takes time and you must be patient and not try to buck the tide."

Just words—that's all Bill is except when he's near and allows the draperies to be cast off of things. Oh, I am yearning for him again, for our old intimacy, for his daily 'phone call, and the rare bliss of his kisses, which come so seldom and are so sweet.

JULY 18. Now that the day is dying, and in about two hours the automobile will be here to carry Jeff [her dog] and me to the train, I am consumed with excitement. There is an impatience that comes with nearness to wanted things that is wellnigh ungovernable. All this; the rocks, and the waves, and the sunsets and sunrises seem suddenly unreal. I feel detached from the life of the past six weeks. I am straining ahead with hope while all the time the cynic in me is hanging back with fear— fear of nothing. Nothingness is the most terrible tragedy that can happen to a person like me. I am always sweating along in deadly fear of it.

JULY 23. New York. Yesterday Bill came. Mother was away, we had the place to ourselves, but I felt strangely shy of him, I didn't want him to kiss me because I so wanted him to, if you know what I mean.

JULY 24. Last night mother and I had dinner together, then she went out, and later Bill 'phoned to find that I was alone, so down he came. We sat and talked in the dusk, and then we took Jeff for a walk, and then home again to the little apartment and sat talking until late. I hardly know what we said. We were both in that tranquil state that comes sometimes between peo- ple—we did not feel restless, he did not kiss me, and I felt somehow that whether he did or not it was all the same.

SEPTEMBER 9. Ogunquit. How did I think I could ever give you [her journal] up? It has been good in ways, and I have been more in myself, more in my life, more vitally a part of outside things—but though I shall never go back to driveling I shall come to you at intervals. I shall always need you. I need you now.

Things begin to happen as soon as you stop expecting them. For long, slow weeks the days and nights dragged by intolerably, and I lived despair in all its old, sick repetitions that I know so well. Then I had a letter from Mrs. VanderKley of *Vogue*. She requested that I call, and since then I have been writing book reviews for *Vogue* at a liberal rate of compensation, and making a success of it. I have now submitted sixteen; only one of which had to be changed. *The Times* and *The Herald* have been printing my poems; *The New Pearsons* has taken "The Death of Thais" and paid me $10.50 for it; and I have had a wonderful letter from Kofoed, rejecting "The Spiderweb," but stating frankly that it was too advanced—too sophisticated—for a lesser publication like *Brief Stories!*

It will be a week tomorrow since I left home. Mother and I have taken a new apartment on Greenwich Avenue so I will never return to Thirteenth Street again—she moves to the new place October first, and I will stay here anyway until then. This place never seemed so beautiful to me before. I have attained no calm of body, but an exquisite calm of mind—a new control of my mental senses. A wild blue autumnal sea shakes out its white plumes all day on the rocks below our shack, and there is a rare privacy and silence in which to live and create. The books Mrs. VanderKley sends keep me busy, and I am to write some articles for *Vogue* also, while I am here.

Just now, and for as far into the future as these eyes can see, I want only the thing that has been denied me; want only that flesh that is—or professes to be—cold to me. I give myself no hope, but I cannot change the course of my heart's destiny any more than I could change the roadway of the stars.

SEPTEMBER 27. Last Monday Bet, her dog Pete, and her baby left for good, bag and baggage—but I have stayed. I have discovered a new world of ecstasy: the solitude that is being alone—not lonely. Except for an occasional nod, word, or exchanged courtesy with the artists who still remain here in the Colony I have been utterly by myself, with only Jeff. And I have been happy! How I have written! Good God! My pen seems charmed these days; my brain a flashing meteor that I cannot check in its plunging flight through unguessed realms. It is night now—the sea roars and pounds, a fire burns bright in the grate behind me; Jeff sleeps: I am at peace. I have only one tragedy left—the only one I have ever had—virginity.

SEPTEMBER 29. Sunset. The sea is a great still green pond, and the tranquil sky bends down above it, softly rose and lavender with the reflected colors of the sun. It has been a warm, golden day; the trees and bushes shining russet red with leaves; apples and pears falling to the ground in heaps from laden limbs. I am almost tired of this beauty; it hurts one, haunts one, de-

mands some expression other than mere writing—demands
human contact. Yet I am alone—alone.

OCTOBER 3. The artists here grow warmer—dined with Ade-
laide the other night in her studio and last night she dined with
me. Izzie and her tall, bearded lover, (whom Bet and I called
"Christ" between ourselves) are most interesting people. She
paints and he sculpts. He would do well to sculpt himself, for
he is a beauty. Everyone save these two, and the Kuniyoshis,
are gone now, and it is nice having less people. I generally go
to town in the late afternoon and come home around by the
Marginal Way which follows the sea along high cliffs. At that
time the sun is sinking, a red glow in the west, and the sky
over the sea catches the reflections, and the sea burns here and
gleams there, exquisite, dark, and brooding. It brings to mind
something—night, storm, wide spaces, other-lives—there is no
name for it. One catches it, loses it, wonders a bit—forgets.
But the beauty remains printed indelibly on the brain. As long
as I live I will be able to shut my eyes, draw breath, and behold
the great ugly magnificent sea stretching from rocks to skyline.
Always it frightens me, takes my breath, inspires me with
strange, exotic dreads; being woman, I therefore love it. Yet it
is a love mingled with dislike and often weary boredom. I tire
of its eternal flatness. Why doesn't it get up and go somewhere?
Since it won't I shall, but not before the middle of the month.
I have no thrill of home-going.

Thank God, I have almost acquired the mental isolation
which is the only solution to my problems and the one toward
which I have been struggling thru all my dark hours. It is the
goal toward which my life has been unconsciously moving. If
it shuts out the little illusion of love, it leaves mind and body
free and satisfied—is more necessary?

Having now partaken of lunch—three bananas, baked beans,
peanut butter on bread, milk—I would like nothing better than
to hie me to some ocean cove, but whenever I thus try to utilize
nature I am reminded of Wilde's dissertation on her discomforts!
Truly, as he said, any carpenter can make a chair fit one's back,

but a natural seat among rocks or grass is bound to be one of discomfort, despite the poets!

I have found the missing link between me and these artists around me. Splendid people all, of fine independent views and excellent breeding and no small amount of ability in the direction of their art, no doubt, but not an ounce of humor in the lot of them! It is beyond belief, at times. They take life with such a tremendous seriousness—no more than I perhaps, but something within me will not allow me to exploit this seriousness. These people are, without selfishness but in the most natural and unthinking way, wrapped up in themselves, their work, their problems. So complete is their absorption that no thrust, however clever, can break through, or find an unguarded chink in the armor. Perhaps I am suffering from bruised pride— I have cast forth a few gems of wisdom and wit, to behold them dead ere they left my lips. This sort of thing is stultifying. I have my delicious jokes with Jeff alone in my bungalow, and be it said he possesses the responsive spark to perfection. He senses my every mood, turns silly and lolls on his back when I am in a silly humor, wags his tail and grins appreciation when I am clever, and sulks in a corner when I am out of temper with the universe.

OCTOBER 14. I have turned out reviews with an inspired pen, specially since receiving the October 1 *Vogue* and beholding my *first prose in print*. What a solemn moment it was! I shall never live that moment again—but I am not sorry. It was a rare jewel, an exquisite flower, set in the framework of daily life; a thing to be looked at always, but never repeated.

I received a letter from Dad saying, "I am absolutely staggered by your reviews. They are wonderfully well done. You seem not only to have a masterly English but a keen sense of analysis. You have a wonderful future in the world of letters, my dear, and the rewards of that kind of work are very great if sometimes slow in arriving. I cannot tell you how great an impression this latest work of yours has made on me. Also it has made me very, very proud." One of the strangest things in my life is my emotion towards my father. Before I came here the last time I had a final break with him—a terribly bitter break that I will not detail. Yet I feel drawn, as always, however unwillingly, to his genius, which I inherit from him. I wrote him a few days ago—he wrote me. A strange situation. I shall try to discount all personal antagonism in the future (I will see him only rarely, as usual) and remember that his weaknesses are mine too.

My happiness usually lies in such trivial things!—it seems that the smallest, most foolish little incident can deflect my mind from what it considered a tragedy before. I hired a bicycle for a week and took long rides through the beautiful country. It made all life look different. I spun along flat, smooth surfaces, or down swift hills, between brilliant woods and hills and fields on one side, and the misty blue sea on the other divided from me by wide, yellow-green marshes and patches of trees. Those rides were golden—no other word describes them. And pedalling home in the dusk, with a slender red moon dangling low in the western sky, and home-going limousines gliding by me in a flash of light, and my little cabin and my two dogs awaiting me. . . .

Ah, that brings me to another story. I used the money that Mother sent me for return fare to buy a little female Airedale, only a few weeks old. Why, I couldn't say! I never intended to do anything less, than to invest in a bitch. Nor do I know what I shall do with her and Jeff in a New York apartment; what Mother will (or will not!) say; or how I am to properly explain the expenditure just now, when we are so low on funds. They had her on sale at a farm house, she was adorable and I had a whim to own her, and here she is. I have resolved henceforth to always do things that way. In thought and speculation lies a fearful labyrinth of evil. The impulses of the soul and of the flesh, when instantly obeyed, cause no trouble. I ask God, or Whatever Is, to grant me the courage, the nobility, to follow this Law. I am convinced it is the only possible one for me, and for people of my fibre.

I have made acquaintance with a red-headed artist, something over thirty, who drives me home to the Cove in his car from the Post Office of an evening. He lives in a big house, down a little hill from my humble cottage, where also is an attractive woman of about thirty-five with several young sons. Bet and I always called him "the tutor," but since he is evidently not that, I can only wonder, and hope—charitably—that he is a friend of the invisible husband (that must be, or have been) or a cousin or whatnot (whatnot, I am afraid, in less charitable moods). He is a strange person—we have been shyly sizing each other up all summer but owing to my blindness I never gave him an opportunity to speak—several times I have passed him with a blank stare, only to realize afterward with a terrible qualm that he had raised his hat to me—or started to. He has a peculiarly cruel face, white and tense under his curly red thatch; which makes all the more attractive his shy, boyish manner when you talk to him. I used to think his stare insolent—now I see that he is rather in awe of me. Indeed he seems to have a sort of muffled, inarticulate passion for me. I don't doubt he has!—I know all the earmarks! It is the sort of thing men always feel at first, before they decide they'd rather die than marry me, and *will* die if I don't yield to their immoral demands! I often think of how few men have proposed marriage to me, and of how many have wanted me! Oh, how I hate to leave here— I shall probably never see "Whatnot" again, and I know that will hurt him as much as it will me—an idle hurt—the sort of regret that has no personal pang to it.

   OCTOBER 20. Still here! Didn't I say that henceforth I would follow impulses? When Lorent closed the shacks I came across the shaky little creek bridge with my family and belongings and settled down in a cosy little studio-shack belonging to a Mr. Staples of the district. To be sure it meant $15 for two weeks rent, $3 for wood, two weeks more on the hired typewriter, telegrams to Ma and *Vogue*, etc. Penniless but proud, I *stayed*. The result is a Nor'-Easter (or a South-Easter or something Easter) which has lasted three days now. The great grey waves plough in huge walls against the rocks, the winds blow and the rains do descend, but I sit happy within, reviewing the books that pile in one atop the other, dreaming contented little dreams the like of which I never knew before, busying myself with a thousand loved little details of my cabin—happy! Even the rains cannot dampen me, so to speak. At night how safe I feel, snug in my little cot, with the two dogs on their blanket by me, and the drops pat-pattering on the roof.

The October 15 *Vogue* reviews are *all* mine—eight of them—signed "W.W." What a thrill I got out of that! Dad writes, "I think you have arrived," but *I* know the snags ahead—and how much depends on the novel I am writing.

Later. A telegram this morning—Sis' [her sister Harriet's] little girl was born yesterday. Both fine. Sis—with a little girl. Everything in me stands still before the sweetness, the wonder, of that fact. A little girl, one of us, to grow up into the same sort of eager, bitter childhood that Sis and I lived together. A little girl to doubt and question and wonder, with all our own thoughts and imaginings. God grant her some such twin-companion in her every thought and act as I have found in Sis. I can ask no greater thing for her.

Over at the house where Red-Head lives I can plainly see a group of men and women—inartistic, happy-go-lucky city folks—laughing joyously over something. It goes into me with a cruel stabbing pain—just ordinary people blessed with a sense of humor! Here I have grown so accustomed to the frozen silences of ocean and sky and *artists*—delightful things, all, and all equally devoid of humor—that this group of people make me remember our little kitchen on Thirteenth Street and Salty and Bill and the rest of us standing around having a gay cocktail, laughing deliciously at nothing, and all so happy . . . a time dead beyond any resurrecting. It is a hard, cold thing to know—a bitter certainty to harbor.

NOVEMBER 3. New York. Home again. Our new place is big and light and airy. The last week at Ogunquit was wonderful. Izzie and H. and I were the only three artists (?) left in the Cove and we ate our meals together over a roaring fire, played bridge, and all came home together on the day coach to save money.

I arrived in New York last Wednesday morning. The only

excitement has been a tea to which I went yesterday afternoon with Dorothy Greene. Given in the apartment of a musical manager, where I met many singers and actors and one reformed blackmailer, who was the only person who paid me any particular attention. I spend my days walking my two dogs and writing book reviews.

What a great lonely city it is! It is like the sea which stretched so wide and wintry from the frowning rocks of the Maine coast. Somehow I love and hate it, perversely, as I loved and hated the sea. Its roar deafens me, its surge frightens me, its clammy coldness invites me . . . And I sit quietly, writing book reviews. Quietly?

NOVEMBER 11. Salty is back in town—he has been trying to locate Bill. Yesterday he met him quite by accident on Broadway, and the two of them came down here last night to see us. We had a casual and gay party. . . . Bill was correctly dressed as always, but sans overcoat and very lean and pale looking. He confessed to me that the past two months have been hell—he is without money.

Salty is taking the four of us to dinner Tuesday night. I wonder why Bill wants to go about with us, after . . . Oh, well, there's no accounting for men. Perhaps he'd do anything for a square meal. Tho, if that were the case, he would have availed himself of my ill-concealed passion, instead of fleeing from it as he did. Not, thank God, that it matters any more. I am as indifferent to him as to everything else. I am a machine that writes, and occasionally lapses into a state of gnawing hunger. . . . Finally, unfed, it writes again.

NOVEMBER 26. Just before Mother went to Utica somewhat over a week ago we had our foursome party. Once when I was alone with Bill, he said, "Damn you! Its a good thing for you I have traditions back of me!" Something of an admission for him!

While Mother was away I had one party after another with people, various and sundry. So much to drink that my face is white and drawn and my brain stands still. One night I had invited Bill and Salty for dinner, but Salty had to refuse suddenly at the last minute, and Bill came without knowing. We had such a casual dinner! Like two friendly indifferent people who like only to eat and discuss literature. In the evening we went up to see Sis and the darling little baby and then he and I walked all the way home from 66th Street down the Avenue, our old spirit of intimate camaraderie somehow stealing back between us.

This week-end was the crashing climax of a 'elluva week! Saturday night a mad party with a bunch of Dorothy's friends; Sunday a bunch of Buell's friends carried me off in an automobile, [and] we sat over drinks and cigarets all afternoon.

Bill and Salty were invited here for supper last night, but when Buell and I came in I was in no condition to entertain— Bill fixed supper and I floated presently out to the dark living-room and lay down on the sofa, leaving the three men at table. As I lay there my blood grew hotter and hotter and an anguished desire caught at me. I whispered foolishly: "God, if you will let Bill come to me, as he used to, alone in the dark, I will always believe in you hereafter." I heard them laughing and talking, eating and drinking, in the back room, and I writhed with pain because I could not believe Bill would ever kiss and hold me again . . . and then he came. He entered the dark room softly and sat on the couch beside me. Pride did not exist in me. All, all melted away save the need of him—I clasped him to me and he rained kisses on my mouth. After a while we were quiet, he sitting holding me tenderly while we talked.

Looking back on last night it is like a strange dream. Why did he kiss me? Why did he say, "The knowledge that you were thinking of me is what has helped me thru these past hellish months"! How could he lie so passionately? Is it because he pities me?

NOVEMBER 30. All day the rain has fallen in wide grey sheets, and I have hung about the house wishing to God that the whistles wouldn't blow. The whistles that blow in the New York harbor on a wet and rainy day are the saddest thing in all the world. I am so restless and strange these days; the ability to write has gone out of me, just as some physical power might go out of one's body—I can hardly get my book reviews out, even. My thoughts are so queer lately, the sort of thoughts that paralyzed me with terror when I was sixteen, but now I regard them indifferently. It is so easy to be vile in this life that I wonder how long I shall escape my fate! I dream at night of bodies crushing down on me—of terrible satisfaction—of unholy cravings. I wake exhausted, and ready to go out on the street after some sort of love. But I keep going along on the mad wistful hope that the good things I want will some day come to me. And, too, there are moments so beautiful! Moments when a boat whistle, or a chord of music, or only the sunshine lying across the pavement, can wake in me such a hunger for the good and beautiful! Then I want to fly to my pen and pour words out of my soul, pile words to the roof, to the sky, to the top of Nowhere! My desires are so fearful! The good ones are far more terrible than the wicked ones.

My life is like the unanswered prayer of a weary, tired human. I am not sorry for myself (though I would like to be—it's so easy) because I know it's my own fault; the fault of my difficult temperament, that is. In me lies all good and evil, and through lazy, negligent, pleasure-loving ways I have fostered the evil, and totally neglected the good. I daresay at twenty-one I am, mentally, as great a roué as ever lived. Long ago I think I said in you, Journal, that if Alwyn would love me I would be very good and if he didn't I would be bad. Mentally, though not yet physically, I am bad, whether or not Alwyn had anything to do with it. There is always a sweet refuge, a "very present help" in drink, but that indulgence is so obviously an inheritance! If one cannot have one's own vices, one had better get on without. And so there is really only the eternal, pitiful pulling at a cigaret, the "wild party," the writing and straining forward. When I replace these with anything else it will be something more evil, I am afraid—since I have almost forgotten to hope for love.

DECEMBER 21. Life has been rather conveniently "full of a number of things"—parties with the Speaks and their crowd, a ball at the Commodore Hotel with most of the U.S. Navy present, a party at Sis' house which included Bill, and one blessed evening when Bill came to see me, and we sat for hours talking, just as we used to do. We have never been closer to each other than that evening. I have had some good poems published lately and my book-reviews have made me wellnigh burst with pride! I have been sort of happy "after my fashion".

CHRISTMAS DAY. It is strange that the young men I meet and laugh and play with have no faintest attraction for me— and yet how I yearn for love! . . . . . Oh, inexpressible, voiceless yearning that is in me! I wish I might once have been happy! If I could look back on a time of great fulfilment I would have an untouched peace in the place of confusion that is my heart.

◇ *1924* ◇

JANUARY 3. Grey, rainy days, how I hate you! You remind me that I am almost twenty-two, and still unloved. You remind me that beauty is a brief thing. You remind me that death hovers over me on dark wings. You even make me want to think of death . . . .

I don't for a moment suppose its the weather that ails me. Too much New Year cheer, no doubt! I am exhausted, mentally and physically, unable to see things as they are. Straight normalities have a dark and crooked look when I am low and fagged. I cannot write any more—it requires the living death of loneliness and solitude to make me write—and no writing ever done is worth it.

JANUARY 15. There's philosophy in toothache or in nothing what is. All night I groaned, shrieked, cursed God and died; but this A.M. I went to the dentist, and was shortly relieved. Now, for the first time in this long while, I'm no atheist . . . there must be a God to have made dentists!

Some good times, and a new beau: one Tommy [Lorin Thompson], thirty-five, of the Speaks crowd. *Vogue* struck me a cruel blow by informing me that no more books will be sent me for reviews for a long time, as they are too crowded for space to use my reviews "at present," and already have a large supply of them ahead. Finances are discouragingly low, and bills are collecting, but I suppose Mother and I will pull through as we always have. I don't much care, if only I can do some worthwhile writing again—my pen has lain in one place so long that it fits my fingers awkwardly this morning. I composed a brief story on the typewriter the other day and took it, with the sketch "To Want," up to Mrs. VanderKley of *Vogue*. She is to read them and pass them on to Mr. Frank Crowninshield of *Vanity Fair*. But I know the answer beforehand so have hardly thought about it.

The only cheerful thing that's happened in a year was the toothache—because that stopped.

JANUARY 22. I have been reading Oscar Wilde again, for days on end. I suppose no-one could ever understand that curious passion I have always felt for his writings—it is to me, when I read him, as tho I sat in the warm presence of some infinite Love: I believe it to be my love of self, for in the arrogant individualism of Wilde's teachings, I see my rebellious spirit perfectly crystallized in words, and adequately expressed. Some subtle, exquisite kinship lies between my spirit and his—between my pen and his, so that half the time I do not know if I am penning my own words or words of his that I have read until they are an irrevocable part of myself.

My dearest mother has gone to Utica for a visit, and I am alone. There is no love that can outweigh the intellectual need of silence and isolation at times. And I am not lonely as I have such good friends to go to. Spent today with Charme Speaks in her apartment on Thirteenth Street—we talked and read in the atmosphere of books and sympathy which is so pricelessly beautiful to my hungry heart—so vital to my starved senses.

I have had the chance of a publicity job at a salary of $75 a week or more! But have not even tried to put it over, since it is not writing, and write I must. I have written Uncle "Charley Mike" in Washington, to arrange for me to call on his good friend Bob Davis, of great literary note here in New York, that I may show him some of my work. I have written an essay on "Oscar Wilde and Modern Review"—a gem. It is the same with everything I write; I do nothing with them but put them by, because I shrink from seeing editors, and it is no use to send manuscripts in.

I sit, with a glass of exquisite sherry wine, the soul of leisure. When I read Wilde I feel that I must be drinking wine slowly, or smoking an expensive cigaret.

JANUARY 23. It is very nice, having a man in love with you. Tommy seems to be—he had Charme Speaks invite me (and himself) to dinner tonight. Saturday night we all went on a party together, down at the Samovar. It is also nice for a change to enjoy the attentions of a man with some money! I can't ever remember having had a beau that wasn't penniless.

This afternoon I went in to see Dad in his office at the Cunard Building, as I frequently do. He is willing to arrange an interview for me with some newspaper editors, as I want to do some Sunday feature stories. I am so delighted, for with Dad's pull and my ability I should get something good.

I love the great twilight canyon of lower Broadway—I can dream it is some fairy place of shifting lights and shadows if I shut my eyes and ears to the noisy little men who hustle, two and two, everywhere, gesticulating, mouthing, and exclaiming. How different, though, is my world, from the world that is there. How secret and clean and sweet is the world of my thoughts, books, writings and dreams, and how far removed from the bare ugliness of office-rooms, and the mad rush for money! How can people live, when it is only for the sake of dying! I live to create some definite—or indefinite—part of me into a thing of eternal life; to express my being and my spirit so that that expression will live in the minds of people just like me who will follow after me. People unlike me—the swarms of money-makers— will not know I have lived, any more than they know now that I live. But my kin-people, my spirit's brethren will know that I have been, that I have drunk the evening shadows of a New York street, that I have loved the lights and faces in restaurants and dancehalls, that I have walked on Fifth Avenue in the brilliant glow of a sunny morning. And they will understand my yearning for far places, for foreign seas and green fields and brown hills and bright flowers that are in other lands than mine, and for great cities that I have not seen, but that I know and love through the love and knowledge of my spirit's brethren who have gone before me, and left me these things—as I shall leave them, in my turn.

JANUARY 30. I shall have little time for you [journal] now, because I am working hours a day on my novel. I want to finish it before June 1 in order that I may send it in to the Little, Brown & Co. contest—or perhaps to one of the Harper contests. Anyway I shall do something enormously wonderful with it, the gods granting me the concentrative powers necessary to its completion. I am turning all my heart's hungers and all its despairs into my work.

Last Sunday Dorothy [Greene] and I went to Dr. Guthrie's church in the morning—St. Marks' in the Bowery that has become so famous owing to its stand in the recent religious controversy—never have I been so completely lifted out of myself, so moved, and so impressed. Dr. Guthrie is all that a man of culture and intellect, and a student of letters could be in the pulpit. He gave life a new purpose for me. He regards religion as a thing to be understood through beauty and the arts—he said things that expressed my most pagan feelings, and yet he was always subtle—never undignified. God is to him the Great Unknown, and as such he worships him. Dor and I sat so tense all through the service that we ached for hours afterward. In the afternoon we went to a concert (orchestral) at the Metropolitan. It was an exhausting day, emotionally—but it started me off writing again with an inspired pen. Only, I have found that an inspired pen is not what I need. I need a pen that can plod along for hours together, making its own inspiration, or just plain *working*, as the case may be, but never stopping until it has accomplished its purpose—which is, just now, to make the name of Winifred Willis ring down the years, even unto the third and fourth generation of them (editors) that hate me.

FEBRUARY 12. For nearly a week now I have been living in a room at 40 Perry Street, in the Village. I have written divine music—words, words, words—words that rhyme, words that don't . . . .

It was all my own doing. I felt desolate indeed the first night I slept here, out from under my beloved Mother's roof. Every time a fire engine shrieked in the night I fancied that she was in terrible danger, every time her dear, beautiful face and eyes rose before me my heart cried out to her. But it is only in solitude that I can write, dream and live—solitude is life; solitude is self, the *essence of self*. I put love away from me and came here.

My dear new friends keep me amused and happy. One Sunday Charme had a tea at her place where I met many literary and theatrical people who had formerly only been names to me. Another night I dined with the crowd at Heywood Broun's table at the Algonquin, though H.B. wasn't there . . . I find that as men like me and become my friends, women dislike me and say things behind my back. One is grateful for a few real women friends, such as Charme and Dorothy. I make friends because I am beautiful and clever—and because I am beautiful and clever I make enemies. So be it.

Last Sunday Charme and Charles Speaks and Tommy and I spent the afternoon in the Museum of Art.

When people criticize me for having a good time, they cannot know the hours I have sat alone stretching my aching arms to the great world of life and color and laughter, longing to be one with it—oh, if they knew, they could not be so cruel as to blame me for my love of joy and happiness and admiration. It is the breath of life to me, and I have so long been without it!

FEBRUARY 14. This A.M. I have finally completed and sent in my novel for the Harper contest. Just now, late, I came into my little room alone and all the past quiet studious days of books and poetry melted away—crumpled up like a dried leaf that you squash between your fingers. I laid my head down among the dear books and cried within, "Oh my love, when will you come and set me free!" I cannot differentiate any more between real moods and theatrical ecstasies, but one hurts as much as the other, so what matter? And I am alone in a great city crying for my love to come while I am young and beautiful. Oh, I shall grow old and cold, and he may never know me as I am tonight!

FEBRUARY 15. I have been so happy today! for a story came

to me, beautifully complete. I wrote the end of it early in the day, and shall do the first half tomorrow. It's the only way one should write stories. I never can rest until I get the climax off my mind. I read what I'd done to Charme, then we went up to Thyra Winslow's apartment on Forty-ninth Street for a while, tea-ed at the *Mirror*, strolled down and bought tickets for *Rain*, and back to Charme's where Charles and Tommy took us to dinner and the theater. We saw *Rust* at Greenwich Village Theater. When I see such stinking truck I know the world is waiting for W.W. Such parrot voices, such parrot lines! Stories are the same, poems are the same. How long, oh Lord, shall the voice of thy servant be dumb? And yet the *Herald* publishes my poems one after the other, such fearful rot that it makes me ill to read them! But the good poems I am saving for a worthier market, and in the meantime I need the *Herald* checks something fierce!

I am so happy in my little room, but sometimes I wonder if I am losing my Mother. I suppose no one could ever understand how I love her. It is not necessary that anyone should. Some facts just exist—like Alwyn. They are not to be explained, they are like the stars and the sun and poetry and the desire to write and seas and sunsets and—Mother and Alwyn. All these together make God; and God—well, God just *is*.

José is a sweet, fine boy, a great singer, an ardent lover—but will he make Mother happy? I call him a boy for he seems one and looks one, but they say he is thirty-five years old. Mother seems about thirty, so *that's* alright. So long as she is happy I am content, but I know no passion can fill her need of me, her love of me. I must cling to her silently, until she finds she needs me again. God bless my mother.

FEBRUARY 18. Tommy, Charles, Charme and I have such pleasant hours. We walk through frosty afternoons, tea at Village restaurants, dine and dance—always in the Village. And how precious these hours of conversation and recreation, coming after hours of hard work. Ah, love may be wonderful indeed, but is anything more exquisite than that sensation of relaxation and enjoyment following upon intense mental effort?

My passion for literature is peculiar, a human, physical passion; a warm upward surge thru my entire body. The hours alone with a loved book or some piece of writing of my own, are like hours alone with a lover. It is a very beautiful, simple life; a very chaste passion. I wish I were incapable of any other.

The letter from Robert H. Davis [of *Munsey*] has come.

"If that's the case why don't you drop in some day and see me? That fact that I used to dine with Charlie Michelson at Uncle Mike's house in Brooklyn before you were born removed the handicap that an introduction from him might otherwise inject. Come, therefore, on your own account. I will be glad to see you.

"I am leaving town tomorrow to be gone until Thursday, after which date you are welcome as flowers in Brooklyn.

Always sincerely—"

So, Friday next, I shall take manuscripts in hand and journey into a new country.

MARCH 1. There is no telling what surprises may spring from the commonplace—or what seems commonplace. I have thought of Tommy as one of the finest, best and kindest men on earth, and as nothing else. Even when he asked me to let him take me to Europe this spring for a honeymoon, I didn't feel any particular thrill. He has loved me almost from the first in a quiet, restrained sort of way that made me merely admire him. Last night I put on most becoming evening clothes and he called for me, resplendent in dress suit, and we went to see *The Miracle* (a stupendous production) then to dance at the Deauville Club till four in the morning. I don't know what did it. Was it the vague half-light, the seductive music, the perfect dance floor, the perfect way we dance together . . . or just *him*? Anyhow, we taxied home at four and he came upstairs with me. He took me in his arms and kissed me, and after a little of that I was hungry for more. I began daring him to stay, feeling sure he wouldn't. He was so big and vibrant and alive in my lonely little room—I couldn't bear for him to go out of it, and leave me. He went downstairs, dismissed the waiting taxi, and came back. I was not a little alarmed when he carried me to bed from a chair in which I had taken refuge, and proceeded to doff his jacket and shoes and lie down beside me. Yes, I was afraid, and he knew it, so he lay motionless for a long time. Then he reached out and drew me into his arms, and put my head on his breast, and we lay still together in the dark. Once at daybreak he awoke and drew me hard against him and kissed me, but that was all. In the morning I had a ripping headache and after coffee he made me lie down and sat beside me rubbing my head for a long time. After he left me I went about all day in a daze, my blood throbbing hot to the memory of his big man's body lying against mine, his strong, gentle hands on my hair . . . Yet tonight when he and I went with a crowd to dinner at the Samovar he was the same old reserved Tommy, quiet, dignified except for his eyes that cried love to me. He has strangely dashed the sweet security of writing and dreaming great achievements—he has even made my wonderful letter from Bob Davis, lauding my stories with their "fine style, vigor and realism" sink to unimportance. I *will not* marry him, but I want him terribly. He is all male—and I am all female. He hasn't a literary or artistic idea in his head—and perhaps that's why I love him.

MARCH 4. Oh, it is spring, spring, spring today! The air is warm and soft, the sun lights the world, and hurdy-gurdies jangle in the streets.

Tommy and I are going out to his home near Bronxville, taking Jeff, the dog—Tommy's going to keep him for me. I'm going to stay all night—there's a couple there, Dick and Nan. Tommy has a car and we'll ride today, and walk with Jeff and Cinders (his dog) and—oh, we'll have a good time!

Last night we dined at Charles Street. When we came home I lay in his arms. He wants to marry me but I don't intend to marry him. We can be happy without that for a while I think. When I *know* we shall not tire—when we have lived and loved together for a time—then I may marry him. A more thoughtful, generous, gentle, understanding husband no woman could find. His heart is wrapped up in me and my career. He wants to take

me away into far countries, to give me all that my heart desires—
but could any man or anything do that for me?

But today it is spring, and we are going to be happy—that's
enough!

MARCH 7. The old gloomy pessimist in me seems to leap up
the more insistently when I am happy—because I am happy.
My Tommy seems too good to be true—I didn't know God
made men like him. He is like a woman for tenderness—he is
utterly selfless where I am concerned. He adores me just as I
am, with all my faults and failings and vices, with all my selfish
self-absorption . . . and yet he is so vitally a man! So big and
clear-eyed and healthy. What a beautiful two days we had in
the country! How sweet it was to wake in a great white bed and
lie hearing the birds, and seeing the endless blue sky out of the
little Dutch latticed windows . . . Dick and Nan both work in
the city, and when I awoke in the morning it was to find Tommy
bending over me, asking me if I meant to sleep all day, big and
laughing in his white shirt sleeves. Then he would run a tub
for me and fix breakfast while I bathed. Then we would idle
away the day alone together; tramp miles through the muddy
country roads, talk and read in the big comfortable living room.
The house is set back in an old apple orchard and in summer,
when the leaves are thick and green, they form a solid wall
against the sky. Just now, the bare limbs twist up silver in the
sunshine, and the early spring wind blows wet and fresh and
sweet from the distant fields. When we walked I wore an old
hat and flying coat of Tommy's (he was an aviator in France
during the war) and rubber boots of Nan's, and when my pale
cheeks grew pink Tommy would bend down and gaze at me
with such happiness in his eyes it sort of made my throat get
tight—he's always worrying about my health, and the way I
abuse it sitting indoors at the typewriter, and smoking and
drinking and keeping late hours.

Today I took two more stories down to Mr. Davis. At 4:30
Tommy came for tea here with me. I had to go up to Sis's for
dinner as Grandmother is visiting there. Tommy took me to
the subway and somehow for the first time I found it actually

hurt to leave him—you hate to leave a man at dusk, just when lovers are going out to dine somewhere together . . . I don't know why. It's one of the queer things New York does to you. Love in New York is lights and dancing and restaurants and cocktails and the continual excitement of changing faces and new places. Queer! I wonder if I could love on a farm?

MARCH 11. Happiness is a new and terrifying experience. Am I in love? Unanswerable. I only know that I am happy.

The weekend was spent at Tommy's in the country. Sunday was a great lake of light, and we seemed to swim through it; past hills and rivers and estates and fields, drinking the beauty of the world, the early spring in the chilly air, the near sense of each other.

Last night the whole crowd of us, including John Speaks and Dorothy who were in town for the weekend, went out to dine and dance. Tommy was divine last night—when we came home I kissed him as never before. I worship him sometimes. When I lie back in his arms and give him my lips I forget everything else except the sweet, gentle, greedy feel of him. He showers me with such a passionate adoration as I never knew existed. His thoughts are never removed from me, his eyes are always on my face, his body is always crying for one touch from me, for the nearness of me. Yet he is so dignified and reserved in his love—it's that of a man, not the sickly puling of an infatuated boy. He is every inch a man, bless his inartistic soul. His wonderful gentleness makes him all the more irresistible when he turns fierce and hungry. And he thinks me the most brilliant genius on earth, which never displeases me.

MARCH 17. Among other beautiful things that have happened I have sold my first short story. Robert H. Davis bought "The Hour Before Dawn" for *Munsey*. Paid me $60, but oh, how sordid a detail *that* is. It only means a new gown to please the eye of my beloved.

Oh, I want him for my lover, my husband, anything! I love him, I love him! He has become the whole world. He is like a vast, lifelong peace after the black, howling wilderness through which I have always wandered . . . God, God, don't take him away from me!

MARCH 18. I write in the above date, and then I just sit and dream, and can think of nothing to say but that I am in love.

Each time he comes to me now in my little room I think it will mean surrender—I told him yesterday, as I lay in his arms, that I thought Charme and Charles considered us lovers. "We are—almost," he breathed against my lips . . . . Yet I am still reserved—aloof—afraid of the tumult in my own body when he is near. Strange! all the philosophy, all the deep thought and genius, all the intense passion of creation cannot change a woman unloved into anything more than a virgin when she feels the insistent desire of her loved one . . . . *how I love him!*

MAY 7. We are soon to be married—I have been unable to write in my Journal, or indeed, to write anything of any consequence, because my heart is too brimful of love. I did not know love could be so perfect, and yet so quietly certain. I thought love had to be daring, dangerous, beyond the pale, or somehow out of the ordinary—now I see that love is only a man and a woman: Only Tommy and me.

Yet even now sometimes when I look into his eyes, or remember his loved face in his absences from me, a fierce anguish, a terrible despair, grips my heart. How terrible that he is all, *all*! His warm love enfolds me, envelops me, stands between me and the cold loneliness of life—yet sometimes a chill old memory blows thru to me; then I want to turn and cling to him and never let him go beyond the reach of my fingers.

Whenever he is away from me fear tugs at my heart-strings.

MAY 24. This is my wedding-day. Tommy and I are to be married at 5 o'clock. This is the attainment of happiness and the beginning of life.

◇　　◇

Afterword

The marriage lasted six years.

In her journals of that difficult time, Willis's realizations of their incompatibility alternate with self-reprisals and resolutions to change herself at any cost to save the marriage.

There were some periods of happiness, such as that surrounding the birth of their son, Andy, in 1926. Financial difficulties added to the strain and in 1930, after Winifred suffered a nervous breakdown, she and Tommy were divorced.

Winifred Willis continued to keep a diary for the rest of her life, sometimes with lapses of several years. Over time, the journals became less and less tied to external events; instead they came to reflect Willis's tremendous internal struggles with the roles of mother, wife, writer and woman.

Her second (1932) marriage, to John Speaks (brother of her old friend Charles Speaks) was extremely happy. During those thirty-three years Willis wrote for *The New Yorker*, *Saturday Evening Post*, *Ladies' Home Journal*, *New York Herald Tribune* and many other publications. Her play, *Byron*, was well regarded both here and abroad, although it remained unproduced.

Yet Willis was never the writer she wanted to be and her journal bears witness to her frustration and anger. She herself speculated that fear of competition with her second husband, who had become a successful writer in Hollywood, may have contributed to the blocks she struggled in vain to overcome.

Winifred Willis's journal was her major work. She carefully preserved the neatly typed pages and made notations and corrections over the years. Although she allowed no one to read it during her lifetime, she wanted this record to be published after her death.

She died in 1982 at the age of eighty. Her journal was prepared for publication by her sister, Harriet Willis Sabine, and her friend Evelyn Harter Glick.

◇ ◇

THE DIARY OF

Eleanor Cohen
Seixas

Columbia, South Carolina
1865–1866

◇ ◇

◇ ◇

Introduction

Nothing is known about Eleanor Cohen Seixas beyond the facts she gives in her diary. She was a favored child of a moderately prosperous Jewish family in Columbia, South Carolina. Her life had not always been sheltered—her family had suffered difficult periods when she had taken in sewing to help make ends meet. But nothing in her early life could have prepared her for the events of February 17, 1865, when Union troops stormed the city and burned it almost entirely to the ground.

Her account of those days, and the months that followed, records strengthened family bonds and loosened romantic connections in a world turned upside down. Eleanor's diary, already a well-established habit, helps to sustain her in this period of hardship and uncertainty.

Seixas is clearly a woman of strong character despite her pious vows of obedience. She admits to being "quick tempered" yet takes care in her journal to express anger only toward acceptable targets—such as Yankees and New York City, "too large too gay and fashionable to suit poor me." She does not appear to question the established order—certainly not the institution of slavery: "I am accustomed to have them wait on me," she says, and to her this is justification enough.

"Poor me"—probably Eleanor didn't believe it, for she was a "survivor" who wasted little time on self-pity. Invariably she directed her energies squarely toward the future.

◇ *1865* ◇

Columbia, FEBRUARY 28. I have been in the habit of keeping a journal for ten years, from the time of girlish beautitude "sweet sixteen", up to the mature age I have reached, 26: All the labors of years, all the records of my girlish triumphs, of my "first love", all have been destroyed, and yet I am determined to recommence the labors, to rebuild from the ashes of dispair, a new record, and enthrone "blue eyed hope" as the presiding deity. I am the eldest of three daughters, and the connecting link between two sets of children, having three brothers elder than myself, one brother and two sisters younger. I was for many years the only daughter and in consequence was much petted and indulged. My dear father's fortunes have been sadly varied, my first recollection is of a sufficiency, every comfort, then came wealth, when I reached womanhood all of life's choicest gifts were mine, but the wheels turned, and we were poor, very poor. Father labored day and night, and could barely make both ends meet. I was young hopeful and energetic, I set to work and by doing various kinds of fancy work [needlework], at which I was adept, I earned enough to clothe myself except shoes without calling on father, peace then smiled on our land. But a revulsion came, the Union was destroyed, the federacy formed, and "grim visaged war" with all attendant horrors desolated the land. The war brought money to father's coffers, and soon he became a rich man, rich alas, only in confederate money. Now all I wished for was mine, and even goods at fabulous prices were bought. So I will leave him and describe myself. At sixteen I fancied, if I was unmarried at 25, I would surely be an old maid and feel inclined to resign all gayety, now I have reached 26, I feel nearly as young I did then, and wonder, if it is possibly true, that I am so old. I am rather small, have a good figure, rather pretty, dark complexion, black eyes, and a quantity of straight black hair of which I am rather proud. Small hands and feet, with a bright expression. I am well educated, have read a good deal; and am called intelligent. I have had several beaux and love affairs, and was privately engaged to be married at sixteen, to one I thought the perfection, of a man, now with increased years, and maturity of judgment I bless God I did not marry him, I am quick tempered, but warm and loving he is jealous, passionate, dictatorial, and harsh, and had I married him, my life would have been an endless quarrel, or I would have sunk into being a slave! But God kindly spared me, and tho at the time I suffered, as every woman must, when she sees her idol shattered, yet I now, and have for years blessed God, that I did not marry my "first love". Dear journal I suppose you think as I am still Miss Cohen, 26, that I am an old maid, No, for next month was to have smiled on my wedding, now *indefinitely* postponed. But I am betrothed, and to one who loves me truly, fondly, and with his whole heart, and I return his love, yes my noble, precious, darling, come what may, my heart is yours I have been engaged six months to Mr. B. M. Seixas. He is very good looking gentlemanly, good hearted, liberal, honest and upright, and devotedly attached [to] me. My precious love, what would I not give for a glance at your dear face! But I must postpone until tomorrow the relation of the facts that destroyed my journals, postponed my wedding and separated me from my lover.

We are now in the fourth year of the fearful war that is now ravaging our land. in my last journals I had an accurate account of every detail, how determined the enemy were to possess dear old Charleston, how they shelled the city and we were hurried away, how my brave city, and forts held out, but this precious record thank God it lives in my heart & in the heart of every true Southern man, woman and child. But at last the dear old place has been evacuated, and is in possession of the yankees, land of my birth, home of my childhood, dear to me as life, my heart bleeds for and with you, and any sacrifice on my part, could be made, I would *gladly freely* give it; for your precious sake. The yankees now possess nearly every city of importance, yet the fire of patriotism, and the determination to be free, swells every nerve of our determined land. After the fall of Sav[annah], Columbia was threatened, but we could not bring ourselves to believe that Sherman could gain so great an advantage as to come so far into the heart of our state. I was to be married in April, all was bright before me. Mr. Seixas left here on 7th of February, promising to come again in March, and in April to come to claim his promised bride, vain hope! When he left me I felt a foreboding of evil, and begged him to remain here. I made him reiterate again and again, and tell me repeatedly of his love, and vow again and again that nothing should wean his heart from me. On the 16th the Yankees shelled Columbia without notice on the 17th the city was evacuated by our soldiers and surrendered by the mayor, Oh! God can I ever forget that day, can time with lethean draughts, ever efface from my memory the deep sorrow, the humiliation, the agony of knowing we were to be under the yankees; that our beloved flag was to be pulled down and the USA flag, wave over the city, that flag, that carried loathing to every Southern heart, that flag whose sway is ever characterized by villainy, by outrage and violence of every kind! The report was that private property would be respected, and we all set quietly at home trying to nerve ourselves for the trials, gold and silver was hid in all imagineable places, provisions were scattered and so the day passed in feverish expectation but as dark approached all felt unhappy. As the evening shades drew darker the sky was illumined with crimson, it was a fearfully windy night, and as we watched the sky, we heard the awful cry of fire, Oh God can I ever forget that night, but after a while we heard only Main Street was so burned, we gathered together in a room at the top of the house, and as we gazed we saw new fires, burst forth in every direction the flames were seen, leaping and dancing assisted by the winds in the work of destruction, and the air was filled witl. torpedoes, shells, hand grenades and all the most instruments of evil doers, the exultant shout of the infuriated soldiers met the ears, and from every heart went up to God a prayer that he would lull the wind stay the flames, and put mercy in the heart of our foes vain hopes! As well might we hope to have mercy from a lyon. We at home did not think the fire would reach us, but it did so rapidly, and were urged to put a change of clothing in a bag and leave our house we did, and as I left all my comforts, all the accumulated treasures of a life time, the letters of loved absent ones, pictures of our precious relations, tokens and souvenirs of childhood, a feeling of fearful desolation came upon me by this time the streets were crowded with the "vandal foe", and as we reached the street, were greeted by curses too fearful to be entered in my book. We met crowds in the street, almost a procession of men women and children, & what was most remarkable, was the calmness of our people, our women and even our children behaved with fortitude. We knew not where to go, our party was large & many children, the flames seemed to encircle us like a belt, and the heat was so great that our faces were scorched, and blackened by smoke! we went to the country with barely food enough for a day! starvation, or death by fire, seemed *inevitable*. After we reached the woods, we were surrounded by drunken soldiers, father was fearful for our lives, and brought us again to the city, at this crisis I fainted, and remained so nearly an hour. We went to a house, and immediately after I revived we moved again to the street we were compelled to abandon our clothing, for father & mother had to support me! and thus we were houseless, homeless, and without food, or clothing, in one night we were, brought from comparative wealth and luxury to abject poverty. After wandering for many hours, we were advised to seek refuge in the "lunatic asylum"! and hither we bent our steps, words are inadequate to describe the scene, that greeted our eyes old men tottering under the weight of some trifling bundle, that he valued, young girls weighted down with heavy packages some had clothing some food, while some convulsively clasped an ornament a picture a package of letters, and some had nothing, but were walked quietly along as if stunned! after many delays we reached the asylum & went to the chapel, which we found crowded there we remained four days without mattress, pillow or anything but the hard floor to lie on, and almost in a starving condition, I never imagined I should be so near actual starvation, from Friday night until Saturday night, I had only a small slice of corn bread to eat, thick and heavy made of meal & water, while we remained there we suffered in every way that human nature is capable of suffering, want of rest, food even, water! without a change of clothing, or privacy to change it in. The fire raged fearfully all night, but on Saturday perfect quiet reigned, the vile yankees, took from us clothing food jewels, all our cows, horses, carriages, & ct and left us in a deplorable condition after stealing from us. Sherman with great generosity, presented the citizens with five hundred cattle, so poor they could hardly stand up. No words of mine can give any idea of the brutality of the ruffians, they swore they cussed, plundered and committed every excess, no age or sex was safe from them, sometimes after saving some valueless token, it was ruthlessly snatched from our hands by some of their horde. Our noble women [were], insulted by words, and some I have heard of in deeds, but none came under my knowledge for I myself, God be praised! I received no rude word from any of them. I did not speak to them at all. Nothing can tell the quantity of plunder they carried off as Monday they left us, and though we feared starvation, yet were glad to be rid of them. Our family, much to our joy removed to Melvins who was not burned out we stayed there two weeks, then removed to Uncle Jacks, he and his family have gone to Augusta, left Grandpa and Aunt R., and gave us, his house, and provisions, he is immensely rich, and has been very liberal, and kind to Pa. The drawing room, which was the scene lately of so much gayety at Alice's wedding, is turned in to a bed room. All my trusseau was burned and stolen, and oh saddest of all I know not where my precious love is or if he is a prisoner wounded, or dead. This is the heaviest trial, April was to have been our bridal, now alas it is indefinitely postponed, I feel truly as if my fate was a hard one from the pinnacle of happiness, I have reached the *lowest depths* of despair, life seems worthless, I have no energy no spirit, all are gone, Oh my God, teach me to bear my burden. Oh my own love I never knew how precious you were to me until now.

MARCH 3. Slowly and sadly the months drag along, tis six months since my engagement, not six months since I knew of and returned my darling's love, but six months since my fathers consent, was formally asked and given and all but the last have been months of perfect happiness to me. No word yet of Mr. Seixas, and strange to say, many letters, have [been] received and many persons come out, I have perfect confidence in him, but I am very miserable, for a dread is on me that my best beloved may be a prisoner, or sick among strangers, with no loving hand to tend him, nightly I wet my pillow [with] my tears, and intrust him, now nearly my *all*, to God's protection. Everything jogs quietly along, wagons come and go, and letters from loved ones serve to cheer our dark lives.

MARCH 7. We are comfortably fixed at Uncle J. the family numbers 23, and I am kept busy for I do nearly all the house-keeping attend to the milk make butter & ct. No news yet of my darling, and time drags slowly along, my dear father is about beginning life anew, his fate is hard. All my friends or most of them have proven themselves *true*.

Fannie I can never forget, she offered me the half of all she had, she found out what I required and gave it to me, & acted like a sister, so did Isabel. All the clothing we have was saved by Rose our faithful servant, she & Helen were true so was Lavinia I shall ever remember her devotion to us she gave us cotton homespun and behaved like a friend. Ben who we be-lieved faithful left us, or said he was forced to.

MARCH 30. Thanks be to God I have heard of my intended, yesterday on Hyams return from the office, he told me there was no letter for me, only one for father, with a deep sigh I turned away to hide the tear of disappointment that daily fills my eye, when I receive the same reply. Father broke the seal, and commenced reading. "At Mr. B M Seixas request" I sprang to his side and said "father *dont* jest with me", he said I am not jesting, read child, and placed the letter in my hand. It swam before me, I was so excited, but to my great joy, I read that the writer a Mr. Thomas wrote me to tell me that Mr. Seixas was well, and had with two others opened a store in King Street, and was making a living and urged father to come down as soon as possible. Of course I am very happy to know he is well, yet there is a pang deep and sore at my heart. Unless he expected us down, and he had no reason to think so, it seems strange to me that he should willingly as it were separate himself from me. To no human being however would I express this thought, for though it looks strange to me I doubt not he knows *best* and is doing what he considers, *easiest* for both of us I will not allow doubt of his truth to cross my mind, no! no shade of suspicion shall mar the bright purety of our love and although I cannot prevent a heaviness of my heart *sometimes*, yet I battle with it and try to believe all is right. A gentleman came out last week, from the city and brought five hundred letters, and yet not one for *me*. Tis very hard to bear, and I pray to God to grant me strength, not to murmur or repine.

APRIL 4. My Mothers wedding day—thirty-three years married! and it *was* to have been mine, but God ordained it differently I bow in submission, to Gods will, and struggle to say thy will, not mine be done. And I could easily bear the postponement of my marriage if Mr. Seixas was only here, to share with and lighten my trials. the day dawned brightly, the sun gleamed with an added lustre, and as I threw open my window, I hailed it as a omen of good, oh I do hope, ere long I will get a sweet loving letter, that will dispel the faint doubts that will come, *some times*. I think if he tried to send a letter to me as hard as I tried to send one to him, I might have got one, but men occupied with business, do not feel as we do, and I suppose he thinks he is working to keep us together it matters not if we don't hear from each other. Spring with all its thousand beauties is here, the genial air the perfume of a thousand flowers greet me, and cheer me when saddest. Columbia is a lovely spot & even in the places where the fire has fearfully devastated, nature is doing a great deal to atone for the ruins. The wild jessamin blows, and trails for the want of its accustomed pillow, which formerly was its support. Snowdrops, roses, and all of Gods most perfect work gladden our sight. And from my heart of hearts, goes up to God thanks for his most beauteous works, these sweet tokens of Gods goodness, do much to reconcile us to the vandals destruction. They could have selected a *better* season, if any season is *good*, for such atrocity.

APRIL 16. Joy is mine dear journal I have had a letter from my most precious love he is well and doing well, is doing business in Charleston in dear old King st., he expects us down but says if "Pa don't come, he will come for me, and be married, oh! happy I am to be reassured of his love to read his fond letter, and know he loves me as fondly as ever. And yet there is a sad struggle in my heart, if to leave my dear parents in their time of trouble, our cause and country in her darkest hours, to follow him, or to allow him to come for his wife, and find her unwilling to return with him, I do not yet clearly see my duty or if I do, I fear I don't see clearly for the path of duty is seldom adorned with flowers. Father Mother and all here, think I should go, I am getting ready the few things I have to do, oh it is sad to see what my trusseau now will be and compare it with what it might have been. But my love loves me not for fine clothes.

APRIL 20. A dark heavy cloud dims the brightness that has illumed my life since I received Mr. S's letters, father called me, and told me a friend had told him that there was much bad feeling excited towards Mr. S. owing to his intimacy with the yankees, and some even declared he was in their *pay*! and had pointed out rebel property, and that his life was not safe if he came up, father said he wished to write him not to come up, for the present, farewell to all my hopes of a speedy marriage, and saddest of all he may come and be arrested, oh God have pity on me I have suffered *greatly*, spare me *this*.

APRIL 21. A sad record today of crushed hopes, wasted life and fruitless exertion. Our noble General Lee with thirty thousand men, were surrounded by two hundred thousand men, and were compelled to surrender. Johnson and Sherman met and agreed to suspend hostilities for the present and not to renew the fight without two days notice, during this truce a peace will be arranged, but what a peace, and although I am glad aye very glad to have the fearful loss of life stopped, and to feel once again, the security that peace alone can give, yet it is fearful to know that we are conquered! by superior numbers all the gallantry of our soldiers, all their suffering avail nothing, we struggled for freedom, but found it not. Oh God fill us with fortitude to bear this reverse.

APRIL 30. Politically I have much to say, no peace yet agreed upon but negociations are being carried on, and people generally think peace will follow. Abram Lincoln, was assassinated in the Washington theatre, by a man who exclaimed "death to traitors Virginia is avenged", so our worst enemy is laid low and Seward the arch fiend was also stabbed, and today we hear the glorious tidings that the yankee congress had a row, and Andy Johnson was killed. God grant so may all our foes perish. I had a short letter today from Mr. S. but it told me he was well, & loved me so I am happy—

JUNE 2. I cannot but blame myself for my long neglect of this dear old book but really I have lived in such a whirl that I entirely forgot to note events important as they are. Peace has come, but oh God what a different peace to the one we prayed for, we are conquered by superior numbers, Sherman and Johnson declared an armistice since then the war is over we know not on what terms, slavery is done away with. Our noble Jeff Davis as well as all of our great men are prisoners, even the governors of the several states have been arrested, confederate money is worthless, and greenbacks rule the day. Columbia and all the principal are garrisoned by yankees, how it makes my southern blood boil to see them in our streets. Yes we are again in the hated union and over us again floats the banner that is now a sign of tyranny & oppression. Johnson was not killed & is now president, sad, sad is the change since the days of [George] Washington. My brothers are all home after fearful deprivations and hardships, thank God they are spared, poor Josh Moses the flower of our circle was killed at Blakely, he was a noble man, another martyr to our glorious cause. I have had several letters from Mr. S. he is well and doing well and truly loves me & he says he can't leave business to come before the roads open but I have written so often to beg him to I hope he may come Pa has gone to town, we expect him daily, when he comes I will know when Mr. S. is coming, I am all ready would to God he would come soon, I am weary of uncertainty & long to see him.

JUNE 23. This book is a sad record of broken intentions I

resolve and reresolve to write weekly and yet I fail to do so nor can I plead want of time for of that if nothing else, I have plenty Pa returned and brought me a letter from Mr. Seixas containing the greatest disappoint I ever had. I felt certain that if Mr. S. did not come with him he would soon follow, but to my grief he wrote he would not be able to come, he feared he could not come, until August, for business had not been good, and he feared he could not afford to marry at present. Independently of my sorrow at not seeing him the trial was more bitter owing to the fact, that all my humble preparations were completed even my clothes done up and every one expected my marriage, and as I could not give out the reason, persons think it strange. Oh God! my trials *this year*, have been great, grant I beseech thee, they may soon end, another source of trouble to me is that Mr. S. wants to go North, this is natural, for his family are there, but oh! I dont want to go, my feelings are yet *too bitter*, to go among them I cannot so soon forget Sherman and while I hope to love Mr. S.'s family I fear some remark may call forth my Southern blood, and it would be truly disagreeable to have any dispute, besides Fathers loss is so great he cant give me a trusseau, and I do dislike going among *total* strangers, who will value me for my dress, destitute as I am of so many things besides if Mr. S. is poor, it will be a great expense and I think we ought to study economy, Mr. S. does not write satisfactorily, he speaks of buying furniture, and I think it far more pleasant and economical to board at first, he is also not very attentive in writing and though *I dont doubt* his love, it makes me very unhappy. Our servants born and reared in our hands, hitherto devoted to us freed by Lincoln! left us today, it is a severe trial to Mother, and quite a loss to me among them, went Lavinia a girl given to me by my grandmother very handy & who had promised always to remain with & when I was married to go with me, Mr. S. was so pleased he wrote me to tell her if she proved faithful he would take her North, and show her as one faithful servant, but she went, she behaved better than most of them she offered to come to me in town & do anything she gave me notice & showed regret at parting this is one of the fruits of the war. I who believe in the institution of slavery regret deeply its being abolished. I am accustomed to have them wait on me, and I dislike white servants very much. My brothers are all home & in no business father's circumstances are very bad, what he will do God alone knows, it is hard he is an old man a good husband and father & son at his time of life to start fresh is hard. Next week is Mr. S's birthday, & I have written him and sent him a small picture of myself I hope it will please him.

JULY 6. It is nearly two weeks since I have heard from Mr. S. his negligence is very painful to me, and though I dont doubt his love yet this annoys me much, for if he is so careless to writing, per chance he may be careless in other things after marriage, but I hope not. The fourth was celebrated by the "freedmen", they had orations, a barbecue, fireworks, and a general jubilee, it was a sad day of humiliations to me, our cause is lost we are conquered and feel the yoke. Mr. Seixas wrote Pa he hoped to be at North by August 1st so I guess I will be married late this month oh I hope I will not be again disappointed, tis five months since I have seen Mr. Seixas and I do yearn to see him Oh! I think with pain of having to go North for although I long to know his family yet I feel *too* bitter towards them, to desire to go North & besides, although I have now a neat comfortable trusseau, very nice for Charleston but oh not fit to go North, and besides I dont feel like going where fashion, and dress rule the day. But Mr. Seixas wills it so, I *must* submit Time glides swiftly by, oh hasten time and bring me to the care of my best love. For I do long to see and be with him. Patience & trust in God, and all may be well.

JULY 9. I feel very anxious and unhappy although I try not to show it I have not heard from Mr. Seixas, for two weeks I fear he is sick and if it is not so, it is equal pain to be neglected he has never even acknowledged the receipt of my picture. I dont doubt him but he is too inattentive. God grant I may soon hear.

JULY 26. Grand news dear old book, I guess this is the last entry Eleanor Cohen will ever make in this book, for next Wednesday God willing I will become Mrs. B. M. Seixas, this event long long looked [for] is at hand, and yet I hardly realize it I don't yet feel either scary or nervous though my whole being is pervaded by a kind of serious strain of thought, and I feel fully that "I am leaving the love tried and true Going to the love untried & new"—I have ever been an indulged petted daughter had my own way considerably & entering on my duties, I feel that perchance I will have to give all this up. I know Mr S. loves me, and I love him with my whole heart, am willing to make sacrifices for him, and all I ask is that he will continue to love me, to be patient with my high temper, and above all be *just*. I had a telegram yesterday, look for him every day, tis six months since I have seen him, and my heart yearns for him— God grant me strength to be a *good true* wife, show me the clear line of duty. I expect to be married next Wednesday at four o'clock leave at five for Winnsboro, to go North—It seems to me to be very hard to go away among those who were so lately our enemies and as my heart is filled with "southern fire" I fear I may by look or word, say things that I might not do, but I will try to learn to keep quiet, truly I fear the change from deathlike quiet of Columbia to the whirl and confusion of gay New York, will almost set me wild—I am calmly quietly happy, I regret much that neither Alice nor Sis will be with at this time, but am thankful that Fannie my first true friend is here in accordance with a childish promise she will be my first bridesmaid—My wedding will be very private very quiet

AUGUST 2. My wedding day, can it be, long thought of, long hoped for here at last—I am very very happy, fully satisfied of Mr. Seixas' love, yet feeling a shade of deep pain at the severing of old ties, leaving my darling parents [to] go among new relations; today I cease to be a girl, and enter on the duty of "a wife"—God grant me strength to act correctly to make him happy & above all to live in the fear and love of God—Can it be that today maidenhood ceases Oh! This getting married is no trifle, but a event that gives use to *grave serious* thought— My new life is full of anxiety & care, and my old one is not free from it, but my faith in God is strong and blue eyed hope cheers me with the reflection, that all cares and troubles will

be shared by one who is dearer to me than life and the full
conviction of his pure true love seems to render me happy, he
is strange & we strange engaged people, yet I feel fully satisfied
with him, increased knowledge of his character has made me
love him better. It is a strange day, for August, cool & like April
alternate gleams of sunshine and of cloud Oh I hope it wont
rain while the ceremony is going on, or until I leave. The wedding will be quiet, at two o'clock by Mr. Jacob Cohen, leave
at four. This event the crowning glory of woman's life this giving
up herself to the one who is her glory—teach, oh! Lord thy
child to act with becoming behavior, let modesty and purity
direct my life let truth and prosperity be my guide and if I can
be loved by my new master as by my family all will be well. I
can write *no* more, this is the last dying effort of Eleanor H.
Cohen Spinster——

Entry number one of Mrs. B. M. Seixas.

Richmond. AUGUST 6. Yes I am a bride, a wife, four days married, but I must start at the beginning. The sun shone clearly,
brightly while I was married, all said I looked better than I ever
did before & I feel did look well I was very plainly dressed
white swiss muslin high & long sleeves trimmed with valien-
cienes lace a lace barbe at my throat my hair beautifully braided
a white illusion that enveloped me and a few natural flowers,
all passed off well, the glass broke, the ring was on my finger
& from every side I received kisses, & congratulations for Mrs.
Seixas, Mr. S. was very nicely dressed he wore a suit of black
except a very handsome white vest he looked remarkably well
he was serious and felt fully the responsibility of his position
my cake was splendid & after eating it & drinking my health
I hastened to my room & donned my traveling dress—We left
at four in a confederate wagon drawn by four mules I was in a
gale of spirits, laughing, gossiping & teasing Mr. S' life out of
him I felt the parting and had to show my excitement either in
tears or smiles so as a bride I preferred smiles I made Mr. S.
laugh until he was weak he was kind gentle tender & loving.
We arrived at white oaks in time to take the car, Mr. Goodwin

of Columbia was with us & gave us no peace telling every body we were bride & groom

AUGUST 30. I feel quite ashamed of my neglect of my dear old friend but for four weeks I have lived in such a whirl that it was impossible to write. We had a delightful time coming on, memory will ever rest joyfully on my bridal tour—we stopped Friday night in Raleigh, then in Peterburg, Richmond, Philadelphia, Washington, I saw all the battle fields, and cannot describe my feeling in leaving Richmond for then I felt I left the "sunny south" home of my birth, my choice & my heart. We stopped at the best hotels every where, each one was better than the other until we reached Philadelphia, the Continental there surpassed anything I ever dreamed of, we had two rooms parlor and bed room, furnished with green velvet, marble mantle etagier mirrors and in superb style, We arrived after six days travel in New York City, we met Mr. Seixas' father at the wharf they greeted me very kindly put us in a carriage and drove us up to the house 129 West 38th it is a large four story house, imagine my feelings in going to see perfect strangers, his Mother wept over us and all greeted me with affection. I was taken to my room a nice large one all ready for me and I love them all already—My experience of married life is that there is no true happiness in single life, yet marriage without love must be intolerable only deep pure holy love can ever fit a woman for what she has to undergo, my dear husband is kind & affectionate of course he has faults, as have I, but I will try to cure mine, and bear with his, his greatest fault is that he never thinks seriously he is always light hearted, & life is not made of sunshine *alone,* as we all know. He has determined to stay in New York, and this has pained me much for I don't like this place to live in, it is too grand too large too gay and fashionable to suit poor me, and I wanted to live with my beloved family, the separation from them is too hard—but as a true wife I try to reconcile myself to my husbands will I have visited theatres, ice cream saloons & ct and I am forcibly struck by the contrast between the prosperous North and our poor desolate south yet is she dearer to me in her desolation, than this gay heartless country.

I have not been well & have yearned for home and "Ma"—
The first year all say is hard I am obeying my husband, my
honeymoon is over, a glorious one it has been.

SEPTEMBER 10. While my husband is taking his Sunday
nap, I will scribble off a few lines, I am very happy as far as
my husbands love goes, but as I continue to feel unwell I long
to be at home oh I am heart sick & home sick—I hope to see
Susie Oakes tomorrow & will be glad to see a home face I shall
also cheer my heart by going to see B.—& talk of home.

◇ *1866* ◇

JANUARY 1. —I feel very much ashamed of myself to think
I have allowed so long a time to pass, but now at the new year
I must take a retrospective glance at the past present and future.
My husband will live in New York and I have reconciled myself
to it for he is so good so kind I must be happy my marriage life
is a truly happy one and I cant feel grateful enough to God for
the blessing he has given me in my precious husband—His
business is as good as we could expect and life looks brightly
to me, my parents expect daily to go to Charleston & I will go
home in two months to stay three, dear old journal let me whisper to you that a womans crowning glory will with Gods blessing
be mine this year, I will become a Mother Oh how my heart
thrills at the word yes please God in May I will have a pledge
of love given me in "*our baby*," as we love to call it, the blessed
assurance of my husbands love I can hardly believe it that I will
be a mother, my dear husband has liberally supplied me with
materials & I am busy making up a baby wardrobe.

Charleston—Home again tho' not to me the home of old for
since the war every thing is changed. On the 3d of February
I left New York and my husband to spend some months with
my parents and to be with my dear Mother during my confinement but could I have guessed how I would miss my husband I would have turned back the night I left if I could, I was
not so sick as I expected to be and arrived safely in due time,
my dear father was at the wharf, and I drove rapidly up to the

boarding house where my family were staying, the war having deprived them of the means to go to housekeeping I found my darling Mother looking well, and oh so anxious & happy to see me, they found me looking better than they expected me. The city in these parts that are not burned or shelled looks bright with an unfamiliar brightness, strange faces, new forms, and signs, take the place of the old loved ones—Yankees crowd the street & colored soldiers, and other "freedmen" may at any time be seen smoking their segars, in the day time! My friends crowded to see me and though I missed many familiar faces as some were married, some dead, some still refugees from home yet it was pleasant to see some, my visit opens pleasantly but after one weeks sojourn here one of the heaviest trials that has ever befallen our family (by no means unacquainted with) overtook us my beloved father was attacked with small pox, My room was immediately opposite to his and in addition to the fears I entertained for him, I was assailed by 1000 on my own account the dread of being taken sick and having no one to nurse me. Father thank God is well, praises be to God, none of us caught it from him, and tho' it was a great expense to him, still it has ended well, his business is fair and I hope he will succeed. They are all devoted to me and save that I am separated from my dear husband I am perfectly happy—All my baby things are done washed and in their place, and as I look on them I cannot but be thankful to the best of husbands for his generosity to me in giving me such nice things and in such abundance, he has truly made me happy. He has sent me several boxes and writes often sweet loving letters. My time of trouble approaches rapidly God be with me, and grant *"our baby"* as he loves to call it may be well and perfect.

APRIL 23. Poor Aunt Rachel after years of suffering she is now free was attacked by pneumonia after her other illness and though she had two Drs, nurses, blisters, and every care nothing could keep her here, she died on Thursday night. Ma said the last prayers for her. her life has been full of cares and as a single woman, she enjoyed not the holy ties of wifehood and motherhood. Isabel is to be married on May the 16th. If she is as happy and has as good a husband as *I have* I ask *no* higher boon from heaven for my little pet. May will be an *important* month for both of us, for she will become a *wife*, and I a mother, during its course Oh God grant all my excitement may not injure the tender luck under my heart but that it may be a *perfect*, well formed healthy babe one calculated to render its father & myself happy. I have not heard often of late from my husband hope to hear today.

◇   ◇

Afterword

And thus the diary ends, on what must have been, to Eleanor, a
strangely familiar note. The original manuscript is evidently lost; a
typescript is in the collection of the American Jewish Historical Society, which has no other record of its author. The fate of Eleanor Cohen
Seixas and her unborn child is not known.

THE DIARY OF

Martha Shaw

Topeka, Kansas; Colorado
1890–1893

Martha Shaw (*Kansas State Historical Society*)

◇ ◇

Introduction

Martha VanOrsdol was born in Iowa in 1867 and moved to the Kansas frontier at the age of five. Buffalo still roamed near Winfield, the newly founded town where her father and stepmother settled with Martha and her two younger sisters. Martha's mother had died when she was three; she did not get along with her stepmother and left home at sixteen to look for employment.

For the next six years Martha lived on her own with a great deal of freedom. Her diaries of this time record many beaux (she appears to have broken several hearts, and one rejected suitor attempted suicide); and dances and hayrides often lasting until the wee hours. During this time she moved to Topeka, where she met Johnny Shaw, a mail carrier eight years older than she, who hardly seemed to interest her at first.

But Johnny was persistent; after a year of courtship, despite strong reservations, Martha became his wife. The marriage developed problems almost from the start; Johnny drank and had a violent temper, and Martha suffered several miscarriages.

Martha wrote in her diary every day, as she had since the age of fourteen, even when she was too ill to jot down more than a few lines. (Her lifetime output totaled more than 4000 pages.) Her melodramatic style was clearly influenced by the popular romantic fiction of her day, but the emotion it reflected was genuine, for Martha felt things deeply and never seemed to doubt where she stood on any issue. Normally energetic, she avoided any display of weakness, even in front of her own family. Only in her diary, which she kept totally secret, did Martha allow herself to let down her guard.

◇ *1890* ◇

SEPTEMBER 4. Our *first Wedding Anniversary*, and the year has been *so full* of tears. I *cannot* admit, even to myself, that I am unhappy, and yet I *know* I am *not* happy. Johnny has an ungovernable temper, and I never know when he is angry at *me* or some one else, but whomever it may be, he takes his *spite* out on me. I *know* he loves me, is *proud* of me but he lets his temper rule him and make him unkind.

OCTOBER 3. In bed all day with high fever. It means I might have been a mother, but will not this time. *I'm sorry*.

OCTOBER 4. In bed all day again and my *fever very high* Johnny went to Forepaugh's *Circus*, tonight and left me *all alone* in the house. I felt hurt, that he would go and leave me at such a time, with only his own *pleasure* in mind, while *I* am sick at home because of him. But I let him go with a kiss and a smile and he *never dreamed* how my heart *ached*. I find him a very selfish man.

OCTOBER 16. I wonder what the future has for me and I *dread* it, because of the *forebodings* that come to me.

OCTOBER 21. Went Shopping this afternoon, but my Shopping *always* means buying *bare necessities*.

OCTOBER 27. Johnny *coughs* so much, I am dreadfully worried.

NOVEMBER 5. I so love to be at home, tho' it is none too happy because Johnny is so cross most of the time and his cough worries me nearly sick. I believe he is *going into Consumption* and will *never* get well, and it *nearly kills me*. *He* believes he will get strong, and *never suspects anything serious*, and I *must be brave* and never let him know the terrible *forebodings* and *premonition*, that comes to me.

NOVEMBER 6. *Never a day passes*, that Johnny *doesn't take his drink*, and I am so *radically against such things*, so of course *am most unhappy over it* but never oppose his wishes and allow him to keep liquor in the house all the time, which *he would do anyway, for he knows how bitterly I hate the stuff* and know it's harmful to him.

◇ *1891* ◇

MARCH 20. Not at all well. I was two months, or more, in Maternity and had so much hoped, and was *so happy in the hope* of being a mother, only to meet with most bitter disappointment this morning, so have been in bed all day. O it is dreadful.

MARCH 22. Sisters folks all down today, where I try to keep quiet, but must stay up, for I cannot tell them of my *disappointment*, since I had not let them, know of my expected joy, wishing to keep it for a sweet surprise. How full of disappointment is this old world, *especially for me.*

MAY 1. Johnny is so cross, he causes me to shed many tears. However, he has *"cursed"* me so many times for the tears that come unbidden at a cross word, that I have gotten so I can control them better and keep them back, until alone and only let him see my smiles.

JUNE 7. I get so deathly sick of mornings, and I am very sure it means "maternity." I have been sick this way, on other occasions when in such a condition and I know its symptoms.

JUNE 18. I went to town this afternoon and bought me a dress of French mull—Lavender. I always have to ask Johnny's consent before I buy anything for myself and take him along or show him a sample.

JUNE 21. Wonder what it would seem like, to have a husband who was kind and good, or how it would feel, to be happy.

JUNE 24. I *have to make a fight*, to *be allowed* to *become a mother*, for Johnny says, *if it is a fact*, that I am pregnant, as everything indicates, I *must* do *something* to prevent it; that *he is not ready to commence* to raise a family and that *I shall not bear the child.*

JUNE 26. Every day, I coax and coax Johnny, to "lets raise a family;" let me bear this child, and tell him, *how nice, "our Baby"* would be, and he gets so angry, he curses me, until my heart *can bear no more* and I go away by myself and *cry* and *cry.* I want the little one, Oh! so much and he *will not* listen to it. He says *"sometime* we will have a family, *but not now."* He is a *good* man, in so many ways, yet ill-*natured, unkind* and *selfish.* I feel it is wrong to prevent this new life and *he*, as honestly, *sees* no wrong; for my *suffering*, he cares *nothing*; soon over, he says. *How unlike the man I thought I was marrying.*

JULY 2. Oh! I wish I did not have to be sick. I am still coaxing Johnny to "*lets* have the child." Let the little one come.

JULY 5. Other men, seem so kind to their wives, I wonder if they really are, or whether it is all *sham* as in my case. Johnny pays me *lots of attention, before others* and makes folks think he is very sweet to me; he would never let anyone, know he ill treats me, *yet there is hardly a day passes* without *his cursing me, for the most trivial thing.*

JULY 6. I get so sick, I can hardly do my work and it makes Johnny so cross, but he has *halfway* consented, that there will be *no preventing* the birth of a child. I *do not see*, what *makes* him such a man; he is jolly and witty and everyone likes him yet his ungovernable temper, *loses* him friends and makes me unhappy.

JULY 10. Johnny has *at last* given *full consent* to the coming of the child, and I *am so happy*, but *he growls* and *grumbles about it.* O just to *think* of *being a mother*, is *unspeakable joy*.

JULY 11. Busy, though all thro' the morning hours of every day, I am so sick, I can do little. *What strange emotions, the thought* of *motherhood brings to one; such sweet joy and loving expectancy* and *the willingness to go thro' untold suffering*, for the *blessed joy* of being a *mother. O, God help me* to be *just the kind* of a *mother I ought to* be.

JULY 19. If I could only live happily with my husband, it seems to me, I would have nothing more to ask for. *Loves me, yes!* as he would love a fine horse; just because it was his, and a little better than anyone else owned.

JULY 31. Morning sickness is getting to be *all day* sickness, with me. And Johnny gets so angry: says there *"won't be another damned child,"* if he has to get sick over it and me sick all the time. I don't see how he can be so wicked. *I am willing to suffer* as I do, *for blessed Motherhood.*

AUGUST 10. Hot day, but a good breeze, so I have felt better but I cramp so at night, I can't sleep and so sick during the day, that I get very little rest at anytime and can neither eat or drink, without becoming terribly sick, so my life is most miserable.

AUGUST 16. I get *so hungry* for *kind words* and *sympathy*: I know it is just Johnny's way, to be indifferent, and that he loves me, but he gets angry at some one at the Office and is then ill-natured and abusive at home and it is so hard to bear, especially now, that maternity, causes me to be so sick and *I so long for sympathy.* But I am thankful he has at last become reconciled and *looks forward with pleasure to the coming of our little one* and does not think of it as an added burden.

AUGUST 21. No day *without* sickness; well, it means *untold joy* after awhile, so I *shall patiently endure.* I just talk to the Lord about it every day and ask Him to *help* me bear it; I have *no mother* and *no one,* I feel *free to go to for sympathy* and *comfort,* beside, everyone has troubles of their own and *would think mine amounted to nothing.*

AUGUST 31. For some time it has seemed as if Johnny's health, was failing and we begin to talk *Colorado* again. I pray God to spare me this sorrow.

SEPTEMBER 2. Working a little on *"Baby things" for the little treasure* thats coming to me: the *very thought is so precious* and *all so strange* and *mysterious.*

SEPTEMBER 8. Johnny is *beginning* to *cough considerably* and Dr. Menninger says he *must* go back to Colorado again and for us to *go in a wagon* and *we are considering it,* or *Johnny is,* for *I don't see how I can take such a trip.*

SEPTEMBER 9. It seems as if my *"cup of bitterness!" was almost full. Maternity keeps me sick all the time* and Johnny's *health* is failing and he *is so cross to me, because I am* sick and *can't help it,* and now I *must think* of *leaving my home* and *dear friends* and go to *make a new one among strangers.* I am willing to *sacrifice* anything for Johnny, *only it's hard.*

SEPTEMBER 10. I walk the floor most of the night in pain, but Johnny sleeps and *never* knows. I keep all my suffering and tears to myself. I get a little sleep during the day in a Rocker.

SEPTEMBER 11. I wish Johnny was a strong, healthy man; he is so ambitious and plans such *great* things and I have a *presentiment*, he will *never* be *well again* and that *I will not raise my child*.

SEPTEMBER 14. We *have fully made up our minds* to *move* to Colorado and *will drive thro'*. It *breaks my heart to leave my friends here*, but we will go *where my father* and *sister live* and that *will be some compensation* and we *must go where Johnny can live*.

SEPTEMBER 21. Johnny traded a *"lot and a half"* out on Redden Ave, and a young cow, today, for a team of big gray horses, wagon, harness and some tools, and so we have *made our first* start, toward a home in Colorado. If it *were not for the hope* of Johnny's *regaining his health, I would be most unhappy*.

SEPTEMBER 24. We talk and plan, every day now, for our Overland trip to Colo. While my heart is so *full of sorrow*, because I *must leave dear friends*, I *smile happily*, and tell Johnny how *well* he will get (and I *am sure* he will never get well) and how we *will prosper* in our *new home* and *say all* the *encouraging things* I *can think of*, while I *feel the opposite*.

SEPTEMBER 30. I *beg* Johnny *to go on to Colorado* and *let me stay here, until my little one comes, but he won't do it; says other women have taken such trips* and *I can, but it will be an unusually hard trip and so long, I do not see how I can ever stand it*.

OCTOBER 1. We hope to *start soon* for a *new home* in Colorado and *my heart is very heavy*. Doctor says we *must go on a farm*, where Johnny *will work in open* air, and to do this, we *will be fifty miles* from a Railroad and *there will be many deprivations*. I can *have no nurse, no doctor, no help*, when *my little* [one] *comes*. I *beg* Johnny to *let me stay*, as our rent is only five dollars per month and my aunt Sarah Ogden a *fine nurse would stay with me* and I could *have the care, that is a woman's right at such a time*, beside the *long drive will almost kill me, but he won't hear to it*, and *his selfishness almost makes me dislike him*.

OCTOBER 18. [Johnny's family] here today all day and they *never dreamed* of my condition. I am [in] *good shape* and *carry myself well* and have been *so sick* all the time, that I have eaten *barely enough* to *keep me alive*; so *have not taken on any fat*, in *fact am poor*.

OCTOBER 19. Johnny coughs so hard it distresses me and

there is *no doubt* it is *consumption*, tho' he won't have it so. I pray God, to make him well and strong again.

OCTOBER 20. I am not sick so much, in afternoons, anymore and I am *so thankful*. I don't think anything could be worse, than this dreadful Maternity sickness.

NOVEMBER 1. I am getting so poor some are afraid, my little one will not live to come to me, but what can one do.

NOVEMBER 7. *Everyone thinks* it *is dreadful* that Johnny *intends to make me drive thro' to Colo.* with him *in a big wagon* and *especially this late* in *the Fall. I have asked him* to *let me go on the Train*, if I *must go at this time*, but *he won't even let me do that. I never quarrel* with him and he *never sees ought but a smiling face, however much my heart may ache*, but *this heartless treatment is beginning to make me lose my love for* him.

NOVEMBER 12. We finished packing and loading our wagon this afternoon, and bid all our neighbors good-bye this evening; and so at last, it is good-bye to home, and away to the West, for a *new* home and *new* friends, in a *new* country, almost a Desert. But I am *willing* to make the sacrifice, if it will but restore my husband's health. Our friends think him, very selfish to *compel* me to take such a trip in my condition especially, when I could as well go on the train. This late in the Fall, will even be harmful to him and I will suffer greatly. Woman will sacrifice everything for the man she loves, why will *he* not do, *half* as much for her.

NOVEMBER 13. Well at last, our journey has commenced and to-night after only a few miles of travel, I am *very* tired and the jolting of the wagon, caused me to *suffer much*. We were late in getting away from Topeka, leaving about 3 o'clock; the weather fine and a lovely evening. From our camp to-night at Mulhollen Hill, or a little West, we can see the lights of my beloved Topeka, and it makes my heart ache; when shall I see them again. But *for an ever present* God, I would be in *utter despair*.

NOVEMBER 14. A cold, chilly drive. Rained all day and the roads terribly hilly—we got "*stuck*" on one hill. With our heavily loaded wagon, we only reached Dover, 20 miles from Topeka, at dark this evening, and I am so weary and heart sick.

NOVEMBER 16. Passed thro' *Harveyville* at noon. Bought some good, *Home-made bread*, at a little house in the Village. Very cold today and snowed some, but we keep warm as we have a stove in the wagon; how *hard* this *shaking*, as we drive along over *rough, frozen roads* and never a word of sympathy. Johnny gets so cross, if he *even* thinks I feel badly: well, I thank God, for giving me a heart, that can keep its sorrow to itself.

NOVEMBER 21. We passed thro' *Marian*, a nice, thrifty looking, little town, late this afternoon and are in camp, three miles West tonight. Turned *very cold* and *wind blows a gale* and only that we are in a *hollow* I believe it would blow our wagon over, heavy as it is. We see some fine country and some especially pretty places but the trip *is so hard*, I can't enjoy *anything*. I am not so sick anymore, but I *suffer* dreadfully, from the *jolting* of the wagon, so I get out and walk as much as I can, but I am getting so heavy and it is *so hard* for me to climb in and out of our high wagon over the side-boards.

DECEMBER 2. Passed thro' *Dodge City*, this morning and tonight are camped 20 miles West at *Cimarron*. *Cold* and the *wind blows a gale*. We *drove in beside a large empty store building* and are *pretty well protected*. The roads are *something terrible* and *sometimes* it is *wholly unsafe* for me to be in the wagon. The journey is *so hard*, that *many times*, I *lie on the mattress* behind Johnny and *cry my heart out* and *he* thinks *I'm sleeping*. How *blind most* men *are* and *how utterly indifferent, to what women suffer. Some times, after a hard days journey*, I can feel no life and my *heart* is *agonized, lest my little one be dead*.

DECEMBER 5. *Six degrees below zero last night* and we had no shelter whatever. About 4 o'clock, we came to a Ranch house and stopped to enquire the *better* road, as *two roads forked here*. It was *commencing to snow* and the people *advised us* to *stay* with them *over night*, as a *Blizzard* was *imminent*, but Johnny *would not listen* to them. Oh! *I would have given the World* to *have stayed*. Well, we drove on and the *storm grew worse*, and *soon* was *dark* and the *little travelled* road, began to *fill*, and my *heart beat anx-*

iously; finally when we could *no longer follow* the *dim trail*, to *either go ahead or turn back*, and the *wind, snow* and *ice* was suffocating us and we *could hardly force our Team against it*, we *made out* a *dim black shadow*, near the road, which *proved*, an *empty* and *locked "Claim Shanty*," so we drove up beside it and are camped, with *no other protection* and *completely lost and only those who have been lost in a Blizzard know the agony.*

DECEMBER 6. The wind was *blowing so hard* this morning, that I *feared* to look out of our *closed wagon*, lest the storm *still be raging*, but when I *found heart* to do so, the sun was shining and a dim depression, showed we were near the road, but Oh! the *terrible anxiety* of the past night. Lost in a *terrible storm*, that might last, on *these barren Plains, for days* and our poor horses, tho blanketed, had to *stand out in it all, as also our faithful Watch dog*, Joe, a fine Newfoundland, whom we *might* have *kept* in wagon, with us only for Johnny's *impatience*: and we might all have been comfortably housed, had Johnny but listened to the *kindly* Ranch people.

DECEMBER 7. We reached Syracuse, our last City in Ks. nearly noon, and found my father there, with Team, to meet us and take part of our load. And he took, a *mighty big load*, off my heart, for there will be no more anxiety, about roads. After dividing our load, with Pa and eating our dinner and getting some supplies, we started out on the last hundred miles of our journey. We are *cozily* camped among some low, sand Hills, and I can sleep happily because Pa is here and I feel safer. He protested about starting out with us after dinner as we could reach no house, to make our camp tonight, but we told him we were used to it. He was *shocked* to think we had not camped each night, in a town, where I could have had some comfort, and care if needed.

DECEMBER 10. Reached Pa's Ranch, Belle View, at 11:10 A.M. and I *could have cried with joy*, that my *long hard journey was ended, only* I *was too tired and sick*. We were *four long weeks* on the journey, who would not rejoice at the end of it.

DECEMBER 11. Enjoying *blessed rest* at Pa's today; I *wonder* if it *won't seem like this* in Heaven. Oh! it's been so hard, and I am sure my unborn little one, became tired too.

DECEMBER 26. We went over to Mr. James Wilson's this afternoon, to complete arrangements for the renting of his farm as doctor told Johnny to go on a farm, so to be out in open air much as possible.

DECEMBER 31. And so ends another year of my life: I *think* the *most unhappy, I have ever known.* Johnny is so *unkind* to me, but *more* through his *selfish, indifferent, nature,* than that he *willfully means* to be unkind; but *it is not possible* to live, *happily* with him and *were it not* for God's *mercy, I could pray to die.* My *greatest joy* is my *expected Motherhood* and one would *think, this coming joy,* would make him kinder, but it *does not. He does not spare me in the least:* there *is not a profane, low, vulgar, filthy name he has not called me. His vileness is almost unendurable.*

◇ *1892* ◇

JANUARY 5. In our new home today. Old Mr. Wilson is to board with us; quite a nice farm, well improved and everything furnished—we give a third of the crop for rent and board him. Doctor said *only hope* for Johnny was farm life and I pray, he *may be restored* to health, but there comes to me such a *strong presentiment* that he will never be well again and that my beloved child, yet unborn, will not be with me a great while. I *wish* I could get rid of such a feeling, for it is terrible and I *cannot* give up either of them; and pray God will not take them from me.

JANUARY 15. There is running-water and a fine Spring on this farm and a good *well* at the door; the kitchen is stone, and detached from the house; a fine large barn and hen house—we are unusually comfortable, for to be living in the West, fifty miles from a Railroad.

JANUARY 16. The days seem long, till the coming of my child, whom *I* shall have *no* part in naming. Johnny says if a boy, it shall be named for him and if a girl, he shall name it for his cousin and I can have no "say so" about it. *I could not be* so selfish with *him.*

JANUARY 19. Waiting the coming of my little one. I wish I might have a nurse and a good doctor, but none here.

JANUARY 23. No day, could *be more grand,* than this one has been and I felt *strangely buoyant* when I arose this morning. About *10 o'clock* I began having pains and they have continued *all* day, *increasing in severity*—but I *have had so much to do,* and *found* I could *stop* them by stooping over, so I just stopped them and *went on with my work. Washed* a few pieces, *ironed* a little and did *much baking.* I *scrubbed* my kitchen after 4 o'clock. *Oh! how I have suffered* and Johnny *never guessed* I *was in pain.* He and Mr. Wilson went to town, late this afternoon, and *I* was *left alone.* It *seemed* to me, if *motherhood* was near, I would have to go to bed, and since I have been able to *endure* and *go on* with my work, it surely can't be that. Tonight I was *suffering* so *dreadfully,* I *could not eat supper,* but *sat* down to the table and *held a paper* in *front* of my face *as if reading,* so they would not see my face in pain and Johnny *scolded* me, for being *"so interested in a Topeka paper, that I could not eat:" how little he knew.* But I kept everything to myself, until 11 o'clock tonight, a *most severe pain,* which I *could not* hold back, *made* me *groan* so *loudly* it *awakened* him and now he has gone for *my stepmother* and I *sit here alone,* with *everything* in *readiness* for the coming of the *little stranger.* When he returns with Ma, he will go *five miles* in *another direction,* for Mrs. Gordon who is *all* I can have to help me thro'. But she is the mother of 15 children and knows all about Babies. I am *just sitting here waiting* for the folks to come so think *I'll read, between pains.* Well here are Ma and Johnny—he made a quick trip—Ma is *so surprised* that I am *able* to be up. And *now* Lyman [her brother-in-law] has come at 1 o'clock with Mrs. Gordon and tries to jolly me. *I am still on my feet. I make all go to bed.*

JANUARY 24. Today, at 12 minutes past 1 o'clock P.M. my *precious,* "wee girlie" came to her mother. The *dearest, sweetest, little, treasure, ever* a mother had. The *blackest* hair and the *blackest eyes, big* and *round* and *full.* I *thank* God *with all my heart* and *soul* and *being* for my darling. But *what* a *time we had, to get her.* motherhood was *all* but *impossible*; by *stopping* my pains, I *had worn* them *out* and *nothing could be done* to *bring them* on, and *part of* the time I lay *exhausted* and *unconscious*, until in *sheer desperation*, Mrs. Gordon, *tore me*, with her *fingers* and *pulled* baby *away*, *scratching* the little *forehead* and *almost crushing* the *head until* was a *great ridge across* the *top, big* as my *finger* and the darling was *black* with *strangulation*—the *cord twice* around her neck. She came *without* a *pain* and *as soon as she was here, all suffering ceased* and I feel *strong as an ox*. In an *hour* and a *half* after she came, I had *eaten* a *meal, hearty enough* for a *Harvest-hand*. I *didn't suppose* they would let me, but *they did* and tonight I *know* I am *strong* enough to get *supper*. And they are *all surprised*. We named Baby, Mabel Inez Belle.

JANUARY 25. A fine day they tell me, tho' they won't let me see outside and I feel as strong and well, as if there was never a pain in the world. Oh! my sweet, blessed Babe, you are worth all the suffering you cost your mother, and more. And how proud your father is of you; but thro' it all, Johnny gave me but one sympathetic word: yesterday morning, he came to my bed-side and placing his hand on my brow asked in a sympathetic voice "Are you suffering much Mattie? Well you will have to try to bear it now:" the only kindly words I have had in all the months, and they brought tears of gratitude.

JANUARY 27. I wanted to name my girlie, "Inez Belle" but Johnny says she shall be *always* called *Mabel* for his cousin. We weighed the precious mite of a baby today and she weighed 9½ pounds.

FEBRUARY 9. When Johnny is cross, what a little comforter my baby *"treasure"* is. I *know* I have some thing to live for. Johnny quarrels with Mr. Wilson and that too, makes our home life very unpleasant. Mr. Wilson is very old, somewhere near 80 and the two men cannot agree about the management of *anything* but Johnny is *almost invariably* in the wrong.

FEBRUARY 10. *My baby dear, you and I, will love and love, if all the World goes wrong. Mother's own dear precious girlie, how I thank God for you.*

MARCH 10. Wash and iron and bake, make beds, sweep and dust, wash dishes, do mending, milk and churn, look after chickens, chop wood too—I wonder if a woman is supposed to kill herself for a man, who has temper like a Bear. But then one marries *"for better, for worse"* and I do not believe in divorces, tho' down deep in my heart, many times, I could wish there was a way out, when I am *cursed* beyond endurance.

MARCH 17. I do not see, how anyone could help loving children. *My heart is full all the time, of the joy of my Babe* and I can better bear Johnny's abuse, because *I have her.*

MARCH 25. Johnny is over his cough and seems well and strong and I believe, in as good health as he ever was. Yet, *I* do *all* the hard work and getting out in the storm, to save him in every way I can; and it seems like the *more* I do for him, the *more* unkind he is to me.

MARCH 27. My little love grows and grows and is so strong— sits alone and can raise up by herself. I sometimes wish I could take her and go away off, where we would never see her father— he curses me so and is so ill-tempered, I am afraid she will learn to do the same, when old enough.

APRIL 13. How my heart has to suffer extremes: extreme joy with my baby, extreme unhappiness with my husband. How can men be so cruel, as many of them are: Johnny's temper is dreadful. One evening he went out, to shoot Jack rabbits by "moonlight" and the dog followed and frightened the rabbits away, which made him so angry he was going to shoot the dog, who seemed to have a sense of danger and ran to the house and I opened the door and called him in, so not to let him repeat his offense; but Johnny followed determined to kill him, and my pleading for the dog's life, because Baby and I need him, when left alone and he our only protection, only made him more angry and when I stepped between him and the dog, still begging for the dog's life, he became insanely angry and drew his gun up and aimed at me, to shoot me. I was paralyzed with fear, as I saw his look and could only turn to my little one sleeping on the bed and thought, "who will take care of my precious one" and in that instant she moved and attracted his attention, and he lowered his gun and left the room without a word. Baby had saved my life, but O the horror I suffered in those moments.

APRIL 26. My 25th *Birthday.* Only 25 years old and think of the *world of care* I've had.

MAY 3. Baby is cross and fretful, and everyone thinks Johnny is letting me work too hard, and have told him, we won't raise her, if he does not do differently; of course *he* doesn't think that way.

MAY 4. Baby coughs, but does not seem to have more than a slight cold, but it makes me anxious.

MAY 20. How I wish there was a good Doctor in this part of the country, that I might consult him for my little "joy-girl", instead of using *all* the remedies, *all* the old "grand-mothers" can think up, for *all* the "diseases," one ever heard or dreamed about.

MAY 24. My blessed little "sun-beam girl" is four months old today, and such a joy to her mother: there would be little to live for, without you, my precious one. Oh! God keep her well.

MAY 25. Johnny has not been well, since his trip to Syracuse, Ks.: that is he coughs and it seems to grow worse. And baby love is not well so my heart is heavy with care.

MAY 28. My little treasure seemed so much worse today, that we took her away down to Vilas, to a Mrs. M. E. Martin, a sort of "Homemade" Baby doctor, and she says, there is very little hope, that my darling can live. Could a mother ever hear more cruel words—why it stunned me, crushed me; my Baby *must* live, or I'll die.

MAY 29. Johnny took me over to Pa's this morning where I will stay while my precious one is sick. My heart is so *utterly crushed* and *broken*, I cannot stay at home.

MAY 30. At my father's. My "wee girlie" see.ns brighter today, but my spirit is crushed. I am wholly undone. I only seem to live because there is yet life, in my sweet Babe.

JUNE 1. Little Inez is so sick, I hardly let her out of my arms day or night, but we think she is getting better, very slowly.

JUNE 8. Baby about as usual and we went over home this morning, to get some of my clothes, then went up to Lyman's and finished packing my trunk, to go to Topeka, Ks, with my baby, to get a good Doctor, and if she gets well, I'll be in no hurry to come back to a cross man. I shall at least take a good, long rest.

JUNE 10. I took the train at 2:30 this morning for Topeka, Ks. with my little sick darling.

JUNE 11. Dr. Menninger came this morning; says baby is a *very* sick baby, but will get well. It *is* her teeth, as I suspected, and she has Brain-fever; O it is so terrible.

JUNE 16. Dr. came again today, and baby grows better, but my heart is heavy in spite of his reassurances, for something tells me I must give up my heart's treasure. Oh! if I could but get rid of these dreadful premonitions.

JUNE 19. Inez is better. Johnny writes nearly every day and addresses the letters to Baby.

JUNE 22. Baby is doing nicely but had to call Dr. M. to see *me*, for I am all worn out with loss of sleep and rest, and care and anxiety and I have a very sore breast: in fact I am *sick*, all over.

JUNE 25. My precious one slept peacefully and seemed quite a well Baby until 12:15 P.M. when she went into a "spasm" and by 3 o'clock had had *five very* hard ones. Dr. M. got here at that time, stayed some time, working over baby; she kept getting worse and he returned at 9:30 Baby very low. Telegraphed for Johnny.

JUNE 27. Retta Shaw stayed up with me tonight, and helped me care for baby and once when baby seemed dying, Retta said to me, "*she is dead*, there is no need to give her medicine," but I *could not* give up, and I forced the medicine down her throat and she revived, and from 1·30 A.M,, was better, and "nursed" two different times but at 9:30 this morning, she grew worse and death commenced: there were no more spasms, but one knew she was suffering dreadfully, and with a broken heart, I bowed to God's will and said "Oh! Lord, I give her back to thee: I cannot see her suffer longer." At 10:05 this evening, while I held her to my aching heart, God sent the Angels for her and her terrible suffering ended and *mine* commenced. Mrs. Pettit and Mrs. Johnston were with me when baby died. Every one else were in bed asleep. I don't know when I have slept.

JUNE 29. Oh! the emptiness of my arms, the loneliness of my heart. Oh! God, ease this terrible heartache. Johnny arrived, from Springfield, Colo. at 4:30 P.M. and is *crushed* by the loss of our darling.

JUNE 30. We buried our little darling, in the Topeka Cemetery at 5:30 P.M. Tho' my heart is breaking, stunned, crushed I can say, "Thy will, Oh! God, be done." And in some way, I know God will help me to live, without my "wee girlie." And I do thank Him, with all my broken heart, that I've known the blessed joy of motherhood. Heaven will be a brighter place, for my little one's being there.

JULY 4. Fourth of July, and we went with the Herman's to Garfield Park, this afternoon. They need not think to make me forget. I just long to be alone and cry my heart out.

JULY 8. I wish I did not have to meet people, for my heart is so heavy, I *could pray to die*.

AUGUST 5. Johnny and I went to the Cemetery this morning to say goodbye to a precious little grave, and he cursed and swore and was so abusive, because I took some wild flowers and put on the little grave. They were all I had, and I had no money to buy any better ones. My "wee girlie" even so young, loved flowers and I've seen her hold and look at flowers and play with them and reach for every flower she saw any one have. With a last good bye, we took 2:40 P.M. train for Colorado. Train was terribly crowded and very hot. But I was almost insensible to any discomfort for my heart was so torn with grief, that I must leave even the body of my precious one; that I must go so far from that little grave. I wonder how I've lived these weeks without her. Oh! just because I cannot die. Oh! if I *might* lie beside her, to stop the pain of my heart.

AUGUST 8. We went to Pa's this morning and will stay until can make other plans, for I just *cannot* go back to the house where my "wee girlie," my little "joy baby" was born.

AUGUST 13. We are still with my father. I try to be brave and not let any one know, how my heart hurts, for I know it makes them all feel badly, to see me grieving. I cannot even go to Johnny, because he worshiped our little one, and her death has seemed to make an "*Infidel*" of him. So I give them my smiles, write my sorrow here, save my tears for the night hours, and pray that God will change Johnny's heart and make him a Christian man.

AUGUST 25. My heart is so lonely, I could pray for another child. I am almost frantic at times, to be a mother again, but Johnny's health is so poor I dare not think of it; it would be wicked.

AUGUST 26. Sometimes I almost think God did not know how lonely my heart would be, and how it would just ache and ache, and hurt me so, or He would not have taken from me, my "*wee girlie*".

AUGUST 27. We have made up our minds to move into Springfield, because I cannot bear to go back to the house where my precious baby was born; and then Johnny is not strong enough to farm—the work is too heavy.

AUGUST 31. We moved today into Springfield, a mile and a half from Pa's, and I was compelled to go to the Wilson farm, to pack our things. The house seemed *haunted* with Baby's presence. I am very tired tonight and heart sick. Oh! It's very hard to live without my Baby and yet I cannot die.

SEPTEMBER 6. So little to do in a small home, and the hours drag, heavy with sorrow: if I only had a kind husband, to whom I could go and cry out my heart's grief, I think my heart would not get so weary, but on these pages is the only place, I dare *let go* of myself. To every one, and in every place, my grief must be concealed, and I must be all smiles, as if there was no such thing as sorrow.

SEPTEMBER 30. Johnny says now, that we will go to Calif. soon. He is so restless and not well.

NOVEMBER 4. Johnny is so abusive, he has driven from my heart all love for him, and he does not *dream* that his cruelty has killed my heart and it cannot love him. I would be so glad of my freedom. Oh! this is such a terrible thing, but the human heart is not capable of enduring every abuse and continuing to love. I stay with him, simply because, I believe as a Christian, it is my duty to do so. I do not believe in divorces. I do not quarrel with him—always I give him kind words and a smiling face. I've left nothing undone I could do for him. I pray for him but my love is dead.

NOVEMBER 5. Johnny left for Lamar Colo, this morning with a load of Rye to sell.

NOVEMBER 10. Johnny has sent me no word, as to how he got along on his trip, and I could almost pray he would never come back, but would run away and leave me. Oh! for freedom—

NOVEMBER 14. Johnny says he will divide with me, what little we have and I can go my way and he will go his, and Oh! I could shout with very joy, at the thought of freedom from such a life, but I feel it is my duty to stay with him, so I turned down his offer: it is the first time he has ever hinted he was unkind, or talked about our unhappy life, and I told him I would stay with him, because if he was to get sick, he would need me, and not everyone would stand by him. I know that consumption has fastened upon him, and no change of Climate will ever cure him, because he *will* drink and takes no care of his health.

NOVEMBER 28. Went up town with Pa and Johnny this afternoon to pack our household things. This settling in a new home, and so soon "tearing up" and going again, takes the heart out of one: it is so hard for me to give up my friends. We could have the Post Office here, and there is, at least, a good living in it, and an easy one, and Johnny's health will be as good here as anywhere. No one wants me to go away with him, but if *he* insists on going, I feel it *my* duty to go with him: no one else would look after his welfare as I would.

[Los Angeles] DECEMBER 22. We awakened this morning to look out upon green lawns, bright flowers, trees in fruit and bloom: the fragrance of Orange blossoms, and the songs of birds, in the air: a blue sky and bright sunshine over all. Great dark mountains, snow-capped, loom in the near distance, and it's a beautiful sight; a *grandly* beautiful one, but a weary, homesick heart, cannot enjoy these things. I would give it *all* to be back where a little grave is covered with snow, in the homeland.

DECEMBER 26. It is all so strange, to come from the snow into the sunny summer time. It is like we had gone to another world.

DECEMBER 27. We went to see a Dr. this morning about Johnny's lungs: he told us one lung was entirely gone and the other badly affected, but could cure him. Johnny believes what he said about *cure*, but *I* know it's only a question of time, until consumption will end it all.

◇ 1893 ◇

JANUARY 21. I went to town this afternoon, and then to see a Mr. Busath about work, for *I have got to go to work.*

JANUARY 22. Mrs. Busath came for me to come down to the St. Angelo and help wait on their Boarders at mealtime and I went down at 4 o'clock. Was a big crowd for Supper and while I am so thankful for the work, pride made it embarassing for me.

JANUARY 23. I went down to the St. Angelo this morning at 6 o'clock to help Mr. Busath for Breakfast, stayed to help with Lunch at noon. Came home at 2 o'clock, went back at 4 o'clock and got home again at 7 o'clock after helping with Supper, or Dinner here. I am to do this each day and receive $20.00 per month and my three meals a day, which will be a big help. Our money is running short and Johnny is unable to work. I could get a place, to Clerk in a Store, but could have no time at home: and this way, I can get Johnny's meals for him and be home afternoons so it is much better, every way.

JANUARY 24. I find it very embarassing to meet so many strangers but they are all so lovely and Mr. & Mrs. Busath so kind. Mrs. Busath will be a mother soon and how I wish I could know this great joy again. My "wee girlie" would be one year old today, if living. O little "joy girl" how mother's heart aches for you.

JANUARY 25. Went to the St. Angelo as usual today. I get home in time to get Johnny's Lunch at noon. Leave things so he can get his own Breakfast, when he doesn't want to go to town and get it and I get his Dinner when I get home in evening.

FEBRUARY 19. It seems hard, to have to be from home all the time, yet I believe it is a blessing, in that I do not have to be so much with Johnny and run the risk of taking consumption, for he coughs dreadfully and the smell from his body is sickening: smells like his body was dead: wish I did not have to sleep in same room with him.

FEBRUARY 20. 17 blocks to the St. Angelo walked four times a day, is 68 blocks, or more than five miles a day, beside my work at home and the St. Angelo, *all for a man* who gives *me many curses* and very few smiles. I give *him* my heart's sincerest prayers. In Colorado, I could have the P.O. with salary for a good living and be with my loved ones; instead I am here doing this, not for love, but because I am trying to live aright and believe in my duty as a Christian. I will not leave a thing undone.

FEBRUARY 22. Drew my first month's wages this evening when Mr. Busath gave me a $20.00 gold coin, which I brought home and gave to Johnny, and was happy to do so.

MARCH 31. Another awful fog. Johnny sick—in bed most of time. I am so afraid I will come home some evening and find him dead. He thinks when the rains stop, he will get well again, but I know it is the beginning of the end and there is no hope, but I dare not let him know. I must keep him in good spirit and cheery, *if cranky*.

APRIL 24. Johnny grows *worse* in health every day, and there is no chance of recovery—the only question is "how long can he last." I would gladly give him my health, take his dreadful disease and die, if God would let me.

JULY 22. Tonight after Dinner I quit work, and am home to stay, for Johnny has grown so much worse, it is not safe to leave him alone any more; and any way, we will soon go home to Topeka, if he lives until we can arrange things. He thinks he will get well when we get back home, where it is warm and dry.

AUGUST 2. Mrs. Cook came with her carriage, to take us to

the Depot. Johnny with some one on each side of him, to half carry him, managed to get down the stairs and to the carriage, almost in state of collapse. At Depot, Conductor picked him up in his arms and carried him into the train. I know, just ahead a little way, death is waiting to claim the one to whom I'm bound: it may come on way home and my heart almost failed me. I scarcely could get courage to make the start, but the sick one so longed to get home, so I've made the start and pray God for strength and to take us safely all the way.

AUGUST 5. This morning I awaken, with only the day between me and home, and still my husband lives, tho' awearied and much worn. . . . We arrived in Topeka about 5:30 P.M.

AUGUST 16. Johnny slowly grows weaker and I am with him day and night. Have not undressed to go to bed, since I left Los Angeles. He won't let anyone else care for him, so day and night I sit by his bed-side, getting what sleep I can in a rocking-chair, and I never seem rested.

AUGUST 24. Home with Johnny, who will hardly let me from his bedside, long enough to eat my meals. I wish he was a Christian; it is hard to see him dying an unbeliever, an *Infidel*. I pray God to change his heart.

AUGUST 31. Johnny, is so ill-natured and abusive to me, that his brother goes after him, sometimes and *"hushes him up,"* telling him, he ought to be ashamed of himself for abusing one, who has done so much for him and does all in her *power* for him, day after day, uncomplainingly.

SEPTEMBER 4. Today is Johnny's and my 4th wedding Anniversary and what a long *miserable, unhappy,* four years it has been. "Four years full of tears," and I have tried so hard to get J. to be kind to me, but he can't be kind to any *woman*. He abuses his mother, more than me and she is such a good woman.

SEPTEMBER 27. Went up town for "morphine" this morning, as Johnny has to have it all the time; the only thing that keeps him alive.

OCTOBER 5. Two months this afternoon, since we came home and not *once* in all that time, have I had my clothes off, only to change to others, nor have I been in bed. I sleep in a chair beside the bed, that I may minister to his every want. Several times I have lain down on the floor on a pallet, but he does not like to have me do so.

OCTOBER 17. Johnny's conscience seems to *give him a twinge* once in awhile and he *feels remorse*, for his *unkindness* to me and he said to me today, *"that I had done everything in the world, for him that a woman could do* and *no other woman*, would ever have *lived* with him and *done for him*, as I have, and when he *gets well*, he is going to *join the church*, and will be a *better man* and be *good to me."* Ah poor man; my heart is *filled* with *pity for him*, but he *crushed my heart long ago; killed all the love of my heart.* I could *never love him again, never* and could such a miracle happen, as his restoration to health, I *would not live* with him. I stay *now*, because *he is sick* and *helpless*, and it is *my duty*, as *one who tries to be a Christian.* But he *died to me, long ago.* When I felt *my love dying*, I *fought* to *retain it*, but *no love can live, under such cruelty.*

OCTOBER 21. Johnny has been real "flighty" all day. Just about half conscious. I sat up *all* night, last night alone, with him, not daring to close my eyes.

OCTOBER 26. Who but *God* and *those* who have gone thro' the same experience, can *know* the *strange, conflicting* emotions of my heart. *Tonight I am utterly alone* and *miserable. Tonight I am a widow. I am free. My heart* would *cry out in very joy, because it is freed from a wretchedly miserable life*, and *my heart is breaking with pain, heart-ache and utter desolation*, that *thro' death must come its release.* It has been such a *fine day* and Johnny *wanted* me to go to town on an errand, so mother came and staid with him and at 2 o'clock P.M. *I kissed him good-bye and went to town*, he saying as I left, to *"hurry back for I like to have good-looking girls sit by me." When I came home, he was dying.* I called Dr. Lewis at 5 o'clock. J. became unconscious about 6 o'clock and *died at 10:5* P.M. and tho' the room was full of *people*, I was the *only one* at his *bed-side.*

OCTOBER 27. Brother Jim would not consent to keeping the body until Sunday, because he died of consumption and so we buried him this evening at 6 o'clock: and *tonight I am so wretched*, that I *feel dazed* and *as if I must awake from some terrible night-*

mare. *Four years ago a Bride, hoping to be happy. Tonight a widow in abject misery. I know* my *heart aches* as *much over his death,* as if *I had loved* him, *for it is terrible* to *have one die; not a Christian,* and *especially one who was much to us at some time in our life.* But *God knows* the *tears* of *my heart* and *the prayers of my heart for this man.* I have striven to do what God would have me do.

OCTOBER 29. Went up the Cemetery this morning and took the flowers to Johnny's Grave and some to put on my *wee girlie's.*

OCTOBER 30. Putting things away and burning many more, that I may have no reminder, of my unhappy life. My Wedding Veil and gloves, were buried with Johnny.

NOVEMBER 2. I feel as if a great load had been lifted from off me and my freedom is actually a joy, tho' I sincerely grieve, that death should be the means of this thrill of pleasure, at being free from such a miserable life.

Martha Shaw Farnsworth with four of her "Sunday School Boys" (*Kansas State Historical Society*)

◇　　◇

Afterword

Johnny's death left Martha with no source of support, and she immediately accepted a job nursing a Mrs. Farnsworth, mother of Fred Farnsworth who had been a friend of Johnny's. Living in their home, she noted in December: "Oh! how good it seems, to have everyone kind to you; how restful. I never hear complaining, nor an unkind word and I feel as if I had been let out of prison."

Martha's experiences with Johnny Shaw had given her a horror of marriage; she resolved never to marry again. Fred Farnsworth, however, was determined to change her mind. In April of 1894 Martha wrote, "Fred makes an *ideal lover; all devotion*; and if I could give him a year's trial as a lover, I think I could make up my mind to marry him."

They were married that May: "Oh! how I *shook* and almost fainted," Martha reported. But the marriage was an extremely happy one that lasted the rest of her life.

To her sorrow, Martha had no more children. She compensated by "adopting" a number of boys, over the years, from the ranks of her Sunday School pupils. She also devoted a great deal of time to politics, especially the Kansas movements for prohibition and women's suffrage.

Martha Shaw Farnsworth died of hepatitis in February of 1924. "What a fine heritage this kindly woman left," said a Topeka paper, "the good she did will live for ages."

Plainswoman: The Diary of Martha Farnsworth, 1882–1922, edited by Marlene Springer and Haskell Springer, will be published in 1986 by the University of Indiana Press.

◇   ◇

THE DIARY OF

Carole Bovoso

*California, France,
Spain, New York
1967–1979*

◇   ◇

Carole Bovoso *(Paul Plumadore)*

◇   ◇

Introduction

Carole Bovoso is a journalist, poet and painter who was born in Washington, D.C., grew up in New York City and Saratoga Springs, New York, and was educated at Bennington College.

Her journals, both visual and written, have been an important part of her creative life since she was a child. "My journals are an end in themselves," she says, "they have their own life. But I also use them to transform ideas: as a source. Both visual and written work emerge from the protective womb of these private pages."

When this series of journals begins, Bovoso has been working as a painter in New York, creating oils and acrylics and showing them in local galleries. She is visiting two women friends who have just moved to northern California. It is January 1967, just before California's "summer of love." ("Love" in its various forms is a connecting thread throughout Bovoso's diaries.) "Although it certainly seems like it now when I reread the '60s passages, the experiences I describe weren't drug-induced," she explains, "Then, the very air in Golden Gate Park was psychedelic; it was mostly a contact high."

The flowing, stream-of-consciousness style of these journals takes us even deeper into the "internal landscape" of the writer. In such writings, real time and place sometimes become irrelevant as the logic of the unconscious mind takes over. Dreams and fantasies, written down, become less elusive and more actively feed the artist's imagination. These techniques have been used by artists for centuries. Through them the reader can come closer to the mystery of the creative process.

◇ *1967* ◇

California. Waking up—outside light is gleaming on silver pools of water—limpid in the morning—fairy like and magical. It is like some secret thing going on out there. I hesitate to look— I look briefly—it is too lovely. I slip back in to darkness and bed and you waiting for me.

JANUARY 1. Slowly I am trying to consolidate—to make my life framework more "controlled" by me, less of a run-away life.

It seems good—The effort is good.

[*San Francisco*] *JANUARY 15*. I am so high with love, high with myself.

We went to that mystical park—do I dream—how the light was then? I have never seen that light before. A. and B. and I parked and the squirrel—California squirrel small & well fluffed—I gave him one of the chocolate covered cherries. He had never had one before—he loved it and took it up the tree where he sat eating it—the juice dripping down.

There was a big river of water—we crossed over the bridge and it was through the looking glass—no one but us. A quiet path and that light beginning already—a soft brown path, trees all around us—bushes & the water on one side—and there— "What is that up there?"

A bear escaped from the zoo. It *was* a bear—it was a bear— for so long—yet walking until it was a rock, a huge rock in the middle of the path. We passed through many different countries—came to the gateway to the desert—huge palm trees towering above us in a natural archway. We rest on a horizontal rock—we twirl in the curious calm spot of the war—Vietnam waiting now for the sub to pick us up—surfacing slowly.

A. gives me 2 beautiful yellow orange flowers—wild & lovely. Then we are at the Japanese garden. It is almost dark and yet some light magically keeps coming through—there is Buddha smiling in the darkness exuding power—we wind in and around the orient over stepping stones placed over low pools. Oh it is lovely—

I have seen B. before we entered the garden. We stood on

the other side—she followed across the road—how close we held her in our hearts—she alone there crossing the perilous street. A moment of high tension, a moment of love, great love. Something breaks in my soul—she has entered in.

It's You—Or The Mirror Book of Lovers

[Bovoso here begins an experimental work, ideally suited to the journal form. This ongoing narrative is written directly to the reader (You) whoever that may be. As she explained the concept, "though faces, bodies and personalities change there is only one lover, one other, the elusive and essentially illusory 'you.'" In the narrative, "Events, countries, dates blend together, time sequence is shattered." Bovoso imagined an ideal edition of the book with a cover reflecting the reader's face, and printed on waterproof material so it could be read at the beach, in swimming pools or bathtubs—"all places that spark memory."]

Its you—Its you, she said

Costa Brava, Spain. White walls—the heat of day surrounded us each afternoon—cool bedroom—our heated darkened bodies you would love me you never tired of me we never slept you & I tasted of salt of air. How big you were—those pictures show us sparkling, sparkling—they seem to have "in a happier time" printed under them.

I arrived before the dawn—sleeping in the back of the taxi that drove me 150 miles from Barcelona. I slept—I woke when we would stop to ask directions. The driver would sing to keep himself awake. Sleep, sleep, he would say—we will find it—do not worry—and I happy to be on my way lay back again. How good to be on the way.

The house rose straight up—beyond. The bright planet venus had guided the driver and I—brighter in the Spanish sky steady over the mountains—around the winding curves. Then dawn was coming and the house like a form transplanted from another world rose, shining white. You came to the door sleepy—my darling I have arrived finally—you are warm as I often found you—warm, vulnerable somehow, glad to see me.

I have thought of nothing but you these weeks since we last parted. Another airport goodbye—another emptiness—all New York empty of you and your apartment now a stranger to me, now cold toward me. A fear stays within me. Knowledge of an end to your love, a limit to your love. A cold edge of mortality to your love.

And I am still there in Spain holding back this wild fear—that becomes smoothed by kindnesses, by your warm self—being so much who you are—another Lord of the Manor—a gem. You conquer me on your Spanish beaches—pebbly pools of clear water transfix me—my darkened skin. Inside me all is dark sleeping—now stunned by your force. You now have my love—how is love an accident—we did not intend it, did not want it much. Each in love (or falling in love) with someone else.

Walking down your winding stairs—wet in your boat slapping on the waves—spread out in ecstacy you make love to me riding the waves back to the shore. I love you darling—both battered by this sun I move slowly in the water you watching me and you take me to you—Carole, you say my name and take me in your arms watching every move I make.

Later in the exquisite pain of New York and your return we both watch [this moment] in the films we have made—you thinking of me less and less—more and more of she who approaches, your obsession. The sun is not yet out of my head—and yet I have known—tried to fight to protect myself. Driving back and forth from the country [Saratoga]—another mail and no letter—Rereading your last card—how good I am at reading your mood, your thoughts, the degree of your interest—the slant of your writing, which pen you used.

Trying to listen to the voice of reason oh my god another mail—all those letters I didn't mail you—one said "I hope it is all going well for you." I knew you were with her—

a silence coming across the ocean to me more & more *nothing* coming across to me.

I work harder, harder, the only pleasure these rides—these long solitary drives 200 miles and I am ready for more. When my radio plays "Will I see you in September or lose you to a summer love?" constantly they ask the question for me—reminding me that I already know the answer.

Your greatest strength is in your silence I tell myself and wait for your first letter. It comes when I have just returned from the country—there waiting in the mailbox. I am not elated for I know it will tell me—what I know. This state of suspended agony is about to end—hot in August far from my beach I read it in the bathroom—it is there that I read—"she is here." Yes I knew she was there. I read it all—all over quickly scanning for the meaning—see the ending, your continued love your kisses your abstracted kisses—your constraint. Your gratefulness—I have been so good—not complained—

What use my complaints—I sit in the living room with your letter "I don't know how long it will last. I think it will be over by my return." I feel the sinking, sinking in me, my mind already searching for ways to survive just this *day*—then I can survive anything. How will I go to work I am due there in an hour—how will I do anything—I am saying, Oh my God aloud. I take a drink of scotch—a long drink and sit reading again, studying the writing, each word and comma, each pause, for signs of love.

Yes, I see you "love" me and I see that "it" will not be over. And that it is over for us. I feel like someone has died—sick.

How many letters before I finally mail one—how many torn—rescued from sealed stamped envelopes—because the tone was wrong or something I didn't mean or something I meant too much. How I sickened myself with the thought of you. I really thought of nothing but you, with horror I would try to stop it—Oh stop it, stop it.

That time when we were in Mexico love, as I wrote to

you, told you—you were a super-you. I was sick—ever so slightly sick the entire time—I did not tell you how odd I felt. The altitude—some latent fragility—you slow your step to mine—my tall beauty of a man. I waking in the morning thinking it is an earthquake so great the sound and find it is my heart, my blood pounding through.

You take me into your bed in the morning kissing me in your hard way, once offensive to me now my craving— kiss holding me close to you up against your wide expanse of chest—I memorize every inch of you. You marvel I am so wet when you touch me—I have awakened wanting you, familiar in a strange place.

Such sensuous heat—pushing down on us, winding back the long road from Taxco—you drive faster still the heat stays with us. I am yours inside this power moving under the sun.

Later after Spain it was like that. July in New York on the road—back and forth I push my car and feel what we felt together a few months ago.

[*New York City*] My fury keeps coming up.

D. you elude me—say you love me—that much—is it even true?

Then you act like it doesn't matter—and probably it doesn't.

Doesn't any of it matter to you? Is it all sex is it my brown skin—perhaps you never loved me—you turn me around but is it real?

At the party I wanted us to be like star points—revolving through the people, through the blinking lights—and then you were angry most of the night—sullen and even mean. What a disaster—and I didn't want to sleep with you. I wouldn't have made love with you. If you hadn't fallen asleep it would have been an argument.

You wore my little heart around your neck on your purple sweater and then you went away. You had the nerve to go away.

"Don't play with me, 'cause you play with fire."

[Bovoso's relationship with D., the painter she lived with, was ending.]

FEBRUARY 15. I sit here in complete confusion—yet some torpor, some dulling of the senses today aides me—and a slight feeling of being unwell allows each positive action I take to appear an enormous advance.

I feel in need of advice—since a move seems near. Faced once more with the problem of—myself—still me—yes—as all quiets down and I find myself once more in the same situation. Good advice would be—to consolidate—to settle my precarious finances—to focus more carefully on one thing—one outlet. That is why it was so simple at the loft—all my work was cut out for me. Here was love—a task—and a challenge—all simplified for me. How could I resist falling deeply in?

Now my mind is ever active—trying to avoid errors—yet knowing them to be in a sense, unavoidable. Faced with my many limitations—my multi-faceted past—out of which I strive to make some sense—to what end, though? It is the continuation of the mystery. How I would like to be and how I am.

Am I trying more—or less—to be as I would like myself to be?

Good questions.

FEBRUARY 16. [Dream.] I prove myself to you [D.] You say "I am in love with you—don't you understand?" All is settled and we are in the wars together—all night there are battles being waged. It is clear to you that I have loved you well and beautifully for some time and that you really know now what to be "in love" is—what "to love" is. There is great happiness between us.

[Dream.] I am on a train with the 3 men in my life. My life patterns seem to involve groups of three most often—and I seem perversely capable of loving more than one person at a time. 3 is also my astrological number, Mercury being in the 3rd house.

Paris. 1 MAI. An old lover—it never occurred to me. Yesterday E. and I sat in the parc—under the warm and lovely sun—the air so light around us—quiet and peaceful!—happy—

loving—we talked. He described the theory—the object vs the word—the great difference between the two.

Last night in my dreams I was going to have a baby—any moment. There was no mention of who the father was—it did not seem to be of importance. I was trying to get to the hospital—or somewhere—because I was sure I was going to give birth to the child "à l'improviste"—although everyone else was more relaxed—(my grandmother, my mother)—not believing it could or would happen so suddenly.

[*New York*]
Dreams of flight
wide space
looking for the plane
various strange aircraft
and finally I spot it—
J., a magic boy.

[Bovoso had met J., a young actor, in New York. He was to share her life for the next fifteen years.]

MAY 28. The most beautiful birthday ever
Stoney Point
a waterfall
hundreds of the loveliest people
good food—flowers all around—paper in the trees
nets on poles—a children's pond—love—sun—love.

JULY 18.
Thoughts of you [J.]
wild joy in my heart
at what you say to me
I contain myself and wait
You are so real.

Mirror Book

Even now, after all this time has passed—in moments of despair a deep cutting slash will go through me and cut through to that underlying pain still left from you. And it colors and overshadows the pain of the moment and I wonder at you, thinking the loss of you greater than any other loss, loving you again (not liking you or me for wanting you). I think then what's the use.

OCTOBER [Dream.] J. has died—but resurrected. Big old apartment—happiness & joy but once alone in apt. with him a great terror & fear comes over me. I try to flee—he follows me—flight down fire stairs in building—hear him opening door at top—escape outside—through a playground. He runs and catches up with me—and I am no longer afraid. I say do you know I really love you? and we walk on.

[Carole and J. moved together to California where they lived together on Mount Tamalpais. In 1969 she gave birth to their first son, Alessandro. Disillusioned with the United States, they moved to Europe where their sons Santiago and Antonio were born in 1971 and 1973. For the next few years Carole Bovoso kept journals of drawings rather than words. She recorded her dreams and those of her family daily.]

◇ *1973* ◇

[*France*] *SEPTEMBER 5.* [Dream.] At college again am taking a co-ed course in football—realize after first class that perhaps I should have taken a karate or jiu jitsu class but it's not too late to get into one.

OCTOBER 1. [Dream.] We go to have dinner at F. and G.'s house. Soup, fish are being prepared—but somehow we don't get to eat—altho everyone acts as though we have. We leave and they are all smiling and we are slightly bewildered.

Later I am going home in taxi, and think—I've left Santiago somewhere—but remind myself that this is a dream and it is unlikely that I would ever leave Santiago anywhere.

OCTOBER 2. [Dream.] We are in bed when I look out the window and see 2 people coming—I wake J. and say guess what we have company—and he groans. Nevertheless we greet them and turns out they are saying good-bye, as they leave that day. I talk with girl & we walk along—she apparently is going off somewhere alone and they are both sad & apprehensive about this parting. I tell her I understand—but that she is young and must see & do many things in her life and it will all work out O.K. She says something like "far out" meaning a compliment to my wisdom.

NOVEMBER 5. [Dream.] Traveling in Italy—anxiety over bags & valises—objects left, perhaps missing.

◇ *1974* ◇

JANUARY 15. [Dream.] My grandfather comes to me and gives me two sheets of paper, saying this is the footprint of your great grandfather and this is the footprint of your great grandmother. They are beautiful outlines which have been colored with pencils.

FEBRUARY 3. [Dream.] I am deciding to go live in California with B.—H. having died. I think of the kids, living in California. I think I will keep my name Carole Bovoso and that will be the kids' names.

FEBRUARY 9. [Dream.] I am President Nixon's private secretary—don't like him but am loyal.

FEBRUARY 20. [Dream.] K. and P. come and take part of our window. I say no—now we have no window—and I yell and make a fuss but K. rushes off with it, and I watch them getting on a motor bike piled high. They go away.

J. wants to get married—he says next time we go to town. He likes the procession. We meet a lady in a restaurant there opposed to mixed marriages. I confront her and discover she was in love with a mixed man & it turned out badly.

◇ *1977* ◇

[*Spain*] *JULY 9.*
"Their devotion to each other was total"
Since I last wrote half of a total devotion has gone (Nabokov).

Since I last wrote the moon has changed its tactics completely—

It comes up over *there* now at 3:30 A.M.

It's not the same one that went down behind the mountain rolling like a paper cutout—

It does funny things in its middle the waning crescent face a butter blur—something is happening—

Since I last wrote everything has changed.

[Attached clipping: New York, July 4, 1977: "Vladimir Nabokov, 78, dies in residence in Switzerland . . . . According to the novelist's widow, 'he had been very sick . . .' Vera . . . was his confidante, typist, chess partner, scrabble adversary . . . . Their devotion to each other was total."]

AUGUST 17. Not a fixation but a point of reference.

Since I last wrote everything has changed. I have come back [to the Costa Brava]. You are not here, your house now owned by someone else.

I just walked in from our country house, my paintings under my arm, wearing my big boots for easy walking—my cape 7 years old now and still flying. I round the first bay, the second bay—the boats are slapping at their moorings, bells dully clanking—a sailboat puts out to the choppy sea. The lights of the white town become more numerous as the dusk fades to night. The evening crowd strolls—I see on the faces of those who pass me that I am beautiful. I thank god for being beautiful, more beautiful than 10 years ago—what a miracle—you would desire me still—but then there were not many women you did not desire, from 9 years to 69. But perhaps you changed after your marriage—I have no way of knowing, only a progression of dreams that keep me in touch with my feelings, or lack of them, for you.

The tall long legged jeaned high heeled girls, the graceful skirts, the beautiful men café-sit beside the sea as I walk by complete. I think fuck everything.

I am an artist. I am walking with an entire show of my work under my arm. This is who I really am.

And yet your presence in my dreams reminds me that although I rarely think of you, you are still with me in some important way.

The light is on on your upper terrace. I resist knowing the resident of your stately abode—still blissfully ignorant I duck into the gallery [mounting a show of her work]. Yes—I am here. I have come back.

Since publication of the little book—I only call you the C.T.L. except when talking to J.

[Carole Bovoso's book *The Coffee Table Lover*, based on *The Mirror Book of Lovers*, was published in 1976 by The Country Press. A sequel, the poem "Piramida Negra," was included in the collection *Piramida Negra* in 1980.]

AUGUST 28. I am amazed at the way one night at the Gallery the paintings will seem beautiful to me—another night silly & vacuous.

Self-image is such a fragile concern.

[SEPTEMBER.] It is a small, diminished anima—vibrant in its essence—that arrives at the station with children in tow. Evangeline crossing of paths at the station—

Costa Brava behind me no matter what.

We gypsies are on the move again.

My strength, febrile and tense carries me—baskets, bags, stuffed toys, babies and all—

The only solace being that at least I am not pregnant too.

OCTOBER 8.

Faire un voyage
dans le rêve—
être le rêve
rêver d'être—
être le voyage
voyager
être

[*Barcelona*] *DECEMBER.* There is both joy and sadness in intoxication: there's almost a latent melancholy in these radiant paintings [by a friend.]

The very magic of the colors, an unusual light and the space of the paintings enclosed like a mirror, all contribute to give us this feeling of inaccessibility. It is comparable to the mystery of the difference between men and women, and of the distance between man and the world surrounding him.

"The separation between man and the world which makes him think . . ." Jean Grenier said. But once we are aware of this separation and the surprise is over, innocence can be reborn again and its miraculous wonderment.

◇ *1979* ◇

[*New York City*] *MARCH 18.* [Dream.]

I danced for a lady
who was giving classes.
We each had a turn
and I took mine.
I felt good—and
proud after.
My motions were
strong—and at the end I went over
on my head & shoulders.

I looked for clothes
in a crowded closet
then accidentally
defused a bomb—an H-bomb
underneath—Red Alert
Red Alert—everyone cried.

[In April, Carole traveled alone to Paris, aware that her relationship with J. was ending.]

Paris. EASTER MONDAY. I resolve to make better notes of the passage of time. Time is—or rather I should say events have become—more a blur than ever before—for several reasons, among them my workload [writing and teaching] which really pulls and scatters my mind.

I have just arrived—via an Icelandic flight—squeezed between two men. Every seat a student of German. Several hideous hours in Luxembourg train station—a luxurious ride to Paris. Two middle-aged American ladies let me put my bags on their cart piled with luggage—"no porters Dorothy"—"But how are we ever going to manage through to Brussels"—"We'll manage—don't worry Margaret—we're managing *now* aren't we?"

A taxi-ride during which an Algerian driver lectures me on nuclear politics—"I would blow them all up—every one"—then leaves me at the wrong corner. I find the house—Paris—still deserted—Claude & her son & and Kafir his cat waiting for me.

I sleep until 2:00 P.M. the next afternoon—a sleep of disturbing dreams—but a good sleep.

EASTER TUESDAY. Slept late again this morning—must need the sleep and the intense dreams. Perhaps I came to Paris just to get some morning (and afternoon) sleep.

In these dreams—

There is a big party in a room—I dance a funny sliding dance—slipping & sliding—enjoying myself—but then worrying that the noise is annoying I stop. Earlier in an apartment like my old (childhood) apt., J. has told me he wants divorce he's met someone else. He is cold and distant—I am profoundly hurt.

Take the elegant & silent Metro—with a minimum anxiety I find Carol O.—an American free-lancing with her husband in Paris. She serves me spinach salad and we have a nice talk—I leave so she can get back to her work. It is rainy & cold—so glad—since I've brought boots, sweaters, wool dresses. Nothing too summery at all.

SUNDAY APRIL 22. Paris. Saturday (yesterday) full—lunch with radio-personnage—*late* to Pierre-Jean's where Cordelia awaited me—dash to theatre—arrive in plenty of time after all. Theatre packed with chic queens—Pierre-Jean a wreck—me too—I've had to retrace steps on Metro to recover this book left in café phone booth! Horrors! Anyway—after Raisin [Lorraine Hansberry's play *A Raisin in the Sun*] which is a bit long (my period starts coming in middle of it!)—but good in parts—they feed me omelette with ham—salad cheese & fruit. We talk about N.Y.C.—about the theatre—acting—screenplays—the idea of a group of people taking each other to the top. They call a taxi and I go through night time Paris trying not to worry that I'm taking the last of my money! almost.

Lunch today with one of those cold, civil Frenchmen—very unsettling.

MONDAY—on the train.—I think I've finally had enough of Paris for a long while. Paris—Parisiens seem on the decline—more than ever before. The goal is to get something from me—from the U.S., actually, which looms high in their perceptions.

Another night of waiting for sleep—thinking—trying to stop the thinking. I'm beginning to chart [periods]—is it glandular?—Or—coffee (French)—I did have some in P.M. But in N.Y. this usually doesn't bother me.

Thoughts for Blondell.

[Notes for a performance piece, "My Readheaded Aunt from Red Bank," choreographed by Blondell Cummings and performed by Bovoso and Cummings in 1980.]

You're always approaching something or going away from something—or perhaps *it* is approaching you and you're going away from *it*. What is it?

Sometimes there's a confusion—something always surprising about it—is it something good—or is it something unwanted? I always mourned it crazily when I wanted children so badly—thinking of it as the blood of unborn children.

Now—oh is it early? So soon—it must be irregular—but what was the last date? Nerves—on the edges of myself—bursting to explode, it seems—then it flows—I sleep peacefully, securely—I feel better. So *that's* why I was so upset—is everything only glandular after all—and why don't I chart it out so I'll know next time. These days (months) I seem incapable of doing so, incapable of making a mark on paper to track it.

When I used to *pretend* I had it—I marked meaningless xxxxs on my calendar—filled with yearnings—10 years old.

Joan and I had the secret in the school courtyard—It is in this sentence—She wrote a short sentence on a slip of paper—at the end a . (period).

We had found each other. It was such a joy. But she had "gotten" hers whereas I—did I really *pretend* I had it? Yes. And I convinced myself as well that on certain days I was different. We tormented our 6th grade teacher Mr. Williams with requests for being excused from gym—and when he seemed difficult about it we went to the school nurse, a young Eurasian woman who soon became our pal. She came to the room one day—she'd promised she'd talk to Mr. Williams—and she whispered to him at the front of the class. Joan and I sat like little angels, in suspense—watching, then with strange satisfaction as Mr. Williams' light brown skin turned deep red. He looked furtively at us—and said a polite good-bye to the nurse. We were vindicated.

When I *really* got my period I was 11—on my way to ballet. I noticed in the changing room. La Sylph asked me why I wasn't coming in to class. I stuttered and stammered, embarrassed and flustered—I don't have the money, I lied—I left my money home—I've got to go home.

That's alright she said—her one bad eye hidden behind the covered lens of her glasses—pay next time. No, no—no! I said—I can't—I've got to go home. She looked at me and must have known something was up—I think she asked if I was alright—and then she let me go. I rode home on the subway—flushed with emotion—standing out, I was sure, in the crowd. I rushed to tell my mother—it was a Saturday. She got me pads and a belt—the symbols I had wished for, for what seemed like ages. Now I had them—they were *mine*—my pads, my own belt. I lay in my room in my bed—not ill, no, but delicate—the shades drawn.

Tears came to my eyes. I cried from sheer joy. Later Pop, my stepfather, came in to congratulate me.

"Congratulations—you're a woman now," he said.

I was very proud and not embarrassed. I cried some more and went to sleep, on the threshold, it seemed, of everything I wanted in the world.

APRIL 23. Iceland. The memory of a color—the colors certain lovers used to wear. Is it that a lot of blonde-red-type men like to wear pink pants—or do I happen to be attracted to men who wear these colors? Brown belts—blues—greens—thick blond moustaches.

I've been channeling too much energy into J.—am now going to divert it to the children and myself. That was the answer the dream was giving me, sphinx dream.

I am overwhelmed by the intensity with which I love—it must be overwhelming to others too.

Big revelation—ahah.

[New York] MAY DAYS—
These days—
I live more in my mind—
loving my mind because
you are so much there.

When I was a child the excitement of May welled up in me as it does now. It was and is my birthday month—my month—and I was filled not only with anticipation but with the very joy of having that anticipation.

We planned a picnic for my birthday. Pop would drive us up in the green cadillac—I prayed it would not rain. We made fried chicken, devilled eggs the day before.

May Days. I have given her the gift of a lover.

Because he could accept her affairs with the other woman, she found herself more passionately drawn to him, as if her openly flirting with the love of another woman had been a test of him in some crucial way. She has hurt me deeply, I wanted to write and perhaps to say—but then that is not such a difficult thing to do—given my state of isolation, my state of almost primal sensitivity.

—I don't fail people—

—I won't fail you—

Words spoken to whom? Past lovers—future lovers—existing loves. Words that well up to the pen.

It is really too late to draw back my hope that there be no crucial heartrending disappointment this time—not like with M. or with J. More importantly there are parallels here that leave me breathless—and yet I sense that this will and can be a complete, whole and beautiful experience.

"Women move me to deepest feeling, of pleasure and loss. As if they are eternally mine yet never wholly belong to me." *Dubin's Lives*. Malamud.

Dearest M. how I love you—

I want to protect J. from himself—but it is so hard and I've spent so many years of energy in this direction. I want to protect my family—myself.

MAY 27. Made love with [K.] my poet lover—one of the happiest moments of my life. A beautiful birthday present—a book and a *poem* of such beauty—like the experience of being with him.

This month of May has been my special time.

Dearest K.—

I felt you so worried last night—and I want to say something to make you not fearful. How fear bounces off itself and prospers—don't work on the fear side.

But in the morning I replay your voice and it is full of the fearful joy of discovery—and "not forgetting."

It is our discovery—yours and mine—and this morning on my birthday I sense it is you and I having been born again—both together and separately—strong together, strong in our separate entities. And in some mysterious ways I have given

birth again (as goddesses are wont to do—to their own lovers)
to the places—high spots over mountains and clouds in which
our love resides. Let us go there often.

JUNE. [Dream.] Sitting around a table in a room—with 2
women & K. One of the women is talking to the other—oh
yeah, oh yeah you read that part in my journal when you were
staying at the house—that's great that's okay I don't mind.

As I listen I grow more and more alarmed and finally blurt
out—Don't read my journals—

And I see them nearby—my old ones—the ones that were
once stolen and mutilated [by a jealous lover]—and I realize
that she *has* of course read them. I suggest this to her and she
is silent, fiddling with something. K. sits beside me, suppor-
tive—wearing white.

[While teaching a journal workshop, Bovoso gave an assign-
ment—to describe the "undeveloped heart"—and then did it
herself.]

The undeveloped heart belongs to those who fear to live
fully—to experience joy and pain in depth. Fear of pain—of
being hurt, rejected, ridiculed—fear of being unhappy—un-
accepted—of being less valuable than others (less beautiful, less
talented or intelligent)—physical differences, age differences,
social differencs—all the causes of untold suffering, often silent
and sometimes more verbal.

The layers of attitudes with which we cover these so–called
failings are perceived by others as ourselves. And we, through
long years of practice come to view ourselves as these shells—
outer casings whose sole misguided purpose has been protection. What we have instead of protection is a wall that not only
keeps us from others while causing all manner of misunderstandings—but keeps us from our own selves as well. The very
act of struggling to hide the real and vulnerable in us takes
precious energy—leading us farther away from what we could
call "the fully developed heart."

As Jean Cocteau said—"Dare to live to the very end." To develop one's "heart" takes unlimited courage.

[another journal exercise]

Hangups through the years

childhood

> *knees too ashy*
> *legs too thin*
> *hair too kinky*
> *most people are white and I'm not*

adolescence

> *legs too thin*
> *no hips*
> *no breasts*
> *hair a problem (not straight)*
> *don't know how to swim*
> *boys (I want them. Do they want me?)*
> *most people are white and I'm not*

late 50s 60s

> *hair*
> *swim (if I get my hair wet it dies)*
> *men. orgasms can I have them? the good kind?*
> *women. I want them. Do they want me?*
> *How smart and clever am I? enough?*
> *Am I not truly hippy enough / too neat and dressed up?*
> *unable to let loose enough to just let it all hang out in the street?*
> *Am I pregnant?? Am I black enough?*
> *I wish I could drive then I'd be truly wonderful.*

60s continued

> *hair—lingering but less strong (also afraid I don't want an Afro)*
> *swim—lingering but less strong*

age—everyone I know keeps getting younger
children—no one else has them—everyone thinks we're cute
my body no longer perfect
hips (too many)
writing. I hate anyone who dares look over my shoulder while I'm writing

late 70s

hair, swim, age, body—linger in moderation
How good a writer am I? enough?
Time (I have none, just when I thought I'd figured time out)
Energy (I have none, just when I thought I'd figured energy out)
Sickness (dear god don't let me get sick)
Money (I have none, just when I thought I'd figured money out)

JUNE 28. I feel disgruntled this morning—the [poetry] reading was one of those learning experiences—but it was a dispersal of energy that I found wasteful. Too many people who were not focused on the work at hand.

Of course disgruntlement is also and always stemming from a personal dissatisfaction—my own anxieties—need to gather energies to me at the moment. Need to complete the [Village] Voice piece today and get a good handle on it. Today is my first free day [from teaching]—I want to celebrate.

I was pleased to feel integrated more into J.'s work—and afterward to have J. congratulate me on the reading—and ask my opinion which I gave—And realizing that much of my hurt—alienation in past has had to with J. *not* (seemingly anyway) valuing my opinions.

For me too, in this sense it was like giving birth—and I am glad to release it. I also see with even greater clarity what a waste of energy certain negative emotions are—jealousy, inadequacy, lack of self-worth—such a waste—spoiling the present and creating more difficulties. *Always Value You* in other words—dope!

JUNE 30. A nuit blanche with my lover—we created a plateau of delight—a place in which we lingered loving each other with infinite care and great joy.

The elements of work and sex—*love*

We are able to love each other in so many different ways—different levels. The different manifestations of our love.

JULY 2.
At last the promise
of my very first kisses
has been fulfilled.

JULY 14. J. a puzzle to me these days—back and forth between personalities—the public & the private. Sometimes I feel there is much left, sometimes I wonder just how he cares. What would be the signs—is it only hardship for him?

I feel resentment about feeling resentful.

In the playground—again. I've spent some of my deepest moments in playgrounds around the world. Poetry comes in playgrounds. This morning felt as though the first in which I'm fully aware of my new freedom—from daily time-clock punching. Slept on & on unable to fully open my eyes (still it was only 9 A.M.!)

Really—the necessity for dreams.

JULY 13. K.'s presence in my dreams—as a motivating, directing factor—filled with wonderful feelings.

[Dream.] At Martha's Vineyard [On vacation with K.]

Going to sleep K.'s kisses—being jet black beads—red rubies later—weaving in and out, floating away. Images of—coming back with a start—a tangle of arms legs—my body against his—heat—and words—laughter and its aftermath.

JULY 22. Dream. I am with a group of people—a party is going to happen—or is happening—a costume party. J. comes up and says he's going—is only going to stay a moment—he is so tired—he's going back to bed where his lover is.

For K.—at Martha's Vineyard
There's a right way to say
this—and I'll get to it later—
you see the connections of
things. The links—
The connections of things—

like the way a poem—
wants to come but can't
without—
until—
the right first line.

I feel as if I am a totally new person sexually—nothing of
the past applies—as in the dream in which I rescued the child
from drowning in the deep pool, feeling her alive to me.
I am that reborn child. Shining—finding a new way.

K.—These last sweet pages of my journal—a book for me,
for you—the continuing fruit of words floating between us when
we first spoke and knew each other and told each other our
dreams.

These feelings are for you as I sit on a bus [to Saratoga]—
missing you—but feeling you with me—inside—so it is alright
for a while at least. These feelings in the dark—so tired—and
wanting the falling into the soft bed—the breathing body, yours
beside me. A word is spoken in the night—I kiss your chest,
your chin—your neck—you hold me as only you have and can.
Sleep claims me as these bus people return to their seats—I
think of us traveling—of all the sights we crave.

"He was interested in my work—*very* interested" (Georgia
O'Keefe speaking of her relationship with Alfred Steiglitz)

[*New York City*] There are times when the children are gone
and my lover is not here, when I feel so devastatingly alone
that I can't imagine who I am. So I still must define myself by
these other beings.

[Some time later] I am sitting here in that state often known
as poetic, vacillating between guilt at not doing some other work
that I've cut out for myself, and telling myself to let it go for
another hour. Time, today, has been moving at a speed to my

liking. My researching and toying with it have seemed to increase its elasticity. I find my mind is filled with my writing,
even when I am not actually putting it on paper. This is nothing
new of course. But it's not always easy to remember that one
is working when there is no tangible evidence (the writer's lot).

I see that being a writer and inhabiting different characters
is akin to acting. The actor's interior is always changing to fit
the role. In me there dwell a million roles. . . . Antonio is here,
now covering my eyes so that I can not see, asking how I know
what to write with my eyes closed. What I know is not what I
see. What I know is all in my mind. Yes, I tell him, this is like
a diary, "or somepin." It's about the same, eyes open or closed,
I tell him.

So when my character is in love with a former lover, I sometimes grow confused and think my present self is in that state.
Or is it true that almost anything is possible within this creative
state, and that whatever we create we *are?* We strive so for love,
and it is right here. Past pain, past love, present pain, present
love all become as one. My heart is irreparably modified,
opened, ripened. A desirable state. What I have wanted is the
infinite and to "make love real"—to prove love's transcen-
dence. The difficulty lies not in my belief, which is heroic, but
in my attempt to prove it not only to others but to myself. No
proof is necessary. I feel strong again, enough to stretch myself
out, enough to actually relax, to read a book I'm dying to read.
I feel as if I have healed myself with my own words. I am making
myself well. Writing is my cure.

◇   ◇

Afterword

"These diaries record my process of working through the concept of romantic love," Carole Bovoso says. "Gradually, I would be able to free myself from this pursuit. By 1979 I was beginning to put more energy into my work, my career."

At that time she was living with her three sons in New York, writing, and teaching poetry to children in New York City's public schools. She was also teaching journal workshops, expanding upon insights which grew out of her diaries, and dream workshops based on her ongoing study of dreams.

Carole Bovoso is a frequent contributor to the *Village Voice, MS* Magazine, *The Christian Science Monitor,* and *Vogue.* She was a contributing editor to *Essence* magazine, and has written for many other national publications. She is the editor of *Letters,* a literary forum for women and men, and producer of the *Letters* radio program on WBAI-FM, New York City. She has produced, written and performed in events at Franklin Furnace, The New York Shakespeare Festival and the Manhattan Theatre Club in New York City.

She is presently director of the Writers in Performance Series at the Manhattan Theatre Club. Bovoso is the author of the forthcoming book *Foremothers,* to be published by Summit Books in 1987. *Foremothers* is a biographical/autobiographical work which was inspired by the discovery of the 1868 diary of Frances Anne Rollin, her great grandmother. Rollin was a writer whose journal is the earliest known by a Southern black woman.

THE DIARY OF

Marie Barrows

*Montgomery, Alabama; Savannah,
Georgia; Paterson, New Jersey
1876*

◇   ◇

Introduction

The 1876–1878 diary of Marie Barrows is probably one in a series which she kept; its precise handwriting and controlled style suggest that she was already a practiced journal-keeper when she began the book. This single volume, documenting an eventful year and eight months of her life, is apparently the only one to have survived, and nothing else is known about its author.

Three major themes run through the first years of Barrows' journal: her love for Captain Streeter ("Diamond"), the man she hopes to marry; her continuing ill health; and her struggle to obtain a divorce from her estranged husband, Gus Barrows.

Marie Barrows was originally from Paterson, New Jersey, where her parents were still living. Her legal residence was in Connecticut, although she had resided at some time in New York City. When the journal begins, however, she is in Alabama, apparently visiting relatives, while Captain Streeter is in Savannah preparing his ship, the *Gardner Colby*, for a long voyage.

During the heart-wrenching days before the couple's long separation, they stay in the same house in Savannah; one can only speculate on the relationship between this married woman and the worldly captain, for as she describes a typical evening, "I think of the sweet hour I spent in my darling's arms, seated in the big hollow chair, before I went to bed, and he went down stairs to smoke." Later, faced with gossipy neighbors, she writes, "I *know* I have done nothing for which I ought to blush, but 'people will talk you know.'"

During her protracted legal battle, Barrows is forced into something of a vagabond existence. Apparently her family does not know of her relationship with the Captain; but when she stays with them in Paterson, talk of her marital estrangement circulates in the neighborhood, causing them embarrassment. Her aunt and uncle in Brooklyn refuse to take Marie in, and so she spends a good deal of time staying in boarding houses and the homes of friends. To further complicate matters, a number of her acquaintances know both Gus and Captain Streeter. She can confide in no one but her diary.

Marie is in poor health throughout this period. Evidently she has gynecological problems of long standing, and although she enters hospitals in New York twice for treatment, it is not clear whether she is actually helped. The diary records, in code, each menstrual period, usually accompanied by moderate to severe pain. In addition, she constantly seems to catch whatever ailment is around, and she notes that her poor resistance is probably worsened by the emotional strain she is under.

◇ *1876* ◇

JANUARY 1. Arrived in Montgomery at 7 o'clock A.M. after traveling all day and night from Savannah. The family were at home to welcome me and wish me a "Happy New Year", yet all the good wishes cannot fill the void in my heart since I left my own dear Diamond. After a pleasant, though wearisome day, I went to bed early, but not to sleep for my heart was *homesick* for my darling.

JANUARY 2. A dreary, dull, rainy, miserable day, and I am as miserable as the day, crying wearily in my heart for my absent loved one, but obliged to sit up in the parlor and *be entertained*, until I am almost wild. Wrote to Gus and Capt. Streeter, but oh, I *wish* that I had never left Savannah. I am *so homesick.*

JANUARY 6. A most beautiful day, and everybody is so kind to me, but I wish myself back in Savannah with my own precious loved one. If I could only see my darling just for one hour, it would be better than all the pleasure they can crowd into my visit here.

Wrote to my Darling, and hope to get a telegram in the morning telling me to come back to him before he leaves. Oh, my precious love, if I could only see him once more I would try to be content, and bear the separation.

JANUARY 7. I knew my Darling would not disappoint me, and I believe from his letters, he has missed me very much. This A.M. I received a dispatch to come to the "Pavilion," and he will meet me. I need not add that I have been bright and happy all day. Called in A.M. on Dr. LeGrand, and got weighed. Only 107 lbs. but I hope to improve. Sent dispatch to my Darling that I am coming. I am very tired, but *very happy* that I am going back.

JANUARY 9. Oh what a blessed, happy, joyous Sabbath it has been to me, for I am once more with my own Diamond. I left Montgomery yesterday.

JANUARY 10. I have been alone nearly all day, but have been happy and contented every moment, for I have been sewing and writing for my darling, God bless him, how I wish I could do something for his comfort and happiness, but I can do very little only *love him with all my heart*. We spent the evening at home.

JANUARY 11. Capt. went down the river at 5 ½ A.M. to get the Ship down to Venus Point. I have missed him all day, and was lonely, but happy in knowing that he was *near* me, and would soon return, yet it makes me realize that the great charm Savannah has for me, is in being with him I love better than all the world besides.

JANUARY 14. Cooler, but very pleasant with fire in my room. This is my last night in #16 and tomorrow I leave my darling, for he has secured my passage, and I sail on the "San Salvador." I can only say God bless and Keep my precious one, and bring us more happily together on his return to me.

JANUARY 15. God help me in my loneliness! God comfort my precious loved one in the lonely weeks and months which will be his while he is far away from me. It has been a lovely day, and though sometimes it was cloudy to me, I found it was only the dimness of unshed tears, that *would* come when I remembered that each revolution of the engine was bearing me farther away from my best beloved. After I lost sight of my darling, and we were steaming down the river, I went to my stateroom for a little while, and having become calm and composed, I went by Capt. Nickerson's invitation to the Pilot House, until we passed the "Gardner Colby" and "National Eagle" (Capt. Sears) at Venus Point where they were lying for the rest of their Cargo. The Capt spoke of how *clean and neat* everything looked about the "Colby" which pleased me. After lunch, and when we had got out to sea Capt. N. came for me to promenade, and with the aid of his arm I succeeded in walking very well, but I kept wishing at every turn that it was my darling's arm I was leaning upon. The Capt. was very kind and gave me a cordial invitation to his Room, at any time, and entertained me there until 10 o'clock reading and talking.

JANUARY 16. This new life without my own dear Diamond is a great trial, but I will try to be brave, and contented as I know he would wish me to be, and will put forth every effort to bring about our future happiness.

I wonder if he misses me to-day as I miss him, and if the room seems lonely to him, when he comes home and finds no little Rosebud to clasp her arms around his neck and hold up her lips for his warm, earnest, kisses. My own true, loving Diamond, how I wish I could meet his kind, tender looks tonight, as I lie in my berth, with no one to come to my bed-side, and lean over to kiss me good-night, but I will pray for heaven's choicest blessings to rest upon him while he is away from his own faithful, loving little Rosebud.

The weather has been delightful, and the sea so calm that no one has manifested any symptom of being sea-sick. It makes me think of what Capt. said about the lovely weather he will be likely to have and the bright pleasant days we would spend together if I was going out with him, but we will wait patiently for one year.

JANUARY 17. Fine weather and good westerly wind which would be favorable for the "Colby" if she sails today, as Capt. N. says. We are making splendid time and present appearances indicate a possibility of breakfast in New York, which will make a quick passage.

JANUARY 18. We passed the Highlands about 4 ½ o'clock A.M. and run up in the fog until we got opposite Governor's Island [New York], when the fog was so dense that it was impossible to proceed, and we had to anchor until 3 o'clock P.M. Then the thick veil was lifted and the panorama revealed to view, amply repaid us for seven hours of waiting! It was the most beautiful view I ever witnessed. *Hundreds* of vessels of all sizes lay at anchor waiting for the fog curtain to rise, and the sun came first *peeping* and then *beaming* down upon us, until the shores, the shipping and the Bay were all lighted up with a flood of radiant glory. How I wished my darling could be with me to enjoy everything that is beautiful and pleasant, but he will be away from me for many a long weary day, and I must try to be happy and cheerful, as I know he would wish me to be, yet he cannot blame me for the sad, lonely feeling I have in my heart, without him.

I took the 5 o'clock train to Paterson, and got *home* in time for supper. Mother was most cordial in her welcome, and dear old tender-hearted father wept, and said, "I am *glad* to have you back, for I thought I should never see you again". To-night I am in my cosy little room, and wish my darling could come with his good-night kiss and his fervent "God bless you," while I clasp my arms around his dear neck, and nestle close to his warm loving heart.

JANUARY 19. A pleasant quiet day spent at home, unpacking my trunk and fixing up my things generally. Rec'd a letter from Gus. [He] sends me a Check on Nassau Bank, New York for $10 and says he is improving, his limb is better. It appears that he has moved to Brooklyn. He writes very plausibly, but I cannot tell anything about him, for he is such a *consummate liar*!

JANUARY 21. Father is having the front of the house painted, and as the painter knows me I have to keep *dodging* him so mother laughs at my being kept such a close prisoner, but I assure her the imprisonment is pleasant, better than when I was in Montgomery with my heart *aching*, and my lips obliged to *smile*. Here I can *rest* and *think* of my own absent darling. Wish I could send a letter to my own dear Diamond, but it will be *three months* before I shall be able to. Had a long talk with father and mother, and they both approve of my determination never to live with Gus as his wife again. God help me to be *true to the love in my heart* and *true to my own womanhood*.

JANUARY 22. I have spent a quiet day at home, *"with closed doors"*, as mother laughingly remarked, when she left me after dinner to go to brother John's; but I amused myself by preparing supper for the two dear old people, and everything looked cosy and cheerful when they came home.

JANUARY 23. John came to see me this P.M. he being the only one except father and mother, whom I have seen since my return. I have not mentioned my determination to John, but he tells father that he approves of my leaving Gus, only he does not want me to leave, and then go back, of which there is no probability.

JANUARY 24. I am thinking of the *night before Christmas*, just one month ago, when my own dear Diamond and I spent the evening at Capt. Dickerson's, and on our return laughed at the bon-fires, the horns and crackers, but I think more of the sweet hour I spent in my darling's arms, seated in the big hollow chair, before I went to bed, and he went down stairs to *smoke.*

There is no variety in my life at present, for I still remain "sub rosa," but father and mother advise that I go to uncle John Stout's to board until my future is decided. They say if aunt Joanna will take me, I can have my home there, and keep my trunk there, but can spend as much of my time here, as I please, until I know how to carry out my future plans. God help me for I hardly know which way to turn, but I *want to be free.*

JANUARY 25. I open my eyes in the morning with a loving "God bless my darling," and at night I close them with the same petition. It is now 11.20 P.M. and if he could look in on me now he would kiss me lovingly and say *"Go to bed, darling,"* so I will do as I think he would wish to have me.

JANUARY 26. Mother went to Brooklyn to see aunt Joanna about taking me to board until I can decide upon my future. I hope all things will come out so that *the end may come soon*; and I may know what to depend upon for the future.

JANUARY 27. I wonder if my dear Diamond would like to look in and see me with my apron on, *keeping house* for father, getting breakfast, dinner and tea all by myself, and I wonder if he would praise my coffee, and omelet, for breakfast, or my dinner for two, which consisted of cold boiled tongue, mashed irish potatoes, corn, and tomatoes, and apple pie with a cup of coffee which father said was *first rate*, for dessert. I wish my darling had been here, I am sure I would have given him *ham and eggs* for I had some very nice ham, and fresh eggs right from the coop, and I know he would have liked the nice light biscuit that I made for tea, which were a grand success, though only made by guess, but he would have smiled to see the dough all over my hands and the ring *he* slipped on my finger, *with a wish,* guarded by a smaller and tighter one, lest I should lose it in the dough, for I would not remove it, as I did my others. It is now 10.30 o'clock and I confess to being a little tired, and fear I have been trying to do too much for my strength. Last night I hoped to see him even in my dreams, but woke up annoyed at the persistent appearance of our *old Preacher*, who used to grace the opposite side of the table! Why *he* should intrude upon my slumbers, I know not, but it would be a comfort if I could see my own darling even in a dream.

JANUARY 28. There are tears in my heart to-night, and it is with an effort that I keep them from my eyes. Oh I have so *longed* for my own dear Diamond and my heart has ached with a lonely, heavy pain, all day long, but I must not lose strength or courage for I shall need both in the dreary future that is before me. Poor dear father looked at me anxiously as we sat down to supper, and remarked that I looked pale and sad but must not get down-hearted, for I was *at home* and no one could take me away from its shelter, so long as I wish to remain. I blessed him for the kind words, but they nearly made me lose my self-control, and brought a choking sensation in my throat, which I finally overcame, and smiled back on him and mother who has returned from a fruitless visit to uncle John and aunt Joanna, as they do not think it best for me to go there. I have written a letter *for father* to Dr. Reynolds to inquire about [Gus'] accident. Oh if I could only *prove* what I know is really true, I could then know what course to pursue, that would bring happiness to myself, and my own dear Diamond.

JANUARY 29. It is 10.30 P.M. and I am ready for bed after an evening of anxious looking for Gus who wrote to father that he would come up to spend some Sunday soon, and so we looked for him but presume that the stormy weather and bad walking prevented him of which I am not sorry, as I do not feel well, and would have to go to Miss Wylie's to stay until he left. He writes father that his limb hurt him *before* I went South which is something new to me, as he never complained of it any more than usual. I do not comprehend why he should misrepresent things so unnecessarily, and when it cannot be any benefit. I have one precious comfort in my own dear Diamond. I can *believe* him implicitly, and have the fullest confidence in whatever he says and does.

JANUARY 30. A beautiful clear cold day, with a westerly wind which I hope may send our good ship on her way. Strange that each change in the weather only affects me as I hope or fear for my darling's safety and success, and yet the weather here is no criterion of what it may be where he is, but I naturally think of him.

I am not feeling well to-day and father says I look pale and sad; but it is only anxiety of mind, and if I was happy with my own dear Diamond I would soon be bright and well. How well I felt in [Savannah] when I was with him, and how much I improved until everybody said I was the picture of health! I have not been out anywhere yet. I think I shall go down to New York tomorrow and see Dr. Roof and make some inquiries about Gus, as well as to consult him about myself. Gus did not come up to-day as we partly expected, though he kept us on the *qui vive* all day in expectation of his *unwelcome* arrival.

JANUARY 31. It is only 8 ½ o'clock P.M. but I am so tired that I know my precious old Diamond would advise me to go to bed if he was here, so I send him in thought a loving good-night, and will soon be courting sleep upon my pillow. How I wish I could nestle close to my darling's side, with his arm around me, but alas, he is far away, and I am alone and lonely.

I have been to New York to-day. Dr. [Roof] told me that Mr. B's leg was nothing serious, or to complain of, but that he was a very irritable man and that at the worst the sore was only [a small one]. Dr. advised me to go to the Hospital and I left him to make the arrangements and dispatch me.

FEBRUARY 2. I received a dispatch from Dr. Roof this P.M. and replied that I would be down on the 9 o'clock train to-morrow, but it is not decided where I shall go, probably to the "Lenox" *H—otel*. I wonder what my own darling would say if he knew where I was going? I do not think he would disapprove of the course I have taken, at least I hope not, for I want his approval in all I do. Oh, God grant that I may be *free* to love him when he returns, for I do love him with all my heart, as I have never loved any one else. Perhaps this is my last night at home for some time, it seems strange to go out *alone* into the world again and I *wish*, oh I wish for my own dear Diamond, but he is far away, and this is my *first decisive* step towards making myself *free*; I have written a letter of explanation to brother John to show Gus if he likes.

FEBRUARY 3. I took the 10.20 A.M. train, for New York. Met Dr. Roof at the Lenox Presbyterian Hospital, Madison Avenue and 70th St. at 3 ½ o'clock P.M. He made arrangements for me to remain, when I was assigned to Ward 1, Bed 9. My entrance to the Ward was one of the most dreadful ordeals of my life, and I thought if I could only fly away and be with my own darling—I would willingly encounter hardships, privations, and anything that might befall me.

FEBRUARY 4. Another dreadful day, and after spending the night in uncontrollable fits of weeping, I have cried almost incessantly all day. But Dr. Charles Roof the House Physician has been very kind, and offered to do all he could for me. I have been so lonely and homesick that I could have died, were it not for the hope of sometime seeing my Diamond.

FEBRUARY 5. A clear pleasant day. Dr. Hadden, the head physician said he would examine my case on Monday. Dr. Roof gave me a pass to go out until 5 o'clock P.M. so I went to Mrs. Carey's and arranged with her to board me any time I desired to go there, paying $6. per week. She was very kind and made me feel how sweet it is to have true friends raised up in time of need.

Miss Woolsey came up to see me, and very kindly said she would transfer my bed to the corner where little Dora Dunn lies next to me, and give me a screen, which was done while I was out, and for the first time I feel as if I could lie down to *rest* without that *terrible frightened* feeling when I look around and see the forms in the white beds all around me. Now I am screened and shut in by myself, and I can *smile* a little as I think of my Darling.

FEBRUARY 7. I have passed through the ordeal of examination, and Dr. Hadden says my trouble is only *temporary* being a retroflexion of the uterus, but that there is no ulceration or inflammation, and the parts are all in excellent condition, showing careful medical treatment heretofore, so I feel more hopeful of getting well and strong.

I wonder if my own dear Diamond saw me here what he would say. Well, I feel that it was a good way to break loose from all the old ties, and strike out for myself, so I think he would not disapprove.

FEBRUARY 8. Dr. S. W. Roof came in to see me. He does not agree with Dr. Hadden in regard to my course of treatment and requests that Dr. Banks shall come and make an examination, before I consent to use the Supporter proposed.

FEBRUARY 10. I would like to-night to look into the Cabin of the *G.C.* and see a certain old Diamond that belongs to me there. I *know* there would be an hour of sweet happiness for two people who are wishing for each other. God keep my darling safely.

FEBRUARY 12. Dr. Hadden adjusted one of Thomas' Pessarys for me, and I went to walk in Central Park. Dr. Roof called, and told me Mr. B. had been to see him this A.M. and was *very much excited* when he heard where I was!!!

FEBRUARY 13. I spent an uncomfortable wakeful night, and all day have suffered much irritation from the wearing of the Pessary; but I retained it until night.

FEBRUARY 14. Valentine day. My dear Valentine is far away, but I will send to him over the wide ocean my sweetest love and kisses. I have been very nervous all day, thinking about Gus, and praying that all things may combine to bring myself and my darling together ere long.

FEBRUARY 15. Another visiting day, but I sent word to admit *no one* to see me, as I fear Mr. Barrows may attempt to come.

FEBRUARY 16. A bright pleasant day, and I have decided to leave here so I have settled everything up with Dr. Roof, who says I am *right*. Mrs. Carey received me very kindly, and says I can stay with her either a long or a short time, *just as I please*; so here I am, rooming with her at 136 East 40th St. in a plain but respectable neighborhood; and I hope it is for the best. If my own dear Diamond could see me tonight, I think he would put his arms around me, and say "I am glad my Rosebud is no longer among those rough, dreadful class of people", and yet I believe they all learned to like me, and I did some good even among them, especially to the poor little Dora, who had never been taught a prayer until I taught her, "Now I lay me down to sleep".

FEBRUARY 17. I am much disappointed that father nor John have neither of them written me a letter since I came, and Mrs. Carey thinks they are real mean, but I think they are only careless, and do not realize how much I need a little word of comfort and encouragement. Well, I will try not to complain for *little* troubles, where I have greater trials to encounter. God help me to come out victorious over them all.

FEBRUARY 21. Not feeling well all day, and had such severe pain in my left side that it almost threw me into a fever, so in the P.M. I went with Jennie to the Drug Store, and got some Iron and Alum to take, and also some mustard leaves, which did me so much good that I sat up in the evening and played Whist with the young folks.

FEBRUARY 22. Washington's Birthday, and a beautiful bright day, but I am not feeling well, and have spent it very quietly. Oh, if I could only get strong and well, I could then grapple with my fate.

I have heard no word from Paterson yet, and am heartily sick of the way *friends* act, sometimes I think I will quit and leave the country and drop everybody, for I almost wish I could drop out of life. Were it not for the one sweet love I have in my heart, I believe I would *die*. I do not want outsiders to know that I am here, for then G. might find out, and annoy me.

FEBRUARY 26. Received a letter from father, saying that he had returned a letter Mr. B. sent in his care to me, with a note saying that he did not know where I was.

FEBRUARY 28. A very stormy day and my cold is not any better. Mr. Story called to see me and we had a very *interesting* conversation, he had been to see Mr. Barrows this morning, and he (Mr. B.) told him I was improving, and would be home in two or three weeks! He has moved back to New York and is boarding on 12th St. I did not say *much* about my absent Darling, but I smiled as Mr. S. said "He thinks a great deal of you, *and you know it*", which more near the truth than he supposed.

FEBRUARY 29. A cold disagreeable day, and we are all sick. In the P.M. Mrs. Carey and I went to the Homeopathic Hospital, but were not pleased with the appearance of things.

MARCH 1. I went in P.M. to see Dr. Roof; who made appointment for Friday. I am glad my darling does not know how much anxiety and heart ache I have, else he would be grieved for me during his absence.

MARCH 2. Have not been well all day, and suffered much with my side. Think if I could see my own dear Diamond it would do more towards getting me well than all the Doctors and medicines in the country; for anxiety is wearing me out by inches. God help me to get the affairs of my life arranged.

MARCH 3. I kept my appointment with Dr. Roof, but trembled lest he might have told Mr. Barrows I was to be there. Dr. made examination and found the cellular tissue of the peritoneum much inflamed, with slight ante-flexion of the uterus, so he advised me by all means to go to the Woman's Hospital and is to see about it on Monday.

MARCH 4. I walked up to 49th Street to see Dr. Porter, at the Woman's Hospital, and engaged to go there on Monday; so I wrote Dr. Roof. Received letter from John enclosing one from Gus to him! begging him to try and effect a "reconciliation", and vowing "his love and faithfulness"!

MARCH 5. Have prepared my things to go to the Hospital but feel a little heart-sick, and lonely, with a dreadful *longing* for some word from my own precious Diamond. I did not dare to more than peep once at his picture, for the tears would come, and the lonely feeling kept tugging at my heart-strings, until it seemed as if I would fly away from everything, and go to meet him; but I know how impossible it is for me to do so, and I must be patient.

MARCH 6. Went by appointment with Dr. Porter to the Women's Hospital at 11 o'clock. Was sent for to the Examining Room and immediately examined. Dr. Roof called to see me, and told me Mr. B. had been to see him about his limb, and Dr. told him I was coming up here by his advice.

MARCH 7. The loveliest day of the season, and I was surprised at a visit from brother John, who thinks I look dreadfully worn out, and says I had better go home, but that is not the best course I know. In the evening the nurse gave me a hot syringe bath, which did me good, and I hope to sleep during the night.

MARCH 9. A charming day, and very spring like, so that I would be out doors if I could but at 4 o'clock I am to be under Examination from Dr. Thomas, and then I hope to know what is the matter, and what treatment I will require.

Evening. I have been through more than one trying ordeal to-day, and not the least was having a letter offered me by Dr. Roof, and which I returned through him to Mr. Barrows, refusing to read it. I do not feel happy nor encouraged tonight, and my heart is full to overflowing with tears. Oh if I was only strong and well, but I fear from the present aspect of affairs that I may not be well in a long time. If *God* would come to my aid, how soon I might dispense with the aid of medicine and doctors.

MARCH 10. Dr. Anway came to give me a "little scold", and told me to go out for a walk which I did in P.M. Am feeling more happy and contented, and find the ladies very pleasant in the Ward. As I sit here in my own little chair, or lie on my little white-curtained bed, there is not an hour in the day but I am wishing and praying for my absent darling. Poor fellow, how he would worry if he knew how weary and lonely I am, and how I have to count every dime I spend so that I may have enough to pay my way and carry me through.

MARCH 14. Mrs. Crowell called at tea-time, we had a long talk which has quite disturbed me, though I feel provoked at myself for feeling so badly. She had seen Mr. Barrows yesterday and he had seemed very humble, and wept bitterly when he talked about me, but I do not forget that he has made *me* weep many bitter tears, and I pray God to keep me true to myself. My heart is very sore to-night and I long to be alone, but it is one of the dark hours when I find being surrounded by others, a sore affliction. I could cry out with the agony that is in my heart, but I have to hush it up and keep the tears back, because of those around me.

MARCH 16. Dr. Thomas did not come to-day and so my case is yet undecided, which is a great disappointment to me. Miss Pitt has been very sick all day, and I am very tired from rubbing her head, for she seemed to want me to be with her all that time.

MARCH 18. I sit here and wonder about my absent loved one, yet I feel that the time will come when I can be a source of comfort and a blessing to him, and repay him in some little measure for the life he has heretofore led.

MARCH 25. Have been suffering much pain all day, and did not see Dr. Thomas who performed an operation on the tumor case in the back room, and took only ¾ of an hour from the time she passed through the room going up stairs, until they brought her down after the operation. It was a solemn scene to see her walk up in all her strength and be carried down on the table, as if dead. God help the poor woman.

MARCH 30. A trip up stairs to see Dr. Thomas has marked the eventful day, and he has decided that I need not remain longer but come occasionally to see him.

MARCH 31. Have been working on my wrapper, and got it all finished and it is much admired. I think my old Diamond would call me his blue-bird if he should see me in it, instead of his Rosebud. Dr. Anway advises me to remain a little longer to use the treatment, and so I shall stay another week.

APRIL 1. I received a letter from Mary Mott which is the first one I have had from any one this week, but I presume my friends do not intend to be negligent or careless, yet I do not understand why they do neglect me, still I will not murmur, for I know they love me devotedly; and while I have my own Diamond I will be content.

APRIL 2. Am feeling, stiff and sore from the effects of dressing up in fantasticals, and dancing with Mrs. Thompson which ended with a fall by Mrs. Jacobi's bed, and frightened good old Ellen almost out of her wits.

Well, we may be a little imprudent, but we have so little amusement here that we make much out of nothing and perhaps it is best.

APRIL 7. Still another lovely day, and I am feeling quite well, but I look forward tremblingly to the change. Had a long talk with Dr. Anway and he gave me much encouragement for my future.

APRIL 10. I remain one more night in the Hospital—my last night—and yet I write this a little sadly, for I believe I have helped some of the poor sufferers while I have been here. God help them—and me.

APRIL 11. A lovely day has passed, and I am in my room at Mrs. Houghton's, weary and half sick, and almost wishing I was back in my little white curtained bed. Perhaps I will be better tomorrow.

APRIL 12. Not at all well and suffering much pain, but am trying most desperately to keep up. Oh, if I should be sick, it would be truly more than I could bear. God help me!

APRIL 30. Well, I have been through the bitterness and pain of a severe illness. Inflammation of the Bowels, which Dr. Pratt says was probably caused by over-fatigue and cold when my system was just in condition for it. Dr. Pratt has been attending me, and for two days and nights my life was merely a *flicker* kept burning by stimulants but then I rallied, and to-day I am sitting up in bed, better, but oh so weak! It seems as if I should never be strong again.

MAY 6. It rained in the night and I wondered if my dear Diamond was where he was exposed to the storms. How my heart goes out in love, strong, devoted, and true, to my dear absent one; it seems sometimes wonderful to myself, as if my whole soul went out in great waves of longing, loving tenderness.

MAY 7. I have spent a quiet day interrupted by a short visit from aunt Joanna. Those visits are a little *peculiar*, being made at times and seasons when *she couldn't do anything else* and so she runs in to *ease her conscience*! Somewhat amusing and very disgusting to me, who would prefer having her stay away!

MAY 9. Rec'd a letter from Mr. Hatchett from Vicksburg, Miss. in which he sends me his picture, a little tin-type! I have laughed myself almost sick over it, and the ridiculous idea of his supposing I cared for the *horrid* little thing! He writes very kindly, but I am a *little afraid* of the man—I know not why for he has always treated me kindly, but there is a feeling of wanting to ward him off!

MAY 12. I sent a letter to father last Sunday night, and have not heard from him in reply which is very strange, perhaps they are not ready to have me at home, and think if I do not get a letter, I will not come! It is very very strange, but I will try not to think hard of them, as they are getting old, but it is very hard to feel that I receive more kindness from strangers than I do from my own people, yet if God will give me health and strength I will ask nothing from any of them.

MAY 13. Received two Postal cards from father. No calls, and aunt Joanna has neither been nor sent to see me all the week, she acts as if she was afraid that I would ask them to do something for me, but she does not know M.L.B. [herself] or she would know better than that. I do not want to find fault with people, but really I am disgusted with some people who parade their religion, and with their long faces and tight-locked purses, tell poor miserable wretches like me that we must "trust in the Lord." I wonder what they would do! Pshaw.

MAY 14. I got *dressed* for the first time to-day, and was glad as I had a visit from father, who came to see if I was well enough to go home tomorrow, when he would send mother down for me. But I said I could not come for several days, as I was not ready.

MAY 24. Took 4 o'clock P.M. train for Paterson. Reached home in time for tea, and they were glad to see me.

JUNE 15. Returned to New York to consult professionally with Mr. King [lawyer]. I went to 6 St. Marks Place, where I saw him, and signed Permission to proceed legally in my business [divorce].

JUNE 16. Wrote to Mr. Barrows in the morning.

JUNE 17. Wrote to Mr. King and sent copy of my letter to Mr. B., then rested for I was weary in body and mind.

JUNE 18. John brought the children up in the evening, and we enjoyed the visit. Father told John about my affairs which did not please me, for I had *asked* him not to mention the matter to John.

JUNE 19. Am waiting anxiously to get some news either from Mr. Barrows or Mr. King.

JUNE 21. Received letter this morning from Mr. King *declining* further connection with my business, because of my letter to Mr. B. I took train and saw him at 2 o'clock. Settled matters satisfactorily having paid him $50.

JUNE 22. Received letter from Mr. Barrows which would have touched me tenderly, had I not had before me his legal Document of 16th of which he makes no mention. Returned the Document with copy of Mr. B's letter, to Mr. King.

JUNE 24. Received Mr. King's *two* letters together, acknowledging receipt of mine, and saying in the latter one that he was ready to see me *at any time*; but it is too warm to go today.

JULY 2. The weather superlatively *hot*, and thermometer 102° in the *cool shady hall*, so what must it be out of doors! We have all succumbed to the caloric influence, and lounge around, panting for breath, and wishing for rain. Eating is an infliction not to be thought of, and *sleep* cometh not even when our eyes are heavy, so we exist in a sort of dull apathy, waiting for some change in temperature.

JULY 3. God give me strength, health and grace as I certainly need, and guide me to success in my present undertakings, so that this Centennial year, may be a year of sincere rejoicing to me. This day I have felt a little nervous from the knowledge that the "Complaint" will soon be decided. But I have had a great comfort to-day for I received *two* letters of June 4th and 14th from my darling, and all is well. He was in Callao [Peru].

JULY 4. The Grand Centennial Birthday! and all the land awoke this morning to the Centennial rejoicing. It has been indeed a glorious day and everything, and everybody seemed well fitted for the occasion. It is also father's Birthday, and he seemed younger for the gay surroundings though he is 68 years old. I wonder if his daughter will celebrate her 68th birthday with children and grand-children as father has done, but I think not, and am sure it would not be desirable unless the years to come brought with them more happiness than the past. Ah, me, what a checquered life mine has been and yet I have had much happiness, with all my troubles.

JULY 6. Lawyer Tuttle came up this evening to see me and had some conversation about Mr. Barrows and my affairs. It was very kind of him to come, but I hope I may not have to place myself under any obligations to him. Oh, I wish I *knew* that I had the means to carry me through all right, I would not remain here, but would go among strangers until my affairs were settled.

God help me until I am safe with my darling, and feel that *he* can protect me with his loving arms from any approach of evil. It seems as if each one who befriends me, seeks to ingratiate himself in my special favor, and I have to ward off evil continually, for I know not from what quarter it may come.

I tremble when I think of where I stand, and shrink from the approach of even friendship, so that I fear I may become cynical and misanthropic, but I will pray that my heart may be kept pure, and my mind *just* in its estimate of proffered friendship. Why should write all this? Because Mr. Tuttle held my hand longer, and with a more pronounced pressure than need be, when he said, "If I can do anything for you, my dear child, let me help you, and the assistance will be given most cheerfully." Well, that was not much from a man who has known me from childhood, and who used to kiss me years ago, as one of his *Pets* when I was a schoolgirl; but looks and acts and *manner* mean much, and I only crave the dear love-light in the eyes of one man on earth. From others I shrink away, and ask only plain, unvarnished friendship.

JULY 10. I am wishing for some clean, cool spot, where I could shut out the world, and keep still until my domestic affairs are settled, which I hope will be *soon* and *satisfactorily*. Indeed

I would gladly pay out my last dollar, if it was all settled, and I could send word to my Diamond by mail of 15th that I was unquestionably free. God help me to keep up strength, and health, and to fight the battle through, though I have to do it *alone* and *single-handed*. Perhaps it is better so, else I would be under obligations, when it is all ended, and I want to *owe no man anything*.

JULY 15. This has been a day of great surprise to me, for while we were at dinner, who should come to the door, and ask for me but Mr. Story! I was utterly astonished, but soon recovered from my surprise, feeling a little mortified at presenting myself in my extremely dirty white sacque, however I shall survive the mortification, for everything here gets so dusty. He staid until the 3.37 P.M. train, and went away with the *reiterated* assurance that he was *coming again*, and seemed anxious about my being "angry because he came", which I was not, but a little annoyed. I had to laugh to myself, when I asked to be excused while I retired to change my dress, and he said "Don't be gone long, for I do not feel like losing a minute from you while I am here"; and I thought to myself, "Well, Mr. Gosh, if you think *I* prize the minutes as you do, you are mightily mistaken, for I would rather spend one wee half hour with my own precious Diamond than enjoy your society all day long"; but I did not tell him so. He talks of his keeping aloof from me for *my sake*, but seems to live in great hopes of the future when *this business will be settled*; but I believe what my darling says, that *he is not to be trusted*. Well, if as I suppose he came out in the sweltering July sun from New York to stay three mid-day hours and *enjoyed seeing me*, I hope he feels repaid, but if he came to *find out anything* he learned that I ask no odds from any man, and intend to come out victorious and *true to myself and my darling*. Mr. Story asked about the *Capt.* but *I knew nothing*. Well, this is a queer world, but in all its vast multitudes of people, there is but *one* whom I feel *perfect trust and confidence in*.

JULY 13. Father spoke this morning about the Saloon Keeper asking him if Mr. Tuttle was here, which annoyed me very much, and made me wish myself away from this miserable place. If I had the means I would go somewhere among strangers, and have no remarks made. It is perfectly dreadful, when I *know* that no harm exists, and I cannot but think that if everybody was as careful to *do* right, and not to *appear* right, there would be less evil in the world.

JULY 16. Oh the weary weeks that have stretched into months since the last Sabbath I spent with my darling. I cannot help grieving when I remember that I cannot bring him, with my unbounded love, the sweet freshness of health and youth; yet I believe he will be happy and contented with his poor faded little Rosebud, who loves him so devotedly. If I thought otherwise, I could never see him again, though it would take from me the only hope of happiness I have in life. I cannot but compare him with those who while they want me to understand how well they like me, are *afraid* to say *"I am her friend"*.

JULY 19. Oh how I wish this dreadful business was over and done with, for I feel as if I could hardly endure this strain on my nerves much longer.

JULY 22. Took 8 o'clock A.M. train for New York. I called on Mr. King, and learned that Col. Tidball had gotten 20 days time in the "Case" so Mr. King had me write to Mr. Barrows saying I did *not claim support.*

JULY 23. Sabbath. A cool pleasant day and very refreshing, but I did not go to church, because I did not want any remarks made about my being here. All day long, I have been wishing I could see or hear from my dear absent one. I do hope I shall get some word from him about the "Note" soon, for my trip to New York yesterday has reduced me to my last 55 cents and I do not like to ask father or any one for money, yet it is most inconvenient not to have it; and I know he would feel badly if he knew I had to "cut so close" in the matter of expenditure.

JULY 25. I have felt nervous and excited all day, hardly being able to settle myself to anything. Probably my nervousness arises from receiving Mr. Barrows reply to my letter of Saturday. I sent copy of the letter to Mr. King in the noon mail.

JULY 27. Received note from Mr. King in which he says he

does not consider Mr. Barrows' letter written in "full good faith," but with a "cautious reserve" and that he hopes to find them ready for *business*.

AUGUST 5. Received a *little note* of July 8th from [Capt. Streeter] but it was a great disappointment as my letters do not seem to have reached [him], and I have written *nine*. The ship sailed July 9th for Astoria, Oregon [from South America].

AUGUST 13. John came to see me in P.M. and gave me $10 which I took because I really need it, but I hope some day to repay it, at the same time I appreciate his kindness. That with $5.50 from father, and about $2.00 he spent for medicine is all I am indebted to them for, but I hope soon to be able to pay them both, and I know my Diamond would rather I would not take their money.

AUGUST 19. After another pleasant rain during the night I feel better and have been more like myself than I have been for some time. Received an encouraging letter from Mr. King, and a Postal Card from Mrs. Fordham asking me to come to Sag Harbor to make her a visit.

AUGUST 23. After a pleasant night on the Sound, I arrived at Sag Harbor [N.Y.] about 8 o'clock A.M. and had hearty greeting of welcome from the whole Fordham family.

AUGUST 26. Have spent a day of quiet pleasure, and find myself comfortably tired to-night. We went bathing and then boating. We had a delightful time.

AUGUST 31. Bathing in the morning, and to Long Beach in P.M. for shells. The last of summer.

SEPTEMBER 14. Received letters from father, Capt. Streeter and Mr. King. About the latter I have much anxiety, but pray that God will guide me in the matter. I feel oppressed with care and responsibility but hope all things will come out right.

SEPTEMBER 21. Received letter from Mr. King with Document to sign for a withdrawal of proceedings, which I signed and returned.

SEPTEMBER 26. Arrived in New York in good season, called on Mr. King who assured me that everything was in excellent condition *for us*. Came out to Paterson and found father and mother both well.

SEPTEMBER 28. Received letter from Mr. King asking for an advance of $75. John advised me not to pay it, and I wrote declining to do so. I know not the consequences, but think I am *right*. Feel nervous and excited, and wish I was away from here. It is worry all the time, so that I am kept in a fever. I have prayed earnestly that God would rule all things.

SEPTEMBER 30. Received letter from Mr. King, more satisfactory than I thought his answer to mine would be, so I hope no bad results may develop from my refusal of an advance to him. When I commenced this matter, I had no idea it would take so long, but alas, when one gets into the spider web of legal proceedings who can tell when they will be extricated. This is the end of summer, and the matter is only about to begin, but I hope the *beginning of the end* may be near, and if what Mr. King says true there will be little further delay. How I hope for the good news to send to my darling.

OCTOBER 3. Met Mr. Tuttle at Post Office, and John was angry because Mr. Tuttle walked down with me. I was provoked because, thinking no harm, I told him of it, and I find they are dreadfully afraid that I shall bring reproach upon their name. I don't think my own dear Diamond would disapprove of anything that I have done and I *know* I have done nothing for which I ought to blush, but "people will talk you know."

OCTOBER 6. Looked anxiously for a letter, but did not get any, and am in a state of uncertainty; wish I was in the State of Conn. having matters and things settled; I pray for patience.

OCTOBER 10. Went to see Mr. King and found things rather dilatory, but unavoidably so it would appear.

OCTOBER 13. A beautiful day, but I have felt troubled and nervous all day, partly occasioned by a disposition on the part of father to talk about the everlasting old "*case*". I hope that this anxiety will not terminate in another sick spell, but that God will give me the health, strength, and ambition I so much need.

OCTOBER 15. Have felt a little unhappy and had a little cry, partly I presume, because I feel lonely, unsettled, and nervous; wishing, oh so much, for my darling.

OCTOBER 21. Am a little surprised at not hearing from Mr. King, but hope his next letter will decide matters for me. Oh, how I wish the dreadful business was at an end.

OCTOBER 22. Wrote to Mrs. Edwards in which I said in reply to hers, "In regard to Mr. B. and his 'domestic troubles' I *think* the least he says the *better for him*, if I judge by the random manner in which he has been using both his pen and tongue which, by the way, I intend to have *legally curbed* unless he keeps within the *limits of veracity*, which is *all I ask*, and *more than I expect*". It is to be hoped she may repeat it to Mr. B. as I am pretty sure she will, on the principle that a dog who will bring a bone, will also carry one.

OCTOBER 30. Called on Mr. King and signed Document for Connecticut Courts.

NOVEMBER 9. Letter from Mr. King. Fixing my trunk preparatory to going to Milford [Connecticut].

NOVEMBER 13. Left Paterson on the 9.30 A.M. train, after receiving a letter from a Montgomery gentleman which displeased me very much, for I consider him entirely too quick to make use of my anticipated freedom, and I would not care for him or his money were he ten times as wealthy and aristocratic. I stopped to see Mr. King and then took the train for Milford. Mr. Smith met me at the train on arriving.

NOVEMBER 15. Am feeling very nervous and full of anxiety, until it seems as if I could not live through the coming trial, but God will give me grace and strength for my time of need.

NOVEMBER 19. A day of suffering and much sadness of heart to me, and a constant longing for the companionship of my own dear Diamond, but he is far away.

Very sick for three weeks and unable to write.

DECEMBER 10. A blessed sabbath-day to me for I made my first visit down stairs since November 16th, and I have lived through *years* of mental and physical anguish since that time. Over and above all comes to me now when I am well enough to realize it, the motherly devotion of dear Mrs. Smith. When I think of her going with me on that *terrible* journey to New Haven on November 22nd, and how she comforted me during that dreadful day, I find my heart full to overflowing with gratitude, for she was the "friend in need" that the dear Heavenly Father sent to me. How I wish I could send word to my Darling that the shackles which bound me have been loosened, and I am now entirely *Free*. I scarcely realize it, yet since November 22nd, with all my suffering from prostration, I have had a *restful* feeling that I have not had in years, and I begin to retrim my sails for my new voyage in life. God grant that it may be happier and more prosperous than it has been.

◇   ◇

Afterword

With her divorce secured and her health somewhat improved, Marie Barrows looked forward to the return of Captain Streeter. "What a surprise our final union will be to all concerned (except us)," she wrote in January of 1877. In February she received word from Valparaiso, Chile that an accident had laid the *Gardner Colby* up for repairs; the Captain would be delayed at least through the summer.

On September 22, having received word that the ship was on its way to New York, Marie joyfully went shopping. After spending $24.14 on clothing, gloves and yard goods, she noted in the journal, "I have not yet got the things I really need. . . . I presume Mother thinks me very extravagant, as she does not know what I am preparing for." On October 6 she left for Sag Harbor to await the Captain's arrival. On the 26th she wrote, "Received two dispatches from my Diamond. . . . He hopes I will be ready to be married, and return with him as his wife. . . . I did not know I could be so serious when the time really came, but I am very happy."

Two days later they were married, and for most of the next year they traveled together on the *Gardner Colby*, going on one journey as far as Java. The last entry in Marie Barrows Streeter's diary is dated September 8, 1878; we know nothing about her life after that time.

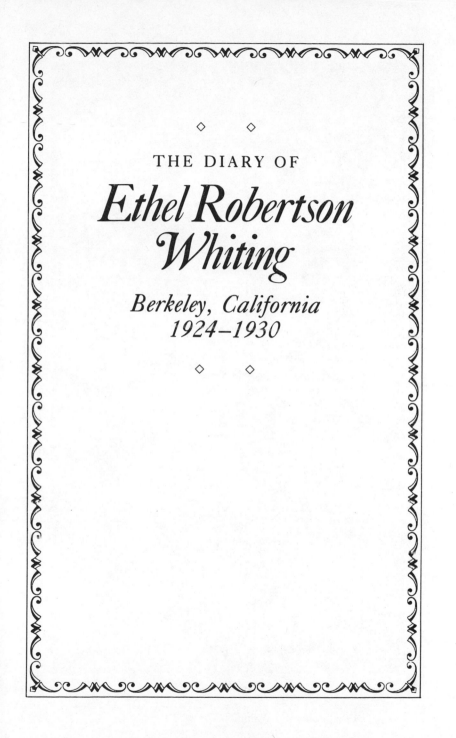

THE DIARY OF

Ethel Robertson Whiting

Berkeley, California
1924–1930

Ethel Robertson Whiting (*Courtesy of Margaret Oxley*)

◇   ◇

Introduction

Ethel Robertson was born on March 12, 1882 in San Francisco. Her mother was a native of the city; her father, from Georgia, had been educated in Switzerland and became an engineer.

Ethel and her younger sister (a younger brother had died when she was three) moved with their parents to the Berkeley hills around 1890. "Just country roads and green hills and gardens—and a view that took one's breath away," she later wrote, "Our part of Berkeley, and our life, was very informal. Often we had no servant and Mamma cooked and sewed. There were interesting, and some decidedly outstanding people about us.

"When we were cut off from our view, [Mother] moved us still higher on the hill to overtake it again. She designed the house herself—an unconventional, redwood Berkeley house. That was 1525 Hawthorne Terrace—a home that revived your interest in life, no matter how black a hole you might be in."

Her mother had a profound influence on Ethel; she "was entirely without pretense or affectation or the desire to do things because they were in vogue with the 'Right People'.   . It did not disturb my mother to defend her opinions with humor and tolerance. I grew up taking for granted that in all families ideas were tossed about at the dinner table, or even at breakfast. . . . heatedly perhaps, but certainly without anger."

Independence of mind apparently ran in the family: "Neither my parents nor grandparents were religious people. They belonged to the Episcopal Church. They loved and respected the tradition, the dignity and beauty of the service, but they thought freely for themselves."

Ethel Robertson married Henry Hyer Whiting of Pensacola, Florida, in 1904. He became a successful industrialist and was known, as well, for his efforts on behalf of charitable and labor organizations. They had two daughters, Carolyn, born in 1905, and Clara, born in 1907, and settled on Hawthorne Terrace next door to her parents.

In March of 1924, after a particularly traumatic year, Ethel Whiting began her diary. She was forty-two and, if she had ever kept a journal

411

before, she did not mention the fact. She addressed her writing from the outset to a grandchild not yet born, and she clearly meant it as a record to be passed on—even adding biographies of the family's forebears. Yet the journal had a personal function, too—Whiting described it as "this troublesome craving of mine to try my hand . . . at freeing my thoughts from disorder and getting them into sight, where I can look them in the eye and see whether I really think them."

The journal entries were written in longhand and transcribed by several different typists. The resulting irregularities in spelling and punctuation have been corrected.

◇ *1924* ◇

MARCH 11. What was it I read the other day? Something like this: "The diarist is about as near as you'll get to the supreme egotist. It is vanity that eggs them on and a lust to be important." That's it. I don't know whether this will turn out to be a diary, but I do want to be important. I want to talk about myself and I want you to be interested. I may as well be honest about it. I don't know whether I shall win, place or even show— isn't that what they say at the races?—but why don't I take advantage of your possible curiosity about these "Olden Days" and use this means of introducing myself to you at my present age—forty-two tomorrow: before I become that faded, outdated, person you may remember—"Oh yes—I do remember my grandmother Whiting, poor thing!" Ah, but I am not like that yet—though slightly the worse for wear.

It is a fixed belief of mine that most of us would like to *write*— perhaps just our thoughts—about things—everything—*and* to have somebody read it. That's the trouble. Nobody wants to read it. Why should they? Each person is busy with his own affairs and for entertainment more interested in a good detective story or the New Yorker Magazine than in Mrs. Whiting's dull account of her very average activites. Nobody except perhaps one's descendants, after they are forty, unless they should be boys.

I shall be lecturing and scolding, writing down my tiresome theories, but you may skip over that if you like. You will be alive and possess the Earth, while I shall have played my small part and passed to the obscurity of the Beyond. You *do* understand that you are not living soul yet, but as I assume that you will materialize in due course and appear in the flesh, I shall try to catch your attention. You cannot hope to make so much as a beginning for years, four or five anyway, so there is no occasion for hurry on my part, but this absurd idea of mine refuses to remain unnoticed any longer.

Behold then—your grandmother!! It amuses me to think of myself as an ancestor, and I know that ancestors are not a dem-

413

ocratic institution, so that very likely you will think it an un-pardonable liberty for me to thrust myself upon you. No doubt you feel that you are Yourself without help or hindrance from us. At the same time it is true that "every man carries his ances-tors within him," so if one of you has my Roman nose (which God forbid)—you may be interested to know where it came from. Don't think too hardly of me because of it, because my father had it and his father before him, so I am no more to blame than you are.

About myself I have dreadful things to tell you. *First*—I am a "Victorian!" That is the worst thing you can say about anybody.

A Victorian in a dress up to her knees, who shudders with distaste at the sight of women smoking throughout an afternoon, drinking too much gin and whiskey, and playing bridge for high stakes—perhaps I shouldn't mind that so much if I played a little better myself.

And certainly I can't agree that it is advisable for girls to go about on motor trips unchaperoned.

As for running off with someone else's husband, in a motor or any other way, I'm against it!

As for my aversion to chewing gun, it falls into a slightly different category—shabby and lowdown as it looks, no one suggests that there is anything destructive about that!

Second—I am a coward! Afraid of mice and Bolsheviki and earthquakes and influenza, *and* the Ocean. "The greyness of the sand and sea and sky, the uproar of the waves, seem to me an utterly sinister thing." Not very bold words, but they de-scribe my feelings.

Third—I like Chopin and Liszt better than Mozart and Bach. This is all wrong and it is awkward for a grandmother to ac-knowledge it. You won't want me for an ancestor. But there it is——it isn't as though I could hope to deceive you. I have read, and I am afraid it is true, that people always give them-selves away to their readers, in writing about themselves. I mean, let them strive ever so hard to prevent it, to hide the egotism, the littleness, the inconsistencies they so absurdly do not want to see in themselves—and don't want anybody else to see—they steal their way through, so you would find me out before we had gone far. I ought to warn you that after this general confession I shall do my best to contradict it all. I shall try to *fool* you if I can.

About my being Victorian,—"Tempora muntantur, et nos muntantur in illud" [Time changes, and we change in it]—isn't that it? And I can't tell you how really hard I am trying to fix myself over in the "new" way. But the fact is that it is so unsettling, so disappointing, and so opposed to what I naturally am that I am not making satisfactory headway. Nevertheless, if I just sit still and be myself, which I would so very much rather do, I am afraid I won't be in the picture at all. Because, you know, the "new" writers don't mean what they say about *being yourself*—and all that—unless *yourself* is radical and against conventions, and I don't want to be radical at all, or only a very little, now and then. No, my trouble is the other way, being too conservative—belonging to the "Late General Grant" period, let us say. Just what Galsworthy calls "stuffy"—very discouraging, isn't it? I am sure that none of them mean one should go on being *that*.

Forty-two: I don't like it very much. It gives me a queer feeling that though there may be another act, following the rules of dramatic form it will naturally have only the *falling action* to offer us, so that we really might begin putting on our wraps and thinking about getting out quietly and decently. You can't help wondering what it is has been, exactly, that you have spent all these years getting ready for

The strange part of it is that everything has turned out so well. As for happiness—I have had more than my share, I know, if it is divided into shares, which I can hardly believe—not very even shares anyway—not share and share alike, even in the long run, or according to our deserts, as so many people appear to think. Knowing that interferes with my prayers. I hesitate to give thanks for my good fortune because it does not seem kind to those who somehow have not come off so well. There must be some mistake for it is hardly decent to assume that Fate has granted special favors to any one person in the face of all the anguish we see about us.

It really isn't clear to me upon what basis we beg to be delivered, individually, from the sorrows that beset mankind. How selfish and egotistic such prayers must appear. "Thank you for doing for me what you did not do for Mrs. Jones next door." No, there is something wrong with that, and how embarassing to have us constantly interfering with the Deity, or assuming any such thing.

The Powers above—if any—must work under pressure undreamed of by our most harried executives, without our jostling each other to get our supplications in for preferment.

Candidly, something in me has fallen short of development, as though I had been preparing for something and not only have not done it but can't even think what it is. (Nothing to help the world, I am afraid, but by which I shall make my mark.) Probably not to *do* but to *be* some still obscure thing. The worst of it is a tantalizing suggestion that there is yet time to attend to it, if only I could discover what it is, and get to work.

I must speak at once of your *Grandfather Whiting*, a wonderful man, your grandfather, not a dashing figure, exactly, not tall enough, and over-weight, a little, but brown, vigorous, eager, and just comfortably handsome for a husband. I am going to talk a great deal about him, but a great deal more about myself. Still, it will be necessary to give him attention. A man with his personality does not stay in the background (personality is a very good word this year—very much used). Personality, dynamic force and whatever all those other things are—your grandfather really has them—as you shall see.

He has worked very hard for years and years, with tremendous enthusiasm and *that* has made him a success and so busy now, rushing and hurrying about being "Chairman of Boards" and so involved in affairs altogether that his days can't accomplish all that is required of them.

Now I shall contrive to tell you in some sort of order, something about the family (though, I repeat, it is myself I want to talk about). Carolyn and Clara, my darling girls, so different in some ways, so much alike in others. I suppose that I may say that Carolyn is beautiful, because she has regular features and a certain peculiar warm, glowing composure in her face, and a true nobility in her expression which reveal her character quite truly—although she has unexpected flashes of rather unreasonable temper too, at times.

As for Clara, though the girls at the really *super* Ransome School with their "rational clothes and rational minds and their hard little hearts" have rather spoiled her natural sweetness, she has an enchanting gaiety and spirit. This gives such animation and charm to her face that it entirely makes up for the slight misfortune of having the family nose. Her eyes are the kind that it simply won't do for her own Mother to try to describe. My children are almost the same size and both have brown hair and pretty, even, white teeth, like your Grandfather's.

Then, this year—the fire, our dreadful Berkeley fire, pretty hard for all of us to take.

Perhaps you have never heard of that fire, although it is so vivid to us that it is hard to realize that it is going to become a fact of the dim past ("One with Nineveh and Tyre"). It came upon us "all on a summer's afternoon," and in ten minutes it had destroyed everything we had, houses, gardens, our dear old trees, silver, rugs, family portraits, books.

I was stupid, not to save anything, and in thinking it over I can't see why we didn't. Only, I wasted a precious half hour—all the time we had—running about to ask the neighbors what they were going to do—what they thought we ought to do. They hadn't thought about doing anything—*No*, no cause for alarm, "don't get yourself all worked up, Ethel," though it did look black and sinister with the smoke growing thicker every minute—queer, of course, still grass fires in the hills are a part of our environment here in California, no need for excitement—no harm has ever been done,—the fire department—best in the country, etc., etc. Well, we just saved ourselves (and the parrot). I had no car at home that day, and Carolyn was in bed after a six weeks' illness—sinus and bad heart. A neighbor drove us away at the last moment, with the garden flaming behind us, and the street trees blazing up in front of us.

A fine sight we made arriving at your Grandfather's office in the City. Grandfather always insists that we brought the parrot to his office too. It does make a better story, but we didn't.

I must say that the poor man took the catastrophe well— "Damned sorry my booze is all lost."—you see he had a good supply in the wine closet to see us through these dark days of Prohibition—and "Did you remember to lock the front door?"

Six months ago now. There, I've made a beginning, Betty, or Anne or Barbara or Phyllis (have I hit it right?) or whoever you turn out to be. It's a pretty poor beginning, I guess, but perhaps I shall improve.

MARCH. The new house is almost finished and it is stunning. I had expected to resent it and have a feeling of disloyalty to the one we have lost when I find myself excited by it. Never-the-less I have a small chill of fear that it is going to look like a model home, open for inspection! It is so very new! It is not going to be easy to handle when we have nothing to put in it that has belonged to us more than three months.

People say that we are taking the fire casually, all of us. Perhaps we are. Experiences of this kind are so overwhelming that they make one wonder whether the whole scheme of Fate may not be casual—certainly things are impermanent.

And then, in our joyful astonishment at finding no one killed or injured we feel that we came off too well to complain. I won't say that it is not demoralizing; I do miss my hand-glass. I have not seen the back of me since September, but even that may have its advantages. It was demoralizing and has left me with a feeling of unreality. This may be partly because of my Mother's unnatural state; she is with me constantly and is confused by what has happened. . . .

You don't mind hearing about our fish pond, do you? We built it ourselves, Beth [her niece] and Carolyn and Clara and I, against the advice of the plumber; the cement man—carpenters, contractors, gardeners and—Grandfather: "If you would only wait", they said, "and let a man do it properly". Can't you see them shaking their heads in dire warning?

But that's just the point, we can't wait—and having a man do it is so expensive. Of course if the goldfish are not happy none of them can justly be blamed. Building it has been fun but I don't advise trying it. It is stiff work and likely to cause you a "heart and palpitations", and fish ponds are apt to end by being too deep on one side and too shallow on the other. I don't know why this should be. However, it does hold water, not a drop leaks out—a very vital thing for a fish pool.

We are planting things around it to grow quickly, and behind it cane which grows tall in a hurry. This will give us one private corner where we may shake off a feeling of being undressed in the street—you have had that dream?

Two important things have happened. First—the girls graduated last week from the Ransome School in Piedmont. I feel a little stunned by their accomplishment. You know that your children will be grown—in the distant future. Now, in the natural course of events, the future is here and it can not be so short a time as it seems to me since the morning they started out in the bus to Miss Talbot's kindergarten—leaving me in tears.

Carolyn took the History Scholarship prize and Clara, considering that she is eighteen months younger and much fonder of the pomps and vanities of this wicked world, came through better than we anticipated.

And that brings me to our second important development: your Grandpapa is to be a delegate to the National Democratic Convention at Madison Square Garden, New York—1924. We are all happy about this because it will interest him and take his thoughts from his business for a time at least. It's outrageously hard to find anything that does that. Marching up Fifth Avenue with the California Delegation, escorted by brass bands, with crowds lining the street will fill his soul with joy.

It is high time that he had a rest and vacation. We have all drawn heavily upon his resource and strength this past year. What with Carolyn's illness, moving us here and there after the fire, building the new house and upholding me in distressing perplexity about my family, it is not be wondered at if he is thoroughly tired out and perhaps a little weary of *us*!

This I understand, but after twenty years there is one thing I do not understand. It simply doesn't make sense:

I search wildly for some hint from Sigmund Freud—or Dr. Anthony, or even Dorothy Dix.

"Dear Dorothy Dix: my husband is a fine man—does not drink, smoke, nor swear (much!)—*But*!!"

But the truth is that while he is usually an altogether charming companion, just as I am convinced that matrimony is a secure and entrancing state—pouf! enters the Heavy Husband, very heavily, and without uttering a word makes it quite clear that I have fallen from Grace and been cast into Limbo. And, isn't it amusing?, the parrot withers me in the same manner by sitting silently on his perch with an air of scornful superiority!

I am undone by silence—and an attitude!

It seems probable that my stupidities are wholly responsible for General Lee's surrender at Appomattox; the San Francisco earthquake—and the impending strike of the Moulder's Union!

Poor Lady Jane Grey awaiting her execution in the Tower of London—stunned and judged guilty. Guilty of what? She didn't know and I don't know either, unless I am always guilty of something. Of being inept or tiresome, or just too great a dunce to cope with life in the twentieth century.

This is almost the only thing I do not like about your grandfather. Oh I am not going to let him off easily, so it is unfortunate that he is unlikely to write anything for you from his point of view. It would be more exciting. Having it all in my own hands does give me an advantage, but not the kind of advantage that helps me when silence continues day after day. A mauvais quart d'heure is one thing, and ten days of being in the center of an awkward situation, while trying to maintain the appearance of normal family life, is quite another.

All kinds of things arise and need to be discussed, but can't be—can't be explained, although other people are involved. All this ought to bounce harmlessly off of my aplomb, if I had any.

So here is an imperfection in the artistic success of our being married; an artistic success is what we would like to make of any career, I suppose. I was sure that we were going to come through with flying colors. I am still so sure that we might have—all things considered. That in my character, or in my qualifications for deft and skillful adjustment must be the reason for my imperfect achievement; a "psychotherapeutic and analytic reason," I mean. There is one for everything, they tell me, only it is so hard to put your finger on it.

Perhaps I am not spirited enough. It isn't my style, you know. Spirited people are likely to be high and mighty, and may degenerate into temper and end by wrecking the family.

Temper is considered very splendid in some situations, I believe, but I am always suspicious of it—ordinary and unintelligent, it seems to me, and a silly waste of time when we have so painfully little of it to waste. There may be people who can allow themselves to indulge in temper, people who have some wonderful thing to balance it. But it is useless for me to consider any such privilege available to me.

I put too much faith in a little theory of mine. One that I had worked out to my own satisfaction and proceeded to act upon and, what is worse, to count upon. It will have to be divided into A and B, and the A part began with being—whatever is the opposite of querulous, irritable or ill-humored.

This A part of my theory was based upon the conviction that being as reasonable and as cooperative as nature allows you to be is a sort of obligation upon all of us, as important as not growing too stout or too pious. Do you know, I still think it is an obligation, because here we all are caught on the same small sphere, forced to live together and dependent upon each other, whether we like it or not, and this is one thing we can each offer toward making the show run smoothly:—agreeable to your husband most of all because he has voluntarily assumed such a great deal: the whole weight of your existence: clothes and doctors, club dues, servants, nurses, and gasoline. He sees you morning—not at noon fortunately, unless he is a professor—and night, very often sick or ugly—even in curlers—poor man—poor man!! Yes, I certainly thought you could be very nice to husbands. It honestly did not enter my head that all this could be taken for a weakness of character, although that may be what it is.

And B—B was a naive little idea that marriage was actually an interchange of understanding and confidence, not confidences necessarily, each partner relying upon the good faith and good intentions of the other. Confidence, not in major matters only, but in every day matters too. Confidence in one's good faith, though possibly poor judgment, in asking the wrong people to tea, for example.

This confidence I thought being thoroughly understood and accepted, things could move comfortably along, allowing each of us a pleasant amount of personal liberty and individual development. And, dear me, how impossible it seemed that we should cramp each other's best style by a failure to give to each other the benefit of the doubt in the thousand trivial concerns of a daily routine—the little adjustments of taste and habit and bringing up.

Well, you can see what a foolish little theory this was to come boldly out into the world and expect to function with entire success—poor immature thing! I have not forgotten the very hour in which I discovered, quite suddenly, that it wasn't going to function with any success at all. Things are not like that. I met with a shocking setback. Why didn't I cry out: "Stop, something vital is being wrecked!" Just what I ought to have done, perhaps.

I still think it a sound basic theory for a satisfactory marriage. If you stick to it without foolish idealism, being prepared to face misunderstandings at a moments notice, it serves for weeks and months between glacial periods.

Here we are back to the reason why the glacial cycle should reappear abruptly in the midst of warmth, harmony, concord, tenderness, love?

At this point you are probably saying:

"Gad: What a smug ancestor we have! Why didn't she take a long look at herself?" Just what I am doing.

No one dislikes to admit her faults more than I do, but after giving it deep thought I must own that there are five or six little reasons—they look little and commonplace at first blush—which formulated and tabulated and set down in black and white, may come to something like that "psycho-therapeutic" and "analytic" reason.

I. My evil habit of sitting up, by myself, until one or two o'clock at night. Not without a struggle can I bring myself to surrender the day, with no assurance that another of equal happiness is to follow. To surrender it at the time when distractions and interruptions have ended—telephone calls, angling the car into a treacherous garage, only to find that it must be taken out again, so forth and so on—at the moment when ones brain begins to come alive and thoughts arouse themselves is asking too much!

II. My indiscretion in trying to talk about Florence Lilly's luncheon instead of explaining why I have forgotten, again, to send for Mr. Snooks, the plumber. It is too true, I *have* forgotten to send for Mr. Snooks. It is only fair to say that I frequently do forget.

It is easy to see how annoying this must be to an executive, who runs all kinds of important matters efficiently.

III. Lacking a commonsense approach to spending—and depending on—someone else's money. I have grown almost modern enough to believe—though by no means modern enough, or clever enough, to carry it out—that earning ones own way would make a better financial balance. It would give a valuable feeling of self respect, and avoid that first-of-the-month accounting, which I dread like a visit to the dentist.

IV. If I could only remember to lock the front door, to see that the cats don't sit on the wrong chairs, that the parrot does not eat the window casings or the legs of the grand piano.

V. This is the last and hardest to put into words. It has to do with forgetting myself and giving, instead of accepting. Giving freely and warmly in a relaxed manner, and not on guard against encountering a chill wind. It is the most difficult, but probably the most important thing of all!

As I came to the end of this lament, the telephone rang.

"I have work to do in the office tonight, can you join me for dinner at Marguard's? Bring along your latest Harper's and amuse yourself later while I work in quiet."

Of course I ran for the train! This has been a custom of ours for years, greatly interrupted since the fire by Clara's tonsils, Carolyn's sinus, Beth's appendix, and various other troubles, all quiet for the moment.

"I'll tear up everything I've written," I thought——but—I didn't!

SEPTEMBER. As it happened we began our new life at 1529 Hawthorne Terrace ten months from the day we escaped from it.

Here we are then, sans chairs, sans silver, sans dishes, sans rugs, "sans anything". This has led to a strange development—my unexpected popularity with gentlemen. To be sure they are all interior decorators, landscape gardeners or in the rug and furniture way. All of them are grieved to find that I have my own ideas. Such conceit is distressing to them. They are patient and regretful but firm—I must be brought to reason! "Now, Madame——the best houses in Piedmont——"

There is no accounting for the fact that we feel entirely at home here—until we look out the window. Then it is bewildering. As the house stands in exactly the position the old house stood in we half expect little familiar views to appear. It gives us a shock and pang each time to see a ruin of bricks and broken cement where my father's house stood next door, and sharpens our conviction that many pleasant and habitual things are done with forever—as indeed they are!

We moved in and the time was getting short in which to prepare Carolyn's clothes for college—dresses and suits and things for [sorority] rushing. Fortunately sewing is my bent (if I have one)! People need to express themselves and sewing expresses *me* while cooking and turning out a line of white, white [clean] clothes displays the skill of the more exemplary. For I have the impression that it is considered more virtuous to express oneself in a good meat loaf, a chocolate cake or sparkling clean windows than in the creation of a charming evening gown.

Well, anyway, in the basement of the Emporium is a table of what they call mill ends. If you close your ears to the noise and confusion and concentrate on them it is possible to find wonderful remnants of the best material. By putting my ingenuity to work with these I was able to turn out exciting costumes—originals, if not Molyneux or Schaparelli! It was fun to whiz along on my new (second hand) sewing machine from eight-thirty in the morning until five o'clock each day—with only a cracker and glass of sherry for lunch.

◇ *1925* ◇

MARCH 11. Another year has slipped through my fingers. A year since that evening when I sat down to see what could be done about this troublesome craving of mine to try my hand—or my head—at freeing my thoughts from disorder and getting them into sight, where I can look them in the eye and see whether I really think them, and if I do, why. I have wasted a powerful lot of time I guess, but I can't say I'm sorry because I have enjoyed it so much.

I remember the evening particularly because my Father was sitting with us reading French with the girls as he had from the time they were small girls and went to Miss Edmonds' French kindergarten: "Let me hear that vocabulary next—and be careful of your *u*—in lcur. It is not loor, you know, and of the *e* in leçon and cretonne. It is these little things that mark the difference between elegant and inelegant French—now that's enough for tonight, and I have a box of chocolates in my pocket."

I did not do well in school. I seemed to become confused somewhere along the way. That's fatal. If you don't understand things step by step you are lost.

Carolyn and Clara have made up to him for my inaptitude, because their heads are clever enough for them to manage all kinds of things. He studied and talked and read with them in a way most beautiful to see; "Should anything happen to them," I remember his saying once, "I should feel that the foundations of the universe were giving way." Carolyn, I think, and hope, is like him, not only in mentality, but in an indescribable, generous understanding. But her eyes can flash fire too. Louis Bromfield has said of a character in his novel *Early Autumn*, that she had a charm that could not be put into words: "Distinction was a part of it, and there was already about her the timelessness that envelopes a lady, no matter the generation in which she appears." I think that might be said of Carolyn.

Does all this sound "corny"? I don't mean to be corny, and I don't know that anything said with complete sincerity can be. But to speak affectionately of those you love for more than two hundred words, and at the same time give the ring of sincerity is no easy matter.

You know me well enough by this time to have some idea of my feelings at the doctor's office the other afternoon, when I heard her mumbling to herself, of course, but most awfully clearly; "um—maybe a tumor—it's just possible—no—yes—move a little this way, please—now let me see. Well I can tell better on Tuesday—Yes, come again on Tuesday Mrs. Whiting—Oh, don't be alarmed, nothing to worry about, very simple," *Sounds* all right doesn't it? But somehow I can't help suspecting that tumors may be a little like comets, not altogether to be counted upon to do the regular thing, whatever that may be, and I am sure I should much rather not have anything to do with them.

Until Tuesday—four days, four really devastating days and in the meantime, nothing to do but to scrape together such bits of courage as one may have. Now if grandfather were obliged to face an operation he would ignore it until the last moment, and then he would simply say, "en passant," "One moment, dear, until I have this appendix out—there—now what were you saying." Impossible heights for me to attain! And on Tuesday she had forgotten all about it, didn't mention it;—"Just a little displacement you see."—Why to be sure! You may depend upon it that I didn't mention it either, perish the thought—down in the elevator and home, almost as though I were escaping from the thing itself. But, you simply can't escape from the *idea* of a tumor. Well, doctors will be doctors.

It has occurred to me that if there is an after life for us we may continue existence on another planet. Perhaps we progress from one world to another according to our development, instead of transmigrating from animal to animal, as the Theosophists believe. I have never mentioned this to anyone for fear they might think it irreligious. I don't think it is. Didn't Christ say: "In my Father's House are many mansions?"

APRIL. It is fatal to linger in the garden these beautiful mornings. The plants are growing and blooming around the pool, covering a multitude of discrepencies in our bird fountain and Roman Seat. If the truth were known these are made from old slabs of cement and scraps of decoration that we rescued from the ruins and fitted together.

The goldfish are fat and happy and do not mind the pool's not being a Chinese pool, a Japanese nor an Italian pool, but just such as one might find in some old half abandoned garden.

Looking dreamily at flowers and goldfish is death to any kind of accomplishment. Pulling a few weeds, tying up one plant and cutting down another, the first thing you know you hear Companile [the University clocktower] ringing for twelve o'clock!

JULY. Clara has "flunked" the Geometry College Board. Awful isn't it? But, not quite so bad as it seemed, at first. When she came home after the examination and told me how impossible it was, I felt absurdly disappointed—not a matter of life and death, after all, only she will have such a wonderful time at college, if she once gets there. Then she really has studied hard all the spring in order to pass these tests and I feel that though she may not fully understand Geometry her mind is at the right point of development to undertake and enjoy interesting work in other lines. She will discover the value of it in later years, if not now, and will have the resources and diversions which result from abstract thought and from enlightenment. Perhaps she may need them very much sometime. I don't want either Carolyn or Clara to be unprepared to meet those years when the things that look so bright to them just now, begin to seem a little faded.

Just as we were at the lowest depth of depression, Grandfather came in, and braced us all up with "that way of his". He escorted Clara right down to see Miss Bridges and actually cajoled her into agreeing that she would give Clara her Geometry credits if the English and Algebra are high enough.

In the meantime, Clara is having a glorious time, visiting [her friend] Katharine L. "We are absolutely convinced, Mrs. Whiting", Katharine told me, a few days ago, "We are ab-so-lutely sure that ideal men do exist because we have known one, now for ten days. So we were right about marriages being ideal too, why we know of simply dozens, anyway, that are, and now, meeting this darling man—without a doubt, the darlingest man you ever could think of—I couldn't tell you how darling—well, we just *know*——". It isn't quite clear to me whether they both mean to marry the same man, and somehow share him between them—but I don't think that can be it. Perhaps twins can be found, alike in every smallest thing; because it hardly seems likely that two really separate men will ever appear to fill all the requirements, in *just* the right way—. Perhaps I am wrong! How nice it would be if I were, and all their dreams came true. But what a man—men I mean, it will take to play the part, because these are very clever little girls, and they will want the twins to be clever too; clever and cultivated and charming and well-bred and handsome. But they are right about one thing, I know, and that is in setting intellectual agreement and companionship, enjoying the same books and plays and people, as the very first and most important thing—right as right can be.

STILL JULY. How lamentable it is that we never do all the things we plan to do. I thought I was going to write a hundred and two letters yesterday—and in the end wrote only two—so that it is positively iniquitous for me to indulge myself in this "Secret Writing" today. My family is spending the weekend at Mortonwood [their country house]; I am alone—"and you will be able to accomplish so much", they said!

Such a time as we have had about Clara's credits—one day they seemed to be in order and on the next some further trouble developed, but this suspense is over and everything ready for [college].

Mount Vernon, N.Y. OCTOBER. Being a worldly person with a hankering for gaiety I jumped at an invitation to travel with a handsome man who has wonderful ideas about exciting hotels, Fifth Avenue, restaurants you read about in "Cafe Society", and Broadway—with the new fall plays.

We never accomplish all we plan for in New York or Washington, but I do *not* miss my visit to Mount Vernon. That's why I am sitting here this afternoon. Mount Vernon is not exciting. It doesn't need to be. It has its own individual charm, which has held its own for a hundred and fifty years with, or without, the approval of the Smart Set.

It has been a heavenly trip, except for one night on Lake Erie. Why are they called "lakes"? The Caspian Sea is not called a lake. It is a Sea, and the Great Lakes are Seas—lashing about like oceans!

It seems that Lake Erie has been placed by Providence in that exact location for the convenience of businessmen, to make a short cut from Detroit to Cleveland, which is what we wanted to do to get on to New York as soon as possible.

Everybody advised going by ship—"so if you think you *could* try a short voyage—"

Now when it is put to you like that you can not allow yourself to refuse, no matter how you dread it, or shake with a nervous chill on the way to the wharf. Your long suffering Grandfather was for changing the tickets and going by train even as the cab reached the pier. But I had made up my mind to see it through if it killed me.

The "short voyage" was pleasant at first because it began by passing smoothly down a river. You go to sleep thinking: "This isn't half bad, what was I afraid of?" It is when you wake about two in the morning——

At daylight I saw that we were approaching a city. "I don't

know what place this is", I said, waking the poor man again, "but I am getting off!" Fortunately it was Cleveland.

I know now for sure that I shall never see the Sphinx nor the Dyurdjura Mountains. I want to go abroad more than I want anything, except to stay off the ocean. The family will go without me. I shall stand on the Battery, or next to the Goddess of Liberty, and wave a sad farewell—unless there [was] a chance that if the doctor gave me a sleeping potion, and the band played all day—as they say it does—I might still be able to make it.

◇ *1926* ◇

FEBRUARY 15. Clara is stepping out with Jimmie Stewart [a fellow student at Berkeley]. Mothers are foolish people. There is in them so great a desire that their daughters may extract from young girlhood the maximum of thrill and unclouded gaiety, that they close their eyes to the threat of potential disaster arising in the wake of that skirmish known as being popular. I am one of them.

Some of the girls [her daughters' sorority sisters] are right down common! Some are very lovely, one feels in them the influence of mentality and breeding. In others these two essentials are conspicuous by their absence. To be without breeding is bad; to be without mentality is worse, but to be without either is horrible!

In saying this I do not express the view point of the [Sorority] House. Of the qualifications which count in "getting by the house" the most important is neither breeding, mentality, money, family, beauty or disposition. It is a flair for wearing clothes well and having dates. A university such as this [Berkeley] is a pattern of any democracy. To each one is rendered, with even handed impartiality, the recognition which is his due, as based upon that one thing alone—personality! Every man for himself, and the Devil, I suppose, takes the hindmost.

But I believe I like individuality better than I do personality, and making one's self felt because of it rather than by adopting and putting over ever so forcefully any one of the accepted "lines" so popular at the moment.

APRIL 26. Unhappily, man does not live by thrills alone; finals are beginning! No more peace of mind this semester.

MAY. Gale [nephew] appeared with a little book of essays, *This New World* it was called, or some such name; about twenty six essays, by Mr. Galsworthy, Mr. Simeon Grunsky, Mr. Gayley, and five or six other brilliant men. "Aunt Ethel", he said, " do you think *please*, that you could read this over before Monday and draw me up a little out-line of each essay——in just a few words, you know, setting out the main thought—so I could memorize them for the English final?" Ye Gods!! Out of the whole book the child hadn't caught a single idea by the tail! "Gale", I said, "My child, we'll make a stab at it". And that was about all we could do. We passed the final, but we can never be the same again. From then on by moving at a high rate of speed, we managed to pass things I had never dreamed of: Gale's Chemistry 2B, Clara's Greek 50—Philosophy 4B— Carolyn's History 2A—, Palentology 1A—Italian, French, and English A, B, C, D, E, F, and G. My poor head was in such a state that it wouldn't have surprised me to come upon Pithecanthropus and that Mr. Sapiens skipping merrily across the desert. . . .

Jazz is responsible for the wild state of the younger generation, they say. It is primitive——but there! Isn't there an éclat for the primitive, the Aboriginal, the unrestrained?

A psychiatrist tells us that Jazz makes its appeal to those who fail to find contest in normal, wholesome activities. It thrills them and acts as a stimulant on their nerves.

A thrill is a thrill for all that. One does not *ask* for a thrill— suddenly it is upon one, and they are too few and hard to come by for me to turn one down. I have heard Papa say that some of us *are* sub-normal, running a trifle below par all the time, so that we actually need some little stimulant to bring us even with the rest of you. It is our misfortune because it opens the way for a thousand little blue devils of melancholy to creep in and lay us low.

If the rhythmic beat of Jazz fills us with the zest and vitality to turn handsprings on the living room rug is it strange that we enjoy it?

Of course, you are wondering what possible benefit society could derive from our turning handsprings on the living room rug—or anywhere—. No there is nothing for society *in that*, I admit, and anyway, I have never been able to get all the way over—but, failing the handsprings, the same vitality is enough to start me on a fresh and joyous spell of cleaning house, mending clothes, writing letters, returning calls! If these fantastic and bizarre cadences give the inspiration to accomplish things——to live——does it really matter why?

DECEMBER 27. Your Grandfather's Christmas present from Janet and Erica [daughters' friends] was a gorgeous pink shirt. A beautiful horse-shoe of diamonds—from the five and ten—was pinned upon its bosom and the expression on his face as he opened the package and debated whether to laugh or to thank them properly, was funny to see. It must be a joke, he knew, but they looked serious and hoped he would like it—it isn't often that he is taken aback. I tell you this to explain how he came by his name "The Unknown" which we shall call him after this until a better one turns up. When dinner time came, he dressed himself up in his white flannel Florida trousers, tuxedo coat, the pink shirt and diamond horse shoe. Wearing a small black mask he slipped out the back way and ringing the front doorbell had himself announced to the assembled guests very grandly "—Enter the Unknown." "The Unknown." They all pounced on it and I can see that it is going to stick.

◇ *1927* ◇

What a pity it is that I have not written a well-organized diary with daily happenings in their proper sequence.

"*JULY 28th* —All drove to Mortonwood this morning, took along a leg of mutton and twelve artichokes. Found windmill out of order. Discovered Archer [nephew] does not like artichokes."

"*SEPTEMBER 13th* —bought black dress—white fur collar and cuffs—real ermine but I fear it is taken for rabbit. Met Florence, ate luncheon at Russian Tea Room, caught five fifteen boat home."

"*OCTOBER 31st* —New terrace below fish pool finished."

"*NOVEMBER 1st* —too cold and windy to sit on it—etc., etc."

Well, it's no good talking about that now, because I haven't.

◇ *1928* ◇

1924——1925——1926——1927——1928!

This is January 1928!

And, of my heart and palpitations—*this* is where the plot begins to thicken: Clara sat on my bed as I dressed to go out this afternoon, recounting to me in her delightful way the little adventures of her morning on the campus: how Mr. Chauncey Wells considers Walt Whitman a great poet; how the half-Oriental, but wholly fascinating and dangerous Mr. Pett, had been smilingly disdainful of her mental fitness to grasp the profound mysteries of his course in Buddhist philosophy. . . . How the entirely Oriental Mr. Chew had insisted that 160 Chinese characters were none too many to master in three weeks . . . "and I'm thinking of getting married in November, Mom . . . . . . Jimmy Stewart . . . . ."

. . . . . Twice I went under, but the third time I clutched at reality, gasped for breath and came up . . . smiling! What does one answer to a sudden thing like that? "But *are* you so surprised Mamma? You must have known" Yes, yes, I must have known—more or less—rather more than less to be sure!

Ah me! What does one answer, feeling a chill of dread? Must one answer happily? Delicately—Yes—understandingly—not to cast so much as the shadow of a doubt upon, or wound, the frail texture of romance (or belief or confidence in romance). Let us turn back for a moment. What was it they said, Clara and Kathryn L.? "He must be clever, cultivated, mature and charming—well-bred and intellectually companionable (above *all*), liking the same books and plays and people—" That's what they said.

Well, it was too much to expect. I wondered at the time, you recall, where even *one* such man was to be found—one doesn't meet them every day. And now we have Jimmy Stewart, good-looking with an engaging manner—but oh so young—young—young. Does one marry a little boy—barely beyond delivering the Berkeley Daily Gazette? Plenty of time, I suppose, for character to develop—but meanwhile, who knows? A husband should be at least three years older, I think, than his wife. The Unknown is seven years older than I am and it isn't a day too much. You *depend* on a husband and you need someone older who can take hold in a crisis. You don't lean on a boy whose entire experience is football and dancing.

How is your grandfather going to take it? Not too well I fear. He has his own ideas, has the Unknown. And so, of course, have all of us. There's no telling whether they are right or wrong. Ideas and beliefs can make themselves appear so right, so reasonable, so conclusive. One puts trust and faith in them through the years and then suddenly finds them out of date.

Whether it is distrust of my own convictions that makes me so hesitant about advising people—even my own children—and interfering with their plans, or whether it is because of being pure bone lazy, I do not know. I do not think I can interfere with Clara. I could not do it tactfully or skillfully. "You want me to be happy, don't you?" Yes—I want her to be happy. This is a very risky business and whatever course I take I shall probably regret.

She must live her own life, she says (and we must live it with her!) I am thankful that November is still ten months off—nevertheless, I understand perfectly that Fate is sticking her tongue out at me, and she needn't think I don't see her!

. . . . And Carolyn? . . . . . This is the year for Carolyn to graduate—from college this time! She has high ambitions to experiment with—being secretary to the Caliph of Bagdad, I think, only Caliphs have ceased to rule in Bagdad; but something like that. Very exciting and quite possible for Carolyn. She knows how to do things, important things, though tenth assistant secretary to some legation under secretary will probably be more like it. It is my opinion that she will find the career of even a tenth assistant secretary carries with it more prestige than any one of us is able to command by reason of our standing as a wife or a mother.

Cooking, walking the floor with sleepless babies, nursing sick children, is not sensational work. It can be done by tender, loving, capable—But alas! tiresome women. Whereas it is beyond imagination that a tiresome person could be Secretary to the Caliph of Bagdad.

What we need is a publicity agent to dramatize our activities. Somebody like Thomas à Becket in the reign of Henry the Second. Remember him? He stole the show from the king himself by moving about London with an entourage of two hundred singing boys in scarlet robes and twenty horses caprisoned in gold and silver trappings. That would be more fun than giving lectures on the Motivation of Parenthood—whatever that means—as one of my friends is doing.

MARCH 1. Clara has gone to bed with a temperature, the "flu" I suppose.

MARCH 3. Clara is really sick and I am worried to death. Her temperature is high—103—and she has a sore throat. Dr. W. doesn't seem to know what is wrong.

MARCH 4. Good Heavens! Dr. W. thinks it may be scarlet fever!

MARCH 6. It could not have been scarlet fever—temperature all gone. I feel ten years younger!

MARCH 9. It was scarlet fever or scarletina! This is what happened—if there could be anything funny about such a miserable fright *this* is funny—"Clara's all in the clear now," Dr. W. said, on Saturday morning, "just a scare, no more temperature, no eruption—by the way I have those two cases of apricot brandy for Mr. Whiting. Suppose you meet me first thing Monday morning in front of the Baby Hospital. I can slip them into your car and no one will know the difference."

"I will be there," I said, and I was there, waiting, when she drove up.

"Better follow me around the corner," she whispered, "too many doctors about."

Whereupon, with due mystery and caution, we very stealthily slipped the contraband from her car to mine and hid it under the robe.

"All right," said Dr. W. "Drive straight home, don't get out, don't leave the car, don't have an accident! If anything does happen say this stuff isn't yours and you have *no idea* where it came from. Call me if you get arrested! How's Clara this morning?"

"Quite all right—coming down to breakfast". I started on my perilous way. Nothing happened. But as I came up the front walk Carolyn came rushing down in a state of high excitement.

"Hurry, Mom, something awful is the matter—Clara's all broken out."

Well of course I rushed to the telephone. "Dr. W. isn't in," the nurse said. "I know where she is. Please get her," I urged, "at the Baby Hospital and ask her to call Mrs. Whiting at once."

In ten minutes she was gasping "Yes, Mrs. Whiting?"

"Clara has scarlet fever after all, she's all broken out," I managed to tell her, forgetting, in my distress all about the apricot brandy.

"Thank God!" she said, "Thank God! I thought you must be in jail!!"

JUNE 15. Oh my heart and palpitations indeed! Something else has happened—something agitating. Next Sunday will be Clara's Birthday and Jimmie Stewart wants to give her a ring. He wants to give her a diamond ring! He planned to talk to the Unknown this afternoon because he goes back to Petaluma tonight.* He wanted me to manage it for him. But there wasn't any chance, so now, he wants me to advise him! This is the time for me to do *something*. But I don't know what to do. I'm

---

* Jimmie Stewart was from Petaluma, a small town north of Berkeley.

no kind of a person to get mixed up in a thing like this. My gracious, when I think of it I'm all in a panic.

"Now look here, Jimmie Stewart," I could say, "this is all nonsense, you and Clara—" so on and so on. Or I could give the Unknown a warning. "Prenez gard!" I could say, because the Unknown is quite in the dark about January 28th. But you see when I think of Clara's confidence in her happiness, it seems too much like treachery. I am going to advise Jimmie to write— I can *feel* that I am—and then sit back and watch the Unknown struck all of a heap. Oh dear, Oh dear!

JUNE 23. You have never seen anyone so happy as Clara is. She is radiant. What a Birthday! She has a ring—she is engaged—she is engaged to Jimmie!

The little white cards are being made ready with the news to shower down on her friends, and on Saturday we are all set to make the thrilling announcement.

It was a long talk the Unknown gave those two—and a serious one, but he was taken at a disadvantage. Permission to give the ring with all that it implies had already been given. It had to be given hurriedly—if reluctantly—by letters because of Clara's Birthday. They have agreed to make no definite plans for a— long—long time.

AUGUST 10. The Unknown is greatly troubled—Clara is not going back to college. "No, no, no!"

AUGUST 15. Nannie Does Something About Something.

(And feels like a fool)

I hate to tell you what happened at Mortonwood on Sunday. I'd much rather not tell you but I think I ought for the good of my soul. I forgot all about being attractive, flew into a nasty, awful rage and made myself ridiculous! I think I had reason to be angry, but having a reason doesn't console one for making a spectacle of one's self and knowing it.

I came out unexpectedly and found the whole crowd shouting and laughing because they thought it funny to see those miserable boys [guests] playing at battledore and shuttlecock with our newly decorated chairs. From the platform they tossed them to Gus and Archer on the balcony above. When they caught them these two tossed them and back when they missed they crashed back on the floor. If the rungs and backs were splintered—that was just too bad!

"Well—they were only country chairs," as Aunt Bernie said. But they were the chairs that Carolyn and I had made so beautiful! With their gay colors they made a difference at Mortonwood and we thought them a real master stroke. They all knew that. It sounds silly, but working on them together with so much interest had given us a kind of feeling for these chairs and the anger that took possession of me had in it something that I might have felt had it been a living thing of mine they were tormenting. I asked them to stop but they were going strong and saw no reason to humor me. "Very well," I said, shaking with a nervous chill, "Frank [brother in-law] will you help me chop down Archer's target and level off that hideous hill he has it on. It's too near the house, it spoils a charming little glade and since he seems to enjoy destroying—for no reason at all—something he knows I like I shall give myself the pleasure of getting rid of the old eye-sore." My teeth chattered but I said it. That stopped them—they stood with their mouths open while Uncle Frank pushed back the squeaky doors of the woodhouse to get the axe and rakes. In silence, like axmen walking to an execution, we moved together to the doomed target, knocked it to pieces, raked over the ground and put the tools away. Everybody looked ashamed (for me). I heard Ave Maria [niece] say: "That was mean!"

"They were only country chairs," Aunt Bernie was saying.

The culprits disappeared in all directions and I went upstairs and had a spell of nausea. There!—now you know.

NOVEMBER 11. Clara was married yesterday—"but Papa we have waited a long time", she argued (almost five months!) It is a strange experience to have your daughter—to have your Clara married. You don't take it in—you do, and you don't.

You wake pretty early because you care so much that the thing you have to do shall be carried through in a characteristic manner. I wish I could make you understand why. It isn't going to be easy to do that. I might make use of a quaint saying of the old South: "I have it to do" but you would think that non-sense. "Why did Nannie 'have it to do', just because it had always been done?" you would say. "Is that a reason?" But that isn't quite it: it isn't simply an obligation. It is more than that. "Why do you bother?" your friends ask. "They don't do things that way now-a-days." "Don't they?" You don't explain that it can make no earthly difference how "they" do things.

You see your family has had a way of "doing things". It is born in you or bred in your bones to know what that way is.

And it is vital to you that this wedding should be in keeping with and—well—a part of or a prolongation of other great occasions which have gone into your make-up.

So you must infuse a certain spirit into Clara's wedding. A spirit made up of dignity, simplicity, festivity and elegance. It must have *tone*—and a bit of dash.

No wonder you wake early! Not that waking before the dawn would do you one single bit of good were it not for a consideration of prime importance: The Unknown is backing you up! His ideas of weddings and yours coincide. That's important.

Almost time!

The Unknown is getting into his striped trousers and his beautiful long frock coat. He looks magnificent!

"How about a good stiff drink?" he says, his eyes twinkling, the way they do. "Your dress is stunning, I like it—your hat is a knock-out too—here you are, 'Happy days.' Keep your head now, don't get all upset".

"Are you almost ready, Darling?" "Nannie's diamond cross! How could I have forgotten that? Just a second, let me pin it here—".

"How heavenly you are! How simply heavenly! a drop of whiskey, dear?"

"No moms, of course not, I'm perfectly all right. Everything's all right." Is it?—If only it is!

Suppose the church should be half empty!

Just suppose it should! But it is not.

"Shall we go first, Mrs. Whiting?" And then you see that it is filled.

"Look me over again, am I all right? Moms—you promised you would not cry!"

"Absolutely not!"

"But you are crying."

"There! He's ending the serenade, the wedding march will be beginning."

Gale steps over to meet you—"Here you go Aunt Ethel—left arm"—You are walking up the aisle at Clara's wedding! At Clara's wedding? "Take it easy, take it easy, why you are trembling." You feel again the warm affection of your father's voice, his encouraging little squeeze on your arm—a long time ago that was—twenty-four years ago.

—a sudden feeling of emerging from an anesthetic—Mr. Hodgkin [the minister] stepping forward as calmly as though it were just any wedding—everybody standing—

Your heart leaps up, it seems to turn right over, and then to stop. Why on earth should it? Why because this is Clara's wedding! This is Clara floating by on the Unknown's arm.

"Who giveth this woman to be married to this man?" "I do". the Unknown says——swept along by fate, unwillingly—almost accidentally, but inevitably. "I do".

Clara and Jimmie stepping briskly down the aisle, bowing radiantly to the right and the left, on their way to—what?

You and the Unknown step out too—the organist is playing that march from "Aieda". And just for one second you have the same feeling you had the time you found yourself leading the Grand March at the Policeman's Ball. It was the last thing you had expected to do in this world, but someone thrust a sheaf of flowers upon you, the band struck up and off you went!

"How do you do? How do you do? My dear—marvelous to see you—yes, twenty-four years ago—the very same church—the same Mr. Hodgkin—they do look happy don't they?"—

You look at the Unknown—the Unknown looks at you. You two are sitting there, alone, in the living room. "Well," he says, "There we are—and I'm hungry!"

Hungry! Why of course, starving! You begin to think how terribly hungry you are yourself.

The front door opens and Dan H. walks in. "Hello there you two, I had a hunch you'd be left sitting here like this. Gosh, what a swell wedding you threw! Come on over to our house. Where is Carolyn? Off with the crowd?"

"No, locked in her room crying because her sister is married and gone forever!"

"I will get her out of this—Ruth's fixing high-balls and fried ham and eggs. There are some peas she is going to warm up too. Come on, let's go. I bet neither one of you ate a thing."

. . . . Fried ham and eggs and warmed over peas and high-balls—how too, too utterly divine!

DECEMBER 11. Clara knows all about handling an apartment. We didn't know she did. If you had asked me I should have said. "No, not a thing, and what is *more*, She isn't interested."

Which ought to be a lesson to me. And it is; lesson number one. For her apartment is altogether right; funny little Petaluma apartment that it is.

She has handled it with unbelieveable skill. She has been so crafty about placing her lovely things that they seem to have formed an entente cordiale with the small town wood work and walls. The result is surprisingly nice and—oh different. She isn't sunk in the mire of Petaluma mediocrity as deeply as I thought she would be.

⌔ *1929* ⌔

JANUARY 1. Carolyn came walking up the walk at eight o'clock this morning, trailing her evening gown, its flashing rhinestone brilliants a trifle dimmed by the winter morning light; Aunt Bernie was shocked to see people in evening clothes at that hour; "Well you never know!——Staying out all night, why that is the last thing"——I guess I had just the same idea two or three years ago. In our day it *was* the last thing——but as I have said "tempora muntantur"—and I have accepted the fact that three times a year, on New Year's Eve, after the big game and on the night of the Inter Fraternity Assembly you may dance all night if you want to and come home when you are ready. It's an unwritten law.

Interlude

(Tempora muntantur has led to my going back over that first writing I did so many years ago—and my Heavens and Earth how Tempora has muntantured! All these collegiate things, not coming home and going respectably to bed—and so on, eight years ago I shouldn't have liked them; but really it is not any darker at three than it is at eleven, is it? If enough people choose to keep going there isn't any difference between ten o'clock and four or five o'clock.)

JUNE 1. New York was as roaring and hysterical as ever, stock market riding high, speakeasies running full blast—thick as peewee golf courses in California. You knock on a hidden door, give the pass word and the counter sign, and in you go. Only we didn't.

We did have cocktails served in bouillon cups at the Café Nino—very hush hush. Eaten with a spoon, old fashioneds are still old fashioneds.

Of course Carolyn and I took the Fifth Avenue bus down to Fourth Street and sat in Washington Square, then walked on through Greenwich Village. From there we took the Sixth Avenue Elevated down to the Battery. This ride in the front seats of the upper deck of the bus, plunging headlong through the excitement of Fifth Avenue, is something we never miss. Nor quaint old Washington Square, nor the walk through Greenwich Village and the trip on the "El" through the slums, and finally the quiet hour sitting on the Battery watching the great ships from Europe passing in and out.

AUGUST 9. Mortonwood. Last night when Clara and Jimmie got here they handed me a big box of candy. Now I don't eat candy, but people often bring it to Mortonwood. So I put it away and thought nothing of it. Only, Clara did say, "Open this when you and Papa are alone!" That ought to have made me curious enough to do it right away, but it didn't and I forgot it.

"Haven't you opened your candy, Moms!" Clara said this morning. Of course I knew then that something was up so I hurried upstairs where the Unknown was shaving and there, inside the cover, was a card, "Congratulations to Grandma and Grandpa—April 1930" ! ! ! ! ! ! ! ! ! ! ! ! ! ! !

OCTOBER 12. Never was anyone in such bounding health as Clara is. No headaches, no backaches, no nausea—*no nausea!* Nothing even faintly unpleasant. Isn't it unbelievable?

Petaluma, OCTOBER 24. Your bassinet is finished, white point D'esprit over pink, with ruffles. I have just tied the last bow and now I'm going home.

Clara and I have a good time. We call you "Little What Not," ("little whoozit", they would say this year) and everything is about ready for you even if you aren't coming until March—or April first, the doctor says.

I can't help hoping you will be a girl—a granddaughter. It is boys who thrill the rest of the world, but my heart goes pit a pat for girls—and I want you to be one. Clara is taking the waves so beautifully. Can this hold out to the end? It seems too good to be natural. "If that isn't just like you", the Unknown says.

The stock market crashed yesterday. Wonder if it is that "fall" we were riding for? I called up the Unknown to buy me one share of Trans America at thirty five. It dropped from *seventy two.* If it only reaches fifty again it will buy me tickets to all the football games this fall. Kathryn and Beth and Carolyn were buying too; everybody is—"shopping for bargains", which ought to send things up in a hurry. But it means ruin for thousands—that drop.

It seems that we have lived through the "Roaring Twenties" without knowing that they were Roaring, gay, abandoned, cynical, and disillusioned!! That's what they say!

◇ *1930* ◇

The New Hotel Petalauma. MARCH 23. Petaluma—Long ago it was the place where we spent the night when we sailed up the Petaluma Creek with Uncle George on his yacht and the yacht got stuck in the mud. Nothing could be done until the tide came up and floated her off. And that is *all* that it was—the place where every so often the Caprice got stuck in the mud. Beyond that for us, it had no existence—the place where we waited, waited for the tide to turn.

Years later, but still before the roads were made for automobiles, it was the place where we left the North Western Pacific Train and waited for the inter-urban trolly to Sebastopol on the journey to Mortonwood. By that time it was almost noon so we settled down to eat a picnic lunch. It was fun because we were all together; we sat on a lumber pile in the station yard and Daddy brought ice cold beer from the brewery across the way—crackers and cheese and beer. The children had a glorious time.

Did people live in Petaluma and pursue the daily course of their lives? I didn't give them a thought. It was the place where we waited for the trolly!

Ten years after that it was a place where the signals held us up on Sunday afternoon—kept us waiting for ten or fifteen minutes because the line was so long, and very likely made us miss a Richmond Ferry.

Now—now it is the place where I am waiting for my grandchild to be born! ! !

A few minutes ago, sitting here, it flashed across me that it is all the same Petaluma—where the tide left us high and dry, where we waited for the trolly, where the signals slowed us down. I see that this Petaluma is a place in its own right, with a life apart from shifting scenes and manipulating settings—because my child lives here.

MARCH 26. Don't think I am being an old busy-body. I swear that I am not, but since my child does live here and can't help being involved with the people of the town it is vital to me to know what manner of people they are.

Clara really loves the country; she has an eye for every bit of beauty it holds—the wild flowers, the lovely morning freshness—"Doesn't the cry of the jay birds send a strange shiver of elation through you Moms?" It does!

It interests her to walk through the lanes, chatting with old timey characters she comes across—a quaint Scotch gardener, and the Irish woman who spares an hour each morning from her rocky, hilly bit of land to clean out Clara's house.

These people are genuine: but when it comes to "the people one knows" I can see nothing in any one of them to justify the theory that it is in the small towns one finds the good, wholesome, substantial Americans—the very backbone of the nation. Coyotes—more like—with their dull spiritless eyes, dressed up and trying for sophistication—their tails in plain sight all the time.

They drink as much as anybody else and conduct themselves in the worst possible manner at parties. Their conversation is narrowed to their own limited interests and if there is anything of good sense and plain wholesome simplicity about them they keep it pretty well under.

Don't worry—I have no idea of saying this to Clara. I'm not trying to make her discontented. But—daughters matter so much—Clara matters!

APRIL 1. Clara calls me every morning about nine o'clock, just as I come up from breakfast. We talk over what we are going to do—shall I go out to lunch with her or is she coming down to the Hotel? Or shall we finish that last small slip of "Little What Not"? Yesterday we played bridge—rather late. This morning she didn't call me. I thought she must be out in the fields picking buttercups and lupin to fix in a stunning blue bowl she has, but at quarter to ten I still hadn't heard from her. Dr. Lumsden had said: "Your baby may come on the first"— and, my darling, you had come! ! !

"Mrs. Stewart is in the delivery room" the doctor's office told me. And then, almost as I turned from the telephone, my head whirling, unreality making my familiar room all strange and upside-down, there was your father's voice: "Duchess, you have a granddaughter!"

APRIL 2. —A granddaughter, a tiny speck with great dark eyes, at whom the nurse allows you to look for just so long— "and how you do look, Moms," Clara says. Margaret Carolyn Stewart, my precious Peggy Carol!

They came to see you today, the Unknown and Carolyn. The Unknown looked at you too—with such a look. He isn't ready for you; he didn't plan you; you didn't ask his advice. You weren't his idea and you didn't even take the trouble to make him think you were. You just came along; that wasn't very tactful. And now you lie there sucking your thumbs without pretending to apologise. You will have to make your own way with the Unknown, my pet.

◇   ◇

Afterword

With the birth of Peggy Carol, the journal's imagined audience becomes real. A new kind of entry appears: "Thursday. Closed your mouth firmly against spinach at noon today. How could we make you take it? You laughed and shrieked and rocked your high chair precariously." (March 1931)

Ethel Whiting continued to write for the next nine years, recording family events (the birth of Peggy Carol's brother, Archer, in 1931; the marriage of Clara to Sydney Murman in 1932), discussions of the books she read and her busy social life. More and more, however, she wrote about a new fascination: politics.

Hyer Whiting had been prominent in the local Democratic Party for many years, and, beginning with an October 1931 visit to Washington, the journal records the couple's work towards the nomination and election of Franklin Roosevelt.

On March 5, 1935, Ethel Whiting re-read one of her first journal entries. She had written in 1924, "Forty-two: I don't like it very much. It gives me the queer feeling that though there may be another act . . . it will naturally have only the *falling action* to offer us."

"How wrong I was!" she admitted, for she considered the intervening years, the time between the ages of 42 and 53, among the most exciting of her life.

Although he never ran for political office, Hyer Whiting served on many important state and national committees. He became a close friend of Roosevelt and the members of his administration, giving his wife an excellent vantage point for observation. Her journal records frequent trips to Washington for ceremonies and consultations, the hard work of campaigns and the stimulation of heated political discussion. She studied the issues thoroughly and often debated their pros and cons in her journal.

But the continuity of this record is abruptly broken, for Henry Hyer Whiting died of a heart attack on July 6, 1939. Ethel Whiting continued to make sporadic entries through the 1950's; the newspaper clippings pasted in the diary show that she continued to read widely and have a lively interest in current affairs until the end of her life. She died in 1974 at the age of 92.

The original journal is still treasured by her granddaughter, Margaret (Peggy Carol) Oxley, a teacher whose four children Ethel Whiting lived to see. A microfilm copy of the manuscript is in the Bancroft Library at the University of California, Berkeley.

THE DIARY OF

Deborah Norris Logan

Germantown, Pennsylvania
1832–1839

Deborah Norris Logan (*The Historical Society of Pennsylvania*)

◇   ◇

Introduction

Deborah Norris Logan, born in Philadelphia in 1761, was a Quaker descended from several of the leading families of colonial Pennsylvania. The only girl among four children, she was raised by a widowed mother who was a prominent figure in the community.

Many of the nation's founders were guests in the Norris home. Their Chestnut Street mansion was adjacent to the State House, an ideal location for observation. The young Deborah had opportunities to witness, firsthand, many of the important events surrounding her nation's birth—including the first reading of the Declaration of Independence, heard from her front yard when she was fourteen.

Debby Norris attended Anthony Benezet's excellent Friends' Girls School, where she evidently was not overly interested in study. Soon afterwards, however, she began a serious self-imposed course of reading which she continued throughout her life.

She was married at nineteen to George Logan, a physician and agriculturalist who later became a United States Senator. They had three sons: Gustavus, who to her continuing sorrow, died at age thirteen; Algernon, who remained a bachelor and lived with his mother all his life; and Albanus, who eventually settled nearby with his wife, Maria, and their children.

At Stenton, the Germantown mansion which had been built in 1723–30 by her husband's grandfather James Logan, Deborah Logan ran a large and complicated household with many servants and a constant stream of visitors. Stenton had one of the best libraries in America at that time, and there she indulged her interests in history, literature, astronomy and other subjects.

Deborah Logan, unlike many of the Quakers of her time, adhered to the Quaker ideals of thrift and simplicity. Although she had servants, she did a good deal of household work herself. "My favorite amusements," she wrote, "are gardening, writing, and reading." Scholarly pursuits were a great source of pleasure, and her researches into Pennsylvania's early history preserved valuable material. She was elected the first female member of the Historical Society of Pennsylvania.

At Stenton, Logan discovered a series of letters between William Penn and James Logan, who had been his secretary. Transcribing and editing the crumbling letters was a massive task, but Logan completed the work, a total of eleven manuscript volumes, by rising every day before dawn.

Logan began keeping a diary when she was fifty-four, intending to record "whatever I shall hear of fact or anecdote that shall appear worthy of preservation. And many things for my own satisfaction likewise that may be irrelevant to others."

After her husband's death in 1821, the journal became an increasing source of comfort and companionship. "The habit of writing in a diary," she noted four years later, "has now become so familiar that I seem lost without resorting to it."

◇ *1832* ◇

MARCH 1. I wish the ceremony of opening the new book was over and I had gotten over the reluctance of spoiling its purity with ugly scrawls. For this is how I perceive my writing will appear with such instruments as the present family of pens. This might look like a pun considering how much I have written about the founding family of Pennsylvania.

MARCH 3. It would have been a pleasure to have the visit of an intelligent friend.

MARCH 11. The blackbirds have come to their old homes in the hemlock avenue. The new gardener wanted to know if he could shoot them but was told by no means. The bluebirds have cheered me with their songs. Reddy [pet bird] has been hung out and the mocking bird has warbled his notes in the dining room. In short, it is like spring.

MARCH 27. I noticed the last patches of snow laying about. Now all has disappeared and green begins to predominate. Welcome spring. We have indeed passed through a northern winter and I am glad that it is over.

MARCH 30. The day was not very satisfactory to me. Things were not ordered to my mind and my niece [Hepsy Norris, who was then living with her] would not exert herself to have them otherwise. She might have easily accomplished this. But such things are of no importance when one glances at misfortune. However, it is well to have things as they should be.

APRIL 1. A very improper hoax was played in Germantown by making a smoke with brush and sending a boy on horseback crying fire down the street. This induced men dressed in their best clothes to take up their engines. They were then hooted at as April fools. I reflected that if the place had been incorporated and a good police established none would have dared play such a trick on the inhabitants.

APRIL 10. [Anniversary of the death of Logan's husband eleven years before.] My mind is sad at the present season. I wish I had Sarah [Walker, a young friend] with me. She understands me and can best assist with her quiet manner. But so it is. She is far away.

APRIL 26. Few, even younger ladies, have more notices and attentions in society than myself. I am waited upon, invited out and listened to with most flattering kindness. I should be unreasonable indeed not to be pleased when I find myself surrounded by polite friends. Yet, in the midst of all this I often reflect upon the counterbalances which I know of. I seek in humility to know myself and to acknowledge that I am blessed beyond my deserts. I must try to be more worthy.

MAY 6. I was not very well and felt weak and good for nothing. Now I experience what my beloved husband felt in his weakness. He had me to comfort and support him. Oh I am glad I did all I could for him. Yet if it were possible to have been one hundred times more devoted I wish I had been so.

MAY 13. My young lady [Hepsy] got into her conveyance by six o'clock. Away they went as light and lively as imagination can paint the reality. Oh if she lives she will often think of these little snatches of pleasure and maybe wish to think kindly of the poor old relation who loved to promote the happiness and innocent pleasures of all those around her.

I strolled down to the inclosure [family graveyard] and was made very sensible of my decline and weakness. I was almost unable to ascend the little acclivities in my path. But I had a pleasant, solitary walk and got some apple blossoms and wild flowers. When I returned to the house my two sons joined me and we had a pleasant conversation over our tea.

MAY 18. I am sitting by the south window in the dining room looking at the dogwood trees. Many years ago I planted them by my own hand; I brought them out of the woods and gave them that location. There is a great pleasure in seeing what you have planted and treasured flourish. I wish that I had prepared even more for my entertainment.

MAY 27. My son [Albanus] dined here with Mary and Dickinson [her grandchildren]. While we were conversing in the dining room there was a knock, knock as children say and Mrs. Morris entered with Margaretta, the little granddaughter, and a younger grandson. So there was bustle enough. But everyone stayed to tea. As Beck [a servant] remarked afterwards, "that little girl and boy ate all the cakes. They mounched and mounched and mounched." A classical line, my dear reader!

JUNE 9. My view to the westward now meets the odious railroad. Even now when I am a little used to the invasion can I scarcely bear to look upon the intruder. And it may justly be asked, "Of what great public utility is it to be?" Is the answer to carry backwards and forwards cumbersome machines drawn by one oppressed animal which are filled with passengers whom the novelty of "something new" has attracted? One would have at least hoped that the president of the company would have had greater regard for the horses. But even this is wanting. And now I suppose their great inducement is to make all the money they can. Then they will sell out and the road will remain a monument to their folly.

JUNE 16. I have just received a visit from a very young man who promises to be worthy. He is Peter McCall. I believe I gratified him by taking him up to the library and showing him some of its contents.

I would not be vain but it is somewhat gratifying that an intelligent young man should covet an introduction to an old woman; one who hates fashion, lives in the past rather than the present, and who consequently does not make parties where he might meet the gay and beautiful.

JUNE 30. It is impossible to keep pace with things any longer. I am scarcely in a position to write. I have boils and sore fingers, a very unusual countenance for me. We have company every day and a great deal to do.

JULY 6. I cannot help observing that changes in the modes and operations of life are not at all suited to the quiet and care which old age covets. And these abominable careless and slothful [servant] girls of mine who neglect and—but I will not complain for it is no remedy.

JULY 18. I am feeling very poorly and I am hardly able to hold up my head. And Lodge [dog] is also sick. He recognized us and wagged his tail but would neither eat nor drink.

JULY 20. Dr. Betton kindly came to see me when he heard I was unwell. He said I have had a little fever. But I was better when he saw me. Lodge was with me all day and all night. He is a very sick dog.

AUGUST 23. I spent the afternoon writing in the library alone. Then I took a pleasant stroll, got grass seed for the birds and material for the flower pots. I drank tea alone with Lodge as my waiter (waiting for every bit he saw me take). As soon as it was dark I lighted my lamp to sew and made a cap and a towel.

AUGUST 29. I was at the inclosure where my evergreens and indeed everything I have planted grow luxuriously. I have been looking over Sister Fisher's diaries [Sarah Logan Fisher, her sister-in-law]. They are full of *excessive* tender expressions towards her husband and children, *too* minute details of sickness and anxiety of various kinds and unhappy Tory sentiments and wishes. I would certainly obliterate these were the books mine. She has written in the most kind and partial manner about me. But it all led to the reflection of man's walking in vain show. How transitory and what a mere shadow does the past appear! I had to think this as I stood beside the grave of my husband.

SEPTEMBER 17. Our folks are busy washing. Algernon [a grown son who lived with her] has gone to town and Hepsey to visit a sick neighbor. I am (where I most covet to be) in the library with Lodge sleeping on the floor and the shutters darkened as in summer time.

What a pity! Liddy Jones is here and wants to see me. She will talk me to death. She lived here some twenty years ago. Her coming today is not desirable to me.

SEPTEMBER 18. I have had a return of influenza which is quite troublesome to my head and breast. My eyes are weak and full of tears and my handkerchief in constant requisition. New York is said to be now suffering from this epidemic and it is starting here with me.

SEPTEMBER 20. Today was rendered remarkable by a visit I received from two distinguished old bachelors. It was really an agreeable visit, much more so to me than morning calls usually are. My guests had a certain tone that savored of the good society of former times. That is, conversation was more interesting, politeness better served and an impression that they wished you well at parting. After they went Albanus took leave of me, intending to set off to the Pocano Mountains after grouse. I think this scheme is imprudent at the present time and cannot favor it.

OCTOBER 6. The day was embittered to me by what passed between my son and my niece at the breakfast table. He has been vexed at her impudence and she will not listen to a word without resentment. And when she has extorted words from him which he certainly does not mean and would never act upon she broods over them, weeps and incriminates him. She will never see her own error or acknowledge it.

OCTOBER 13. I had Mocky and Reddy placed in a warm spot to make them happy. I dressed two glasses with flowers. And my animals, attached as they are by petting and kindness, follow me from room to room to stay where I stay.

OCTOBER 15. The summer season always appears the longest of any of them to me. I am at a loss to know the reason why unless it is from a dislike of the heat and a dread of the diseases which often accompany it.

OCTOBER 19. My birthday. I have completed my seventy-first year. And I was up by dawn though I must confess I do not in general rise so early now. Perhaps this is to be my last birthday.

I have fed my chickens and my dove, my mocking bird and my Reddy. I have cleaned my greenhouse and planted some slips. I have carried down rich earth to nourish some favorites at the inclosure. And I am cheerful and comparatively happy. Oh dear reader when one hundred years shall have flown what would thee not give to see things as I behold them now! My heart gladened as I passed through the hall and parlors at the bright sun shining through the clean panes and the house rubbed bright and looking so pleasant. My flowers are still blooming in the cut glass on the table. They are dearly prized for they are the last; the frost has killed all their fellows in the garden. To add to my pleasure the guinea fowl and their little ones of all sizes are under my window.

DECEMBER 31. I think I am cured of the folly of expecting to grow better. Experience has made me a little wiser. And one of the lessons that she has taught me is the proper estimation of the faults and weaknesses of my own character. I may resolve and resolve but indolence and habit completely frustrate the good intention.

⋄ *1833* ⋄

JANUARY 18. I was engaged in putting up the winter's beef and we had no company—nor news. I was alone, with industry to prevent ennui. Often while I am at work thoughts that breathe are presented to my mind. Some persons never imagine what they would see if they would accustom themselves to a little introversion of the mind.

JANUARY 20. I spent the evening alone with my faithful animals laying round the stove with full bellies. This certainly constitutes dog paradise.

I should like it if these books were preserved for a few years so as to have the stamp of antiquity bestowed upon them. And if any of my descendants or others should be so interested in my character as to be pleased with details about me, I should like a picture of my morning and evening hours to be preserved. I spend them in the old dining room with the great improvement of my coal stove and lehigh coal. I have a low green cushioned chair which I found in this house fifty years ago. But repairs and new covers still make it respectable. Then there is a table under the south window. Its board is rubbed bright. A few cherished plants are put on it daily to get nourished by the sun beams. Our ordinary dinner table stands under the window. Occasionally it has a small green bench with more plants on it. Then there is my little maple desk containing my ever wanted books and writing materials. Its drawer is usually open when I sit near it. There is a mahogany stool covered with a very white square board. I use it as a table and sit before it to write. Then there is a nondescript place on the hearth between the stove and the chimney wholly unknown in architectural embellishment. It is kept clean and white washed and affords room for plants and the etcetera wanted for the fire. Lodge usually sits at my side between me and the stove. Often he has the company of a black buck cat. Reddy hangs above the desk in his nice new cage and poor blind Mocky is near by. This along with my work basket and books is a pretty true picture of my winter establishment.

But dear me! What folly to think that in a future day anything will be enquired after or thought interesting about so feeble a being as myself. Daily we see the wise, the virtuous, the great, the powerful, the rich—those whose places in society we thought would not soon be filled—die. And after their obituaries and the may-hap of their funeral pomp, they are seldom mentioned, their services appear to be forgotten and the sluggish waves of oblivion begin early to wash away the traces of their footsteps upon the earth.

JANUARY 25. At present we have too great a variety to read. It fares exactly as it does at a table too plentifully furnished with delicacies. You do not make as agreeable a meal as if you had fewer things. I do not read much; certainly not enough to keep up with current literature. And I hardly know any one who does who has any other occupation to attend to. But surely, if I might give advice, a few choice authors of merit would go further to reform the taste than this inundation which is daily issuing from the presses. Much of this material is ephemeral.

FEBRUARY 9. What will come after this dream of life? I feel my bodily powers decay—my appearance. Oh how changed. I feel a kind of ebbing of strength to which no flow returns. I do not wish to complain. It is right to submit to the law of my nature. And I do so. But I feel I ought to be quickened in my preparation, for what is to follow is inevitable.

FEBRUARY 13. I often think of my dear mother. This morning I thought that she would have been made more outwardly comfortable by some of the improvements which we now have; especially the defense from the cold. And as to her mental trials, as I have gone along in life I felt sympathy that she had so many and they were so severe. These great perplexities and difficulties were not monetary ones. She had a good fortune at her own command. And I rejoice that she had it.

FEBRUARY 18. Pens, books, and the needle always afford a resource. And they did today.

MARCH 3. I had to attend to the greenhouse stove and felt uneasy lest the frost should now destroy my plants on the verge of spring when I had taken such good care of them all winter. Besides this I had my patch work and sewed squares together. Now that I am left to myself a little I feel like a bird who sits quietly in some secure retreat and plumes itself, happy to escape from observation. Although I wanted to remain alone the dogs pleaded so hard for a share of the comfort of the stove that I could not deny them. And these white beasts, their ermine diversified with a little brown, are accordingly basking in its warmth. I had my tea—not alone—but the canine company behaved themselves well.

MARCH 7. When snow first falls its purity dazzles and delights the eye and poetically seems to be the regal robe of winter. But when it is shoveled out of the paths and switched about and dirtied, partially melted and in a thawing state, it looks dreary. It looks that way now.

MARCH 25. My neighbors were here in the evening and I did what I could to make their visit agreeable. I see and feel my own inability to do much good. But I try what I can to confer a little comfort and strew a wild flower now and then in the paths of those who are too often hurt by slight or coldness in others towards them.

APRIL 1. I was making an oyster pie in the kitchen when a knock at the door announced George, the butcher boy. He had come with a fine show oxen above two thousand weight to see if I would engage some of the beef. I thought he knew me better than to think I could contemplate the fine living animal and then eat of his meat. I would not go to see him but all the women did. And though I was forced to order some to be sent, I am sure that I will not touch it.

APRIL 2. I have not much to tell. It was a day of receiving my rent [on property in Chester, Pa.] but I had a small balance since repairs had to be paid. The consideration of what I shall do next to pay off my debts oppresses me very much.

APRIL 5. The weather was very warm and spring like and the grass grows like magic. In the evening I was seized with a bad colic but obtained relief by peppermint and going to bed.

APRIL 9. At present my mind feels sad and my spirits are unusually depressed. The failing state in which I see my brother's [Joseph Parker Norris] health has most deeply touched me and many awful and affecting reflections are presented. This morning I got up after distressing but unconnected dreams in which remembrances of my dear husband were mingled. I know how to guard against superstition—but I feel that I have arrived at an awful period of life.

MAY 6. I am writing in the library for the first time this season. It has become as hot as summer, very dry and dusty with a high wind. My spirits are below par today. I want the kindness of encouragement and assistance and I want money. I feel helpless and feeble, unusual to execute my usual tasks. The passenger down the slope of age is in need of supports.

MAY 11. I had expected the rent from my Chester house but I was disappointed. My son brought me no money. I feel weary and out of spirits.

I wait calmly and patiently to emerge out of this ocean of work.

JUNE 2. As I was quite unwell I very naturally thought of what a scene would be presented here in the morning if I should be found dead! But I crave pardon for recording such things.

JULY 27. Robert my gardener gave the warning that he should leave this place. This did not grieve me for I told him that it was very well. But in the afternoon he behaved with the utmost insolence to my son. I think he must have been heated with liquor for no provocation was given. No one ever hated these occurrences worse than I do. I have no talents to cope with them at all and they make me nervous and distress me. I am now suffering from this cause.

AUGUST 8. My brother has again been considerably indisposed. I see that his constitution is breaking up fast. But I may yet assert my primogeniture and perhaps go first!

AUGUST 31. The worst about having company with me in the house is that I have no time to write. They kindly, as they suppose, help me in my little domestic tasks when I would rather do it myself in my own way. I do have time to go into the library with my book and work in the mornings. Then comes dinner and the siesta followed by company at home or going abroad. This is succeeded by our agreeable evening parties round the table in the dining room. We do not think of departing until the clock strikes eleven. So pass my present summer days. If I were left a little more to myself in the morning I would have more time to write and do some things which are now of course put off until a more convenient season which may never arrive.

SEPTEMBER 14. It is vain and most probably will be diverting to those who shall read this hereafter that I should complain of not obtaining time to note down the incidents of my insignificant life. But really, of late it has been the case and it extends to many other affairs that press upon me and ought to be attended to. But the constant current of company which flows to the house at this time prevents me.

SEPTEMBER 16. I passed my time satisfactorily by myself and had a little ramble to gather berries for my birds towards evening. I enjoyed the autumnal scene which was very beautiful.

OCTOBER 1. Cares press upon my mind at this time. I want to pay all my debts and settle my affairs. And my [Chester] property which has been offered for sale for some time has had no bidders. And the weakness of declining years demands quiet and repose from all harrassing thoughts and perplexities which I now sensibly feel.

OCTOBER 3. I strolled over the ruins of my garden, down to the inclosure and beyond the avenue on the other side. And I felt sensible of my declining strength. But still, much enjoyment was left for me. The afternoon was beautiful and the scene was so likewise. Yet it was mingled with that slight shade of melancholy that leads to serious reflection—and suitable at once to the declining year and my advancing stage of life. I had my tea and passed the evening tranquilly though alone.

OCTOBER 19. And now I have got in the order of time to the nineteenth of October which is my own birthday, which has now reached the seventy-third, a long vista of years when we take the protracted term of human life into consideration.

I must here I suppose give some account of my entertainment on account of my granddaughter's [Lis] marriage. I found that I could not entertain more than twenty people at dinner without confusion and inconvenience. The day before, from seeing the preparations going on, I became more at ease about the event and set cheerfully about at those minor things that I was capable of doing to help others. We had sent someone to market in the morning to buy provisions and all was now in good train.

Things progressed. In due time the waiters arrived. The table was laid and looked handsome and I was dressed to receive my guests who came one after another in rapid succession. I had no anxiety about the cooking of the dinner because I had hired a first rate cook from Philadelphia to whom I paid a five dollar note for her services.

The day glided away. It was spent as such galas usually are. I know not of any great satisfaction or conversation worth remembering. It was certainly very pleasant to receive my valued friends Dr. Betton and his wife at this house upon the joyful occasion of their only child being united with my fair granddaughter.

OCTOBER 22. I am not well myself at this time and my spirits are depressed at seeing my dear Algernon low and poorly. His toothache has caused him to suffer. He is not used to this circumstance because he has not often had it. And now that I am upon a dental subject I may as well mention the trouble which I have had with a rebellious one of my own. My few remaining teeth are white and firm, and decreasing in number, they have increased in value. But one, the only one that has varied originally from the strict line of uniformity by growing a little back from its fellows, has of late broken forth from its moorings and become loose. It vibrates backwards and forwards most disagreeably. Moreover, it has assumed a tusk-like appearance and is considerably higher than its compact brethren—a thing I used to think so ugly in others. But it is of an ivory whiteness and has no speck of decay. Yet I fear I shall have to take it out for it hinders my speech. And who can do without talking who enjoys the gift and loves conversation as much as myself? But I ask pardon for all this impertinence and will proceed.

OCTOBER 29. I prepared gruel for two sick neighbors besides ordering my greenhouse and feeding the pets. And I feel better for the employment. But how my life glides away!

OCTOBER 30. I took up *The Rambler* [one of a series of essays by Samuel Johnson]. It contains reflections on mankind's proneness to complain about the shortness of life and yet go on to waste in the same desultory way what yet remains of it. I am convicted of doing this myself.

NOVEMBER 4. My tusk tooth which has been very troublesome for some time came out today. It was quite a release and yet I miss it sadly. It is quite sound and white.

NOVEMBER 21. I do not have a pen I can write with. It is a wonder that I am not in a thundering bad humor. I will write no more on this page. It looks too ugly.

DECEMBER 14. I completed the sale of my pretty little lot of land near Chester. I did it with very painful feelings at first but then I concluded to do it with a conviction that it would be best to do so and relieve myself from debts and interest which I have to pay. I obtained a pretty good price and now the thing is done. And I hope that my affairs will get settled and my mind made easy.

DECEMBER 25. It is now Christmas day and it is astonishing to perceive how soon the seasons get around. It seems shorter and shorter every year. Time does not halt at all with me and has besides a pair of monstrous wings to help him in his flight.

I was alone for most of the day and made mince meat for pies, always expected at this season.

DECEMBER 27. After company I have the trouble to clean

and fix up next day. And now I find such things more troublesome with the increasing infirmities of old age.

DECEMBER 31. There is a sort of thraldom in too much society which renders you unable to do as you like and obliges you to relinquish the employments which you wish and ought to attend to. I wish to be left a little to myself. And this day I was so. Rain came and the roads are tremendously bad. I looked over papers and put my desk and drawers to rights. And now on the last day of the year I have the thoughts and reflections which seem to belong to the season. Upon self examination I do not find that I am one bit better than I was this day a year ago. And I am one year older, nearer to eternity, uglier and more infirm, passing rapidly down the steep of age. What can I do but try to turn inward and endeavor to gain strength from prayer and those reflections which clothe me with humility.

◇ *1834* ◇

FEBRUARY 3. My eyes which had begun to become inflamed yesterday became worse and felt badly and looked worse than bad. My son prohibits the use of pens, needles, and books so I dare not let him see me write.

FEBRUARY 7. My eyes admitted of no employment. I got up however to tea which Albanus took with us. I was ill, I think at night and felt myself in no state to meet the stroke of death which will not be much longer averted.

MAY 4. I am sick of the world, the wickedness and confusion of it and covet only retirement and to cultivate the best of affections. There is nothing now comparable to the sweetness of long ago remembrance. Perhaps I only now remember the beautiful, the good and the agreeable of other days and have lost sight of what was otherwise. But so it now appears to me.

MAY 23. We have a pair of scarlet tanagers about the garden and have heard of small flocks of them seen in the neighborhood. The seventeen year locusts are now rising from the earth. The fowl and even the cats and pigs eat them and I expect will get fat upon the plenty which they afford.

JUNE 14. The temperature, the prospect, the fresh green, the quiet, the balmy air and the songs of birds, the distant voices of the laborers, the crowing of the cocks and my Reddy's cheerful chirp all reach my ears as I sit at the south window in the library. I might have added the monotonous voice of the locusts who are here yet.

JUNE 18. I think to go to Somerville [Albanus's home] to tea, but am so fatigued with going about among the plants and pets and flowers that I now can scarcely stir. I am very broken and decayed of late. I feel it. But if it kills me, I shall at least die a natural death. And the state of repose after such fatigue is a rare enjoyment which an Epicurean might covet. Women in general in easy circumstances (ladies I mean) are much too artificial and sedentary to enjoy either good health or unsophisticated pleasure. My eccentricites (as I believe they are called) have procured both for me.

JUNE 21. What a pleasure it is to get even a few minutes by myself in the library. Yesterday I did not obtain it. Mary has to be considered as too much of a guest to be left to herself except at the time which I must devote to repose. The conversation could have been quite agreeable if Mary would have prattled less.

AUGUST 3. I have liberated most of my squirrels. Although they are pretty and amusing they became too troublesome for me to keep. If they can only imagine to take care of themselves it will be well. They seemed restored to their proper element in ascending the tall hemlocks in the avenue.

SEPTEMBER 22. I am seated in the library with a new pet, a very pretty tabby kitten in my lap. I left Lodge on the carpet in my room. Just now I feel so much in my own element that I am sorry at the day's decline, for the sun is hastening away.

OCTOBER 25. Sarah and I were, as might be expected, good company to each other all the time we could snatch for conversation between the war of the elements in the reign of chaos called house cleaning. The old dining room is to be newly painted. Oh how disagreeable it is to put a new coat on an old back—except that it will hide where Lodge tore the mouldings off the doors years ago in his attempts to get out of the room. In my eyes it will be no great improvement. Cleanliness is enough with me. I leave elegance to the elegant.

◇ *1835* ◇

JANUARY 5. I have a fire in the Franklin stove every day and evening. It is quite unavailing as to comfort so that I am determined if I live another season to substitute a coal stove in its place. Then I suppose I shall wonder why I bore the inconvenience so long.

JANUARY 10. In the afternoon we had the agreeable interlude of having the parlor chimney swept. No other variety.

FEBRUARY 6. This book is only to myself. I should not venture half the folly it often contains if I were in the habit of showing it to others.

FEBRUARY 8. If I am not mistaken today will hereafter be remembered as "The Cold Sunday of '35." Even the coal stove was inadequate to secure enough warmth for me.

FEBRUARY 11. I went to town. I always (almost) bring something home for the various members of the family [her servants] when I go to town. And upon my return they come in to see what I have brought and to receive their gifts. They call bringing in the various articles "unloading of the ship." It is a gratification to me as well as to them. But in another sense it does not make much impression. They will remember the kindness by and by—when I am here no longer.

MARCH 5. Yesterday was passed as well as can be expected. I have plenty of girls (not very efficient though) to do my work and a large family of people and more cats than catch mice. Unless I do things myself nothing is done as it should be.

MARCH 16. I had the fattest turkey that I have had this season as well as delicacies for a desert, but nobody to help eat it, though I had invited guests. I did not enjoy my meal at all.

APRIL 11. I have been for a walk for the first time this season and it was a melancholy one. I felt my own decay. And I saw my rural domain, as if in sympathy with its occupant, exhibiting marks of age and need of repair. And I said to myself, "all these things are warnings and let them have their desired effects."

APRIL 27. I had an agreeable time in town [Philadelphia]. Yet it had mingled feelings. It may be supposed in the first place that I feel the saddening influence of years and that after you have three score and ten there is not much pleasure to look forward to. I have added nearly four years to that number— and yet—if vexations did not assault me—and as long as affection and respect would cherish, I could find much to interest and please in life and society. In some tastes and pleasant views of things I certainly do *not* seem old. But my readers cannot judge for themselves for when they are perusing this book, I shall have passed "the bourne from whence no traveler returns." And it will be only from my book that I can be judged. But dear reader, be candid. Invest me with all the dignity and wisdom which your conscience can allow. And in no account consider me in the light of a vain or foolish old woman (that is, so foolish as to be vain).

My last day [in Philadelphia] was spent gratifying my love of seeing antiquities and whatever is curious in nature or art. J. F. Fisher had invited me to visit the Philosophical Society's Hall. There were rare and beautiful books. And I mentioned a work I had long wished to see, but almost despaired of it. Indeed I did not know if a copy of it was in this country—[a book on] Egypt published under the patronage of Napoleon. "We have it here," said John Vaughn and an immensely large book was placed on the table.

The subject was Thebes and the details most curious and astonishing. To be carried back ages upon ages the mind requires time to comprehend it and is ready to ask "Can such things be?" Well, there is a difference in thus going back to the primitive ages. My mind goes like we used to travel: over rugged roads and by long stages. But many people make a kind of railroad and steam boat excursion of it and see nothing of the long extended train of time, whole races of people and dynasties of kings. The birth and extinction of empires which these ruins have witnessed—I believe I have a passion for living in the past.

APRIL 30. I am not yet quite settled since my return home. I am displeased with myself for *pottering* about and doing little, a thing displeasing enough to others—but not to be helped, I think in my case.

MAY 15. Dickinson came to say that he was going back to school tomorrow. He sat by me and gave me an agreeable ear of his company. This is the secret of being agreeable to old people (and perhaps to others). Attend to them, hear what they have to say, and at least *seem* interested in what they tell you. Never interrupt them in the midst of a story with an "Oh yes, I have heard all that before." But listen as if it were interesting and new and let your manner be kind to them. Dick practiced this today and I was happy in his company and he left a highly favorable impression.

MAY 19. Sewed at the patchwork, liked it. The variety of its little details amuse me much more than sewing on another scale does. And I keep at it once I sit down to it—by choice. And sometimes even a book lying near me does not tempt me to put it away. I sat at it—amused—after all were gone to bed.

JUNE 4. I passed the day quietly but not very pleasantly— my memory grows so bad that I cannot remember particulars.

JULY 22. I was quite unwell today but made the best of it to prevent my son from being uneasy and moreover to secure myself from a lecture, for I never complain but it is somehow sifted out that I am to blame from exposure, exertion or anyway else that is possible.

AUGUST 14. I have rarely passed a more distressing day then this proved to be. The dinner hour approached and my son came in to dress. He was in his chamber when he was taken with violent spasms. Dr. Betton was sent for . . . I was vexed beyond words, but I kept my presence of mind so as to know what I had best do. He continued oppressed and ill, though in a lesser degree, throughout the afternoon.

AUGUST 26. Algernon has scarcely eaten any breakfast. My

heart is sad. Oh how melancholy it is to see the withering decay of such a manly beautiful human frame as his.

OCTOBER 9. I am totally occupied in doing all I can for my poor invalid. Indeed I seldom obtain half an hour to sit down except during the evening, my only time of rest when I am not asleep, when I sit in his room.

OCTOBER 31. In the days which have elapsed since I last wrote there have been fluctuations of hopes and fears in my mind with regard to my dear Algernon.

NOVEMBER 8. Several days of suffering have passed for my dear son whose spirits are now ready to give way.

DECEMBER 19. My dear and tenderly beloved son! My advisor, my friend, my protector and the object of all my anxious care and solicitude is no more!

DECEMBER 30. There is no describing the state of my mind: grieved, unsettled, agitated and overwhelmed. I am without adequate words to express my unhappiness. Here is a void never to be filled and though time may blunt the edge of sorrow, yet its secret fountain lays deep in my heart and my beloved Algernon's loss will ever be felt and deplored. The feeling is a sacred one.

◊ *1836* ◊

JANUARY 13. I never was in any state of mind more hard, more miserable, less productive of good than that in which I now am.

FEBRUARY 15. I cannot describe in how many ways my loss is present to me. I pass by his deserted chamber, the places where I used to find him and in bitterness of grief regret the vacancy. I see the things which he used, the clothes he wore— all here, but his loved self that I can see no longer.

MARCH 31. Gustavus [grandson] came in the afternoon to stay here as his future home.

APRIL 4. I felt (as I always shall) the greatness of my bereavement. And today on the account of my concerns I feel sick at heart when I reflect upon how I am to do. And when they come to consult me about what he always directed, I feel how inadequate I am to the additional care and charge of things. Gustavus is as yet unaccustomed to it.

APRIL 5. It begins to look like spring. But oh how unlike its cheerfulness is my poor heart. Yet I always enjoy its returning comforts to the poor animals.

JUNE 15. A good deal of company has been here. I apprehend that they paid me a pleasant visit from the satisfaction which was expressed. People seem to think that when they get here and view the remains of the olden times which I have about me that they are transported into the times themselves. They think and talk differently then what they are in the habit of doing in the world. To be candid, this suits me very well, for I have lived so much out of it for a long time and my thoughts flow in such a different channel, that I had rather say but little about its concerns.

JULY 25. My memory now has become so treacherous that unless I commit any circumstance which I may wish to remember speedily to paper, it is ten chances to one that I forget it altogether.

JULY 28. I have company daily and sometimes I am almost ready to say "too much."

SEPTEMBER 2. On one of the early days of this week I had the company of my dear brother. On my part I could have wished better, for after having looked for them in vain all the moonlight evenings, I had been prepared for their visit with nice queen cake and jumbles and good relishes all that time. Now that the best had vanished, they came. However, I was very glad to see them and the welcome of love would overlook deficiencies.

SEPTEMBER 17. My family affairs, though I have people about me in plenty, cause me more fatigue than I can bear.

OCTOBER 25. I do not know what has come over me as to my diary. I do not take the pleasure in writing that I used to do.

OCTOBER 27. I feel the loss of my beloved son in all things. At present there is a kind of derangement in everything which he used to wisely control. Nothing seems to go on right. I feel my own inability to manage my own affairs. I want help, essential help. Oh how sadly I feel intellectual decay.

NOVEMBER 2. I am sensible that I have not managed my affairs to the best advantage. And indeed I seem incapable of it. I have debts to pay and money is wanting. What to do, I know not.

NOVEMBER 12. I have, I believe, fifty pens, and not one that I can write tolerably with. Few things now interest or amuse me and at times a gloom that I cannot describe covers my mind.

◇ *1837* ◇

JANUARY 6. The papers today give a mournful account of a distressing shipwreck and loss of human life.

I felt very sad at this intelligence and went to rest in a melancholy mood. But my future acquaintances, I mean the readers (perhaps now unborn) who hereafter shall peruse these pages, I say I must hope such who have not known me in life will not figure me as morose, melancholy and averse to the innocent enjoyments of life, and suppose that I delight in brooding over misfortunes and disasters. This is not the case at all. I am naturally of a cheerful, lively turn of mind, though I am now but ill at ease and very unhappy compared to how I used to be. The death of my dear, dear son has cast a gloom over all my prospects in this life and altered the aspect of all things about me. Yet still a cheerfulness lights up when I see the faces of my friends and enjoy their society.

JANUARY 12. While laying down in the afternoon I had some very serious thoughts. It brought home to me in an unusual manner the only thing we are sure of; the certainty of death and the "remorse" (John Randolph's word) that will attend my soul if I now triffle and put off the preparation for that dread day. I hope I shall not forget the impression. I hope I shall profit by the feeling. But I have no opinion in my own stability. I have no confidence in myself!

JANUARY 30. I have not spent the day at all profitably. I do not feel at all justified. And I am famished for intellectual food. But in the evening Sarah and I had some agreeable conversation.

APRIL 13. My dear Albanus brought me sixty-five dollars from my Chester property after defraying expenses for repairs, taxes and so forth which everywhere devour much of my means to live.

I have been all this morning packing up my clothes and preparing to go to town for a week to the [Friends'] meeting. And a perhaps superstitious presentiment says it may be the last time. So under such a feeling—I put up my book, depositing it in my Beloved Algernon's desk until (if I live) I come back to my retirement.

APRIL 26. I got home on the twenty fourth. But yesterday I could not write and now that I have time to sit down to it I find alterations which do not at all accord with my liking. My pens have been scribbled with, the ink emptied out and the little glass washed. All of this was not only unnecessary but mischievious. I hate thin ink. I hate my things to be meddled with. I hate change of almost any kind. And I perceive it shall be days before I get settled. Nothing is for the better and I am sick. So much for disturbance and being put out of my way.

MAY 9. I feel as torpid as a tortoise and as if I should like to withdraw into my shell for a month at least.

JUNE 17. I have been busy this morning putting my old halls to rights and bringing in a few flowers. For I cannot resist the temptation when I see their morning loveliness and know that the bright beams they have cherished will accelerate their decay. I cannot help wishing to perpetuate their bloom a little longer in the house.

JUNE 19. Several days have passed and I seem to have no leisure and certainly no inclination to write in this book; which ought not to be. Sadly, I forget things especially when left a day or two. I believe however that I have not had much to insert for I have not had much company and I have heard but little to communicate.

JUNE 22. I know that I am anything but fit to leave this world and yet I seem tired of life and my mind seems as if it had lost the power which it once possessed of turning from pleasant subjects and only entertaining those which administer to its comfort. I wish I could feel more in harmony with what is good and agreeable—but I do not and am extremely dull.

JULY 23. I hear of things which interest others but they do not reach me. I seem as a sojourner at the feast of life when others are risen and gone. When my turn comes, if you think I dare to hope in Christ, mourn not for me but rejoice at my liberation.

JULY 24. Upon reading what I wrote yesterday I am sorry that it is written so despondently although I feel no better than I did when I wrote it. I feel rather worse for I have fatigued myself too much this morning. And though I have slept and bathed and dressed since, a sense of weariness is full upon me. Now I wish some agreeable friend would drop in and enliven me—for it is seldom that I want company as I do today.

JULY 28. I hear the hens prate. The horns blow for breakfast round the neighborhood and the steam carriages rattle along the railroad and I bless my stars that I do not live more in the hurry and the vortex of the world than I do.

AUGUST 2. I have been helping to put the house to rights. That is doing the *little* arrangements of every day and I am fatigued and exhausted with the exertion. Is this not one of the messengers to tell of what is fast approaching? And shall I not heed it?

AUGUST 3. A dreadful hot and dry spell of weather. I hardly know how to live along; to make any exertion of any kind seems as if it would kill me. I shall be glad on my own account when the summer is ended.

AUGUST 6. Yorick [dog] now attaches himself to me and stays mostly with me. I have lost so many of my pets that there seems a void for him and he is an affectionate animal.

AUGUST 7. Reading over what I have written on the opposite page it seems hardly credible that with so little insert I should think of keeping a diary. But the truth is I have become so used to writing in it I go to it naturally.

This reminds me of what more I might have said in commendation of "poor Yorick." He is one of our old breed of dogs and was given away three times when he was young. He would not stay with his new masters though each time he was a distance of many miles. Once he swam the Delaware above Trenton and came home. This proof of attachment has gained him exemption from any further wanderings.

AUGUST 8. The most oppressive spell of heat! I am overcome with it—languid—fatigued and my limbs trembling under me—almost dead!

AUGUST 17. I am now in the library by myself. No one in the house but me. I hear the people at work on the farm as they pass with their cart. In the interval there is no other sound except the loud ticking of the library clock.

AUGUST 26. We were at home yesterday and through the day had a good deal of company which sometimes fatigues me. And I feel how necessary quiet and seclusion and freedom from care is for the season of old age. I have a family that will not do without constant looking after. As soon as I relax I am sure that all exertion in others is at an end and I am mortified and worried with things neglected and out of place which, when you have friends in the house to witness it, is very upsetting.

SEPTEMBER 1. I hear the black cock crow, I know his voice and this leads me to think how many of my favorites [pets] are gone. And a special regret is felt for poor Tabb. [Her cat had died.] Her place at this time is proposed to be filled by a kitten.

SEPTEMBER 6. The anniversary of my marriage. I believe all who were present on that day at my mother's house except my brother and myself are deceased.

OCTOBER 15. I am very hum-drum at home. Yet if I had a little more money and things were a little more neat and in order about me I could still have some enjoyment though sorrow and disappointment have cut off my best domestic prospects.

OCTOBER 22. Mew, mew, mew. I have a little cadet of a cat here which I should like to install in poor Tabb's place if she will only behave herself. Tabb did not make this disagreeable noise. It is abominable.

And here I may as well tell that I have lately met with an

accident which has hurt me a good deal: coming out of my room in the twilight of the evening I did not perceive that Yorick had followed me and lay on the carpet near the door. I fell over him and cut my face. My nose bled and has to be covered. My eyes are blackened, but not beautified, and my left arm is very much incapacitated from use, besides other bruises. I sent for Dr. Betton and he most kindly came immediately and visited me since. Except for the inconvenience of my arm I am at the present time as well as can be expected.

OCTOBER 26. I look as if I had been in the wars. My nose (the best feature in my face) is covered with a huge black patch.

DECEMBER 5. I am so perplexed with domestic affairs that I feel as I do not like to feel—sad and irritable. But I will not complain. I will try to do as well as I can though at this time vexation and heaviness are in my heart and tears are in my eyes.

DECEMBER 13. A very busy day spent in salting and putting up the meat, chopping sausage meat and making pudding. We pretty well succeeded. And now there is a world of labor to scrub and scour and clean again.

DECEMBER 15. I have run about all day. Few, very few use half as much exercise as I do. (I mean of women in such a rank in life that they might be excused if they wished from the exertion.) But I believe it furnished me with health and in some degree wards off infirmity and decay.

◇ *1838* ◇

JANUARY 2. I had two hands hired who came last night, foolish girls who were frightened at their own shadows at going up to bed and raised such a clamor with their fears that I had to let them lodge in my room. But what they saw, or what they feared I can by no means understand.

JANUARY 5. Without one word of reproof or quarreling or any reason plausible or the contrary, I have found myself deserted by all my female servants except the cook. They have all gone off, clean off! How I shall get along I know not. If company were to defer visiting me—that would be desirable at present.

JANUARY 26. I miss my pretty Tabb most exceedingly. When I used to come out of my own room I used to find her sitting on the outside of the casement of the dining room window waiting for admittance and the poor black cock was on the pavement beneath ready to be fed and saluting me with a crow. I miss my favorites and want something that will look up to me with confidence and love.

JANUARY 28. My mind is in a pretty good frame for the idea of my beloved Algernon is my constant companion.

FEBRUARY 25. Lis [granddaughter] is to me as a dove that I would continually nestle in my bosom and like a cordial in the cup of life to delight and exhilarate my old age.

MARCH 2. I cannot write with the least freedom with these odious pens doctored up and thought very good by Sarah—but not suiting me at all—dreadful—worse and worse! Most hateful!!!

MARCH 6. I have got a cold, stiff neck and pain in my back but I feel lively and not inclined to make the most of it.

Now pray try to write this page fit to be seen. I think of all his scholars my good Master Benezet succeeded in making me write "plain and easily to be read" as he always recommended.

MARCH 20. It is not often I feel so very lonely as I now do. Well the recipe, I suppose, for such a state is to read—good books of course but such mutable beings as myself sometimes want amusing ones. And in such a frame of mind I lighted upon Sir Walter [Scott's] *Life.* Oh how I should have liked him. But I am afraid he would have discerned more in me to laugh at than to have liked. But any how I could have told him many things from real life that a touch of his wand would have transformed into rare gems.

MARCH 26. I wish I had something entertaining to put down. But this is not in my power unless I could fib and invent something. When I was young I had a fertile imagination and could dress up a fiction as nicely as most. But a very worthy and sensible gentleman, a man of high honor broke me of this propensity by cautioning me against its indulgence and by asking "Are you sure it is true?" I have often reverted to this with advantage.

APRIL 5. Yesterday we had a good deal of company.

Sarah has been washing ribbons and starching. And I have tired myself to a fatigue like sickness in doing very, very little of putting away things and pottering in the greenhouse. I can hardly bear up under the languor. I did not think I was so weak.

APRIL 9. The sun now shines out cheerily. The sweet Reddy and little canary can go out of doors and hang in the open air. When prisoners have been so for a long time and are treated kindly and well provided for they are more at home in their confinement then if let out. In the present case freedom would be fatal to the dear little creatures. So they must stay and live with their kind mistress.

APRIL 13. The note of preparation has been sounded and we expect to go to town today. "Going up to Jerusalem to the feast" for it is a religious solemnity which is mixed (and I trust it is no crime) with a pleasant feeling of seeing your friends' faces and going to their houses at a convenient time (for everybody is prepared and glad to have you as a guest). Yet now that the day is come I think I hate to leave my pleasant home—my old fashioned mansion and all my conveniences clustered around me: the little desk and board where I write and the sweet red rogue in his cage above it—whistling now at the top of his voice, and the little canary, a lively fellow. Well, I trust I shall find you [birds] alive when I come back—like the country mouse—to my cheese parings and bacon. So closes this entry. Heigh Ho!

APRIL 22. I had a satisfactory and refreshing week in town. And now that I have returned home, my mind is solemnized by the truths which I have heard and the considerations which have been suggested to it.

MAY 13. A fine, bright clear day. But alas! the last of my dear Sarah's sojourn with me at this time. Breakfast is brought in as if in mockery to me for I want nothing to eat. And here I sit inert and desultory. Oh! I wish I could accurately describe how

Stenton, "My old fashioned mansion" (*Courtesy of The National Society of Colonial Dames in Pennsylvania, Stenton*)

torpid and dull and good for little I am, dwelling upon the past and living upon the stores of memory.

MAY 27. Just now I took a stroll in the garden and seeing some weeds near a plant which I wanted to cultivate I stooped down to pick them up. It was but a very little effort—but that little convinced me of the change in myself. It is a rapid diminution of strength. My God! prepare me for the parting scene. I have no dear Algernon now to bitterly regret my death. My beloved Albanus will mourn tenderly for me, yet he has another home and affectionate family to console him. Poor dear Algernon had only his old mother.

I am alone in the house without a creature to speak to except Puss. And she answers me by her caresses and climbing up on my shoulders to the great discomposure of my handkerchief so I look like a witch.

MAY 29. A truce with complaints although it is a foggy morning. I have a fire in the stove and my sweet Reddy sings delightfully. Poor little canary is sick. He sits huddled up. I must try a little saffron for him.

MAY 30. I have just had a severe trial—greater than I am well able at this time to bear because it will impeach my prudence and it will make my beloved son think there is no end of my difficulties. It is in the shape of a bill due to the butcher which has not been paid up and has accumulated beyond what I expected. I am indeed grieved and ashamed and know not what to do. I however withstood his solicitation to procure the money, or any part of it, from the bank, which I positively refused to do. Now I am but too unhappy—nervous—strongly excited—and miserable! If my dear Albanus does not upbraid me I shall rejoice in his forbearance.

JUNE 4. I sat in the little parlor with the doors opened through the hall and the moonlight sweetly entering through the vine covered window. I fell into a reverie of the past. The beauty of my old place struck my fancy this evening as being of a singular description and very great.

JUNE 11. I am exceedingly unwell but I am afraid to complain for fear of having the doctor sent for and my liberty abridged.

JUNE 15. Enfeebled by my age and the warm season I surely may take an invalidship upon myself, especially when the state of lameness from the extreme tenderness in my feet is taken into consideration.

I am now alone. There is only a little puss who seems to wish to make my acquaintance. And here a thought occurred to me of how very unimportant a being I am. I regret it not. Yet I stand upon an awful spot. My day of life is nearly at a close and my most important work not keeping pace with its shadows. Much to do—penetence and prayer befit such a wasted life.

[MISTAKENLY DATED JULY 3]. As I have been sitting upstairs a disagreeable event has considerably discomposed me. And I could not even weep as women do when they are hurt either in mind or body. But it is not worth while. The business however must be attended to. It is a debt due of about seventy dollars which I must pay this week.

JUNE 28. I have been in a great mistake lately about my dates. But now I hope I have correctly ascertained that I am right.

The dates here are all wrong. But in my unimportant life it is no matter. It is not known certainly now who built the large pyramids.

JULY 1. Old Mrs. Morris and Margaretta drank tea with me. Mrs. Morris is a hardy old lady. She is very peculiar in conversations: When she gets on a subject, she perplexes it so much and brings into the discourse so much irrelevant and foreign matter, that it is almost impossible, with the closest attention, to follow her. She however is satisfied with what she has done and does not always require that you should reply, or that you should have understood her. She told me today that she is in her seventieth year.

JULY 3. I prepared to go to bed. But in my own room I met with a bad accident from the window sash. Its ropes are broken and have to be propped up. In setting it to my mind, the prop slipped and the sash fell heavily on my left hand. It hurt and pained me sadly. This morning I am glad it is not worse. But it is bruised, swelled and helpless.

JULY 4. The hand is swelled but not near so helpless a paw as I feared it would be. Now the little cat is sitting up on my shoulders washing my neck with her tongue.

JULY 5. Puss is sitting at her post. She would make a warm tippet for winter. In looking over this page I am surprised at my folly in keeping a diary. The only excuse allowable is that I have formed the habit.

JULY 12. This morning it seems like I am standing before

the mouth of a heated furnace; very little air and a broiling sun.
I shall give out! The little cat will seat herself nowhere but on
my neck and shoulders.

JULY 17. I am happy in the library, undisturbed but by Puss.
There is a kind of melody in the air like the distant chime of
bells. Is it imagination or not?

In seeing Dickerson [Mahlon Dickerson, a friend] I had to
inquire after his female relations. He has ever been remarkably
kind to his female relations and I respect men that are so. Many
that are not deficient in affording us protection nevertheless
make us feel our dependence.

JULY 20. There is a dead calm. Not a breath of air. No motion
in the foliage. I have slept and bathed and dressed clean but I
am much oppressed with the heat though seated in the library
with all the facilities of obtaining a waft of air. How I pity the
poor men and oxen at work. I am suffering almost from a sense
of suffocation. I cannot sew nor write nor do any thing.

JULY 22. Oh for a good and kind servant that would consci-
entiously relieve and help me. Oh for any one to take thought
and give me assistance. Youth is thoughtless and blames age
without consideration or pity. Those who live with you ought
to try to alleviate your vexations. I am sure I should be thankful
for such help.

Here is a little puss who follows me about and will lay in my
lap—though it is inconvenient to write under such circumstances.

JULY 28. I left the dining room for the hall where the beautiful moon beams fell on the pavement and a faint breeze somewhat allayed the heat. Oh what a hot sultry night it is.

JULY 29. My heart throbs, my hands tremble and my limbs
almost fail to support my poor weak frame. Yet I reproach myself
for the complaint. Have I not mercies and indulgences that
many a better person is without? I have!

AUGUST 7. Dickinson stayed all night and breakfasted with
us. Now he has gone, the most pleasant companion that I
have—for Gus, with very kind feelings, will not talk.

AUGUST 13. We all of us know that we are fleeting beings

passing away like shadows. We are here now and speedily disappear. The reflection presented itself so powerfully that, if I could, I should like always to retain the impression. After all it comes to this: "What shadows we are and what shadows we pursue."

AUGUST 24. In thinking on the subject of myself I believe I am thought a singular woman and in some respects I am so. I prefer being by myself (unless I have good company) and I prefer the contemplation of former times to the present, though many are now conspicuous on the great theater of human affairs who would do honor to human nature in any age.

AUGUST 31. The day was spent at home without company and I was content to be without for I had my work, my pets and daily amusements. All was as it should be.

SEPTMEBER 2. In the morning the first bad news that assailed me was the information that my poor, pretty Reddy was dead! And there in the bottom of his cage lay the little lifeless remains of my late cherished favorite. I believe I have had him a full fifteen years. My beloved Algernon bought him in the Jersey market—brought him in his little corn stalk cage home in his carriage, covered with a silk handkerchief. He presented him to me, a precious gift, and I have cherished and loved him ever since. Ann [servant] and I buried him this morning in the garden.

SEPTEMBER 8. I never can, nor do, forget my dear Algernon. But there are times when he seems more immediately before me. Oh what a thing is life and what a mystery is death.

SEPTEMBER 15. Passing by a glass in one of the chambers just now, I was perfectly shocked to see myself—so old and so ugly. But what else can be expected at seventy seven! Never mind. Take courage. Nobody expects to find any beauty or even "agreeableness" at that age. But they may look perhaps for a little sense—and so farewell to this foolery.

SEPTEMBER 19. This is the day of the eclipse, Lis was with me. We smoked pieces of window glass and looked at the eclipse in all its stages to the utmost satisfaction of our unlearned intellects.

SEPTEMBER 24. It is a beautiful evening. I have been out twice to enjoy a view of the heavens.

SEPTEMBER 25. It is near noon. I have been running about and gardening in the pots and boxes all morning until I have gotten a headache.

SEPTEMBER 26. My poor little guinea was taken into the kitchen to be fed and sheltered from the storm. There I saw him in the morning. He was very well, only a little lame—knew me, watched for me and loved me. In the afternoon when I inquired of him, I found that something had occurred. And upon pressing to know discovered that Gustavus had him killed to put him out of his misery. Why, he enjoyed life and was happy as any dear little feathered creature could be. His lameness did not interfere with his enjoyment of his little day of life. Oh I am grieved and unhappy and mortified that I could not extend protection even to a little fowl. Now I shall never more hear his cheerful voice nor see the little creature. And I am hurt and take it hard. The tears are in my eyes! I would not for many dollars have been so wounded. I see the other fowls going to roost and he is not among them. I am vexed and grieved.

Well tea time came and my grandson came in to his meal. I received him kindly, poured out his tea and made no allusion to what I felt, which really was a sort of sorrow.

SEPTEMBER 29. You can't think how much I miss and morn for my guinea. It was a shame to deprive me of him so unnecessarily.

SEPTEMBER 30. The house looks dirty. The old dinning room abominably so. I feel fidgetty and disagreeable and am holding in with a curb bridle to keep from scolding. I feel sick.

OCTOBER 1. The afternoon was remarkably fine and I went down to Somerville to tea. The additional ride was a luxury from the goodness of the roads and the beautiful moonlight. The ride was delightful. And here let me mention with satisfaction the improvement I can observe in the manners of the people you now meet with on the roads; no incivility or rudeness and I have very seldom of late seen or heard an intoxicated person. All is quiet and orderly.

OCTOBER 5. I have been sitting disconsolately by myself. I feel weak and enervated, as if conscious that it would not take much to sever the little hold which I still have on life.

OCTOBER 9. [She mistakenly dates the 23rd.]* The nineteenth was the anniversary of my birth seventy seven years ago. Oh how little have I profited by the many opportunities afforded me of good.

OCTOBER 22. As I sit by myself I am not melancholy—but the idea of my dearest Dr. Logan and of our lovely boys are my constant companions. I have lived here longer than any of the family have heretofore done.

OCTOBER 24. I have fed my chickens for I have a hen and a dozen young ones who claim my attention. I see her supplied with food very often. But I have no pets as beloved as my dear little guinea, and pretty Reddy and the little droop-wing canary were and they are gone forever.

OCTOBER 25. I don't know what day of the month it is. I have often thought if one was separated from the rest of the world and on a desert island as Robinson Crusoe was, how important it would be in my estimation to keep an exact register of time.

I am sickish at my stomach. I think I could eat something out of the sea, crabs, lobsters or even oysters or clams if they were nice and well cooked.

OCTOBER 28. It is a pity I am doomed to always have such wretched pens. A good one is a real luxury to me but I seldom have it. They put me in a kind of torture.

OCTOBER 31. Today I received a present of white guinea hens (or rather a pair, a gentleman and his wife) of this description.

NOVEMBER 1. I have been busy at work for to say truth I have too much to do. I am without any one to relieve me of

---

* [Note by Logan] I have made a mistake here in the date. I forgot how I came to do it and it is of no other consequence than that it will probably induce future readers to suppose me much more decayed in mind than I really am at this time.

the care of my plants. And I have been watering them and cleansing the greenhouse.

My beloved Algernon's image is my constant companion. How I have supported his loss as calmly as I have done is a mystery to myself. Yet it is an enduring sorrow.

NOVEMBER 2. It is my last pages in the diary that are not already occupied and I have not a new one ordered. I have to do so, for thick quartos are not so easily met with which are made of the best paper ruled and bound. When I first got the present volume it appeared to be a task to fill it, both for the supply of subject matter and even the mechanical operation of the pen. But the events of everyday life (often it is true very vague and uninteresting) have furnished this one—and the other, if I have anything but a bit of stick [to write with] will progress.

NOVEMBER 4. Gus has brought home to me a large green parrot who was saved out of a shipwrecked vessel. I think he talks the plainest of any bird that I have ever heard.

NOVEMBER 10. I am not well this morning. I think I must do what I seldom do and most abominably hate to do: take physic [medicine].

Polly who was saved from the shipwrecked vessel talks pretty plain and fluently but told us nothing of the disaster.

DECEMBER 11. My dear Albanus wants me to have a nurse to live with me this winter which I must positively but respectfully decline. I don't want her. I cannot have her. I can do quite well without anyone. It would vex and displease me far more than benefit me. If I should be sick and want a nurse it would be different.

I have a worrying toothache and pain in my face and have sometimes born such a thing a week without telling anyone of it.

DECEMBER 15. What a gradual weaning from the concerns of life old age forces on us. We give up (often reluctantly) not only the past times, but the employments to which we have been used. But let me tell the tyro, it is far better not to give up too soon and not to be discouraged at one failure for it often happens that upon another occasion you perform better and get in better humor with yourself.

DECEMBER 18. I have no new nor amusing book to read, no pen to write with, no friend nor companion to talk to. Verily, I am badly suited. I never wielded such detestable pens. It is not often I complain as I now am compelled to do. Yet I am conscious that I do better than most women would.

I am constantly up the first of anyone in this house. I make my own fire, light my lamp, wash and dress generally before anyone is stirring. I have not wasted much of my time in sleep, only and except my afternoon siesta which is a great refreshment to me and not to be dispensed with.

DECEMBER 19. Chopping mince meat and flying about to get lists for the articles wanted for the indispensable mince pies.

Gustavus brought home some birds this evening, a thrush and two little stranger birds to me—in the dirtiest cages possible. But they must be cleansed and taken care of and if they become attached to me there will be affection and consequently pleasure and all those little soothing emotions which arise from care and protection afforded. And if I could but feel anything of the same attachment I had to my sweet Reddy it will be well and I shall gain by the little creatures.

DECEMBER 20. I feel disconsolate and I want comfort and help, spiritual help, and likewise the kind and cordial help which sometimes a fellow creature can bestow—which my dear Sarah Walker has not infrequently effected for me and which I myself have sometimes been so fortunate as to effect for others. And it is truly a great pleasure when one is conscious of really helping a fellow creature in this too troublesome and wayward world.

But oh! here is dinner time and all is still in confusion. And myself, who used to be the life and soul of things here, quite inefficient and incapable to help to much purpose.

I want no dinner for I am sick at the stomach.

I miss my dear Algernon.

DECEMBER 24. Here are all the little animals and creatures depending upon me for comfort and it is a pleasure to impart it.

DECEMBER 26. We have been employed, I fancy, something in the way Mrs. Butler calls "dawdling about." In the afternoon I lay down a short time and then got up to the undefined employment of housing the pet chickens and carrying plants to the sunny places to catch the beams of the afternoon sun.

My endeavors to employ and entertain myself are not very successful this evening for I am in pain and feel impatient and disagreeable with that kind of irritability which is at war with comfort. In the midst of all this puss chooses to lay her length in my lap between me and the book and I can hardly make out to write in this position. I believe I had better put the book away.

DECEMBER 27. It is quite essential to my comfort to have good pens and black ink—and likewise to have the chickens fed, for the poor fellow who was housed up in my room last night and gave a Christmas crow this morning has been turned out of doors, I am afraid without his breakfast.

The parrot occupies the kitchen. One of the parlor birds makes a very singular noise.

Yesterday Dickinson brought me home bound in Morocco leather, of very fine paper handsomely ruled, a quarto sized diary—too pretty by far to be spoiled and be made free by my scrawls for which this book at present seems quite good enough. Therefore, I believe, I shall continue awhile to make use of it.

DECEMBER 28. It has been an up and down day—and with me more down than up.

I do not know when I have felt more uncomfortable than I do this evening though my dog is on the carpet beside me and puss has made for herself a bed on the stool. They both seem comfortable enough. I wish I were so myself.

◇ *1839* ◇

JANUARY 2. I am not very well and seem considerably oppressed. My ankles too are swelled so as to be much larger than their natural size. The feeling is extremely irksome to me though not painful. Oh how I wish I once more had good ink and pens to write with. Then it would be a pleasure to me and beguile the tedium of many an half hour. Now it is a fretful task because of the evil instruments.

Albanus and [his wife] Maria now talk freely of coming up here to live and of our making but one family in the spring. I feel remarkably free (as Friends say) that it should be so and am satisfied from the goodness of Maria's principles that there will be no difficulty on her part. And my dear Albanus appears much to approve it. For one good thing it will be the means of having the old mansion and its grounds put in beautiful order. And we shall have a garden once more. And our united means to live will enable us to do so very comfortably. United we shall only be a family of six persons without our domestics.

JANUARY 3. I was alone last evening and worked industriously at my needle. The needle is a great friend to women.

JANUARY 4. I am old and infirm and want kindness and comfort, no anxiety and care, which however seems to fall to my lot at present. But it will be better when my dear Albanus comes. Then, there will be a renovation of matters and things and I confidently hope the aspect of all will be for the better.

I do not look forward to much longer life. But I sadly want to "set my house in order." I have symptoms of decline amongst which I reckon the swelling of my legs and ankles. But it is not painful—only a sense of weariness oppresses me.

Four hogs are to be put up for pork, sausage made and the feet cleaned. And I am totally inadequate to see after it. I must trust to others. Exceedingly poorly and not able to undertake any part of the work, I have come in. And seated in the dining room I seem quite incapable of helping others or of being pleased myself.

JANUARY 6. I have been up some time by lamp light. The beams of the sun when he first rises at this season come in for a short time and form to my imagination the figure of a pine tree growing out of a rock. But it is very evanescent. Now—it is gone.

I am waiting for my breakfast as are the pet chickens for theirs. I do not feel at all pleasant or efficient. And it is not possible to get along with dowdy help unless you seem smart and capable yourself.

I ought to read good books I know, but my mind is vacant and unstable at this time and I have a bad headache.

JANUARY 8. I am quite at loss to know what day of the month it is. My little maid keeps better account than I do. She says it is the eighth. One thing I know—I am exceedingly unwell, my stomach is not good and my ankles are swelled very much. At present it is disagreeable enough in the old dining room and it seems very dirty to me. Only the sunny picture of the tree growing out of the rock on the wall pleases me. Now that is fast vanishing away. It is gone! The bright sunlight makes the lamp unnecessary. Blow it out.

◇　◇

Afterword

Deborah Norris Logan died on February 2, 1839, less than a month after making her last diary entry. Her beloved Stenton was left to her grandson Gustavus Logan, and continued to be occupied by her descendants until 1900. It is now a National Historic Landmark, open to the public.

Although surrounded by a sadly deteriorated urban neighborhood, Stenton's graceful house and gardens are a peaceful oasis of quiet and green. The house is furnished with antiques of the period 1730 to 1830, some of which are original to the mansion and undoubtedly were used by Deborah Logan and her family. Archeologists working on the grounds of Stenton have recently discovered the remains of early buildings and household implements; the house's basement is contributing to history, just as its attic did through Logan's research there. Debby would certainly have approved.

In 1980, Logan's diary was transcribed and edited by Marleen S. Barr as her doctoral dissertation. I am grateful to Ms. Barr for allowing the use of this manuscript, including her introduction, on which these notes are based.

ABOUT THE EDITOR

Penelope Franklin is a free-lance writer who has kept a journal and edited women's diaries for many years. She has also produced radio programs on women's writing and taught journal writing workshops. Ms. Franklin makes her home in New York City and Long Island.